GUJARAT - I

Between the hills of Maharashtra and Rajasthan to the north and east, the Pakistan border to the west, and the Arabian Sea to the south, Gujarat is a state which is unsurpassed for architectural and natural beauties. Starting from the stunning Islamic monuments of its former capital, Ahmedabad, and the related cities of Mehmedabad, and Champaner, this new travel guide explores the coastal cities of Cambay, Bharuch, and Surat, the princely state of Baroda, the Parsi sanctuaries of Udvada, Navsari and Sanjan, and the hill resorts of Bansda and Saputara. The great Sun Temple at Modhera introduces us to the early Hindu Kingdom of Gujarat based at Patan, with the Hindu and Jain sites of the north.

Interludes in the former Portuguese enclaves of Daman and Diu present another intriguing aspect of life in mediaeval and modern India. The bulk of the book is taken up with the magnificent former princely states of Saurashtra peninsula: Jamnagar and Bhavnagar, Rajkot and Wankaner, Porbandar and Junagadh, each with its lavish palaces and grand urban projects. The world-famous lion sanctuary of Sasan Gir and the wild ass sanctuary near Dasara have to be seen, as do the religious centres of Dwarka and Somnath, and the magnificent Jain complexes at Girnar and Shatrunjaya. You can relax on beaches at Chorwad or Ahmedpur Mandvi, or seek out historic Hindu temples at Bileshwar, Ghumli and Gop. Lothal rivals Mohenjo Daro in Pakistan in its insight into the prehistoric Indus Valley civilization. The book ends fittingly in the isolated region of Kutch, with walled towns, beaches, desert wildlife, and tribes untarnished by commercialism. Gujarat is a great experience that nobody should deny himself.

PHILIP WARD, FRSA, FRGS, ALA is the well-loved author of *Rajasthan, Agra, Delhi; South India: Tamil Nadu, Kerala, Goa*; and *Western India: Bombay, Maharashtra, Karnataka*. A reviewer has said "If you are fortunate enough to be travelling in India, and specially in the regions that he has already covered, then look no further. This is the one book you really need". *The Hindustan Times* concludes: "Ward in one sweep of his pen, with the strength of his convictions to back him, convinces his readers of the reality and the magic that is India".

GUJARAT DAMAN DIU

A Travel Guide

Philip Ward

Oleander

The Oleander Press
17 Stansgate Avenue
Cambridge CB2 2QZ

The Oleander Press
80 Eighth Avenue (Suite 303)
New York, N.Y. 10011
U.S.A.

British Library Cataloguing in Publication Data

Ward, Philip, 1938-
  Gujarat, Daman, Diu: a travel guide
  (Oleander travel books; v. 22).
  1. India (Republic). Gujarat - Visitors' guides
  2. India (Republic). Daman & Diu Union
      Territory – Visitors' guides
  I. Title

  ISBN 0-906672-22-8

Typeset, printed and bound in Great Britain

Contents

Acknowledgments

Foremost and first as always, my wife Audrey made it all possible. In New Delhi and London, the Government of India Tourist Office kindly arranged for my flights; in Gandhinagar, the State of Gujarat Information, Broadcasting and Tourism Dept. kindly arranged board, lodging, car and driver, coordinated by their colleagues in Ahmedabad. The Archaeological Survey of India kindly gave permission to visit Rudramala in Siddhapur and other sites. Mr Anil Mulchandani of North West Safaris, Mohenjo Daro, Ramkrishna Kunj, Sachivalaya Polytechnic Rd., Ahmedabad 380 015 (tel. 441511) is a fund of local information. Boman Desai kindly permitted me to reprint a passage from his novel *The Memory of Elephants*. In South Gujarat I thank the driver Ahil Bhupendra and my friend Basant Kanojia; A.S. Sayyid and Muhammad Razzaq at Cambay; Mrs Goal Sidhwa, Mr Vishwas Christian and Emmanuel C. Christie of Broach; Dr Anil Patel and pro-Narmada Dam activists, and Shripad Dharmadhikary and anti-Narmada Dam activists; Mrs Indira Mafat, Dr K. Krishnan and Mr S.B. Vaidya in Baroda; The Chief Inspector of Police in Surat for allowing me access to streets under curfew during riots; Mr Dara Patel and Dasturji Nushirvan Dastur at Sanjan; Surya Goswami in Saputara and Chintamani in Malegaon; the sadhus at Akshardham and at Swaminarayan temples in Bhuj and Sarangpur; Jain priests and pilgrims at Taranga, Kumbharia, Girnar and Shatrunjaya; Mr R.D. Shah, Mr Harish Barad and Mr Ramesh Bghowda in Palitana; His Highness Shiv Bapu in Bhavnagar; His Highness the former Ruler and his son the Crown Prince in Wankaner; His Highness the former Ruler in Jamnagar; Narendra Giri of Bileshwar and all other hospitable Hindu priests; Mahmud Khan Pathan and all other Muslim imams; Ishwarbhai Mohanbhai Raval in Mehmedabad; in Porbandar Mr Pota at the palace and Gobind the dhow-builder; Mr Kataria, the Superintendent of Sasangir, Mr Japardia, Superintendent of Velavadar, and Mr Rana of Bansda National Park; Mahantshri Tansukhgiri of Junagadh; Rabindra Kumar Lalshankar, a builder at Shankeshwar; Mr Krishna Dev Singh Thakur at Chorwad; Mr Sarfraz Malik and his gracious family at Dasada; Leroy Machado in Daman; Padre Mariano, the artist Michael Ledingham, Mr Bashir M. Kureishi and Dom Duarte de Bragança in Diu. In Bhuj I am grateful to the musicologist Jodia Umesh Prabhulal and in Mundra to Sumarbhai.

Introduction

My intention while travelling throughout Gujarat, and its former Portuguese enclaves now administered from New Delhi as the Union Territory of Daman and Diu, has been to reflect a Western visitor's experiences and to provide enough background details to make the personal impressions more meaningful in terms of history, geography, art and architecture, landscape, and life both human and animal. *Gujarat, Daman, Diu* is a companion volume to my *Rajasthan, Agra, Delhi* (1989), *South India; Tamil Nadu, Kerala, Goa* (1991), and *Western India: Bombay, Maharashtra, Karnataka* (1992) and will, I hope, appeal to the same wide audience.

The population of Gujarat in the twentieth century has multiplied more than fourfold from 9.1 million in 1901 and on present trends is expected to surpass 50 million in the first decade of next century, that is to say surpassing the combined projected populations of Australia and Canada.

1901	9.1 million
1911	9.8 million
1921	10.2 million
1931	11.5 million
1941	13.7 million
1951	16.3 million
1961	20.6 million
1971	26.7 million
1981	34.1 million
1991	41.3 million

All government attempts at encouraging family planning have failed within all communities except among some of the wealthiest and best-educated. The larger the city, the great the centripetal attraction, as we can see from the astronomical increases – more than tenfold in Ahmedabad, Surat, Baroda and Rajkot, but rather less spectacular growth in Bhavnagar and Jamnagar.

	Ahmedabad	Surat	Baroda	Rajkot	Bhavnagar	Jamnagar
1901	185,889	119,306	103,790	36,151	56,442	53,844
1911	216,777	114,688	99,345	34,194	60,694	44,887
1921	274,007	117,434	94,712	45,845	59,392	42,495
1931	310,000	98,936	112,880	59,112	75,594	55,056
1941	591,267	171,443	153,301	66,353	102,851	71,588

1951	837,163	223,182	211,407	132,069	137,951	104,419
1961	1,149,918	288,026	298,398	194,145	176,473	148,572
1971	1,591,832	471,656	467,487	300,612	225,974	214,816
1981	2,159,127	776,876	734,473	445,076	308,642	294,344
1991	2,954,526	1,505,872	1,061,598	612,458	405,225	350,544

The book opens in one of India's great cities, Ahmedabad, which took its present form under the Ahmed Shahi dynasty. The dynasty also created other great cultural centres at Mehmedabad and Champaner, and developed ports at Cambay, Broach, Surat. It replaced the Hindu dynasties of Gujarat, with their capital at Anahilvada Patan, who also created Modhera Sun Temple, the Hindu temple now ruined at Siddhapur, and renewed the Hindu temples of Somnath at Prabhas Patan and Dwarka, among others.

The great city of Baroda has recently expanded into engineering and industry, but boasts one of the two or three best museums in the State. South Gujarat possesses not only marvellous wildlife and cool hill stations such as Saputara and Bansda, but remains a sanctuary for Parsis escaping persecution in Iran. Daman has become a beach resort with a fascinating Portuguese heritage.

If you enjoyed the Jain temples at Ranakpur and Mount Abu in Rajasthan, you will be overwhelmed by the beauty of the Jain hill temple-cities of Girnar above Junagadh and Shatrunjaya above Palitana. Wildlife in Saurashtra is among the best in the whole of Asia, with lions at Sasangir, dolphins and coral reefs in Jamnagar's marine sanctuary, blackbuck and marsh harriers at Velavadar, and wild asses and pelicans near Dasada. Prehistory offers no better site in India than the Harappan civilisation at Lothal.

Princely India survives in Bhavnagar, Wankaner, and Jamnagar, and you can stay in royal palaces at Utelia (near Lothal), Poshina (near Palanpur) and Gondal, for example. Other recommended overnights include a Jain dharamshala in Palitana, a tent camp at Dasada, railway retiring rooms in Dwarka or Porbandar, and beach hotels in Diu, another intriguing reminder of Portuguese enterprise. To avoid interrupting the narrative, I have relegated most of the suggestions for hotels and restaurants to the 'Useful Information' chapter at the end.

Kutch is really an isolated adventure , far from the crowds of Surat or Ahmedabad, and it would be possible to use Bhuj as a centre for a week, departing every morning in a different direction for new explorations of landscape and nature, tribal ways and handicrafts, temples and fortresses.

I should have liked to offer the reader comforting generalisations, but I can offer none, for every day in India is unique, and every meeting with Indians is unique, complex, apparently both changeless and ever-changing, like a river which bears a single name but cannot seem remotely similar to any two spectators in any two places, as it absorbs pollution and pure rain, accommodates playful fish and rotting carcases. I have not the slightest idea who I am, so I am not going to be much help as a guide through India, unless...Unless perhaps the reader comes along with an equally open mind, taking everything on trust and taking nothing on trust. I return to Europe every time a puzzled man, not understanding whether the vivid exoticism of India is more real than the grey, plodding predictabilities of the National Health Service and laned motorways. I listen to Jain temple chants from Girnar, touch an agate from Cambay, and look at my tablecloth from Baroda, my photographs from Pavagadh. Another life is intertwined. If the purpose of life is to increase primary experiences of ecstasy, creativity, awareness and understanding, then Gujarat can provide all of these to a receptive traveller.

I have written the book not necessarily in my own order of travel, but in what I have come to appreciate as the best possible order for anyone wishing to seek out the best that the State has to offer, spending as little time as possible on backtracking. If I had had more time, I should have pursued the Narmada eastward, explored Panchmahals district, and visited Songadh east of Surat and towns in Saurashtra such as Dhrangadhra, Gondal, Jetpur and Surendranagar. My only regret is that I have not spent longer in Gujarat, but then I have always felt the same whenever finishing any book about India.

Gujarat is not a feverishly active tourist destination and, like Daman and Diu, lacks the beggars and touts connected with more crowded destinations. Instead, the visitor will find ready hospitality and it is to the ordinary folk of Gujarat, Daman and Diu that this book is affectionately dedicated.

Illustrations

Nani Daman. Doorway ... *frontispiece*

Chapter VI

Chapter VII

I: AHMEDABAD

Ahmedabad, capital of the State of Gujarat until the new city of Gandhina-gar's assumption of administrative capital status, has for more than five centuries deserved the title of a great city. Even today, despite its dust, noise, and pollution, Ahmedabad remains one of the five or six greatest cities of India not merely by population, but because of the beauty and ubi-quity of its monuments, beginning with its Citadel (1411) and Friday Mos-que (1424) and culminating in its Gandhi Museum designed by Charles Correa (1963) at the Harijan Ashram.

The growth of Ahmedabad, originally dependent like Manchester on textiles, but now more widely based, can be seen in its growth of popula-tion: 185,889 in 1901, 310,000 in 1931, 1,149,918 in 1961, and 2,954,526 in 1991.

Originally known as Asaval and Karnavati, on the east bank of the Sa-barmati river, the settlement was chosen by Zafar Khan (entitled Muzaffar Khan) as the town in Gujarat where he would settle as an independent Sultan in 1407, having defeated the rebel governor Malik Mufarrah in 1392.

The aim was to replace the atmospheric old Hindu capital of Gujarat, Anahilvada Patan, 112 km to the north, with a larger, even more influen-tial Islamic capital.

Zafar was the grandfather of the great Ahmad Shah I, after whom Ahmadabad (now more commonly spelt Ahmedabad) would be named from its foundation in 1411. His thirty-two year rule was marked by mili-tary engagements against Rajput princes of Jhalawar and Champaner, Idar and Nandod. When Idar fell in 1428, its name was changed to Ahmadnagar, and more recently to Himmatnagar. The first great building period we see at Ahmedabad is 1411-42, the reign of Ahmad Shah I. There is a quieter phase during the reigns of Muhammad Shah II (1442-51) and Qutb ud-Din Shah (1451-8), but a new efflorescence marks the time of Ahmad's grandson, Mahmud Shah I Beghada (1458-1511), who also estab-lished the new cities of Mahmudabad (now more familiar as Mehmeda-bad) and Champaner.

Having encouraged the immigration of merchants, craftsmen and arti-sans for more than a century, Ahmedabad gradually declined with the de-cline of its Ahmadshahi dynasty in the 16th century, and the growth of Portuguese power seaward and Mughal power landward. The Mughals took much of Gujarat in 1572, and as a viceroyalty subject to the waxing Mughals it regained some of its glory, but the 18th century saw renewed

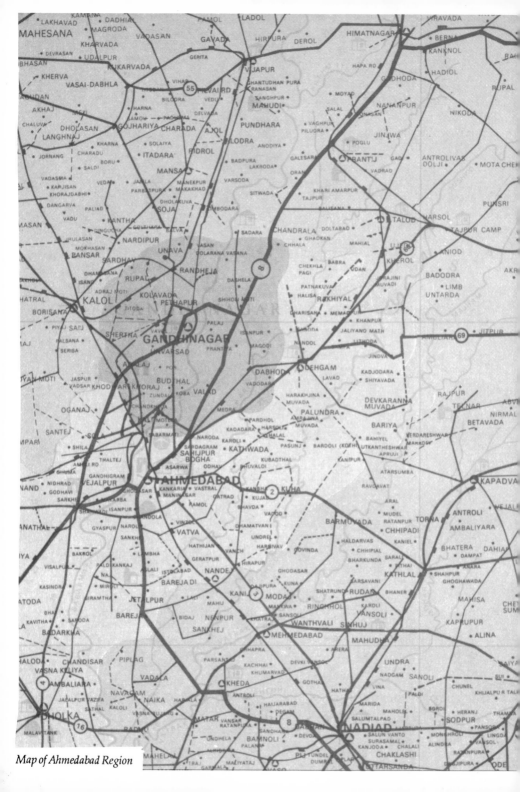

Map of Ahmedabad Region

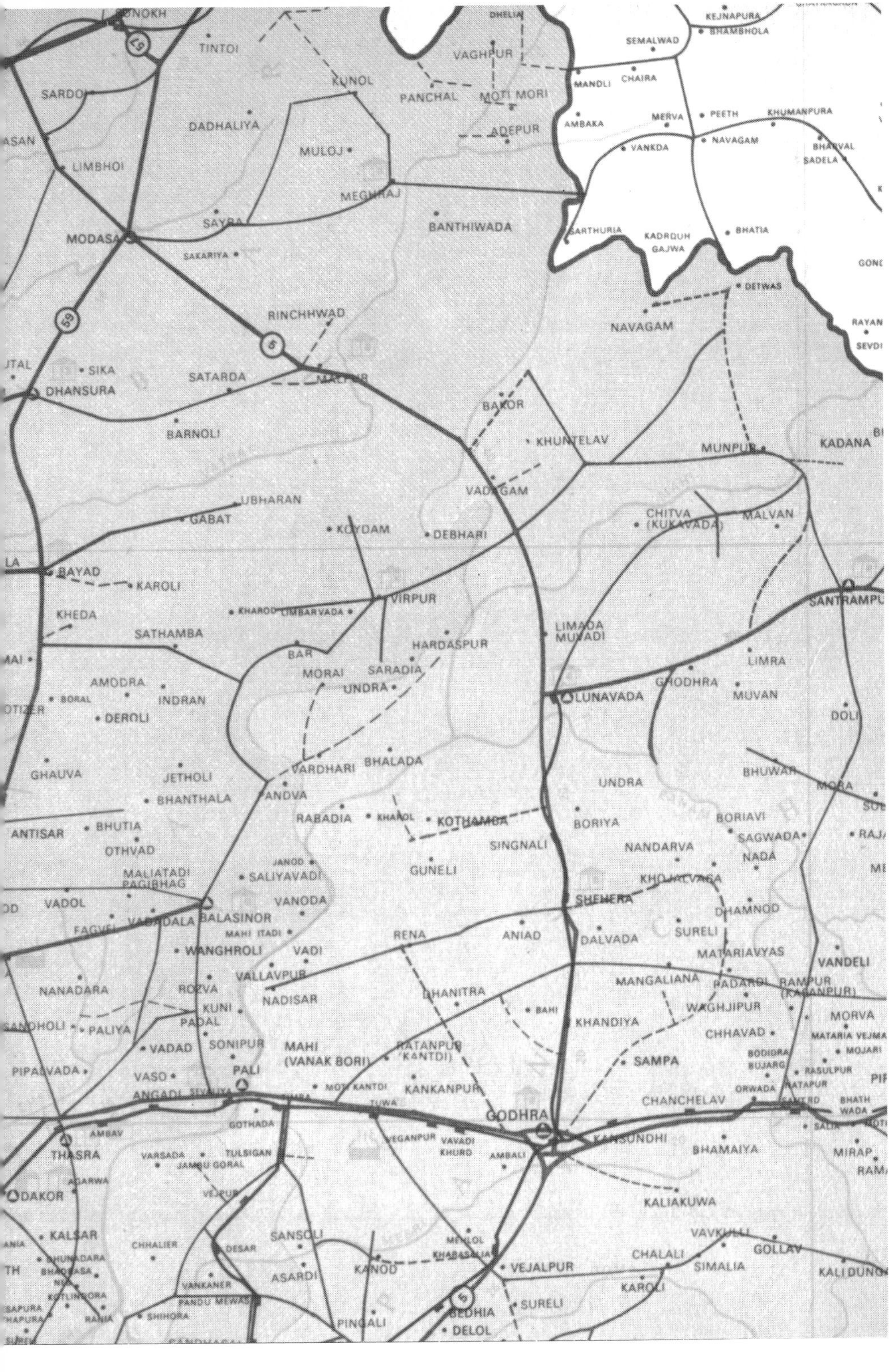

SUNOKH
TINTOI
DHELIA
KEJNAPURA
BHAMBHOLA
SEMALWAD
VAGHPUR
MANDLI
CHAIRA
SARDOI
KUNOL
PANCHAL
MOTI MORI
DADHALIYA
ADEPUR
AMBAKA
MERVA
PEETH
KHUMANPURA
VANKDA
NAVAGAM
BHARVAL
SADELA
LIMBHOI
MULOJ
MEGHRAJ
SAYRA
BANTHIWADA
SARTHURIA
KADRQUH
GAJWA
BHATIA
MODASA
SAKARIYA
DETWAS
RINCHHWAD
NAVAGAM
RAYAN
SEVDI
SIKA
DHANSURA
SATARDA
BARNOLI
BAKOR
KHUNTELAV
MUNPUR
KADANA
UBHARAN
GABAT
VADAGAM
CHITVA (KUKAVADA)
MALVAN
KOYDAM
DEBHARI
BAYAD
KAROLI
KHEDA
VIRPUR
KHAROD
LIMBARVADA
SANTRAMPUR
SATHAMBA
LIMADA MUVADI
HARDASPUR
BAR
MORAI
SARADIA
UNDRA
LIMRA
GHODHRA
MUVAN
AMODRA
BORAL
INDRAN
DEROLI
LUNAVADA
DOLI
GHAUVA
JETHOLI
VARDHARI
BHALADA
PANDVA
UNDRA
BHUWAR
MORA
BHANTHALA
ANTISAR
BHUTIA
OTHVAD
RABADIA
KHAROL
KOTHAMBA
BORIYA
BORIAVI
SAGWADA
SINGNALI
NANDARVA
NADA
MALIATADI PAGIBHAG
JANOD
SALIYAVADI
GUNELI
KHOJALVASA
VADOL
BALASINOR
VANODA
SHEHERA
DHAMNOD
FAGVEL
VADADALA
MAHI ITADI
RENA
ANIAD
DALVADA
SURELI
WANGHROLI
VADI
MATARIAVYAS
VANDELI
VALLAVPUR
MANGALIANA
PADARDI
RAMPUR (KADANPUR)
NANADARA
ROZVA
NADISAR
DHANITRA
KUNI
PADAL
BAHI
WAGHJIPUR
MORVA
PALIYA
KHANDIYA
CHHAVAD
MATARIA VEJMA
VADAD
SONIPUR
MOJARI
MAHI (VANAK BORI)
RATANPUR (KANTDI)
SAMPA
BODIDRA
BUJARG
RASULPUR
PIPALVADA
VASO
PALI
NATAPUR
ANGADI
SEVALIYA
MOTI KANTDI
KANKANPUR
ORWADA
CHANCHELAV
BHATH WADA
TIMBA
TUWA
GODHRA
GOTHADA
AMBAV
VEGANPUR
VAVADI KHURD
KANSUNDHI
BHAMAIYA
THASRA
VARSADA
TULSIGAN
JAMBU GORAL
AMBALI
MIRAP
AGARWA
DAKOR
VEJPUR
KALIAKUWA
KALSAR
SANSOLI
MEHLOL
VAVKULLI
CHHALIER
DESAR
KHABASALIA
CHALALI
GOLLAV
BHUNADARA
KANOD
VEJALPUR
SIMALIA
ASARDI
VANKANER
KAROLI
PANDU MEWAS
SURELI
SHIHORA
BEDHIA
PINGALI
DELOL
RANIA

discord: the Muslims and Marathas ruled Ahmedabad jointly but in frequent discord from 1738 to 1753, after which it fell into Maratha hands until the East India Company took control in 1817.

On the map, the Sabarmati river looks influential, but it fills reliably only during monsoon rain; otherwise it trickles feebly in a wide bed greedy for moisture. Without a navigable river, Ahmedabad relied on road transport for its export trade until the advent of the railway which began service to Delhi on the Western Railways metre-gauge line in 1881. (There is a broad-gauge service to Bombay.)

If you are familiar with the alleys of Banaras teeming with sadhus or the pilgrim-choked streets of Nasik or Hardwar during a Kumbh Mela, Ahmedabad may strike you either as refreshingly secular or numbingly materialistic, depending on your attitude. Numerous mosques, temples and other places of worship can be found, but the city itself attracts few pilgrims: Hindus are more likely to find their way to the new Swaminarayan Akshardham at nearby Gandhinagar, then to Somnath and Dwarka, Jains to leave for Palitana and Junagadh.

The Muslim historian Muhammad Qasim Firishta noted in the early 17th century that Ahmedabad was, "on the whole, the handsomest city in Hindoostan, and perhaps in the world". It is in the light of this fascinating encomium (not from an Ahmedabadi, let it be recalled, but from an Adilshahi Bijapuri from Karnataka) that we should try to understand and appreciate Ahmedabad today. It has retained most of its fifteenth-century features, and its urban and suburban layout, while adding such practicalities as more bridges over the Sabarmati, more textile mills, and more restaurants. But we can pick our way through bazaars and mosques, *pols* and *puras*, in the knowledge that changes have been kept to the minimum in this innately traditionalist society. If one does not endorse the principles of caste and class, sect and guild, one can at least enjoy benefits that come from deliberate adherence to the old ways. Camel-carts mooch noiselessly along the crowded streets of Ahmedabad – and they are the only noiseless denizens apart from surviving pedestrians. Recent communal disturbances must not be allowed to divert attention from the simple fact that Ahmedabad has for centuries been distinguished by enviable communal peace and stability. This harmony is reflected in the most obvious way: in architecture. Stones and indeed complete pillars were brought from Anahilvada Patan for mosques in Ahmad Shah's new capital, which would be influenced by Hindu traditions and by mediaeval Jain Gujarati motifs. Delightful minarets, elaborate tracery patterns, and infinite attention to detail distinguish Ahmedabad's mosques and tombs, Hindu delicacy enlivening the broad sweep of Muslim grandeur. The Bhadra area of the inner city once inhabited by the Muslim sovereigns is named after a corresponding Bhadra fort at Anahilvada Patan dedicated to the auspicious aspect of the Hindu goddess Kali, also the patron goddess of Ahmedabad. Up to Maratha times, state officials and weavers were mainly Muslims, as were the

Bohras trading in silk and piece goods, but financiers and merchants were usually Jains and Hindus. The *sarafi* families could not be called 'bankers' in the modern, restrictive sense of the world, using depositors' money in the main: they dealt in cheques, currency, insurance and acted as army paymasters to princes and farmed land revenues, sometimes indulging in their own enterprises too. Such a figure was the Jain financier and jeweller Shantidas Jawahari, important not only as a servant to the Mughal courts at Agra and Delhi, but as an ancestor to the leading mill-owner of Ahmedabad and exemplar to the shrewd, hardworking Jains of Gujarat responsible for the creation and restoration of great Jain temples throughout the state and in neighbouring Rajasthan.

Shantidas Jawahari and his elder brother Vardhaman erected the temple of Chintamani-Parshvanatha at Saraspur in Ahmedabad in 1621-5, but regrettably this great temple is no more, having been desecrated by Aurangzeb in 1645 and converted into a mosque to be called Quwwat al-Islam (The Power of Islam). Jean de Thévenot relates how Aurangzeb killed a cow in the Chintamani temple, knowing that thenceforth Jains could no longer worship there. He continues, 'All round the temple there is a cloister furnished with lovely cells, beautified with figures of marbles in relief, representing naked women sitting after the oriental fashion. The inside roof of the mosque is pretty enough and the walls are full of the figures of men and beasts; but Aurangzeb, who has always made a show of an affected devotion, which at length raised him to the throne, caused the noses of all these figures, which added a great deal of magnificence to that mosque, to be beat off'. Thévenot might have added that, since it is forbidden in Islam to portray any living being whether painted or carved anywhere, let alone a mosque, Aurangzeb's leaving the rest of the figures intact might be seen by strict Muslims as a concession to the infidel in Ahmedabad at the time.

Many peasants and rulers alike would have been ruined without the moneylenders of the Jain community and their farsighted investments, seeing their clients through bad times as well as good. During Mughal times, Ahmedabad was ruled by an appointed Governor or *subahdar*, responsible for defence, justice and the police force, while the Diwan dealt with finance. The police looked after crime and security, market regulation such as short weight and the forbidding of monopolies, the punishment of drunkards, and the regulation of cemeteries. The financial guilds or *mahajans* took on many of the functions which a modern Western city would assume, such as water-supply, street-cleaning, parks, hospitals and even schools. Charity formed a religious obligation which would have the effect of reducing social and economic inequalities; the acceptance of caste obligations and privileges minimised any spirit of rebellion; divisive political parties did not exist, and a *nagarseth* or city representative would use his good offices to settle disputes that threatened the city, and intervene with outside threats, as when Shantidas' grandson Khushalchand Lakshmichand interceded with Maratha marauders in 1725, offering them his own funds to spare the city. Likewise, *qadis* represented the Muslim communities in secular as well as religious matters, but Muslim guilds seem to have been much less influential than their Jain and Hindu prototypes. The artisans' guilds were called *panches* and their heads *patels*, the latter name having passed into folklore as 'the' Gujarati surname. 'Patel' originally meant *patidar*, a farmer possessing a *pata* or landholding in a village which pays taxes jointly not individually. The name Patel was given not only to this farmer caste, but was also used to designate a village chief. A guild would comprise members of different castes, and caste members would normally belong to different guilds, admission to which would be paid by application or by heredity. The guilds tentacled into virtually every aspect of Ahmedabadi life (and death, with funeral expenses), including wages, standards, competition, caste rules, holidays, charities, and in some ways corresponded to the much later introduction of trade unions. Beyond the civil service, silk industry and paper factories, most people worked at home in a group of homes called a *pol* generally confined to a single caste. A *pol* consists of a single main street open to tall wooden houses and lateral side streets ending in *culs-de-sac* with a common well, common latrines, often its own temple, and gates which could be locked at night. These gates have now gone, but even so it is a great privilege and delight to be invited by a resident to see one of these intriguing old *pols* with their old mansions or *havelis*, which give the impression of having been lived in very intensely. A traveller called Forrest could write in 1903, 'Nowhere does one feel oneself more thoroughly in an eastern city of past times than in the narrow streets of Ahmedabad, thick with ancient houses, none so poor as not to have a doorway or a window or a wooden pillar carved finely'.

Rich residents of these *pols* later felt the need for privacy, and moved out to suburbs or *puras* with gardens and even palaces beyond the walled city all the way to Sarkhej. The Nagarseth's family created the new suburb of Madhavpura in Maratha times.

Some of the surviving *pols* possess mansions of great beauty in need of permanent preservation: these include the Yogesh Shah haveli in Haribhaktini Pol, Vasa haveli in Totlagini Pol, and Gautam Patel haveli in Jada Bhagatni Pol. If your auto-rickshaw driver can't find these, there is always the Samal Bachan haveli in Panchbhaini Pol and the Divetia haveli in Sankdi Sher. Eighteenth-century wooden Jain temples that have survived hazards of fire and age can be seen in Shamlani Pol and Vaghan Pol. It is a pity that the only Jain temple shown on the official day tour of Ahmedabad is the white stone Sheth Hathi Singh (1853) which may be larger, but possesses none of its predecessors' atmospheric charm. Opening hours are 10-12 and 3.30-7.30. While I enjoyed losing my way in alleyways and byways (it sometimes seemed as though – Kafkalike – I emerged from one *cul-de-sac* only to be confronted by two more) – I passed a glassy-gazed woman pulling a leading donkey of a caravan of six all laden with soil, another saried woman pushing a creaking cart full of red earthenware cooking pots roped securely, and a tricycle slowed by its load of flapping aluminium strips.

Harijan Ashram

Raucous Ahmedabad streets can be forgotten as one steps into the quiet compound of the Harijan Ashram. Gandhiji had originally settled at Kochrab in the bungalow of his friend Jivanlal Desai, on the Paldi road near the river. But two years later a terrible epidemic broke out and Gandhiji chose this new site, at that time a snake-infested wilderness. Visitors are shown the simple cottage of Bapuji, 'Respected Father' you might translate it, called Hridayakunj, and Charles Correa, the eminent Bombay architect, has created a harmonious sequence of modular units 6 metres square based on the brick column, the tiled roof, and above all the open vistas through the columns. This imaginative use of cheap materials, including stone floors and louvred windows without glass, distinguishes Correa's Gandhi Smarak Sangrahalaya, his first important commission in private practice (1958-63). The institution is a memorial museum open to the public, a study centre filing some 30,000 letters written to and from Gandhi, and the major repository of Gandhi memorabilia, with a distinguished library.

But you may find more enlightenment in the plain cottage where Bapuji lived between 1917 and 1930, when he left for his historic march to Dandi, a campaign of civil disobedience which formed part of the cumulative drive for Indian independence. He wrote on 22 November 1944, 'The search for truth and the observance of non-violence are impossible without adherence to chastity, non-stealing, non-possession, fearlessness, respect for all religions, and eradication of untouchability and the like'.

If you are tempted to visit Churchill's Cabinet War Room while in London, then do not miss Gandhi's peace rooms in Ahmedabad, with his saying engraved for us all to remember: 'If blood be shed, let it be our own. Let us cultivate the calm courage to die without killing'. It is tragic that such Hindu extremists as the B.J.P. and the R.S.S. have hijacked the dominant role in the public perception of Hinduism, to the point where His Holiness the Dalai Lama nowadays represents the gentle side of Gandhian beliefs in the world at large. But there are disciples of Bapuji here at Harijan Ashram to speak of the twofold purpose of this place: to carry on the search for truth whether immanent or pragmatic; and to forge a new nonviolent community from the old, divisive patterns of life. Gandhiji taught teachers to respect manual labour, reintroduced spinning wheels and handlooms into daily life, celibacy became the order of the day, and liquor, meat and tobacco were prohibited. The ashram forswore caste and with it the doctrine of untouchability, as well as theft, and greed for possessions, and decreed the use of simple, Indian-made articles.

A

Map of Ahmedabad

Playful striped palm squirrels darted among the trees amid the birdsong and profound peace. An ancient companion of Gandhi beckoned to me to examine the rooms of Gandhiji, Kasturba, and guests, and pointed to the hut where Gandhi's 'European daughter' still observed the eleven ashram rules. Gandhi's clothes – just a dhoti made of the cheapest *khadi* and a pair of *chappals* for his feet – lie mute in a showcase, yet how eloquently they speak of the man's self-abnegation. His writing desk and spinning wheel gave me that authentic shock of historical palpability: the man will return through that door at any moment.

A hundred stories of Gandhiji's years at the Sabarmati Ashram jostled in my memory as I wandered through the few rooms. I recalled the dispute with his old friend the textile-mill owner Ambalal Sarabhai, delegated to represent the mill-owners when labourers complained about conditions of hours and pay. Gandhi proposed arbitration, but the mill-owners refused, so Gandhi suggested that the workers should strike and was supported by Sarabhai's sister Anasuya. Gandhiji's method was to gather the strikers under a banyan tree and strengthen their resolve, which day by day weakened until he threatened to fast until death if they did not prolong their strike until victory. He told the workers to keep on strike, but they said they needed to feed their families, so Gandhiji found different work for many, including erecting new buildings at the Harijan Ashram; he told the mill-owners that his fast was not directed against them, but to encourage the workers as their representative. Yet he knew they would be influenced: if he starved to death, all India would blame them. His fast lasted only three days: the mill-owners agreed to arbitration and the three-week strike ended, neither side having lost and non-violence having won. His system of peaceful arbitration succeeded then and later.

The spirit informing Harijan Ashram gave rise in 1972 to the Self-Employed Women's Association, a cooperative founded in Gujarat but now spreading all over India, allowing more than 13,000 women so far to benefit from credit schemes, training, welfare and minimum earnings, giving them social and economic progress and dignity.

If you plan to see Son et Lumière at Gandhi's Ashram, you might like to know that you can sample a Gujarati thali at the Toran Restaurant attached to the Toran Guest-House, a state-operated hotel basic but acceptable.

City Tour

I should love to be able to recommend the four-hour bus tour organised by the City Corporation and leaving Lal Darwaza (Stop 1) at 9.30 a.m. and 2 p.m. But I can't. The greatest monuments (the Friday Mosque complex) are excluded, as is the best museum (Calico Museum in Shahi Baug) and one is best alone in the Gandhiji Ashram. Apart from the Sabarmati Ashram, the tour visits the Sidi Sa'id Mosque, the relatively uninteresting Hathi Singh

Ahmedabad. Kankaria Lake

Jain Temple, the shaking minarets of Sidi Bashir's Mosque, and Kankaria Lake, but without adequate time to visit the island garden, aquarium, zoo and Natural History Museum: again, this lake designed by Sultan Qutb-ud-Din in 1451 should be enjoyed at your own pace so instead draw up an itinerary, ask the bell captain in your hotel to call an auto-rickshaw driver, request a bilingual receptionist explain the route to him in Gujarati and fix a price per hour, including waiting time. The order of visits I have given in the text is by no means the only one, and may not be the best, but its careful progression minimises travelling time in a city bedevilled by traffic jams and pollution. (I wear a cheap throwaway surgical mask bought at my dentist's to protect nose and mouth, but a cycle shop may have similar masks).

My suggestions for a day's tour of Ahmedabad by auto-rickshaw or taxi would be to begin with the Friday Mosque and Tombs of Ahmad Shah I and his Queens, and continue to the Queen's Mosque and Tomb at Sarangpur, the minarets near the rail station, the minarets of Sidi Bashir, the mosque of Muhammad Ghauth al-'Alam, Bibi-ki-Masjid beyond Sarangpur Gate in Rajpur, Rani Sipri's mosque and Dastur Khan's mosque.

11

Lunch wherever you happen to be (there is no shortage of restaurants) and then continue to Ibrahim Sayyid's mosque, and Hauz-i Qutb.

On your way back to the city centre, make sure you stroll around the Citadel called Bhadra, the triple gate called Tin Darwaza, and the mosque and tomb of Rani Rupavati, locally called Rani Rupmati. If you have time to see a step-well, Dada Harir's is in a better state of repair than the nearby Mata Bhavani's and the best-known Jain Temple is that of Sheth Hathi Singh.

The end of the afternoon is for Gandhiji's Ashram (8.30-6.30 October-March, otherwise 8.30-7) and its moving Son et Lumière (in English, 8.30-9.30 on Sundays, Wednesdays and Fridays). You can get a vegetarian meal at the Toran Restaurant opposite the Ashram. The best way of taking dinner in Ahmedabad is by visiting the enterprising Vishalla village designed by Surendra Patel. 4 km outside the city centre at Vasana on Sarkhej Road, it is described by Mr Patel as 'huts, cots, swings, lanterns, clean food and clean air in a soothing rustic environment' and after the pandemonium of the dusty city the change is welcome. You need to arrive before about 8 p.m. to book your meal, then squat down with your drink or wander round the Utensils Museum (open from 10 a.m.)

Flying your Kite
Mid January is the time of Gujarat's Makar Sankranti or Uttarayan, the international kite festival, because that is when the skies are blue and clear, breezes are virtually guaranteed, but the sun never becomes too hot. Day 1, around 13 January, is devoted to the Patang Nagar or kite town in the Police Stadium, where international enthusiasts from Europe, the U.S.A., Japan and the rest of Asia can set up stalls to sell and display their national kites, some flown for exhibition as design models, alongside the many Gujarati types. Stalls of Gujarati food provide refreshments; crafts and arts stalls vary the entertainment, and music and dance platforms are busy throughout the day and evening.

On the second day of the three-day festival visitors are taken to terraces above the town and shown how to fly kites under tuition. At night, illuminated *tukal* kites gleam in the skies overhead. On the third day, the kite-fighting is held, for kites with strings coated in *manja* (a lethal mixture of egg-yolk, boiled rice and ground glass) and *'kata'* ('I've cut!') shrieks announce the winner, as a loser floats limply to the ground or snags on a telegraph wire.

Gujarati Handicrafts
Gujarat State Handicrafts Development Corporation Ltd manages emporia known as Gurjari in Bangalore, Bombay, Calcutta, Delhi and Lucknow; its Ahmedabad head office is opposite Sanyas Ashram, Ashram Road (tel. 46 60 36): a two-storey warehouse of immense variety and interest, concentrat-

Ahmedabad. Sankheda furniture at Gurjari Emporium

ing in a single invaluable encyclopaedic space all the richness of Gujarat's artisans. A brass-covered wooden *patari* or jewellery box from Jasdan near Rajkot fetches Rs 230. Minakari (painted) furniture from the Rajkot family of Muhammad Bashir Bukhari is attractive: one low-slung chair costs Rs 1200, and a set of sofa, two chairs and centre table comes to Rs 5350. A wall-board of clay figures from Chhota Udaipur (Baroda district) is priced at Rs 3000. Colourful Kutchi quilts range from Rs 250-300. Low-priced souvenirs include puppets (now made in Wadej, Ahmedabad, following Rajasthani traditions), hanging beadwork called *malas* (Rs 95) and *ari*, embroidered cushion-covers from Radhanpur, Banaskantha district. The unique Sankheda furniture, rounded and blindingly painted in maroon, vermilion, green and brown picked out with gold and silver, is made by carpenters from Sankheda (Baroda district), who specialise in garden swings (Rs 10,000), rocking-chairs (Rs 1,500) and screens (Rs 6000), though more conventional settees and chairs can be produced for about Rs 8000 the three-piece suite. I am still using every day a block-printed fabric folder (Rs 40) for its durability and attractive appearance. Metalware includes nut-crackers, copper bells from Jhura (Kutch), incense-hangings called *sagdis* transformed into plant-holders, and associated brass *bajoth* now used as low tables.

But of course embroidery is the paramount Gujarati craft: bags, purses, salwars-kurtas, ghaghras, dupattas, blouses, shirts, bedspreads, cushion-covers and wall-hangings: all can be elaborated by the various tribes in their own unique styles: from the regular, delicate *suf* work of the Soda community in Lakhpat (Kutch) to the bright yellow and red *pako* work by

13

Hodka craftsmen. The Jats, Rabaris, Ahirs, Mutwas, Mochis, and Luhanas have rich traditions followed faithfully: look for the tiny broken mirrors embroidered like stars in the sky by the Mutwas, and the gold and silver *mukka* embroidery by the Hali Putra artisans of Kutch. Gorgeous tie-dyed saris from Jamnagar and Mandvi figuring animals, birds and flowers will be priced according to the number of knots, which may number 200,000 or 500,000. At the other end of the scale, a simple Ganesh wall-hanging for display in a living-room might come to as little as Rs 150. The queen of Gujarati textiles is the Patan *patolu* or wedding sari best seen in the Calico Museum and taking six months to a year in the making, at a figure rising to Rs 50,000. A Rajkot *patolu* made in less than a month would fetch only Rs 4200.

Culturally, Ahmedabad can offer few amenities to the Western traveller in the evening: some *bhavai* performances of Gujarati folk theatre can be seen (but of course only in Gujarati) at the Tagore Theatre, Paldi; or the Sheth Mangaldas Town Hall, Ellisbridge. Dance companies occasionally perform, and Indian music recitals can be found in the local press which your hotel concierge can translate and communicate to a rickshaw-wallah. Hotels can also arrange temporary membership of sports clubs such as Ellisbridge Gymkhana, Ahmedabad Gymkhana on Airport Road, and the Sports Club of Gujarat, Navrangpura (for cricket). Films are of course the staple entertainment diet of the Amdavadi, but you can see these potboilers at home: much more useful to spend your hours in the city outdoors, or in the unique museums.

Calico Museum of Textiles

This is a museum even for those who are not interested in textiles, because it is situated in the leafy, aristocratic Retreat in Shahi Baug (Royal Garden) district where the Sarabhai family live in serene splendour. A Jain dynasty of wide commercial and cultural interests, including cotton, chemicals, pharmaceuticals, and the first-rate Mapin Publishing Company, the Sarabhais are involved with dance and learning, as well as the Udyana Botanic Garden, which with the concert hall and museum is sponsored by the Sarabhai Foundation. The Royal Garden suburb owes its origin to Crown Prince Khurram, who succeeded Jahangir as Shah Jahan (if one excepts the brief interregnum of Dawar Baksh) in 1628. Khurram built the royal palace of Shahi Baug in 1622 to give employment during a famine: its garden once extended as far as Delhi Darwaza, covering the whole area now known as Shahi Baug. The palace itself was modified in 1835 by the British, whose Commissioner lived here. Since 1960, it has been renamed Raj Bhavan and occupied by the Governor of Gujarat.

The great Mughal garden beyond the palace confines gradually ran wild, except for land cultivated in private farms. Sri Ambalal Sarabhai's uncle bought some of these farms in 1904 and built a new home as a quiet alternative to Shantisadan, his home in central Ahmedabad. The family moved out in 1915, gradually enlarged the residence, developing the gardens with fountains and ponds, pergolas and greenhouses. He set most of the trees between 1908 and 1964. The botanic garden, library, and textile museum are run by the Sarabhai Foundation as an educational service. Visitors are welcome to this shady paradise from 10.30 to 12.30 and 2.45 to 5 p.m. daily except on Wednesdays and bank holidays.

The Museum divides into two parts separated by ornamental gardens. Le Corbusier's private domestic architecture can be appreciated here at its best, integrating outer and inner, art and craft, light and dark, as it complements the Gujarati-style fantasies of woodcarving on the haveli surrounding the chowk. Here are secular textiles: embroidered *shamianas*, wall hangings, costumes and outstanding carpets, *kalamkaris*, *saris*, and Punjabi embroideries called *phulkaris*. Morning tours here start at 11.30 and afternoon tours at 3.45. But the emphasis is on religion and religious textiles. In the Vaishnava section, a Pustimarga shrine leads to galleries with *pichhwais* and *patachitras* (paintings on cloth) of immense historical value and intrinsic beauty. The *pichhwais* are grouped according to festival, season, and devotional theme. Tours of the religious textiles take place at 10.30 in the morning, and 2.45 in the afternoon. I found the Jain Gallery especially moving, since the museum is a Jain foundation. A painted, domed, wooden ceiling of a *derasar* or shrine in Maratha style had been brought from early 18th-century Patan and part of Sri Ambalal's own private ancestral shrine is shown, behind a reconstructed carved wooden temple in Western Indian style of the early 18th century. Here too are beautiful Jain manuscripts, easily hidden during periods of Muslim repression, just as the shrines were disguised to resemble the homes of wealthy *sravakas* or laymen. I found the most interesting textiles in the Jain Gallery to be painted cotton Shatrunjaya cloths of the 18th and 19th centuries, half maps of the sacred mountain, and half drawings: at once souvenirs of the pilgrimage and exhortations to make it again.

Of the other exhibits, I greatly enjoyed the palanquin of the Maharaja of Holkar (Madhya Pradesh), 17th-century *patola* from Patan exported to Bali, *kalamkaris* made for the British market in the same period, 18th-century tie-and-dye Karuppur *saris*, 12th-century block printing exported to Bali, window curtains for the Portuguese market, Gujarati chintz made for the East India Company, 18th-century tie-and-dye from Bhuj, and above all sumptuous *patola* from Patan, where the only surviving craftsmen – the family of Salvi Vado – can spend anything from six to twelve months of a *patolu* valued at Rs 85,000. A *patolu* is a silk woven with designs in double ikat; that is, warp and weft are coloured in sections by tie-dyeing before weaving, then woven to form intricate multi-coloured designs. Double-ikat is known only from India, Indonesia and Japan, so these examples are of enormous value, both commercial and historical.

Tribal Museum

Apart from the crucial Calico Museum a number of other museums are worth a visit in Ahmedabad: the Shreyas Folk Museum, off Circular Road (open 9-11 and 4-7 daily except Wednesday); the N.C. Mehta Museum of Indian miniatures in the Sanskar Kendra Municipal Museum, Paldi, next to Tagore Hall designed by B.V. Doshi, a collaborator with Le Corbusier here and in Gandhinagar (open 11-12 and 3-5 daily except Monday); the Indology Museum, Navrangpura (11.30-5.30, but closed on Sundays and holidays) which specialises in Jain culture; and the Tribal Museum at the Gujarat Vidyapith Tribal Research & Training Institute (open 12-5 daily except Sunday).

This institute is the only one of the thirteen tribal institutions in Gujarat not run by the Government. Dr Mustali Masavi showed me the work of the Institute, which does research, produces the excellent journal *Adivasi Gujarat*, offers 3-week courses to Class II government officials dealing with tribal people, and 4-day courses to Class III officials. Peripatetic classes are held in local areas for other officials. He sees the key to advancement of the tribals as preserving their lands (threatened by dams such as the Narmada, and encroachment by regional projects and private industry), improving their education, and defending their rights against non-tribal landlords and richer tribals. Untouchability is still a retrogressive factor in rural areas: Chaudhuris for instance don't allow Kathodis into their homes and will not dine with them, and Padhas, Kotwalias and Kolghas suffer similar ostracism.

Throughout India generally, 7% of the population is tribal and 14% comprises scheduled castes, but Gujarat reverses these percentages. Of Gujarat's tribals, roughly 42% are Bhils, 9.7% Dubla, Talavia and Halpati, 9.3% Dhodia, 6.4% Rathwa, 5.8% Naikda and Nayaka, 4.5% Chaudhuri and 4.2% Kokna, Kokni, and Kukna. The Tribal Museum aims to illustrate facets of their lives and culture, because no visitor can aim to see more than a very small number of tribal groups if he concentrates on towns and cities. Most tribals are animists, though some worship Hindu deities in the way that some Pacific islanders attend church as an extra insurance policy.

Rathwas and some Bhils draw magical paintings on their walls to protect their crops, cattle, and family when catastrophes threaten. Hindu potters make them terra cotta clay horses, which are placed in a circle to face a central plaque or stone. Elephant, cows, bullocks, men and women in terra cotta effigy may also be offered to the spirits governing every aspect of their daily lives. Crocodiles are the deities of the Gamits of South Gujarat, elephants of the Rathwas of Chhota Udaipur, and tigers are worshipped by many tribes throughout South Gujarat. Fishing is usually by bamboo traps; hunting by bow and arrow. The usual house is of one rectangular room, but in North and Central Gujarat the house may be surrounded by green bamboo fences to keep domestic animals in and wild animals out. Walls are usually of mud or mud-plastered rushes, and roof-tiles are often made locally.

The Islamic Monuments

A connoisseur of Islamic art in India begins with the imperial and classical style of Delhi and Agra. Other styles may be 'provincial' in the geographical sense but not in the pejorative sense often deployed in Europe to snub country cousins like the obscurer painters of the Abruzzi and Marches compared with the greater Tuscan and Umbrian Schools. These Indo-Islamic schools include the Punjabi (1150-1325), the Bengali (1203-1573), and the Gujarati (1300-1572), as well as the later flourishes of Deccan, Jaunpur, Malwa, Kashmir, Khandesh and Bijapur.

Of these provincial styles – notes the scholar Percy Brown in *Indian Architecture* (Bombay, 1956) – 'by far the largest and most important was that of Gujarat'. Two reasons for this have been defined. The first is that the Ahmad Shahi sultans, though leaning neither to arts nor learning, wished to impose a vision of their might on their subjects and guests. The second is the existence of a caste of artisans adept at all the architectural and building techniques, yet temperamentally willing to abandon the constraints of their own ancestral guild rules in favour of a new order dictated by constraints of Islamic doctrine. Judging by the magnificent results, these guilds felt even freer within the dictates of Islam, and their overlords permitted the reintroduction of details from Hindu and Jain precedent which in the ensemble made a dazzling effect, just like the Norman cathedrals of England, French in their planning but English in their detailed execution. The first period of Gujarati Indo-Islamic building is typified by the Friday Mosque at Cambay (*c.* 1325) and had its capital at Anahilvada Patan, where little remains; the second period covers the early decades of the 15th century, and boasts as its greatest glory the Friday Mosque in Ahmedabad; the third and last period covers the latter part of the 15th century and early 16th, when Mahmud Beghada and his followers tried to outdo the earlier monuments, and crowned their achievement with the Friday Mosque of Champaner.

We shall see the great early mosques in Cambay and Broach, but the middle period is our Amdavadi adventure, beginning with Ahmad Shah's exploratory mosque in the citadel (1412) which immediately sets the scene for our intriguing mixture of styles: a plain, almost severe façade, concealing within a riotous indulgence of twenty-five carved pillars from Hindu and Jain traditions. Its minarets are apparently unfinished, and contrast with the slender minarets of the Khan Jahan Mosque (*c.* 1512) to the south, overlooking the river at the south-west corner of the citadel. A pavilion in the open court before the mosque houses the tomb of Raj Mandlik, conqueror of that King of Junagadh who converted and served Sultan Mahmud Beghada bearing the name of Khan Jahan.

From here we turn eastward from the river towards the English Cemetery near Jamalpur Gate, and north of this is the mosque of Haibat

Khan (*c*. 1424), fascinating for its reuse of Hindu and Jain masonry, possibly even *in situ*. Its turrets look like those on Fairuz Tughlaq's Delhi buildings, as do the five strange new round bastions on the western wall. Just to the north you will come to the mosque and tomb of Nawab Sardar Khan, unfortunately in ruins now but well worth the visit for their exquisite beauty uncharacteristic though they are in Ahmedabad. Both date to around 1685 and are on brick plinths. The mosque is entered by three pointed archways in the façade and the solid minarets (usually Amdavadi minarets have spiral staircases within) soar four storeys high. The three onion-shaped domes in the Persian style carry crescent moons indicating the Persian extraction of the sponsor, Nawab Sardar Khan, who earned Emperor Aurangzeb's fervent gratitude by shutting the gates of the city to the defeated Mughal rebel prince when he fled here for refuge in 1659. The Nawab's neat and harmonious tomb has one large Persian-style dome and eight smaller domes in perfect proportion.

Even earlier than Haibat Khan's is Sayyid Alam's Mosque (begun in 1412), north of Bhadra and very close to the popular Sidi Sa'id mosque. It was built by Abu Bakr Husaini who was given (or perhaps appropriated) the megalomaniac honorific 'Lord of the World', and presents many features of the nascent Amdavadi style: the one buttress at the back of the main mihrab, the now turretless minarets with undistinguished bases, and the even height of the three arched entrances.

You make now for the nearby mosque (built in 1572) of Sidi Sa'id, a nobleman in the service of Rumi Khan, second son of Khudavand Khan Khwaja Safar, Governor of Surat in the reign of the tenth Sultan of Gujarat, Mahmud Shah (1537-53). Sa'id then joined the retinue of Bilal, an Abyssinian general in the army of the last Sultan (Muzaffar III, who surrendered to Akbar in 1578), who died in 1576, and is buried near the north wall. Still an active mosque, Sidi Sa'id can and must be visited outside the five prayer-times for its magnificent pierced ornamental stone window screens, known as *jalis*. The two best examples are on each side of the mihrab and white marble minbar: the other eight *jalis* are less interesting. The finesse of these intricate tree patterns has to be studied carefully to be believed, and is reproduced here to enable the reader to compare such artistry with Mughal glories known from Agra or Delhi. Oddly, this artistic highpoint of Ahmedabad manages to retain its cool invitation in the middle of a tumultuous traffic roundabout at the northeast corner of the citadel. On the corner of this square the former British Library (now moved opposite Gujarat College, near Hotel Shalim) has been converted into the City College.

The greatest complex of monuments in Ahmedabad is concentrated east of Tin Darwaza: the Friday Mosque (ask for Jami Masjid), Ahmad Shah's tomb, and his queens' tombs.

Let us not think that, because Ahmedabad was the capital of Gujarat, early Islamic architecture in the area began here. On the contrary, early

Ahmedabad. Sidi Sa'id's Mosque. Carved screen

Muslim buildings were created at Anahilvada Patan to the north (the Friday Mosque of which only the foundations remain, and Shaikh Farid's mausoleum of 1300), Broach and Cambay to the south (Friday Mosques), and Dholka (Hilal Khan Qadi's Mosque of 1333 and the Tanka Mosque of 1361) 35 km to the southwest. But the sheer variety, number and magnificence of the Amdavadi mosques form an unforgettable experience. It was not that Ahmad Shah himself is to be credited with all of this great fervour: his ministers, officials, and other great men of the period all made their mark in the most permanent of memorials: fifty mosques, and many mausolea. His citadel and palace led by the stately Triple Gate to the northern side of the Friday Mosque, and the area in front the mosque enclosed his own royal mausoleum and that of his household.

The last of the monuments dating from the first quarter of the 15th century is the masterpiece: the great Friday Mosque for which the three previous essays discussed above were in the nature of trial runs. You pass the Ahmedabad Mercantile Cooperative Bank and Delhiwala Perfumeries and enter the year 1424, when the great mosque was completed to the wonder of all the city. Here, as at Sidi Sa'id, we recall Hope's words: 'As to style, it was singular fortune of the Mohammedans [sic] to find themselves among the people their equals in conception, their superior in execution and whose tastes had been refined by centuries of cultivation. While moulding them, they [the Muslims] were moulded by them, and though insisting on

19

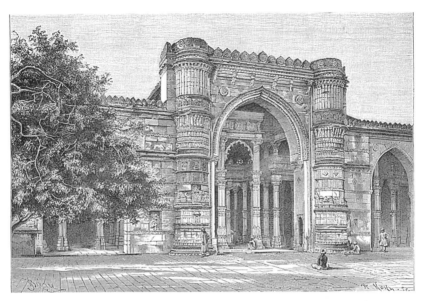

Ahmedabad. Friday Mosque

the bold features of their own minaret and pointed arch, they were fain to
borrow the pillared hall, the delicate traceries and the rich ornament of
their despised and prostrate foe'.

The white marble paved courtyard measures 255 feet by 220, allowing a
dignified pause between the crush of shops and stalls outside and the solemn majesty of the most perfect Muslim building in Gujarat, and one of
the finest in all Asia. You must mentally restore the upper parts of the minarets, destroyed by an earthquake in 1957. The courtyard is surrounded
on three sides by a covered corridor, and on the fourth by the great sandstone sanctuary. The front elevation combines the arch-screen in the centre
with the pillared portico on the flanks, producing an effect of massive
strength (though with those lost minarets offering a vertical play on lines)
with an invitation to light, airiness and depth beyond. Any thought of
heaviness in the minaret-supports is avoided by elaborate decoration and
sudden switches of bands and friezes all the way up.

The interior measures 210 feet by 95 feet, with 260 slim pillars as closely
set as a birch grove supporting a roof with three rows of five domes alter-
nating with flat slabs, the three central cupolas being higher and highly
ornate. The mihrab's quartz digital clock glares out the time in red figures
on black and if the mihrab were missing one would have difficulty identif-
ying one's surrounding as Muslim at all. Havell has admitted that 'even
the most sacred symbol of Islam, the mihrab, is so completely transformed

that except for a small pointed arch, which is as much Hindu as Saracenic, it is only a replica of the door of a Hindu shrine'. The whole plan is based on Hindu octagons or *mandapa*s grouped together, adapting Rajasthani Hindu temples of that time. Each dome is supported on eight columns and built according to traditional Hindu design in horizontal courses by changing the octagonal base into a circle. Side clerestories to admit diffused light served as galleries for the royal ladies of the *zenana*. Burgess noted that 'it is only in the Gujarat mosques of the 14th and the first half of the 15th centuries that these royal or zenana galleries appear' and Fergusson explains how 'the necessary amount of light is introduced, as in the drum of a Byzantine dome, but in a more artistic manner. The sun's rays can never fall on the floor, or even so low as the head of anyone standing there. The light is reflected from the external roof into the dome and perfect ventilation is obtained, with the most pleasing effect of illumination without glare.' The central 'rotunda' surrounded by galleries is not circular at all, as one might expect, but square in the lower gallery and octagonal in the upper. You can explore these galleries and sit very comfortably on slope-backed stone seating.

Next to the Friday Mosque enclosure is the Badshah-ka Hazira, or King's Mausoleum, completed by Ahmad Shah's son Muhammad Shah, who ruled from 1442 to 1451. The great square domed building has a central hall with deep pillared verandahs and four square chambers, each with smaller domes, at the corners. Light is admitted through large-scale *jali*s inferior to those of Sidi Sa'id. Ahmad Shah's tomb in the centre, draped like the other two, is flanked by his son's on the left and on the right by his grandson's, Qutb ud-Din Shah (1451-58). Outside the central domed chamber, but also draped, lies the tomb of Ahmad Shah's brother.

The Tombs of Ahmad Shah's Queens (Rani-Ka Hazira) are normally locked, so just rattle the door, and someone (to be tipped) will come running with the key and wander round with you until you are ready to leave. Regrettably, the *jali*s are of no great quality, but the complex belongs to the same period as the mosque and tomb of Ahmad Shah, and the tombs, out in the courtyard, are draped like those of the royal males. The arcaded corridor again is clearly of Hindu inspiration, and several of the tombs are beautifully carved with find Hinduising detail. The white central tomb with a Persian inscription is that of Bibi Mughali, wife of Sultan Muhammad Shah II, and daughter of the Sindi Jam Nizam ud-Din of Thatta, and mother of Sultan Mahmud Beghada. The black tomb nearby is that of Mirki Bibi, Mughali's sister and wife of the saint Shah Alam.

Scraps of broken kites fluttered in the whisper of wind here in the heart of Ahmadshahi Ahmedabad, where women without privacy empty enamel basins from balconies onto the heads of unsuspecting goats in the street below, and kiddies lurch naked from doorway to doorway. Boys play cricket in every patch of space. Through the window of the Stock Exchange you can see shares being brokered, broked, broken in a world of fax and filofax far from the chewing goats beyond the barred windows.

I finally came upon a sleeping rickshaw-driver, and I convinced him to go to the Rani-ki Masjid. This is confusing because there are several so-called 'queen's mosques' in Ahmedabad – Rani Sipri, Rani Rupmati or Rupavati (depending on whether you say it in Gujarati or Hindi), and Bibi-ki Masjid in Rajpur. So ask for Rani-ki Masjid, *Sarangpur*, for it lies close to the Sarangpur Gate. Malik Qiwam ul-Mulk Sarang, a Rajput converted to Islam, built the mosque in the suburb named after him about the middle of the 15th century. The minarets have been lost above roof level, but can imagined from their charming contemporaries at Bibi-ki Masjid.

The central arched gateway is memorable, and the five large domes within preside over square areas in the sanctuary, the whole enlivened as at the Friday Mosque by galleries and a play of illumination through four *jali* windows at the front, two at each side, and six at the back. The nobleman's tomb and that of his wife have been stripped of their expensive marble facing.

From here my driver Ram Singh drove me with great parping of horns and revving of engine to the shaking minarets of Sidi Bashir's mosque, which was probably built by the same Malik Sarang whose tomb we have just seen. These are pointed out to the goggle-eyed as 'shaking', but then it is likely that most of the great Amdavadi minarets were of this type, including those of the Friday Mosque itself. When the top storey of one minaret is agitated hard enough (as for instance by Robert Grindlay in 1826 and by Henry Cousens in 1905), the other minaret shakes though no perceptible shudder occurs in the mosque between. In fact, imperceptible movement occurs in the stone bridge between, and the shaking is due to the employment as foundation-cushioning of a flexible sandstone called *ita columite*. The original mosque has been replaced by a modern building of no great value. Another pair of minarets at the old railway station have lost their mosque but have been preserved from the early 16th century largely because of their curiosity value. The old railway station itself has been converted into warehouses or 'godowns' as the saying is throughout India, and a dispensary for rail employees.

Sarangpur is the site of the textile market: in these recessionary times 32 of the 65 textile mills in the city have closed down, as demand drops and labour problems rise. To the east of Sarangpur Gate, Bibi-ki Masjid is situated in Rajpur district. It is a great mosque of 1454 erected by order of Makhduma-i Jahan, mother of Sultan Ahmad Shah II, with a royal gallery covered by a typical Hinduising carved dome with a luxuriant spiral pendentive. Chain-and-lamp carvings and florid rosettes cover the five mihrabs. One of the minaret buttresses was destroyed down to roof level by lightning. Returning to Sarangpur westward across the railway line we turn south to the mosque of Muhammad Ghawth Gwaliori, constructed by a holy man called Hajji Hamid ud-Din from Gwalior, who died in 1562 and is buried in his native city. It derives not from the Gujarati tradition at

Ahmedabad. Shaking minarets, near Water Tower

all, but from the style of Jaunpur (Uttar Pradesh), where mosques typi-
cally reuse materials from Hindu and Jain temples, have a central propy-
lon with recessed arch, and solid, unusual minarets. The northern minaret
is 25 metres high, but the southern minaret has been demolished above
roof level. Here you can see how the absence of elegance and the flawed
attempt at awed majesty compares so unfavourably with the local craftsmanship on the superlative buildings we have seen so far and on these we
come to next: Rani Sipri's lovely mosque and tomb by the Astodia Gate
and Dastur Khan's mosque west of them.

Rani 'Sipri' is actually Queen Subha Rai who ordered the small tomb
locally known affectionately as the Nagina or Jewel Mosque. Fergusson
praised it as 'one of the most exquisite buildings in the world' and 'the
most perfectly Hindu of the buildings in the city', which would puzzle

23

Ahmedabad. Rani Sipri Mosque

most visitors if they had not already seen for themselves how Hindu craftsmen had infiltrated their iconography, vigour and delicacy, so that each column becomes a vibrant series of jutting and receding friezes; each screen whirls and winds into itself in sinuous arabesques of infinite (because tail-swallowing) variety. The minbar is lacking. I begged the crosslegged mine host of Novelty Tailors across the street to let me climb his narrow stairs to survey from above the tiny domes and exquisite minarets so appropriate for a queen, widow of the seventh Sultan, Mahmud Shah I Beghada. The tiny rectangular mosque only two bays deep is actually overshadowed by her tomb (hardly an Islamic tradition!), which has one massive dome over a two-storey square plan, and twenty outer columns in a square enclosing another twelve. The stone screens have recently enjoyed good restoration.

24

Nearby, Astodia Road is home to shops selling chemicals, paints, dye-stuffs and textiles, and to a unique internal square-plan mosque made in 1463 by Dastur Khan, one of Mahmud Beghada's favourite ministers. Additions changed the original plan of a sanctuary two bays deep and five bays long with three domes and mihrabs so that now there are three mihrabs and minbar in the centre, two spaces on each side with windows, and two more mihrabs in the end sections. Magnificent *jalis* in the cloister are well worth study, but you need to avoid prayer times as this is a popular mosque in a densely populated Muslim area and it is of course considered as impolite to enter a mosque for curiosity's sake during prayers as it is to enter a Christian church during service. Dastur Khan, or Malik Khasazada as he was also known, is buried in the courtyard near the south doorway. On our way south to Kankaria Lake we are looking at Ibrahim Sayyid's mosque (1540) and a graveyard for foreigners commonly called the Dutch Cemetery. The former resembles Shah Khub Sayyid's mosque near Azam Khan's Palace in the citadel area, while the latter contains tombs of Dutchmen from the Dutch factory here, Armenians who worked for them, and the founder of the English East India Company's Ahmedabad factory, one Mr Aldworth, who died here in 1615 and was succeeded by a Londoner called John Browne who fancied himself a poet and amused the more prosaic factors at Surat with his affected, hi-falutin' poetical style even in business correspondence.

The Hauz-i Qutb ud-Din or Kankaria Lake was devised by the Sultan as a place of recreation in 1451: a regular polygon of (yes, I counted) thirty-four sides with sloping ramps and stone steps. The best feature (if one excludes the children's amusements, aquarium and museum) is a wonderfully-carved set of sluice screens again in most abundantly inventive Hindu style bringing to the needs of technology a refinement unfortunately lost to today's commercial barons and whizzkids.

Rather than spending a great deal of time in these pleasant but by no means unusual surroundings, I recommend continuing southward by rickshaw to Shah Alam's mausoleum. *Rauza* is the Urdu word to use here, from the Arabic *rauda* (plural Riyadh, as in the Saudi capital) meaning garden, but extended to mean a tomb surrounded by a garden, as at Agra and Aurangabad. Muhammad Shah Alam is not the saint Burhan ud-Din Qutb ul-Alam (buried at Batura, farther south) who founded the Bukhari Dervish community, but his son, the spiritual mentor of Sultan Mahmud Beghada. It is interesting to note the influence of these Sufi mystics on the Ahmad Shahi dynasty, who were thus removed from the puritanical strain of the Aurangzeb style of Mughal Islam. The entrance bears Shah Alam's date of death (1475) and the tomb's date of completion (1483) in the village of Rasulabad ('Abode of the Prophet') now known as the village of Dani Limda, 3½ km northwest of Vatva where his father's ruinous tomb can be seen. Islam traditionally has no theological need for saints, but India has reinterpreted Islam in the light of its eclectic origins, in the same way that the original teachings of the Vedas, Buddhist scriptures, and Jain sutras have been similarly reinterpreted, whenever sects diverge. So just as pilgrims visit Hindu shrines and Jain temples, in India it is very common to see Muslims praying at the tombs of shrines as well as in mosques, a procedure heretical to the orthodox especially since over the nearby grave of Sayyid Muhammad Maqbul Alam, sixth in descent from Shah Alam, is a stone tablet reputedly bearing the footprints of the Prophet (s.A.a.w.s.)!

To return to the principal dargah in the complex of four buildings dating from 1475 to 1575, its appearance is in the so-called 'casket' tradition. On the outside a trellised wall has 28 pillars; within this a square enclosure of twenty pillars surrounds an inner square of twelve roofed by a dome which protects the grave. At the eastern end of the southern corridor, seven sandstone tombs preserve the relics of sons and grandsons of Shah Alam. A similar building already mentioned above, commemorating Sayyid Muhammad Maqbul Alam, contains three other graves on the south side. The domes of both these beautiful mausolea bear metal finials showing the *pipal* leaf, symbol of the Gujarati Sultans and of course like the banyan a tree sacred to Hindus.

The assembly hall was built in the reign of Sultan Muhammad Shah II (1442-51) but renovated more than once. Its purpose is to afford shelter for devotees arriving for the saint's anniversary celebrations. The mosque itself is a splendid though atypical construction of open-portico type, with a fine interior whose pendentives are connected by cross arches between pillars which take the domes. The later minarets were completed in 1620, damaged by the 1819 earthquake, then well restored.

If you start another morning at the Bhadra and Triple Gateway, your first call could be at one of the most wonderful post offices in the world, in the Palace of Azam Khan (1636), an honorific concealing the name of Mir Muhammad Baqir, a highly efficient Mughal Governor of Gujarat so devoted to building palace-citadels throughout his state that they called him 'udai' (white ant). Having been used also as a prison, and a hospital, it has consequently suffered numerous unkind cuts and alterations. It gives entry to Bhadra citadel on the north and the modern Bhadrakali temple can be found in one of the outward-facing lower cells of the annexe stuck on to the palace as a caravanserai.

Near the Triple Gateway is a café charitably offering simple meals to the needy at Rs 2 and above. As you pass, you hand money to the attendant. This he hands to the first in the field of dozens of poor people squatting on the pavement outside, where upon the applicant purchases the food of his choice. This ingenious procedure confers merit on the anonymous silent giver, and on the café-owner subsidising it. We shall never remove poverty from India, but we can remove the *stigma* of poverty by such thoughtfulness. I repent now that I paid for only five meals – I had money for many more, but I paid for only five. In Tin Darwaza I bought two fresh notepads to eke out my dwindling supply, and noted in the adjacent meat market: 'Muslims selling goat, beef, mutton in the open air; breakfast available; everything crawling with flies; fast food bazaar open till 2 a.m.; goat-heads staring blindly as if in a Buñuel movie'.

Near Khas Bazaar a Hindu temple has transformed by the ardour of Islam in 1452 into the mosque of Malik Sha'ban, an eminent figure in the reign of Ahmad Shah II whose *rauza* is found at Rakhiyal village. It has lost its minarets, and its central mihrab with the dated inscription is flanked by two smaller mihrabs, but the main feature is the great central dome over 6 metres in diameter upheld by twelve pillars. Though I should never wish to enter sectarian controversy on any side, I find it heartening that Hindus in Ahmedabad seem to wish no harm to these 'mosques' despite the Hindu revival exemplified by the violent removal of the Ayodhya mosque from the site of the Hindu temple there.

Khas Bazaar is also the home of the late mosque of Shah Khub Sayyid (1538), named for the Chishtiyyah sayyid buried north of the mosque, which was actually built by Nau Khan in the time of Mahmud Shah III. It's difficult to find, but a local Muslim shopkeeper will send a boy to show you where it is. Its minarets survive, but the *jali* work has been replaced in ugly concrete, so you have to concentrate on the serene interior, covered by twenty-one equal domes.

If you go back past Malik Sha'ban's mosque you come to the mosque, madrasa and tomb of Shuja'at Khan (1695) close to Red Gate, or Lal Darwaza, recognisable from the mosque's slim minarets. Then along the road northward from Delhi Gate in Mirzapur district you arrive at Rani Rupmati's mosque and tomb. If all these names seem indistinguishable, recall that one Hershey bar is indistinguishable from another, but each is very sweet, and when you have finished one you just feel like starting another. So, if you enjoyed Rani Sipri's mosque and tomb, the contemporary Rani Rupmati's will not seem any less wondrous. Its size is much greater, with an imposing central arch with one truncated minaret on each side, casualties of the 1819 earthquake. The middle part is raised to allow light in, and as we have seen in the Friday Mosque and elsewhere the galleries have dazzlingly carved parapets and the mihrabs enjoy similar attention to detail. The *rauza* of Queen Rupavati (Hindi; or Rupmati in Gujarati, 1430-40) bears another grave next to hers. The height of the upper storey in relation to the lower is more thoughtfully executed 'and this is better designed' than Rani Sipri's in the view of K.V. Soundara Rajan's *Ahmadabad* (1980), the Archaeological Survey of India's indispensable companion to the Islamic monuments. The problem I found was that the welcome growth of trees nearby tended to make a view of the *rauza* difficult.

Muhafiz Khan's mosque and tomb to the east, near Delhi Gate, were built in 1485 to honour Jamal ud-Din, an official raised to the rank of City Governor in 1471.

Situated just south of Qutb ud-Din Shah's mosque, it must be one of the most enchanting Indo-Islamic creations even in the abundant city of Ahmedabad. Hajji ud-Dabir, in *An Arabic History of Gujarat* (London, 1910) notes that this trusted minister of Mahmud Beghada had spent a great deal of money and effort on creating new mosques in Gujarat, and the Sultan clearly wanted to reward his Governor with a work of beauty and even originality, because there are no wings, no large entry in the façade and no full view of the main dome from the front. Everywhere the sandstone carving reaches the zenith of taste, from friezes and domes to minaret buttresses and hollow minarets. I found the simple *rauza* almost equally moving, because of the equivalence of many graves, two (but not the middle two as one might expect) of marble, and other of less precious sandstone. A young lad will help your rickshaw driver to find the nine tombs called Nau Gaz Pir, the Swami Narayan Temple (1850) and a touching Jain Animal Sanctuary. Throughout the *pols* of old Ahmedabad, Jains have set up delightful carved stone bird-feeding contraptions which remind me of those traffic platforms at crossroads in India (and in Communist Europe). These *parabadis* have survived after most of the great wooden havelis in the *pols* have disappeared.

Qutb ud-Din Shah's mosque, near Delhi Gate, is known locally as Pattharvali Masjid, and was built by Nizam son of the Arsenal Keeper Hilal Sultani in 1449 during the reign of Sultan Muhammad Shah II. Its glorious minarets make this visit worthwhile, and a vast congregation indicate its popularity even today within the community. Sixty pillars and corresponding pilasters support a roof of ten small and five large domes; stairs to reach the gallery are found not in the minarets but in the façade wall. Again all mouldings, niches and ornamentation present a marked Hindu appearance. A further surprise occurs in the mausoleum: the Sultan Qutb ud-Din after whom the mosque is named is buried not here but in the mausoleum of his grandfather.

Considerably to the west is the mosque of Shaikh Hasan Muhammad Chishti, one of that sect known in India since the 12th century at Delhi, Ajmer, and Fatehpur Sikri. The sect taught (among many other precepts) the unity of being, non-violence, and non-possession, so it is hardly surprising that in this land of Gandhiji, and of Jain love for all humanity, that Chishtiyyah should flourish throughout Gujarat.

Shaikh Hasan Muhammad, Qadi of Shahpur district, ordered the mosque in 1565 during disordered times; carvings and minarets alike remain incomplete, but what has been accomplished is a riot of Hindu invention, with glorious carving on the unfinished minaret, and on the inner screen of the upper front balcony. Another Chishtiyyah mosque considerably to the north, in the Shahi Baug district, near the Sabarmati, reunites the brilliant synthesis of Muslim pointed arches and Hindu carved pillars which so excites the architectural enthusiast. Amid so many ways of achieving a balance, Ahmedabad provides the connoisseur with a virtual library of effects. My favourite features of the Miyan Khan Chishti mosque are the

Ahmedabad. Miyan Chishti Mosque. Detail

radiant doorwaylike verticals of the superb niches culminating in a gentle arch softening the lines of lintel and pillars. It is a mosque of the closed type and dates from 1465. Its eclecticism matches the vigour of Sidi Bashir's mosque and Bibi Achut Kuki's, for example. The latter lies to the south, and was created in 1469 for his wife by a minister of Sultan Mahmud Beghada called Baha Nek Bakht Sultani, honoured as Imad ul-Mulk Arid ul-Mamalik. The most original feature of the unified Indo-Islamic style here is the provision of arches to support the ends of the gallery in the front aisle. Of the two surviving minarets, one was rebuilt in 1884. Three others at the entrance to the complex fell victim to the 1819 earthquake. I cannot forget the extraordinary panorama from the Miyan Khan Chishti mosque; the biggest power station in India; the reluctant trickle of the Sabarmati in its broad, rocky bed; Subhash Bridge; and Gandhi's quiet ashram.

Step-Wells

One day you must mark down for one or more of the extraordinary step-wells known locally as *vavs* or *baolis*. In Italy we are familiar with decorated fountains such as Fra Bevignate's masterpiece for Perugia, with statues and panel ornamentation by Nicola Pisano and his son Giovanni. But even the finest Florentine well-heads of that great civic Renaissance fade into insignificance when compared to the supreme ornamental step-wells of Western India, from the Hindu Rani-ki Vav of Patan and the Vikia Vav at Ghumli to the achievements of Ahmedabad: Gujarat possesses several hundred step-wells, but most fell into disrepair as alternative water supplies became available. This is a great shame, because they deserve to be maintained for their aesthetic and historic value, but the Government has concentrated on a few exceptional monuments. The first to be seen are the pair north-east of the walled city: Mata Bhavani's and Bai Harir's. The latter is dedicated to Bhavani, an aspect of Parvati, the consort of Shiva or perhaps one might say the Shakti or female energy of Shiva, whose small shrine can be found in the back wall of the shaft. Profoundly Hindu in character, it may date to the time of Raja Karna Solanki (1063-93), founder of Karnavati, a settlement preceding Ahmad Shah's city. Though inferior to Bai Harir's, Mata Bhavani's step-well illustrates the tendency seen already in mosques and tombs to decorate any surface with sculpted friezes, niches, pillars, capitals, railings, cornices and borders.

Structurally, the *vav* consists of two parts: the vertical well-shaft familiar all over the world, from which water would be pulled up by ropes; and the entrance passage, which would be sloping in parts, and stepped in other parts, but roofed to protect from rains and above all debilitating heat. Animals could be prevented from fouling the area and its water by a single gateway at the top. Platforms around the shafts have parapets and stone seat-backs for those who wish to stop and rest.

Step-wells as a civic amenity continued to be provided into the Islamic

Adalaj. Step-well

period, again using the only available Hindu craftsmen so that fortuitously the same sculptural traditions persisted. Close to Mata Bhavani's *vav* is that of Bai Harir Sultani, superintendent of Sultan Mahmud Beghada's *harem*. Inscriptions in Persian and Sanskrit date its construction and that of the associated mosque to 1500: 'this fine building and excellent edifice and lofty colonnade and the four frescoed walls were built and fruit-bearing trees planted with the well and reservoir so that men and animals may benefit.' Spiral staircases in the side walls of the well-shaft give dark yet spotlit dramatic access to each succeeding platform level, as if you were Dante, passing through succeeding *bolge* of the Inferno at the speed of light, all sinners sucked out of view.

Even more glorious is the step-well at Adalaj, left off the main road 18 km north from Ahmedabad to Mehsana. Built in 1498 by Ruda, wife of the Waghela chief Vairasimha, as recorded in a marble Sanskrit inscription in a niche on the right-hand side just before you descend, the oblong step well runs north-south, with an entry at the south on three sides, and a five-storey octagonal shaft. Green parrots dart through the levels, between columns and beams where striped palm squirrels lollop and sit, then sniff and search. Wonderful sculptures include a king seated on a stool beneath a parasol with two bearers, erotic moments appropriate to this sanctuary, the churning of buttermilk, the Bhairava (terrible) aspects of Shiva, dancing maidens and musicians, birds and animals. The well is round at the foot, and beyond it another (dry) well has niches found ideal by local pigeons. A truly magical experience of descent from heat and bustle into the cool, shady depths reminded me of troglodytic dwellings in France and North Africa: Libyan Gharyan or Tunisian Matmata. Elephants march eternally round an exuberant frieze, as do a parade of horses, and another of mythical animals. I walked round the flat gallery at ground level, surrounded by tended gardens, and then retreated below to bask in the balconied compartments, each pillar and cornice, railing and capital alive with scenes carved by master-craftsmen.

Many other step-wells exist in and around Ahmedabad, though of course they are hygienically catastrophic and ought to be sealed up to avoid the use to which some of them are even now put by those without running water. A brick step-well is found in Isanpur district, another of stone behind Madhav Lal Boarding in Shahi Baug, and near the rail station a third created by the father of laureate K.H.Dhruva.

Sarkhej

One of the most significant architectural complexes in the Ahmedabad area is to be found 9 km to the southwest, beyond Ellisbridge, the first permanent bridge across the Sabarmati, a triumph of Victorian iron engineering, and Vasana, a village where you can find the mausoleum of the brothers Azzam and Mu'azzam (1457), craftsmen believed to be responsible for designing the Sarkhej complex.

Sarkhej owes its importance to religious and secular factors intertwined as usual in India. Shaikh Ahmad Khattu (called Ganj-Bakhsh) lived here for half a century as Sultan Ahmad Shah's spiritual mentor, and survived him by four years, passing away at the age of 109 in 1445. The mausoleum in his honour was begun by Sultan Muhammad Shah II in 1446 and completed by Sultan Qutb ud-Din Shah. Shaikh Ahmad is said to have been responsible for persuading Ahmad Shah I to establish his capital at Ahmedabad, and certainly his holiness was so deeply revered that Sultan Mahmud Beghada took the whole complex under his wing, created a reservoir, and decided to be buried here in another impressive mausoleum (1511) connected in turn by a portico to the tomb of Bibi Rajbai, consort of Sultan Muzaffar Shah III (1590).

The saint's tomb, which I found deluged by a charming, chaotic stream of celebrating holidaymakers (why are western pilgrims so gloomy, by comparison?), lies in a building larger than any other mausoleum in Gujarat, its plinth area 31.7 metres square. The central square bearing the massive dome is double-pillared, though the division into two storeys lightens the appearance of the whole. Perforated stone work, brass screens, inlaid marble and expensive gilding illustrate the importance of the man and his message. The associated mosque of the same period has

Sarkhej. Mausoleum of Makhdum Shaikh Ahmad Khattu

five large domes and forty smaller domes corresponding to the pillared squares. It lacks the minarets and arched façades of the Amdavadi mosques, but maintains their jaunty Hindu floridity, like patterns made by the pawmarks of a symmetrical striped palm squirrel dancing across the walls. Sultan Mahmud Beghada erected palaces and a *harem* without a single Muslim arch, but borne by simple square based Hindu pillars crowned by bracket capitals. Sarkhej became a retreat for each succeeding Ahmadshahi sultan, who added gardens and pavilions, and regulated water in the reservoir by means of sluice-gates of the type we have already seen at Kankaria Lake. The palace complex is now ruined, but its grace and charm reflected in winter sunlight over the waters indicate the taste of its sponsor and the brilliance of its designers and artisans, their colonnade with projecting bays and steps down into the lake giving almost the impression of the Udaipur lakeside and island palace in regal Rajasthan. Two local women, returning from laundering their clothes at the water's edge, held overflowing tin basins on their head with an arm crooked at the elbow like dancers posing on a stage.

Sarkhej, nowadays almost a suburb of Ahmedabad, previously stood on its own feet as a independent producer of that valuable dyeing commodity, indigo. Soon after the rains, the plant was cut three times and thrown into lime-coated tanks about ninety paces in circumference, half-filled with water and stirred every day until the deep purple leaves be-

Sarkhej. Palace, with women bringing home the washing

came a slime. When the slime had sunk to the bottom, the water would be drained away and the slime removed to fields, where labourers would mould it by hand into egg shapes cut in half. We know a great deal about the industry in the time of the traveller Jean-Baptiste Tavernier (*Six Voyages*, Oxford, 1925), a French merchant who visited India between 1641 and 1668, who records that Sarkhej indigo was more highly prized than any from other production centres such as Surat, Golconda, Burhanpur, Agra and villages in Bengal.

Gandhinagar

Mahatma Gandhi has been honoured in his native Gujarat by the name of a new port in Kutch, 'Gandhidham', the Ellisbridge district of Ahmedabad has been named 'Gandhigram', and the new administrative capital of the state, after bifurcation from Maharashtra in 1960, has been called Gandhinagar, despite the fact that Bapuji might not have relished more connections with the proliferation of bureaucracy, and might well, if his shade had been consulted, have preferred to leave capital status in the more than capable hands of Ahmedabad. Because Gandhinagar has by no means replaced its industrial neighbour, its State Assembly and Secretariat may look impressive but to me seem merely faceless and repetitive genuflections towards 'Sixties functionalism, lacking even the innovative sparkle of Le Corbusier's Chandigarh, India's first modern planned city since the New Delhi of Lutyens.

After the higgledy-piggledy bazaar of most North Indian cities, Gandhinagar's orthogonal planimetry made me feel glum. Just like Dickens, visiting Philadelphia in 1842, who noted: 'After walking about in it for an hour or two, I felt that I would have given the world for a crooked street'.

The only craftsman making woodblocks that I know in Gujarat, Chaganlal Mistry, lives in Petapur, Gandhinagar. Accommodation is available at the air-conditioned Hotel Haveli in Sector 11, within easy walking distance of the administrative blocks. A double room costs Rs 700 (Rs 850 de luxe), and an excellent restaurant provides Indian, Continental and Chinese cuisine. But the main reason for a traveller's coming to Gandhinagar is for the extraordinary religious complex called Akshardham, Sector 20, J Road, inspired by Pramukh Swami Maharaj, spiritual leader of Bochasanwasi Shri Akshar Purushottam Sanstha, popularly known was the Swaminarayan Movement. As one of the most energetic and influential Hindu revivalist groups currently evangelising in India (especially Gujarat) and the world (especially Neasden and Leicester), it is amply worth three or four hours of even the busiest schedule to fit in Akshardham, devoting at least an hour to Hall 1, half-an-hour to Hall 2, and an hour to Hall 3.

The movement was founded in 1907 by Brahmaswarup Shastriji Maharaj to propound the Vedic ideals as enunciated by Shri Nilkanth Varni (1781-1830), known as Lord Swaminarayan, who settled in Gujarat, established six temples, and pronounced discourses collected as *Vachanamritam* and 212 verse precepts called *Shikshapatri*, while promising to remain ever-present on earth through a succession of saints. These have been Akshar-brahman Gunatitanand Swami, Bhagatji Maharaj, Shastriji Maharaj who died in 1951, Yogiji Maharaj who died in 1971, and Pramukh Swami Maharaj, a Gujarati born in 1921 in a small village called Chansad near Baroda. The scriptural discourses were all delivered in Gujarati, and the headquarters of the movement is in Ahmedabad.

Guides are provided from 7 a.m. to 10 p.m. in English, Hindi and Gujarati every day but Monday, when the site is closed.

Sadhu Brahmaviharidas, my English-speaking guide, had passed 'O' levels in Leicester with 9 A's and 2 B's, but decided to leave the world at the age of 15½ and had spent his last twelve years as one of the fourteen celibate monks in the management team realising Akshardham, from the foundation-laying in 1979 to the opening of the gates in October 1992. Akshardham is not a temple – no puja is performed there – but it can be considered an educational presentation of the tenets of Vaishnavism according to Lord Swaminarayan, who rejected the caste system and widow-burning, saying that the widow should worship God, not her husband.

The fivefold tenets of the Swaminarayan Movement are a pure vegetarian diet (and no onions nor garlic), moral purity, no addictions, no illicit sex, and no stealing. Unswerving adherence to one's guru is seen to be equally important, though in most fields other than religion it is usual for a pupil to advance beyond a teacher for any significant progress to occur, and I could not help wondering why more importance was not attached to Lord Swaminarayan's own guru, Swami Ramananda. 'Some gurus are more important than others', smiled Sadhu Brahmaviharidas, but the movement undercuts that possibility by dictating that you owe absolute subservience to your guru, whoever he is. The saffron-robed *sadhus*, who refer to themselves disarmingly in English as 'saints', come from backgrounds such as pharmacy, engineering, medicine and law to manage the spread of the global movement, travelling to promote 'an addiction-free, morally regenerated and spiritually enlightened society', and they tell me that they have achieved sublime purity through complete renunciation of women and wealth. I must have looked dubious, because most of the sublime purity I have encountered in my life has been possessed by women, and the movement shows no reluctance to utilise immense wealth for its own purposes: the contrast with Gandhiji's little ashram could hardly be more sensational.

Akshardham itself is a fantastic monument in Rajasthani pink sandstone, commemorating the life of someone who taught poverty and non-possession through the paradoxical means of a seven-foot cross-legged image in hollow copper entirely covered in gold leaf, and faced by two smaller figures at the sides, also entirely covered in gold leaf: Gunatitanand Swami and Gopalanand Swami, on a podium lower than Swamin-

Gandhinagar. Akshardham by night

rayan's but higher than floor-level. The great central dome, allowing light in hushed breath, is surrounded by sixteen other domes, and all the 97 sculpted pillars have been carved in traditional Hindu fashion by artisans from Bansipahadpur. Pramukh Swami Maharaj asked the Gujarati architect how long reinforced concrete would last if used in the main hall and when he was told 'about a hundred years' he said 'let us use quarried stone that will last forever', and 6,000 metric tonnes of pink sandstone came from Rajasthan. The only wood used is rosewood from Hubli district in Karnataka, of a quality giving rise to the proverb 'sonu ane sisam sarkhu', 'Gold and rosewood are the same' – it is reputed to resist fungus. The same considerations for immortality governed the choice of non-corroding brass instead of iron for nails and screws. So the stairs leading up to the public gallery are cantilevered, without the use of iron girders. Brahmiviharidas showed me the Hall of Holy Relics including the only known surviving letter from Swaminarayan, written to his guru Ramanand Swami, and his pure wool shawl; he used to climb the trees as a boy in his native village of Chhapaya, Uttar Pradesh, and a fragment from one of those ancient trees is preserved. From here Swaminarayan set out on his seven-year pilgrimage through India, he was appointed spiritual guru at 21 and created five hundred so-called 'paramhansas', or 'ultimate swans' whose names all end in 'anand', or 'joy'. These gold-leafed standing figures surround him in a warm glow. Brahmiviharidas said that we have none such in the present generation. The state-of-the-art display employs fibre-optics, dioramas, and a sound-and-light show set in the Gujarati village of Loj, where the narrator is a banyan tree.

A 25-minute Czech-made 'integrovision' show produces simultaneous images on fourteen screens, dazzling the viewer with images from art and nature, man and animal, suggesting that the answer to man's quest for happiness lies in enlightenment, preferably through Hinduism, and by choice through the Swaminarayan Movement. The Nityanand Hall displays dioramas from Indian culture such as the Upanishads, the Ramayana and Mahabharata, in all of which the figures are blond-complexioned and of extraordinary beauty. Premanand Hall introduces you to Indian mystical poets such as Tulsi Das and Kabir, with special reference to the Gujarati poet Narsinh Mehta, and Brahmanand, an early 19th-century *sadhu* and devotee of Lord Swaminarayan. Nijanand is the hall of universal harmony, where all religions are described in tones of utter tolerance. The audio-animatronics presentation is a diorama in which Swaminarayan, *sadhus* and devotees are seen 'speaking' and listening to music.

Splendid landscaped gardens cover eight acres at present, with a further fifteen acquired for development. A research centre including library, archives, computer centre and seminar hall is being created as the Akshardham Centre for Applied Research in Social Harmony.

It would be easy for a western visitor to suggest that the 5½-crore rupee expenditure on the project (£1.25 million) might more productively have been spent on the Movement's projects for anti-drug drives, relief during floods, famine and drought, and camps for giving blood. In fact, the main threats to India's whole future come from inter-communal strife, and the loving tolerance shown by the Movement's itinerant *sadhus*, and the religious festivals such as the bicentennial celebrations of 1981 promote harmony and understanding absolutely vital to India's peaceful democratic future, reinforcing the appeal for harmony by the secular authorities. Moreover, Gujarat's millennial collaboration between Hindus, Jains and more recently Parsis and Muslims has been largely based on non-violence, a tradition making it safer to walk around Gandhinagar at night than Miami or Manchester.

Mehmedabad

In 1479, Sultan Mahmud Beghada decided to build a new walled town on the river Vatrak, found 27 km south-south-east off the highway from Ahmedabad to Baroda. Though guidebooks ignore the city, it marks a cardinal moment in the Ahmadshahi dynasty, and bears the name of its founder, though 'Mahmudabad' has been changed in the course of time to the slightly disguised Mehmedabad. You arrive by the Kaecherry Gate to find the nucleus of a town surrounded by ruins for miles in every direction. The Friday Mosque bears the date 1948, though the minarets are original. Next door to it in Vav Bazar is a six-storey step-well or *vav* of a type already familiar from Ahmedabad and Adalaj. A local guide called Ishwarbhai showed me the adjacent ruined rice-mill, and demonstrated how to enter through the broken perimeter wall, at the back, encouraged by a swarm of urchins. Nesting pigeons raised their cooing decibels in momentary alarm, but soon recovered their poise. Though unattended and uncared for, Mehmedabad's step-well needs only minimal restoration for a full recovery, and could be easily maintained. My guess is that the water-level is too deep to be useful, otherwise local housewives would use it regularly, as they do elsewhere.

The population of the town is half-Muslim, half-Hindu, yet as at Champaner the whole atmosphere is profoundly Islamic. A ruined mosque still has two fine minarets standing and its walls patrolled by a colony of langurs: Ishwarbhai called it the Bijli Sayyid Mosque, but I have no records to corroborate that name. You can stay at a government guest-house in Mehmedabad, which has its own rail station, and state buses stop just beside the rickshaw-stand.

You'll need an auto-rickshaw for the trip of several kilometres to the village of Sojali. There, above the Vatrak riverbed, stands the imposingly beautiful mausoleum of Hazrat Mubarak Sayyid dated in inscriptions to 1515 and historically crucial in representing the complete and exuberant acceptance of the arcuate style in the tomb architecture of Gujarat. It seems a splendid continuation of Lodi-dynasty Delhi styles explicable by the fact that master-craftsmen from the Mughal capital were attracted by the wealth and aggrandisement of Gujarat.

Mehmedabad. Sojali. Mausoleum of Hazrat Mubarak Sayyid

Its formal success can be traced to the symmetry of its parts, the proportion between main dome and minor cupolas, the creation of *chhatris* over the clerestory, and the great brick platform on which the ensemble poses high above the threat of riverflood. Spiral staircases lead down from the platform's corners; very fine *jalis* add their delicacy, and Hindu-style brackets make their own eclectic contribution. In the main chamber the tomb of the mystic Mubarak Sayyid (nearer the door) is flanked by that of his son, Sayyid Miran, with the rest of his family outside the enclosure. A side chapel has the tomb of a devotee called Sidi Sayyid. As you patrol the fine, deserted place, as tawny in its sandstone as the riverbed below, striped palm squirrels flicker like automata among the sixty-six pillars.

The attendant, Alam Shah, explained that at the annual *urs* or festival here on the tenth of Ramadan between five and seven thousand Muslim foregather.

I bounced back in the auto-rickshaw along the 4-kilometre track from Sojali to Mehmedabad, then 750 m from the town in the opposite direction I came to another ruined brick mosque from which most of the stone facing had been robbed away. Overlooking a great artificial reservoir, Ishwarbhai conducted me around the Chandra-Suraj Mahal (Moon-Sun Palace), a ruined pleasure-palace which would have induced swooning in 'Vathek' Beckford and painters of the Romantic and Sublime. Perimeter walls of Old Mehmedabad stretched away above the tussocky ground which is all that is left of once-royal gardens. At Bhamaria reservoir in the town, overlooked by a prosaic water-tower, dhobis wash laundry on the banks, and migrating water-birds dip and glide for fish. Ishwarbhai showed me another circular well of the Mahmud Beghada period, with square windows, twin arches, and a colony of bats squeaking and whirring. Altogether, Ahmedabad epitomises citified Gujarat and Mehmedabad, just half an hour away, exemplifies the rural aspects of the state, at once quiet yet vibrant with historical echoes.

Dakor

There is a full moon ('Poonam') festival once a month at Dakor's Sri Krishna Temple and special trains depart on that day at 6.50 from Ahmedabad (arriving at Anand at 8.20 and leaving Anand at 8.50) and getting into Dakor at 9.40; and at 7.25 from Anand arriving at 8.15. The latter returns from Dakor at 8.35, and the former at 2.10 p.m., arriving at Ahmedabad at 5.40 p.m. You will know the date of full moon day (which of course changes every month) from notices at all rail stations concerned and from the newspapers. Huge numbers of pilgrims come for the year's major festival, Sharad Purnima, during the full moon in October-November.

I arrived in Dakor by road, 43 km east of Mehmedabad on the road towards Godhra, and my taxi-driver asked in the bustling narrow winding streets for the 'mandir' ('temple'). Everybody knows what you mean: the temple of Sri Krishna at Dakor is one of the most celebrated in India. It derives its name from an ascetic called Dank Rishi whose ashram stood on the bank of the Gomti reservoir, Dankpura being reduced to Dakor.

I removed my shoes at the entrance, where just past the silver-plated gates tired sari-clad women sorted *chappals* into twins. Signs in front to the white temple exhorted pilgrims in Gujarati and English: 'While worshipping the Deity beware that your pockets are not cut by tick-pocketers' and 'Photography of Ranchhooraiji is Prohibited'. Between the triple doorway and silver-plated entrance to the shrine a noisy crowd prayed and talked, chanted and shouted. Some, though prostrate, still managed to writhe and shudder like electric eels; others swayed from the back to touch the marble floor with the forehead. All walls are painted in garish colours, but the idol of Sri Krishna is black, though much is covered with silver and cloths presented by worshippers. Its throne, a masterpiece of woodcarving plated in silver and gold, was presented by the Gaekwad of Baroda last century at a cost of £12,000 sterling equivalent. A young man keen to practise English told me the tale of how a Rajput called Bodana used to make the pilgrimage from his home town of Dakor to Dwarka to pay homage to the image of Ranchhodrai, the aspect of Lord Krishna worshipped at Dwarka. When he grew old and felt no longer able to make the long journey on foot, Krishna appeared to him a dream and told him that if Bodana could no longer come to him, he would come to Bodana. So during his last visit to Dwarka, Bodana removed the idol and carried it off concealed in a bullock-cart. The temple priests, on missing the idol next morning, alerted the authorities who pursued Bodana. Bodana sank the idol in the Gomti tank and would not confess its whereabouts, so the dispute was settled by the brahmins from Dwarka accepting in lieu the idol's weight in gold. Lord Krishna came to the aid of his devotee because, when the idol was brought to the surface, its weight had lessened to that of the nose-ring of Bodana's wife Gangabai. She surrendered her nose-ring and honour was satisfied all round. The temple was built by a devotee of Krishna called Tambeker, whose heirs still administer the temple. Illumination of the idol ends at 12.15 and the temple of Ranchhodrai closes at 12.30. Outside the temple, pilgrim stalls are filled with incense and powder, calendars and oleographs, booklets about Lord Krishna in Gujarati, and plastic windmills for children, combs, mirrors, and trinkets for all the family to take home as souvenirs. The Jitubhai haveli opposite the temple makes a picturesque moment of overhanging stillness in a road zinging with animation, belled sacred cows chewing between parping auto-rickshaws, and fruitsellers shouting their wares above the prevailing racket.

Lunch could be at Bhojanalai, the cafeteria for pilgrims around the corner. From the cashier at the door you purchase food coupons (10-2 and 6-9) and at clean tables you are brought standard Gujarati vegetarian thalis on tin trays which, for Rs 10 including papads and a many refills as you wish, must be today's best bargain anywhere in the world. You may take

Dakor. Jitubhai Haveli

in your own bottled water, but of course no alcohol of any kind. I buy large bottles of resealable Bisleri water from hotels, restaurants, or wayside stalls, and this is always perfectly safe.

Vaso

There is a village called Vaso north-east of Dakor, so if heading for the haveli-town of Vaso make sure you leave Dakor south-west in the direction of Nadiad, then after Nadiad continue westward towards Vaso, which lies almost due south from Mehmedabad.

Nadiad is connected with two great Gujaratis: the novelist Govardhanram Tripathi, author of *Saraswatichandra*, whose home is now a museum; and the late Chunilal Asharam Bhavsar, known as Pujya Mota, who founded the charitable Hari Om Ashram subsequently run by Shri Nandubhai.

Vaso has been transferred from its original situation eight km away because of recurrent disease, so the present town is not ancient: it derives its deserved celebrity from a few magnificent mansions, or *haveli*s. The social

42

history of the *haveli* is described in Sarah Tillotson's fascinating *Indian Mansions* (Cambridge, 1994), and Gujarati wooden courtyard houses in particular have been studied in V.S. Pramar's *Haveli* (Ahmedabad, 1989), so if you wanted to devote several weeks in Northern India to the *haveli* alone, these two books would guide you through cities and towns where traditional carved and painted wooden houses have resisted change: towns like Kapadvanj (east of Ahmedabad), Palanpur and Radhanpur (where the Nawabs' palaces retain their ethereal splendour), and above all Vaso.

You immediately notice a difference: the narrow streets are even, stone-paved, and kept clean: keep going through the town, past the clock tower, until you come to a kind of privileged *cul-de-sac*, where the barking of dogs is heard only faintly. You have arrived at the *haveli* of Vithaldas Amin, sometimes called after his son Anand Prasad Amin. It has been acquired by central government for maintenance and restoration as a museum, assigned to the underfinanced Archaeological Survey of India, but is currently closed and seems to be deteriorating, so if you go there is little chance that you will be able to see the superb centrepiece of the carved and painted ceiling of the first-floor *divankhanu* (reception room) with its flying *apsaras* and *gandharvas*, celestial damsels and musicians. The Amin family now lives in the U.S.A.

The history of this building and the adjacent Desai *haveli* is closely related to the story of Vaso itself because the Maratha rulers of Gujarat in the mid-19th century delegated tax-collection and other revenue-gathering to the Patel family of Vaso, and this family divided into two branches who took the surnames of Amin and Desai, and built these two glorious wooden mansions in the early 1870s.

The Amin *haveli* has four floors, if one counts a small pavilion on the roof as an extra floor. The main part of the *haveli* is its *chowk* or courtyard, open-air hub of the family which connects with most rooms, and protects the family's activities from being overlooked. A room for grain storage and a well preserve the family from hazards of famine and drought. A *parsal* or space in front of the rooms has the function of linking rooms. An *otlo* or front verandah has an intermediary function; in the evening senior members of the family may sit there to greet neighbours, do informal business, or gossip. Many of the columns exist for decorative rather than purely structural reasons and the craftsmen's ingenuity extends to carved plaques, faces of bonding-timbers, panels beneath sills, and a wall-niche with a fine Ras-Lila scene and horses rampant. Gujarat's woodcarving has a venerable history, from at least two thousand years ago, but because it is perishable we have few objects dated back more than three or four centuries. Wooden temples are known to have existed in Gujarat from the sixth century, but after Mahmud Ghazni destroyed the temple of Somnath in 1024, the wooden pillars encased in metal had to be replaced by stone and as each wooden temple in turn fell victim to fire, it would be replaced

43

Vaso. Vithaldas Amin Haveli

in stone – and after the fall of the Solanki dynasty, temples often replaced by mosques. The 19th century was a golden age for woodcarving in Gujarati *haveli*s and *haveli* temples: a great example from Anahilvada Patan has been reassembled and restored at the New York Metropolitan Museum. The Bohra Muslim mercantile communities of Patan, Siddhapur and Kapadvanj east of Ahmedabad adorned their homes with excellent carving, as did the wealthy citizens of Idar, Nadiad, Ahmedabad, Junagadh, Cambay, Broach and Surat.

But arguably the most dramatic *haveli* in Gujarat is that of the Desai family, which you will find in a quiet *cul-de-sac* behind the Amin *haveli*. Everybody in town will guide you there, to Mahendra Desai, a strikingly vigorous, intellectually lucid 77-year-old speaking idiomatic English but writing novels in his beloved native Gujarati. Tall, white-haired, and with heavy spectacles, Mahendra held my hand and asked about my travels in India, the books I had written, the people I had met from the Hindus in Rameswaram to the Parsi High Priest in Bombay, the Jains in Sravana Belagola, the Buddhists in Mundgod and the Jews in Cochin. 'My family was in the insurance business in Calcutta and Bihar', he reminisced, 'then my father worked as a cinema projectionist in Visakhapatnam (Andhra Pradesh) from 1934-9. When Mahatma Gandhi asked everyone to refuse to co-operate with the British war effort, my family took this instruction seriously, and I was sent to jail for a year. When I was released in 1940, I supplied spare parts to the cotton mills in Ahmedabad, and from 1945-9 I worked in the mica business in Bihar. My father's estate had been confiscated by the Government because of his involvement in the peace movement of Gandhiji, and he received compensation only in 1947, on Independence. I now own some fields and estates in Surendranagar and Baroda districts and three villages, yielding Rs 39,000 a year for 14 years, from 1948-62'.

Mahendra's wife brought glasses of boiled water, and retired. 'I have stomach pains and feel quite uncomfortable, but I spend my time writing novels under the pen-name Navinachandra Amin. I want you to meet my mother.' The splendid, indomitable lady, smiling with the contentment of inner serenity, I found spinning, as she had been taught by Mahatma Gandhi. She still spins every day, at the age of 93, and no better tribute to Gandhiji's forceful humility can be imagined. The intensely practical activity, generating financial independence, the repetitiousness representing tradition, the plain utility of the articles produced, the ingenious use of minimal resources, and the fact that one can spin in private or in community, with a portable wheel that can be taken from a bicycle.

'The whole place is alive', smiled Mahendra. 'We have giant cockroaches, pigeons on the roof, but the biggest surprise is round the corner: come.' Of the eighty-odd rooms in this rambling mansion for a great extended family, only three are being used by the three residents left. I thought of the late Satyajit Ray and the great film he would have made of the Desai family saga, the details of the woodcarvings unseen for a dozen years at a time, sudden darkness descending, dawn broadening across the courtyard as the first birds grumbled awake. Dozens of slender columns, wondrously and abundantly unnecessary, still stand soldierly behind their cornucopia of carved brackets. The *parsal*, a passage between *chowk* and inner rooms, has a wall niche scintillatingly carved, and with its original colours of red, yellow, orange, green. A shelf above it drips eternally with red carved droplets. These carvers possessed the demonic drive to fill every square inch that Anglo-Saxon artists reveal in illuminated manuscripts, as you can see in vibrant tendrils decorating the lintels (the lower painted red, the upper brown) over the door from the *chowk* to the inner rooms. Like many other aristocratic doors in Northern Gujarat, it consists of planks bound with iron bands and a layer of carved battens spiked to the planks.

The emphasis throughout the Desai *haveli* is on the ground floor, with its superb columned verandah raised above the ground to avoid flooding during the monsoon, and the first floor, with its generous running balcony and wide overhang protected with corrugated iron. The second floor is by contrast unadorned.

Wherever you look the detail is literally fabulous: mythical *kinnaras*, celestial musicians who are partly birds or horses, *apsaras*, celestial dancers, and on a column in the central courtyard a virtuoso craftsman has recreated that moment from the Mahabharata when Bhima shakes a tree to bring down the Kauravas hiding among the branches. The giant Bhima, leaping off the ground to shake the slenderest of all trees, perfectly vertical, topples fifteen rivals, though the topmost seems smugly unaware of his imminent downfall.

'Here we are', said Mahendra, stopping in a dark corner on the ground floor, as our ears were assailed by shrill but confused whistling in a thousand voices, as if Luigi Dallapiccola's *Prigioniero* had suffered the torture of the damned. I had heard something similar twenty years earlier in a cave near Kuala Lumpur: it was the collective voice of a myriad bats, clustering and resting in pairs up there, sheltered in quivering tenebrae. I did not ask why Mohandas did not summon the pest control services to remove these guests. I knew.

'I have two married daughters, but no sons', explained Mahendra, and again the whole story of the inheritance became clear in a moment. The great *havelis* of Vaso must be preserved *in situ* by a foundation similar to that of the wealthy Sarabhais in Ahmedabad, but where is the money to be found? A new Museum of Domestic Architecture would have sufficient space for arts and crafts to be displayed in every room, although the main exhibit would always be the *havelis* themselves. Let us hope that private or state funds will enable Vaso to continue to offer visitors the vision formerly offered by the Amins and now – for the time being – still hospitably provided by Mahendra Desai.

II: SOUTH GUJARAT

South Gujarat can be divided into two regions: the coastal plain, with populous towns, once-important harbours, and in industrial belt near the Bombay-Ahmedabad highway in the west; and the rural uplands and forests of the east where the state merges into upland Madhya Pradesh and Maharashtra largely inhabited by tribesfolk.

Cambay

The harbours on the eastern shores of the Gulf of Cambay have historically suffered notable changes in historic times, due to changes in currents and bores of the rivers Sabarmati coming from the north, the Mahi entering the sea near Cambay, the Narmada joining the Gulf above Broach, and the Tapti, emptying its water beyond   the   city of Surat as well as the Dadhar, Bhukhi, Amravati, Kim, Mindhola, Ambika, Kharera, Auranga, Par and Kolak. The silt brought down in the monsoon is considerable, but a great tidal scouring effect permits only about 1% of the silt to remain in the Gulf, the balance being carried away by tides.

The major ports of the regions during the Mauryan period (321-236 B.C.) included Bassein (Sopara) south of the Gulf, and Somnath Patan in Saurashtra, but from the 1st to 3rd centuries A.D. Broach (Barygaza in the *Periplus*) rose to prominence, Cambay replaced it as the premier port in the 10th-15th centuries, and Surat achieved pre-eminence in the 16th and 17th centuries, when it was eclipsed by Bombay.

When exploring the South Gujarat coast, remember that unpredictable floods and tides have changed the conformation of the vulnerably low-lying shore almost from year to year. The *Periplus* of the early centuries A.D. warns that 'in the Gulf of Barygaza, the tides are particularly violent' and even large vessels were driven from their course and stranded on the shoals. Despite the dangers, Broach was known to have traded with the Chinese in the 7th and 8th centuries, and attracted Arab merchants eager for trade. Writing in 916, al-Mas'udi notes that the channels to Cambay were as difficult as those to Broach. 'The floods near Cambay rush from the mouth of the bay like a huge mountain' and it may be that the ruins of Naghera, about 5 km from modern Cambay, actually formed the port of early mediaeval Cambay. Al-Mas'udi states that 'Cambay' lay 5 km from the sea ('one league' is the translation) in the 10th century but in 1153, if al-Idrisi is to be believed, Cambay was a coastal town, and we know that it became the seaport of Anahilvada Patan kingdom which reached its zenith in the 11th and 12th centuries. By 1340, the ferocious tides at Cambay had forced ships to anchor near Ghogha on the western coast near Bhavnagar, and in the 16th century the channels to Cambay had silted up so that larger ships with cargo for Cambay had to offload at Diu on to smaller boats.

So one high point in Cambay's chequered history occurred between the 11th and 13th centuries because of the stable might of the Solanki dynasty based at Anahilvada Patan, now called simply Patan or Jhalra Patan, chief town of the native state of Jhalawar, but now just a town in Mehsana district. Another great period began with the transfer in Ahmedshahi times of the capital from distant Patan to the more strategically valuable centre of Asaval, until then a Koli tribal settlement and the new town of Karnavati, which Ahmed transformed within a few decades into a thriving Muslim city, diverting the course of the Hathmati to the Sabarmati to improve water supply. From the new trading and manufacturing city of Ahmed Shah I, Cambay lay only two days' travel. Until the end of the reign of Mahmud Beghada (1459-1511), Cambay retained its importance, though its channels were kept open only by extensive and costly dredging. When George Birdwood writes, in *Inventions of the Indies* (1891) that ' the history of modern Europe is a quest for the aromatic gums, resins, condiments and spices of India, Further India and the Indian Archipelago', he may be guilty of exaggeration, but one should remember that until the 16th century this trade lay at the mercy of Arabs, Africans, and Indians, though the Venetians tried to challenge oriental merchants from its bases in the Mediterranean. It was the coming of the Portuguese, and later the British and to a lesser extent the Dutch and French, that changed the balance of power in what is still known as the Gulf of Cambay.

The Portuguese were ambitious to compete with Venice and Genoa for the East Indies trade and their East India Trading Company's representatives in India, Almeida (1505-09) and Albuquerque (1509-15) recommended control of the sea by interfering with Arab and Indian trade in the Indian Ocean. Allying themselves with the Shah of Persia against the Ottoman Turks and Arab rulers, the Portuguese gained Hormuz in 1508 to control trade through the Arabian Gulf, then Socotra off the coast of Yemen, which enabled the Portuguese to raid Arab and Indian ships bound to Mokha and Aden, then Jiddah in 1512. Albuquerque seized Goa in 1510, Daman fell into Portuguese hands in 1531, then Diu five years afterwards. At this time Gujarat (still known as 'the Kingdom of Cambay') began to decline during the reigns of Mahmud Beghada's successors: Muzaffar II (1511-26) and Bahadur Shah (1526-36). Harassed by the Portuguese from the sea and coastal possessions, these rulers suffered repeatedly from incursions by Babur, who had acceded to the throne as Mughal ruler of Delhi in 1536, and his successor Humayun, whose troops were robbed by Kolis at Cambay in 1539. The vengeful Humayun ravaged Cambay, and the distraught Bahadur had no choice but to ally himself with the Portuguese against his northern foes. The price he paid included the cession of Diu and his income from trade at Bassein in Maharashtra. The Portuguese effectively ruined Cambay by demanding that all trade for Cambay and the Gujarat interior should pass through Diu, and by the period of Ahmed Shah II his territory had shrunk to Ahmedabad and its environs. Finally, Akbar the Great entered Ahmedabad in 1573 and a last despairing attack by Muzaffar III of Gujarat suffered defeat by Akbar's Mughal forces at Sarkhej in 1584. Interestingly, Cambay's fortunes revived under Akbar, who encouraged craftsmen, artisans and in particular weavers to settle there. The Venetian jeweller Cesare Federici lived in Cambay for twelve years after its conquest by Akbar, and reported in the words of his chronicler Fra Bartolommeo Dionigi that 'Cambay was a city of such trade that he could not have believed possible had he not seen it'. The English arrived in Surat in 1608, with a firman or charter from the Mughal Emperor Jahangir.

The Dutch next arrived in India in search of cloth that they could exchange for Moluccan spices and, as the English refused to tolerate any competition at Surat, the Dutch established their factory at Cambay, in or possibly before 1617. By this time the Portuguese ascendancy of the seas had been eroded by Dutch entrepreneurship, and the English knew that they would have to compete for India with the Dutch as well as with the Portuguese, and to obtain the Moluccan spices they would have to acquire the cloth from Gujarat that the Dutch had been seeking to monopolise. The English therefore set up an agency at Cambay for the express purpose of acquiring goods which their Moluccan trading partners desired. So the fortunes of the local people in coastal Gujarat fluctuated with the trading policies of the English, the Portuguese, and to a lesser extent the Dutch. In the late 17th century the English chose to concentrate their activities at Bombay, farther south, thus effectively sealing the fate of Surat and Cambay. We know that the British Government increasingly used the East India Company as a lever to produce wealth and ultimately power throughout India, until the ostentatious splendours of the Raj appeared, often at the expense of local competition and the infrastructure of Indian village life.

The merchant William Finch arrived in Cambay in 1611, and wrote: 'Cambay stands by the sea, encompassed by a strong brick wall, the houses high and faire, the streets paved in a direct line with strong gates at the end of each, the bazar large. On the south is a goodly garden with a watch tower of exceeding height. On the north are many faire tankes. It is the Mart of Guzurat and so haunted by Portugals that you shall often finde 200 frigates at once riding there. It aboundeth with all sorts of cloth and rich drugges.' Thévenot noted in 1666-7 that Cambay was as big as Surat but not as populous, and that the gates at the end were shut at night-time. The town centre market then sold textiles, sugar, cotton, yarn, arms, horse-saddles, agricultural products, herbs and fruits.

The story of the Nawabs of Cambay begins with Momin Khan Dehlami

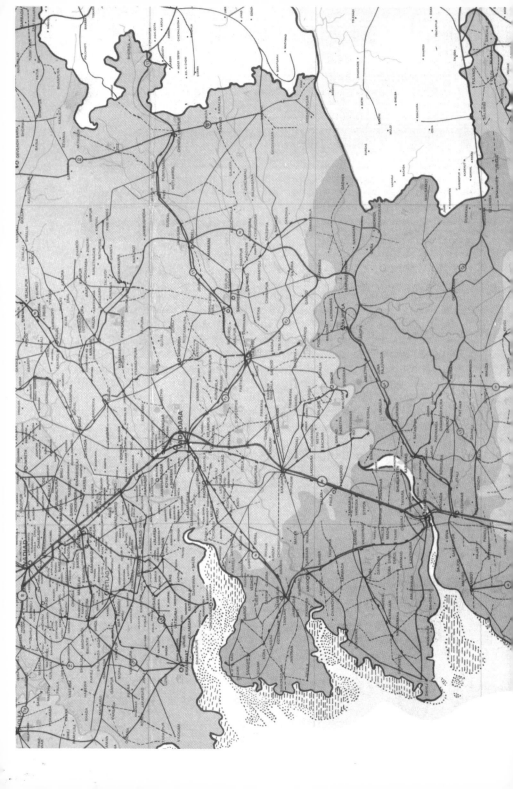

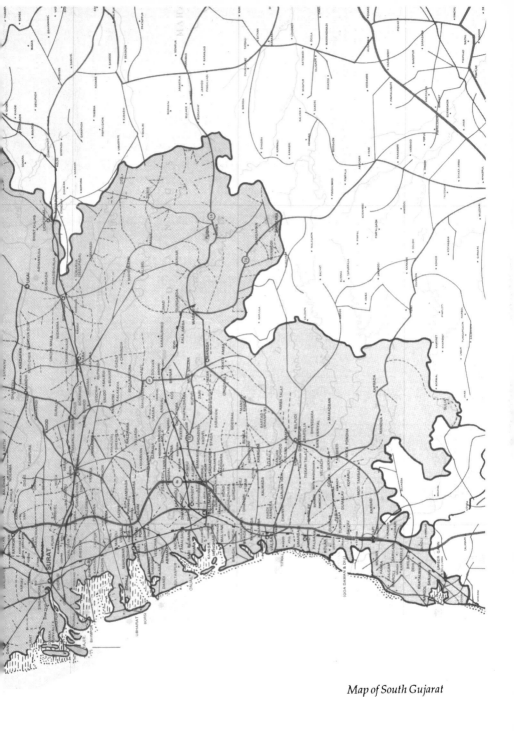

Map of South Gujarat

I, whom the English wanted to promote in order to protect their trading interests against the Mughals in the north and the Marathas from Maharashtra. Momin Khan Dehlami was appointed agent at Surat and Cambay under the Mughals' Viceroy of Gujarat, Sarbuland Khan; after his death in 1728, his son-in-law Mirza Jafar succeeded him two years later. A line of independent Nawabs began to rule in Surat from 1733, and Damaji II took Baroda from him in the following year. When created Viceroy of Gujarat in 1737, with the title Momin Khan I, he was resisted by the sitting Viceroy and had to wrest the position by force with the military aid of the Peshwa Bajirao. This brought with it a dire cost: half the income of Gujarat, leaving him with only Ahmedabad and Cambay. As Momin Khan I weakened, the English at Cambay grew stronger, doing business with their own local agents instead of through the Nawab. The English themselves suffered from internecine rivalry. Daniel Innes, the Cambay factor in 1735, was replaced by Hugh Bidwell, but would not surrender and tried first to raise a mob against Innes and then asked the Nawab to charge Innes with corruption. The English East India Company's directors resolved the internal conflict by sending out Munroe to replace both. Munroe, asked by the Nawab of Cambay to provide defensive forces against incursion by Damaji Gaekwad, refused on the grounds that the English were allies of Baroda, so Momin Khan I retaliated by forbidding the crucial export of indigo, whereupon Munroe ordered the seizure of all the Nawab's ships throughout the Indian Ocean and the Gulf: the Nawab capitulated. Playing off Bhavnagar and Baroda against Cambay, the English persuaded the Nawab of Cambay to let them handle his affairs for him; most orders coming from the palace emanated from the Resident in the name of the Nawab, who found his revenues first eroded, then taken over for 'administration'. The English protected the Nawab against the Marathas and the Gaekwad, and in return took the Customs House and had charge of all goods coming in or out of Cambay. In 1818, with its economy in ruins, Cambay's English Resident was withdrawn and replaced by an executive officer to govern the new district of Kaira, thus removing central influence .and independence from Cambay. All Nawabs henceforth were appointed by the English. In 1857, when the Company's holdings were taken over by the Crown and made part of the Empire, Cambay was given a salute of eleven guns, but the princely state had a tiny area of no more than 350 square miles, and a population estimated in 1880 to be 83,000, a third of whom lived in Cambay city. The British allowed the harbour to remain silted up, because they chose to concentrate trade in their principal ports: Karachi, Bombay, Madras and Calcutta. The rapid and spectacular growth of Bombay, now seen to be disastrous and unmanageable in the last decade of the 20th century, meant that all the surrounding ports nearby would lack adequate maintenance, let alone expansion. The growth of larger ships, and latterly supertankers, would have bypassed the smaller ports anyway, but at least Ghogha, Diu, Daman and Surat should have been allowed longer respite. By 1872, however, the prosperity of Cambay had dropped to the point where active workers formed a minority of the population: 16% in agriculture; 11% in arts and crafts; 2.6% in government service; 1.92% in service; 1.52% in the professions; and only 1.36% in trade. The main crops then were tobacco, rice, pulses and wheat, but indigo had declined and the production of opium had been declared illegal three years earlier.

A new impetus was given to the town with the coming of the railroad, and it is in that direction that a new ribbon of homes and shops is growing. But of the historic gates, only Gavara, Chakamali, Furji and Makai remain. Akbar's suburbs were all destroyed, and the English factory turned into a military hospital and later a rest-house.

Cambay. The agate-bead worker A.S. Sayyid

Cambay's manufacturing base, the forlorn remnants of which we see today, in the early 16th century rivalled that of Ahmedabad. It included ivory carving, weapons, amber, scents and aromatics, turbans, soap, camphor, gold and silver, silk, carpets, cotton, leather, lacquer, and above all the agate industry.

Pliny noted in his *Natural History* (77 A.D.) that Indian agates would heal scorpion stings, and if held in the mouth would quench thirst. Muslims and Kanbis were stone-polishers, and I found a polisher at work just outside the Friday Mosque in Cambay. I selected a perfectly cylindrical agate for Rs 25. A.S. Sayyid, sitting crosslegged on a gunny sack, was continuing an industry that had begun in the Neolithic Age, around 7,000 B.C. and intensified with the Harappan civilisation that spread throughout the Indus Valley zone as far as the Sabarmati in Gujarat, specifically in Nagwada and Lothal, for example. Agate and carnelian beads from this culture have been located throughout northern India, Afghanistan, Iran and Iraq. It is likely that agates have been worked in Cambay continuously, because the mines in Gujarat and nearby Maharashtra (near Aurangabad) have never been worked out. This is because the Bhil groups excavating agate use simple tools. and consequently mine relatively lightly. Once on the surface, the nodules are sorted by quality and colour, and sold to traders who truck them to Cambay, where they are dried in the sun, then heated so that they fracture regularly, then rough-cut, heated again to change the colour by oxidising iron in the nodule to turn it red-orange. After the flaking or chipping process, the bead is ready for grinding, nowadays using an electric-powered emery wheel. It is then drilled and polished: diamonds were used for drilling beads as early as the Mauryan period, in the 3rd century B.C. Agate cups were greatly sought after in antiquity: the Emperor Nero is reported to have paid extravagant sums for such cups from Cambay.

The monuments of Cambay date from Islamic times, but in quantity they are disappointingly few compared with those of Ahmedabad or Champaner. Ala ud-Din Khilji and his Muslim force attacked the city in 1304, and razed Jain and Hindu buildings, reusing their masonry to create mosques. The Baleshah Mosque, 2 km from the heart of modern Cambay, is a ruin set among palms, but the principal Friday Mosque, clearly intended for a huge congregation, was completed in 1325 and stands in the line of Gujarati-style mosques beginning from the model of Delhi's Quwwat ul-Islam Mosque and spreading to all Ahmedshahi strongholds such as Mehmedabad, Champaner, and Broach. The Delhi craftsmen used local artisans to work on local materials, and from their expertise and experience in Gujarat, these artisans and craftsmen would spread architectonic elements from Gujarat across north and central India. Such elements include austere arcades, multiple domes, multiple niches, niched and porticoed courtyards, and above all a growing fascination with the size, number, placing and style of the minaret. At first you can see from Delhi's

Qutb Minar that the Indian minaret was intended as a detached victory tower to signify the new might of Islam in an alien landscape. But subsequently it formed part of the mosque's design and could be twinned, or even quadrupled in a show of strength. The new Islamic rulers created triumphal triple gateways as a sign of their temporal power: that in Ahmedabad is colossal, but Cambay too has a so-called Tin Darwaza, near the S.D. Kapadia High School.

Features of Cambay's Friday Mosque are the intricately-carved stone screens or *jalis* (though nothing here equals Ahmedabad's Sidi Sa'id *jalis*), the arcuated façade of the mosque, facing the great courtyard with a well (where a young girl was drawing water into a brass pot); a glorious marble minbar; a triple mihrab, the central one entirely Hindu in concept, with two attached columns at each side and two free-standing round col-

Cambay. Friday Mosque

umns in the niche, each with five rings between its foot and capital; and women's galleries at left and right, with private steps from the side of the courtyard. The great mosque has a florid double-storey annexe with a magnificent inscribed marble tomb, and the whole stands on a plinth, being virtually fortified by massive high walls. Screens are superbly constructed to allow sea breezes in and keep the strong sunlight out.

Beyond the mosque one descends rapidly through a walled gateway to the tidal shoreline, with its railhead causeway. The trouble for Cambay was that the Bombay-Ahmedabad railway line was routed in 1863 not direct via Broach, but eastward via Baroda, thus at a stroke killing off the trading and communications potential that would have been enhanced by a bridge link across the inlet south of Dhuvaran to Jambusar. At it is, branch lines were run to Cambay north of the inlet and from Broach to Kavi south of the inlet, linked nowadays by boat.

You can drive to the distant sea, with its view on a clear day as far as Bhavnagar, but the overriding emotion on these neverending sandflats is of melancholy, dead cities and dead hopes, of dashed prospects and missed opportunities. White bags of fertilizer await transportation. A line of chattering women carrying brass water-pots on their heads makes its serpentine way. Under the arch, a wit has scribbled 'Lovers' Point' with an arrow pointing towards the drifting sands.

Muhammad Razzaq offered to show me the Nawab of Cambay's Darbar Hall, a wooden summer pavilion within the walls and overlooking the blue, blue, sea. Green rose-ringed parakeets nest in its upper storey, and the desolate hall is used now just to store the Muharram *tazias* carried in religious procession. For the Nawab succession here is of the Shi'a persuasion, even though there are only 32,000 Muslims in Cambay nowadays, compared with 70,000 Hindus and Jains. The Nawab Sarkar-i-Aliyyah lives in Lal Darwaza, on the road to Ahmedabad. On leaving Cambay, past the New Tip-Top Laundry, and the barber's shop called Hair Art, you come to a Jain temple to remind you of Ludovico di Varthema's words on his visit to Cambay in 1504 (*Itinerario*, Bologna, 1885): 'About forty years ago, Sultan Mahmud Beghada captured this kingdom from a king of the Gujaratis, a race who eat nothing that has blood, and never kill any living thing. And these people are neither Moors nor heathens. It is my opinion', continues the Roman Catholic writer, 'that if they were baptized, they would all be saved by virtue of their works, for they never do to others what they would not that others should do to them.'

Broach

As soon as you leave the state highway, the traffic changes character, from 'National Permit' Ashok Leyland cargo trucks and oil-lorries, to camel carts and motor-bikes. We passed the Circuit House (on your right before the town) which is the quietest place to stay, then after the rail station the two-star Hotel Palmland with welcome a.c. rooms, the Dadabhai Garden and the Hotel Shalimar.

'Broach' is the comic westernisation of 'Bharuch', itself a corruption of Bhrigukutch, or settlement of Bhrigu Rishi, a Hindu sage whose descendants and devotees are even today known as Bhargavas. Some Bhargava Brahmins remain in Bharuch still, but others have found more fertile homes inland along the Narmada in Madhya Pradesh. As Barygaza, it was known to Greeks who voyaged there via the Red Sea and Arabian Gulf.

The town lies on the main road and rail network linking Ahmedabad with Bombay, which historically – and recently – should have ensured the town's prosperity. Ironically, the coming of the railways did nothing to help Broach, which owed all its success to its situation on the Narmada close to the sea, where towards the end of the 15th century Western travellers reported seeing hundreds of vessels at anchor. Silt brought down from the upper reaches of the Narmada has gradually submerged the harbour installations of Broach, so that the port is now virtually dead.

Solanki-period monuments have mostly disappeared, leaving only the strengthened riverbanks, the fort walls and parts of an ancient temple. Ulugh Khan destroyed Jain and Hindu temples in 1298. The Friday Mosque is the most valuable monument in Broach, and dates from the 14th century, that is, from the same generation as the early mosques of Patan and Cambay, when the city was governed by a Muslim regent for the Delhi Sultanate. In 1396 Muhammad Zafar Khan defied Delhi and Broach remained subject to the Ahmedshahi dynasty of Ahmedabad until Akbar annexed the town in 1572. The Portuguese had attacked Broach and looted it first in 1536 and then under Menezes in 1547.

In the eastern base of the fort, the mosque is truly majestic in concept, though plain and austere, and reminds one of the simple, uncompromising faith of Islam's early centuries as recorded in the chronicles of conquest. The sanctuary is divided into three, with three Hinduising mihrabs and three domes. The extensive open courtyard, intended for thousands of worshippers, has gates on three sides. Another mosque in the fort's southwestern corner is probably of eleventh-century date.

The factor Nicholas Withington writes in 1613 that Broach has 'the best Calicoes in the whole kingdom and a store of cotton'. Broach had ships of two hundred tonnes riding at anchor. Three years later, Sir Thomas Roe said that he had managed to obtain a firman from Muhammad Khan, the Governor, permitting him to build for the English a house in Broach 'near the Governor, strictly commanding no man to molest them by sea or land or take any custome of them or any way trouble them...' The English might 'buy, sell, and transport any commoditie at their pleasure without any molestation' and by 1622 the English factory at Broach could employ eight hundred weavers producing solely for the Company, who would then trade the textiles farther east, as well as indigo, saltpetre, and later cotton. Bleaching and washing were a speciality of Broach, because of the pure abundant waters of the Narmada. Broach also became a centre of textile dyeing and printing for the Company. Then from 1637 the English moved the textile industry to Surat, and later still to Bombay, so Broach quickly declined.

Of course, the high Fort is the hub of old Broach. You can start from the Victoria Clocktower (1901) and wander the mazy streets to find the Collector's Office, the English Factory in danger of being razed, the Dutch Factory, and the other municipal buildings redolent of a colonial past. The town centre perches on the high riverbank behind the surviving wall reputedly built by Kumarapala, King of Gujarat. Aurangzeb demolished most of the walls in 1660 because the Mughals feared defiance: the town was after all a centre for Jains, Hindus, and the other potential allies of the British. The Marathas naturally took their chances to invade in 1675 and 1686 and Broach finally understood that its continued survival depended on repairing its walls.

Sauntering around these streets, where ruins might be of yesterday or from five centuries ago, I came across a gate which protected a shady garden. On an impulse I rang the bell, and a manservant answered the summons.

'Is your master at home?' I enquired. He shook his head with awesome finality, eleven times, as a fierce leashed mongrel leapt and howled in fury at my presence. 'Madam is present', he replied, and unlocked the gate, ushering me through the shady garden and past the slavering hound. Should I be here, if the master is absent? In a Hindu or Muslim household it would be quite inadmissible to stay, so I hung back until a dignified old lady eventually made an appearance and I divined that she was a Parsi. 'Mrs Goal Sidhwa', she smiled, 'sister of Mrs Perin Jal Vakharia'. She pointed to a comfortable chair and called for glasses of boiled water. 'This is a palace that used to belong to the Nawab of Broach, and is now called Begum Wadi. The Nawab was a great opium-eater, and squandered all his revenues on this and other addictions. The Vakharias (*vakhar* means godown or warehouse) have been in Broach for five or six generations, and you probably know that Broach like most of coastal south Gujarat has always been beloved by Parsis for its hospitality towards us across the centuries. To tell the truth, I don't like this town, and I'd like to go back to Calcutta. My husband owned cinemas there and when I left Broach for Calcutta at the age of 16 I never wanted to come back. But my husband died in 1959 and my sister said I shouldn't live on my own, so I sold the Calcutta house in 1991 and live here now. Of course the mansion is too big – we have six rooms upstairs and down here a large hall, a dining-room, card-room, lounge. I rattle around like a pea in a pod now my sister has gone to Australia for a holiday. I have a cook and a gardener to help out, and a dangerous dog keep out thieves. My dear old Mistry brings me fresh orange juice, and I have simple meals. But you can imagine how I miss Calcutta'.

I wandered in the leafy old garden, peaceful and tropical, well-watered,

Broach. Begum Wadi garden, high above the riverbed

with a summer pavilion dated 1915, and gazed from the ancient wall across distant flats towards the other shore of the Narmada, and the hazy mouth of the river way to the west. I tried to envisage Mrs Sidhwa's nostalgia for the sticky boiling mass of humanity that is Calcutta, but completely failed. Mrs Sidhwa explained that there are three active fire temples in Broach for the significant Parsi minority, and prayers are offered at 6 a.m., 1.00, 4.00 and 8.30 in the evening. I took an auto-rickshaw in the hunt for a fire temple (ask for 'agiary' pronounced *agg-yaree*) but the Hindu driver had no idea where to find one, so I ended up by enquiring at the Christian Spiritual Life Centre on the outskirts of the town. There I was welcomed by Emmanuel C. Christie, English-speaking Director of the conference centre. Rule 1 of the fifteen crucified on the wall exhorted 'Conferees and visitors must not practise any religious activities or motions or worship either by words, songs, actions or meditations except Christian worship'. This organisation derives from the Northern Irish Presbyterian Mission Trust, which first came to Broach in 1840, and set up a hospital which no longer survives. In the Indian tradition of unquestioning, immediate hospitality, I was driven to drink tea in the home of Mr Vishwas Christian ('Vishwas' means 'faith') and there we discussed the difficulties faced by Christian missions in Gujarat. Nowadays it is much more arduous to obtain permission to baptise a convert; an affidavit of 'no objection' must be taken in a court, and both Hindus and Muslims find it almost impossible to avoid ostracism from their communities if they try to do so. Mr Christian showed me the derelict Christian cemetery not far away: 'Hier Rust Matthias de Lairesse van Dol'; 'Hier Rust Iohannis Groenvit 1666'; and a smaller memorial to 'Anna Maria Canevan 1664'. The new Christian cemetery, well-tended and regularly supplied, belongs to the United Church of North India, which comprises Anglicans, Baptists, Lutherans and Methodists. One tomb commemorates 'Mabel Barnes died 18.2.1942 in her 72nd year' and another 'Raju Varghese Kulanada, b. 1950, d.1987. We will meet you one day'.

Our party had now augmented to a battalion of onlookers around my cluster of informants who between them knew where the out-of-town

Broach. Old Parsi Tower of Silence, now disused

agiary would be. It turned out to be located just opposite the Dutch cemetery. Our cohorts poured beyond the sign on the white fortified wall 'Parsees only are allowed to enter this place' in Gujarati and English, and I hesitantly followed. The vaulted white anjuman, or assembly room, was erected according to a plaque 'in Sorabji Jivanji's memory paid by Parsi Homanji Sorabji Rs 700 and the remaining expense by society'. The old, disused round white stone tower of silence or dukhma, where corpses of the faithful are exposed to be eaten by birds of prey, dates from 1309 after the Parsis arrived here from Sanjan, but the new dukhma behind it is dated 1833, and one of the gates above the ramp is dated 1910. This was still being used in 1993. The *Vedas* reveal that the ancient Indo-Aryans buried their dead, but their Hindu and Buddhist descendants cremate them on open funeral pyres – except that the youngest children are carried to the river to ride along the current on little rafts. Parsis by contrast believe that the elements of water, earth, air and fire must not be polluted, and leave the vultures and other carrion birds to pick the flesh off the bones. This does not always answer the theological purpose, for the fields, gardens and roads round about are frequently defiled by scattered fragments of dropped flesh.

As one leaves Broach for the south, one passes Holy Angels Convent School, Broach Textile Mills, the Relief Cinema, and the Hotel Maharaja.

Bridges over the Narmada linking Bharuch to South Gujarat and Bombay first assumed historic importance with the railway bridge built by the British in 1881 and named 'Golden' because of its astronomic cost. A new railway bridge had to be built recently, so 'Golden Bridge' was given over to road traffic, then a further road bridge was added to relieve congestion. It leads to Surat via the oil-rich district around the town of Ankleshwar.

I should have liked to practise the Parikrama, or pilgrimage along both banks of the Narmada. Pilgrims must not carry money with them on their long journey, cut their hair or shave and, once begun, like life the journey may not be cut short. Some charitable donors have provided *sadavrat* or centres of free food along the way, which is often hindered by dense forest and thorn-bush, by dangers from wild animals and exposure to monsoon rains, heat and night cold. That is another journey, for another year. But you can experience the magic of the Narmada, with its island of Kabirwad and huge banyan, by staying at the Shuklatirtha Holiday Home 16 km from Broach.

The Narmada, invoked by the early 9th century Hindu reformer and teacher Shankaracharya in one of his greatest poems, was reputedly one of the places where the Mahabharata was dictated. Kalidasa's great play *Shakuntala* has been alleged to describe the Narmada hills up-country, and Kipling set his *Jungle Book* in the region, which has most recently been honoured by the subtle prose of Gita Mehta's brief, enchanting *A River Sutra*. Coleridge reminded us long ago that 'Poetry excites us to artificial feelings – makes us callous to real ones', so do I dare to take comfort in

61

Shankaracharya's verse against the agony of those made homeless by Narmada dam?

For the Narmada valley has become a highly contentious area with the construction of the Sardar Sarovar Dam. It is now 60 metres high and is planned to rise by another 60 before completion. Funding has been stopped by the World Bank, so India will have to find the balance of the funding alone. Pro-dam activists such as the health-worker Dr Anil Patel point to the fact that Saurashtra suffers a total drought one year in three and in good years can produce only one crop: with effective irrigation from the Sardar Sarovar the dangers of famine and drought would be gone forever, crops could increase from one to two or even three a year, and hydro-electric power would revolutionise the lives of poor farmers and tribals over a wide area. Anti-dam activists such as Shripad Dharmadhikary worry that Gujarat's existing canal network is leaking badly due to inadequate repairs; over a hundred dam projects lie incomplete; and irrigation channels might reach only as far as wealthy cotton plantations nearer to the dam, leaving poorer farmers no better off. Survival International claim that the new dam would displace over 100,000 people (60,000 of them tribal) and submerge 40,000 hectares of land. Manibeli in Maharashtra, Vadgam in Gujarat and two hundred other villages will be drowned, but if we look to the long-term resettlement of people in surrounding areas made increasingly fertile by the dam, to the long-term hydro-electric needs of expanding cities, and the long-term benefits to the region's agriculture and horticulture, not to mention greener pastures for cattle, the project begins to look sounder. There is no real seismic danger, as there would be in the ecologically more suspect Tehri dam in the foothills of the Himalaya planned to complete its first stage in 1998. Environmentalists in Gujarat tend to the conclusion, irrespective of whether Sardar Sarovar Dam is finished, that the best alternative to the once fashionable mega-dams (Hoover in America, Aswan in Egypt, Victoria in Sri Lanka) will comprise very large numbers of small-scale water-catchment areas benefiting huge numbers of isolated rural populations throughout the country, so encouraging them to remain on the land.

Baroda

'Baroda' is the long-established western form of the local name 'Vadodara' or 'Varodara' (retroflex *d* and *r* are interchangeable, as in Gaekwar and Gaekwad), which means the place of banyan trees. Banyans are sacred in Hinduism, so it was a foregone conclusion that any concentration of the trees would give rise to a settlement, which would in turn attract pilgrims, then merchants, in a never-ending cycle of growth and expansion. In fact, the city population in 1872 was 116,274, a figure which saw a general decrease until the 1941 census, when it rose to 153,301. It then rose by 38% to 211,407 in 1951, with huge increases in each succeeding decade: 298,398 in 1961 (when for a time it exceeded Surat's population); 467,487 in 1971;

734,473 in 1981 and 1,061,598 in 1991.

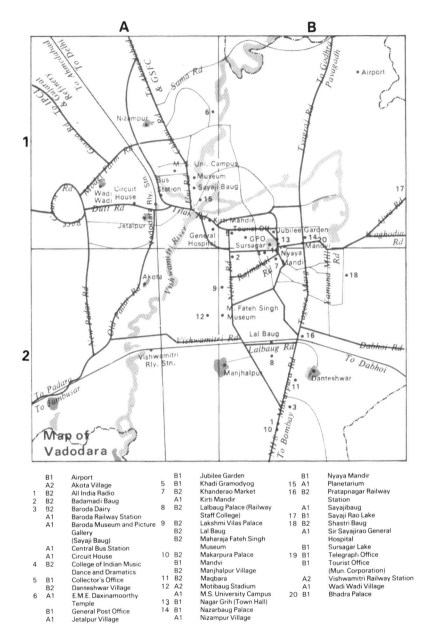

	B1	Airport		B1	Jubilee Garden		B1	Nyaya Mandir
	A2	Akota Village	5	B1	Khadi Gramodyog	15	A1	Planetarium
1	B2	All India Radio	7	B2	Khanderao Market	16	B2	Pratapnagar Railway
2	B2	Badamadi Baug		A1	Kirti Mandir			Station
3	B2	Baroda Dairy	8	B2	Lalbaug Palace (Railway		A1	Sayajibaug
	A1	Baroda Railway Station			Staff College)	17	B1	Sayaji Rao Lake
	A1	Baroda Museum and Picture	9	B2	Lakshmi Vilas Palace	18	B2	Shastri Baug
		Gallery		B2	Lal Baug		A1	Sir Sayajirao General
		(Sayaji Baug)		B2	Maharaja Fateh Singh			Hospital
	A1	Central Bus Station			Museum		B1	Sursagar Lake
	A1	Circuit House	10	B2	Makarpura Palace	19	B1	Telegraph Office
4	B2	College of Indian Music		B1	Mandvi		B1	Tourist Office
		Dance and Dramatics		B2	Manjhalpur Village			(Mun. Corporation)
5	B1	Collector's Office	11	B2	Maqbara		A2	Vishwamitri Railway Station
	B2	Danteshwar Village	12	A2	Motibaug Stadium		A1	Wadi Wadi Village
6	A1	E.M.E. Daxinamoorthy		A1	M.S. University Campus	20	B1	Bhadra Palace
		Temple	13	B1	Nagar Grih (Town Hall)			
	B1	General Post Office	14	B1	Nazarbaug Palace			
	A1	Jetalpur Village		A1	Nizampur Village			

63

The nearest images I can find to Baroda are Mysore and Hyderabad: two cities overwhelmed by the magnificence of their dynastic rulers. Like them, Baroda has never truly assimilated the end of the princely states decreed by the late Indira Gandhi in 1971, when she imposed on Parliament an amendment to the Constitution stripping the maharajas at one stroke of their privy purses and their privileges. What she could not accomplish, in this vindictive and petty nod to a Russian-inspired egalitarianism, was to destroy the popularity that strong, effective, avuncular rule had earned for so many of the princes, though naturally not all. As Mrs Gandhi won her first elections on a pledge to overcome poverty – a promise that could never be fulfilled – she felt obliged after victory to act, but to plan and implement effective long-term economic strategies for popular consumption would have threatened her political survival, so she took the much easier option of plucking privy purses. This crass act did not affect those princes who had already made themselves extremely wealthy through good investments in India and abroad, diversifying into industry or banking, for instance. It simply handicapped those more modest of the 278 little states which between them comprised a patchwork of half India, from kingdoms larger than England to petty states that you could walk round in an hour. The size of each privy purse was determined by size, from a million rupees a month to 200. Added to the coffers of the Indian Government, the total sum was derisory; subtracted from the domestic economy of a sovereign who looked after many servants and employees, each particular amount sometimes proved crucial, and many rulers found themselves suddenly poor. Whether Hindu or Muslim, the princes almost invariably dealt even-handedly with their subjects, though it could be argued that being above the law gave them too much autocratic power.

The former Maharaja of Kurundwad, a tiny state in Rajasthan, filed a suit to claim that Mrs Gandhi's constitutional amendment had violated guarantees made to the princes when Mountbatten persuaded them to join India. Now 88, the former ruler received a rebuff when the Indian Supreme Court rejected his claim. Chief Justice L.M. Sharma pronounced: 'The distinction between the erstwhile rulers and the citizens of India has to be ended in the interests of common brotherhood. In a country like ours, with so many disruptive forces of regionalism and communalism, it is necessary to emphasise that the unity and integrity can be preserved only by a spirit of brotherhood.'

Baroda may not even feel the difference, because the ruling family, like Madhavrao Scindia of Gwalior in Madhya Pradesh, is independently wealthy, with many industrial and landowning interests. Indeed, it is impossible to spend long in the city without discovering the all-pervasive influence of the Gaekwad family. We can look at these palaces first, unless you prefer to visit the Tourist Corporation of Gujarat information bureau in Narmada Bhavan, C-Block, Indira Avenue, popularly known as Jail Road after the Central Jail across the road.

The British had a long history of alliance with the Gaekwad dynasty, from their support of the founder, Pilaji, against his master Dabhade, and subsequently the Peshwa Bajirao I, so his successor Damaji (1732-68) allowed the British to set up agencies in Baroda for dyed and printed textiles to be exported from Surat.

When Beatrice and Sidney Webb visited India in 1912 (*Indian Diary*, Oxford U.P., 1987), they called on the Gaekwad, Maharaja Sir Sayajirao III (1863-1939), a man so learned that he read Plato in the original Greek, and so versatile that he enjoyed equally the economist Jeremy Bentham and Lewis Carroll, and commissioned a translation of *Alice in Wonderland* into Marathi. Sayajirao's perspicacity can be judged from the fact that in 1909 he appointed the great Romesh Chunder Dutt as his Prime Minister, though unfortunately Dutt died very soon afterwards. R.C. Dutt, after whom a main road in Baroda is named, wrote a valuable *Economic History of India* and translated into English verse both the Ramayana and part of the Mahabharata. Retiring from the Indian Civil Service in 1897, two years later he became President of the Indian National Congress. The Webbs visited schools and were told that 'about 94% of the whole population' (of rural and urban Baroda State) had schools accessible to their children and reflected that 'this is enormously ahead of the rest of India, and reflects great credit on the State'. At the time, the Maharaja was one of the three premier princes of India, with a salute of twenty-one guns, ruled two million subjects and possessed possibly the finest collection of jewels in the world.

Around 1909, the Rev. Edward St Clair Weeden, Vicar of Canon-Frome in Herefordshire, was invited to spend *A Year with the Gaekwar of Baroda* (Hutchinson, 1911), a book compiled from letters to Weeden's mother in England, charmingly naive with an authentic period style. Weeden ingenuously once asked Sayajirao whether he had much property in Baroda. 'He was rather amused and told me with a smile that it *all* belonged to him; all the land, all the houses, all the revenue, all the rates and taxes are his personal private property, which he disposes of as he thinks fit. How well and wisely he uses the enormous resources at his command one has not to live very long in Baroda to discover. He lives in the magnificent style expected of an Oriental ruler by his people; but his own personal expenditure is a mere trifle as compared with the large sums which are spent annually on public works and buildings. His position seems to be that of a despotic monarch governing constitutionally; appointing a Council to advise him, judges to administer his laws, departments to carry out the work of administration; and distributing his revenues in such a way as to be for the greatest good of the whole State.' Weeden gives no figures, but W.S. Caine, in *Picturesque India* (Routledge, 1898) records that in 1881 the total revenue of the State was £1,120,00 made up as follows: land revenue, £850,000; customs, £94,000; taxes on castes and trades, £31,000; taxes on liquor and opium, £42,000; forests, £7,000; tributary states,

Baroda. Udaya Narayan Temple (8th century)

£64,000; and justice £26,000.

Sayajirao III was not the direct heir to the throne, but adopted as heir, a custom widely recognised, especially among Hindus of Gujarati and Rajasthani dynasties, to ensure the continuity of any line without male heirs. His predecessor, Malhar Rao (1870-75) had been deposed for attempting to poison the British Resident, Colonel Phayre, with a cup of pomelo juice in which ground diamonds had been mixed, a device he had practised on his predecessor and brother, Khanderao (1856-70). Khanderao's widow was given the right to choose a new ruler, and she decided upon the eleven-year-old who was to revolutionise the life of his people. Major changes involved the founding of a Cotton Spinning and Weaving Mill (1885), a technical school called Kala Bhavan (1890) which later became the Faculty of Technology of the Maharaja Sayajirao University of Baroda, and a City Improvement Trust (1910), which transformed the higgledy-piggledy Old City into a small corner of a great modern city, just as the City of London is a small corner of modern London. If you want to explore the Old City nowadays, proceed east from Sursagar Tank, past Nyaya Mandir. The western gate to Old Baroda is the Laheripura Gate built in 1558 by Khalil Khan, son of Mahmud Beghada. The Tomb of Qutb ud-Din, and a *vav* or step-well in the grounds, dates from 1586, but the earliest extant temple in Baroda is the Udaya Narayan Temple dating from the eighth century but here reconstructed. I saw this venerable sanc-

Baroda. M.S. Hospital (1876)

tuary, above a busy road next to the Sayajirao Hospital (1876) designed in his florid Indo-Saracenic style by the inimitable Major Mant (1840-81).

The Palaces
Since the Maharaja still occupies some of Baroda's palaces, access is severely restricted, by invitation. However, anyone can glimpse from the road the extraordinary ostentation of Lakshmi Vilas Palace (1880-90), one of 'Mad' Mant's most extraordinary concepts, completed by R.F. Chisholm after Mant's death. In white stone inlaid with marbles of various colours, the palace is a riot of columns, cupolas and arches drawn from South Indian, Central Indian, North Indian and Islamic traditions in a fairy-tale of colour and curves, as if an architectural Paul Klee had taken solid lines for a walk; as if an Indian had designed a stage set for Rimsky-Korsakov's *Le Coq d'Or*. The breathless Edward Weeden, one of the earliest of all Europeans to stay in the palace, reported: 'In the centre are the Maharaja's apartments. They are approached by a portico of noble dimensions, under which the tallest elephant with the largest howdah on his back can pass with plenty of room to spare. Three broad steps, on which sentries in gorgeous uniforms are posted, lead into a lofty hall of white marble, opening at the top into a gallery of carved cedar. The hall is paved with a very rare green marble of great beauty which is found only in the Gaekwar's territory, and in the

67

middle is a table of the same marble, at which His Highness can transact any pressing business...'

In another large hall, Sayajirao placed three large stuffed tigers and other trophies; above this the great white marble staircase inlaid with gold and mosaic rises to a gallery which leads to a broad terrace over the portico. Another gallery leads to the drawing-room, library, reading-room, and study. Three courts with palms and fountains separate the dining-room from the billiard-room and the small Darbar Hall. The Gaekwad's private rooms are at the back.

The rooms that Sayajirao built for Prince Shivajirao are on the floor above, while the zenana or south wing for his Maharani are in the style of her native South India. Here is the shrine of Lakshmi, Hindu goddess of prosperity, after whom the Vilas or palace is named. The north wing, in North Indian style, is dedicated to the Great Darbar Hall, with seven domes, twelve chandeliers, and carved cedar gallery. No furniture save the royal throne diminishes its awesome dimensions.

Opposite Lakshmi Vilas is Indumati Mahal, nowadays the hub of the palace administrations and those charitable trusts which the present Ruler delights in. I spoke to his private secretary, S.B. Vaidya, who promised to have me shown the armoury of Shastragadh, and the Kirti Mandir, or mausoleum of the Baroda rulers, with ceiling frescoes by Nandlal Bose. West of the Kirti Mandir is the Kothi, or Secretariat, contemporary with the District Court or Nyaya Mandir (1896), part European Gothic and part North Indian, the whole characteristically Barodan Eclectic. Charles Mant not only designed Lakshmi Vilas, and the Hospital, but also the grandiose Public Library (1876).

The earliest extant royal palace is the Nazar Bagh, in the city centre, originally dating from 1721 but much changed by later rulers, and now looking almost derelict, with a shanty town flipping dismally along its perimeter walls like a horizontal house of cards. W.S. Caine saw Nazar Bagh in better days at the end of the last century when its treasure-room was shown to visitors. 'Huge cheetahs, carefully muzzled, used for hunting bucks, are usually to be seen on the palace steps. The Regalia of Baroda is valued at £3,000,000 sterling. The jewels worn by the Maharaja on state occasions are those shown to strangers. These consist of a gorgeous collar of 500 diamonds, some of them as big as walnuts, arranged in five rows, surrounded by a top and bottom row of emeralds the same size; the pendant is a famous diamond called "The Star of the Deccan". An aigrette to match is worn in the turban. The rest of the jewels consist of strings of pearls of perfect roundness, graduated from the size of a pea to a large marble; wondrous rings, necklaces, clusters of sapphires and rubies as big as grapes; and, greatest marvel of all, a carpet, about ten feet by six, woven entirely of strings of pure and coloured pearls, with great central and corner circles of diamonds. This carpet took three years to make, and cost £200,000. It was one of Khanderao's mad freaks, and was intended to be

Baroda. Nazar Bagh Palace

sent to Mecca to please a Muhammadan lady who had fascinated him, but the scandal was too serious, and it never left Baroda.' Nearby stands the Mandvi, an Islamic pavilion of 1736.

Maharaja Khanderao's own palace has been converted into offices for the Municipal Corporation, so you can wander about in it as in one of Kafka's bureaucratic nightmares.

Shiv Mahal is a palace used for festivals and bazaars. Pratap Vilas, yet another royal palace, was originally commissioned and completed in 1914 for Sayajirao III's crown prince. It can be found beside the railway line off Makarpura Road to the south of Baroda City beyond the Polo Club. You can visit the grounds of this massive two-storey mansion, with its superbly-maintained gardens, because the building is now occupied by the Railway Staff College.

Six kilometres farther south is Makarpura summer palace, though the royal family would spend much of the summer at their English-style residence at Ootacamund in the Nilgiri Hills of Tamil Nadu. Makarpura is not open to visitors, but is well worth a glimpse from outside, with its stunning three-storey Italian Renaissance elegance, anachronistic of course, like most other buildings in Baroda, because although it dates from the 1800s its ethos harks back to those spacious days when maharajas hunted tigers from elephantback with bows blessed by Arjuna.

Baroda Museum and Picture Gallery

If you have time in Baroda for only one museum, the one to choose is the Museum and Picture Gallery both because the building belongs to the hysterically eclectic 'Mad' Mant Indo-Saracenic tradition we have seen across Maharashtra and Gujarat (here with R.F. Chisholm to moderate his eccentricities), and because the collections are first-rate. Purpose-built in Sayaji Park between 1887 and 1894, the Museum was shortly joined by its sister Picture Gallery (1908-14) and filled with choice items acquired in India and overseas by Maharaja Sayajirao III Gaekwad of Baroda, one of the great princes of his time. Sayajirao travelled very widely, and commissioned dealers and scholars to seek out Indian miniatures, European oil-paintings, sculpture, textiles, objects from Japan, Tibet and Nepal, Indian and foreign coins, and collections for the study of science and natural history intended to emulate the various London museums he knew such as the Victoria and Albert and the Science Museum. I explored the excellent library with the Librarian, Mrs Indira Mafat, who showed me some of the rarest books. I purchased O.C. Gangoli's indispensable *Critical Catalogue of Miniature Paintings in the Baroda Museum* (1961) for background data on the many masterpieces, outstanding among which is a page from the earliest Mughal manuscript, the great *Hamza Nama*, about 1565. The Emperor Humayun ordered a manuscript to be copied from Nasir ad-Din Tusi's life of Hamza, uncle of the Prophet Muhammad (s.A.a.w.s.); many of the dispersed leaves are lost, and others are in the U.S.A, London, Berlin and Vienna. Almost of equal value are 32 miniatures by different artists (see 198/8, signed by 'Madho Guzarati') from a *Razm Nama* manuscript dated 1598. The *Razm Nama* is a Persian version of the Hindu epic Mahabharata commissioned by the Emperor Akbar, a tolerant truth-seeker. Since Gangoli's catalogue appeared, there has been a great donation of 109 miniature paintings from the Parsi collector Jagmohandas Modi: my favourite is a late 18th-century Kangra masterpiece showing Krishna vanquishing the great snake, all swiftness, light, grace and magic realism in a harmony of colour-play.

Look for intricate narrative paintings and silver-plated copper trays from Tanjore, a lovely Shiva Nataraja from 11th-century South India, the Ganj-e-Shahid inscription of Qazzaq Khan, Mughal Governor of Dabhoi (1635) proclaiming the protection of a mausoleum, and an exquisite 9th-century ivory-inlaid book box from Nagina (U.P.)

Even if you plan to visit Roda and Shamalaji in northeast Gujarat, it is worth visiting Baroda Museum just for the sculptures removed from these sites, though 6th-century blue schist figures from Shamalaji can also be found in the Prince of Wales Museum, Bombay. Apart from these, the most significant collection in the Indian sculpture section is a series of fine Jain bronzes excavated at Akota, near Baroda, which has been dated between the 5th century (two figures of Jivantswami) and the 8th (a chauri-bearing attendant in *tribhanga* pose on a lotus pedestal).

If you are travelling through Gujarat, you will want to find in Baroda architectural fragments and pottery from Champaner, the carved ceiling from Shaikh Farid's tomb at Patan, and glazed ceramics from Ahmedabad and Baroda. The dying craft of *patola* from Patan and Surat can be seen at their height here.

Tibetan Buddhism is exemplified by mandalas, paintings, temple banners, manuscripts and ritual lamps.

The upper floor of the Museum building contains sections on natural history, ethnology, and geology while the upper floor of the Gallery building contains European paintings, often studio works, copies or relatively insignificant works by minor artists such as 'The Death of Rachel' by the early 18th-century painter Giambattista Cignaroli. Poor examples of works by or attributed to Alonso Cano, Ribera and Zurbarán represent the Spanish School; among the Dutch and Flemings included are Rubens, Teniers, Fyt, Storck, Weenix and Paulus Potter. Among the French, you can see works by Millet, Courbet and Boudin. British artists represented include Reynolds, Turner, Lawrence, Varley, Linnell and Henry Moore.

Western museums have traditionally shown an array of copies of classical works in plaster and metal as guidance to art students, and the Baroda Museum has one of the best selections in India, including the Delphi Charioteer, the Pergama Altar, statues from Pompeii, and a statue of the Emperor Augustus.

The ethnology section features tribes from Gujarat: the Rabaris, the

Baroda. Museum and Picture Gallery. Ambika on a lion (9th-century bronze from Akota)

Gamits from Surat district, utensils and costumes from the widespread Bhils, the Chaudhuris and the Wagharis of Okhamandal.

Maharaja Fatehsinhji Museum

I wish I could be as enthusiastic about the royal gallery in the Lakshmi Vilas Compound, near Moti Baug cricket ground. I was the only visitor, outnumbered ten to one by suspicious peons, twelve to one by pigeons cooing overhead, fifteen to one by screaming peacocks in the ground, and thirty to one by beady-eyed geckoes wandering the walls diagonally: sceptics more than critics. The opening hours are quoted as 9 to 1 noon, and 3.30 to 6.30 except Mondays, and I could not established whether it closed for lunch at one or noon. You would have to overstay your welcome to find out.

The building was erected as the Moti Baug School in 1879, then remodelled and extended as a gallery in 1961. As the catalogue sadly avows of Sayajirao III: 'This great ruler, though not knowledgeable in the fine arts, employed and consulted various renowned artists of India and Europe to choose art pieces to decorate the various palaces in Baroda and other palaces in India'. He also ran a Parisian palace and Room 21 recreates the atmosphere of his living-room there, with Rococo porcelain figures of the Four Continents then known, and an overriding taste for chinoiserie and sentimental mezzotints based on paintings by Angelica Kauffmann.

Sayajirao's advisers included the Travancore prince Raja Ravi Varma, the first Indian to practise oils, the third-rate Venetian artist Augusto Felici, appointed Court Sculptor in 1892, Fyzee Rahman, a disciple of J.S. Sargent; and the sculptor Phanindranath Bose (*d.* 1926), represented in Room 3 by the fine 'Boy with Falcon' (1920), 'On the Way to the Temple', and 'Peasant Girl'. Room 4 recaptures the atmosphere of the Gaekwad style before Sayajirao. The inlaid door, great chandelier, furniture, and the portrait of Maharaja Khanderao formerly adorned Makarpura Hunting Lodge built by Khanderao 6 km south of Baroda City. Among the other formal state portraits is a charming picture of Princess Tarabai, Khanderao's daughter, by Ravi Varma, more of whose paintings fill Room 5. Some are smooth evocations of a Hindu mythology in which all gods and heroes are dramatically handsome, elegant and pallid, and the others are court paintings which attempt to related the Hindu epics to the Baroda of our own times, so that the most successful of the former, such as 'Nala and Damayanti', seems to be paired seamlessly with the aristocratic posture and regalia of Maharani Chimanabai, the first wife of Sayajirao III, and those of her successor, Chimanabai II (1871-1958). I found the atmosphere melancholy as a pile of dead leaves: copies of the Laocoön and Apollo Belvedere, Hygeia, Homer, Aeschines, and Venus Kallipygos from the Louvre or the Vatican seem to yearn for their natural surroundings.

In Room 12 I enjoyed John Seymour Lucas's interpretation of the sculptor Alfred Gilbert at work (1891) and a fine portrait entitled 'The Mask' by

Giovanni Costa (1833-1893). In Room 13 we are back in the realm of official portraits, the best in the room being Fyzee Rahman's 'Maharani Chimanabai II' and 'Princes Fatehsinghrao and Jaisinghrao' (1892) by Sir James Linton (1840-1916). Ravi Varma has a glowing record of 'Maharaja Sayajirao III on the Occasion of his Investiture'. Room 14 is devoted to landscapes, mainly European, such as 'A Moorland Road in North Wales' by E.M. Wimperis (1835-1900) and Swiss lake views by Charles Giron (1850-1914). On the western staircase two austere Jain images of tirthankars seem dislocated in time and space from the adjacent oil painting of two girls picking flowers by G.D. Deuskar. The only aesthetic which has not faded over the last century in this gallery is the Chinese and Japanese tradition: porcelains, bronzes, paintings and sculptures from the Far East remain as exquisite and universal as on the day they were made. On the first floor the landscapes by minor artists (McWhirter's 'View of Edinburgh', Fulleylove's 'Clumber Castle') have not stood the test of time, and Angelica Kauffmann's mezzotints seem pretentious and superficial. Inadequate copies of great European paintings (Rembrandt, Van Dyck, Murillo) merely make one long for the presence of the originals.

Maharaja Sayajirao University

Visitors are welcome to view permanent and temporary exhibitions in the Archaeological Department on campus between 11 and 6 daily; this is a good place to find an expert (Professor V.S. Parekh, or Dr. K. Krishnan) willing to discuss the finds and new excavations, such as the prehistory and palaeoenvironment of the Dadhar river northeast of Pavagadh; the Mature Harappan site (2140 B.C.) 3 km south of Nagwada village in Surendranagar district (seasons 1984-8); and finds from the site of Zawar (200 B.C.-100 A.D.) 48 km south of Udaipur in Rajasthan. A major new Harappan site is being examined at Moti Pipli, 40 km from Jamnagar. Even more poignantly important are the 4th-century finds from the Buddhist site of Devani Mori near Shamalaji now submerged.

The Rest of Baroda

Everybody has their own Baroda, from the stylish modern shopping centres which rival those of Delhi to the wonderful haveli of Tambekar Wada near Dandia Bazar, a merchant's mansion administered by the Archaeological Survey of India. Look for exhibitions by graduates and students of the Baroda Art School, and check evening performances of music and dance in the local morning newspaper, at the Tourist Information Office, Narmada Bhavan, Indira Avenue, or at the M.S. University Faculty of Fine Arts.

In Ahmedabad (the Dwarkanath in Raipur) and in Patan (the Kapur Mahetano Pado) we can see haveli temples created to reinforce the ideal that devotion to a god should resemble the duty shown to one's earthly lord. Such an idea was transformed into a building space by the Vaishna-

74

vites of the Pushti Marga movement begun by Vallabhacharya in the 15th century. R.G. Bhandarkar explains in his *Vaishnavism Shaivism* (1965) that according to Vallabhacharya 'God cannot be worshipped independently in a public place of worship, but in the house or temple of the guru which has therefore to be regularly visited by the devotee with offerings'. This type of *bhakti* cult can be found in the Swaminarayan movement nowadays centred at Akshardham, Gandhinagar: one must show total commitment to religion not only by chastity, celibacy, poverty and prayer, but also by unquestioning obedience to one's guru, whoever he might be.

In Baroda, such haveli temples include the Maratha Brahmin temple of 1763 dedicated to Ganesha, and the Narasinhji haveli temple in Narasinhjini Pol. One must imagine the deity as a sovereign, and the haveli temple as his palatial home. To that end, no expense will be spared in decoration, carving and ritual. You enter Mairal temple by a multi-storeyed gate bustling with attendants, and pass on your right the mushak shrine, for Ganesha's mouse-vehicle. An artificial lake at the left is matched by a fountain at the right, and the main temple has a galleried hall. The dharamshala for pilgrims at the back of the temple seems now to be rented out to local residents.

The family with custodianship of the Narasinhji haveli temple lives upstairs, but you can ask to see the splendid temple noted throughout Baroda for its chariot, paraded through the city every year. The main image is in the sanctuary behind which is the treasury. You might be lucky enough to glimpse *prasad* (the deity's sacred sustenance) being prepared in the large kitchen at the back, but the pool for divine water-games called *jala krida* was closed during my visit.

The Church of North India has its principal Baroda church north of the city in the Residency and Cantonment district. It was consecrated as the Anglican church in 1825 by Bishop Reginald Heber, author of a *Narrative of a Journey through the Upper Provinces of India from Calcutta to Bombay, 1824-5*, but had to be rebuilt in 1838.

Much more interesting is the Friday Mosque, in the heart of the bazaar area, which dates from 1912. The position of Muslims has always been fragile in Baroda. Heavily outnumbered, they have nevertheless enjoyed persistent open favours from successive maharajas, whose tolerance and evenhandedness to British, Parsi, Jain, Hindu and Muslim employees has been legendary. Yet in the past there have been outbreaks of communal violence between Muslims and Hindus even before riots in Surat or Ahmedabad. After the Babri Mosque incident in 1992, however, Surat and Ahmedabad saw the worst of the riots and Baroda remained calm. When I asked the maharaja's secretary about this he shrugged and called it a miracle. But clearly something conciliatory lives in the air of Baroda, as I discovered when speaking to the Friday Mosque's serene muaddin, the white-bearded, bright-eyed Mahmud Khan Pathan. I asked to see the legendary Great Qur'an of Muhammad Ghaus, a fabulous manuscript completed in 1206 A.H., corresponding to 1791-2, and he took me upstairs to the room where it is ensconced, as in a bed, one majestic leaf turned over each day. Mahmud speaks no Arabic – like most Gujarati Muslims, he knows Gujarati, Hindu, and often a regional language such as Marathi in the south or Rajasthani in the north. The mosque itself, empty until midday prayer, slept half in the sunshine of its pleasant courtyard and half in the shade of its ample sanctuary with nine mihrabs and square stone columns.

Baroda's pollution by industries such as chemicals factories and mills is only one aspect of the city, and one which the visitor can easily ignore. Opposite the noisy Central Bus Station and Central Rail Station is the extensive greenery of Sayaji Baug, a municipal garden with Zoo and Planetarium laid out by the greatest of the Gaekwad dynasty. And the annual Navratri Utsav, or Festival of Nine Nights, provokes the city into light, colour, dancing and music during September-October. Navratri is held throughout Gujarat, at small villages as well as in great cities, but Baroda is its cultural capital. Amba Mata, the earth goddess bestowing strength and power against the forces of evil, enjoys especial attention during Navratri by puja in temples and dances of the Ras Garba tradition. These normally begin at eleven at night and continue until dawn at various sites, including Indrapuri and the nearby Surya Chandra Nagar in the east, Ahmedabadi Pol off Vinoba Bhave Road; R.C. Patel Estate and Akota Stadium off Padra Road in the west; the Fine Arts Faculty opposite Sayaji Baug; and Bhawanipura and adjacent Mehsana Nagar in the north.

Champaner

Fatehpur Sikri is the most celebrated abandoned Islamic city in India, though I have made strong claims for Bidar in my *Western India* and now make similar claims for Champaner, a Chauhan Rajput town under Patai Raval, virtually razed and remade by the rampaging Sultan Mahmud Beghada from his victory after a twenty-month siege (1482-4) from 1484 until 1507, when he deserted his new capital renamed Muhammadabad. Like Fatehpur Sikri it was abandoned by court and people, who returned to Ahmedabad in 1537.

The town in the plain has been protected by the two walled forts on the nearby mountain called Pavagadh. The lower fort with its royal palace of Raja Jaisingh Patai Raval clearly deterred invaders, as did a sequence of narrow gates, each visible from the one above. Whoever held Pavagadh could descend at will on Champaner; whoever held Champaner could surround and besiege Pavagadh, so it has always been necessary to hold both, as the forces of the Mughal Emperor Humayun did briefly in 1535, followed by the Marathas (1727-1853) and by the British until Independence in 1947.

Champaner in the plain can comfortably be encompassed in a morning, if you set out after an early breakfast from Baroda 44 km away, though a few monuments are scattered over a wide area. You begin with the massive walls running parallel to the highway, and park by Mahmud's Friday Mosque, or Jami Masjid, an even more exuberant series of variations on the Hinduising ornamentation that you find in its model, the Friday Mosque of Ahmedabad (1423). Anyone interested in phases and styles of Indian architecture will be overwhelmed by the complex beauties and ingenuity of Champaner's designers and craftsmen, for virtually every building is a masterpiece.

British readers tend to equate great Muslim architecture in India with the Mughal Emperors, but there is a similar case to be made for the Sultans of Gujarat, notably Ahmad Shah I and Mahmud Shah known as 'Beghada' according to the *Tabaqat-i-Akbari* of Khwaja Nizam ud-Din Ahmad (translated by B. De, Calcutta, 1913-40) because he had conquered twin forts, and because his moustaches were swept back like horns on a *vegaro*, the Gujarat word for a bullock.

Mahmud proved a worthy successor to the martial Ahmad Shah I (1411-42). Born Fath Khan in 1446, he followed Muhammad Shah (1442-51) and Qutb ud-Din Ahmad Shah II (1451-9), ascending the throne of Gujarat (an area then not of course equivalent to the modern state) at the age of thirteen and determined to prove his strength by supporting the ruler of Khandesh against the invasions of the Malwa ruler, Mahmud Khilji. He took the port of Daman from its Hindu overlords, and in 1470 he created a new town at the foot of Mount Girnar in Saurashtra, calling it Mustafabad, nowadays Junagadh ('Old Fort'); he attacked Dwarka in 1473; created the new town of Mehmedabad, now ruined, south-east of Ahmedabad, and most notably he constructed a major new capital at Champaner after besieging the old Hindu fort for two years from 1482-4.

He allied himself with the Egyptian fleet sent by the Mamluk Sultan against the Portuguese, who were threatening the trade of Cambay and Broach. One naval battle off Chaul was won in 1508, but the Portuguese returned in greater strength a year later and destroyed the Gujarati and Egyptian fleets. When the Portuguese overcame the Adilshahi rulers of Goa in 1510, Mahmud sensibly decided to come to terms with the Portuguese. We have a first-hand, probably high fanciful, account of this man, by Ludovico di Varthema, a Bolognese Catholic of rooted antipathies to all Muslims. 'He has twenty thousand horsemen, and when he rises fifty elephants with riders come to him, doing reverence and then retiring to spend the rest of the day in idleness. When he eats, there are many kinds of instruments: trumpets, drums, flageolets, fifes and many more. The Sultan has mustachios under his nose so long that he ties them over his head as a woman would tie her hair back, and he has a white beard reaching down to his girdle.'

After Mahmud died in 1511, he was succeeded by Muzaffar II, a less fearsome character who lived in a state of tension with the Portuguese intent on seizing Diu from him. Muzaffar died in 1526 and was succeeded briefly by two other rulers before Bahadur Shah acceded (1526-37). He and the Ottoman fleet cooperated in the naval victory of 1531 over the Portuguese, but his long-standing enmity with the Mughal Emperor Humayun proved to be his downfall. Escaping with his men first to Mandu (now in Madhya Pradesh) and then to Champaner, Bahadur eventually fled to Cambay, where he burnt his fleet of a hundred ships to stop them being captured by Humayun's troops, and sailed to Diu, where he finally agreed to the Portuguese request to build a fort, hoping to use their forces as allies against Humayun. Fortunately for Bahadur, Humayun was diverted from his march on Diu by Sher Khan's insurrection, so Bahadur left Diu and reassembled his army to recover his former glory and territories. In 1537 he returned to Diu at the head of an army, but the fort he had himself, ironically, authorised proved too strong and fell to the Portuguese, thus effectively ending the Sultanate of Gujarat, which would be finally extinguished by Akbar.

Mahmud Beghada's new town plan from 1484 consisted of a walled fortress protected by bastions and stout gateways with the royal palace at its heart, surrounded by official buildings and mosques. The Customs House still stands and the sentries' quarters too, but the majority of the surviving

Champaner. Mahmud Shah Beghada's Citadel. Gateway

78

buildings are sacred: mosques and tombs of saints, all else having been robbed away by people hungry for fine masonry. The tombs are ruinous, rather than robbed, and are usually in the form of a domed central chamber surrounded by an arcade roofed with smaller domes, and a pillared portico jutting from one side. The best example can be seen today at the Nagina Mosque, itself a minor masterpiece in the mould of the Friday Mosque.

Guards of the Archaeological Survey of India attend the major sites, such as the Shahr-ki-Masjid and Jami Masjid, and my suggestion would be to show one the following list of monuments and ask him to take you round, saving time. Of course, there is always the chance that you will be commandeered by a guard who knows only Gujarati, or someone with only a hazy idea of history, but that is another of the glorious uncertainties of Indian journeys. Establish a fee before starting off, with witnesses, be genially firm, and smile a great deal in particular while haggling down from an unrealistic charge to one equidistant between extravagance and avarice. The major monuments to see are the citadel known as in Ahmedabad as Bhadra, the Customs House, the Friday, Shahr, Nagina and Kevda mosques, Sadanshah Gate, Navlakha Kotha (that is, costing 'nine lakhs'), Patai Raval Palace, Makai Kotha and Lakulish Temple.

As I was the only foreigner at Champaner that glorious winter morning, it was not for me that a red-robed 'snake-charmer' was exercising his skills, but for a group of local lads, many of them barefoot, perching on the massive fifteenth-century walls. Langur monkeys scampered along the walls, and tree squirrels speed on innumerable secret missions hither and thither. One langur drank gratefully from a fountain installed to benefit the flowers so lovingly tended by the Archaeological Survey staff.

The Friday Mosque, completed in 1523, had been started much earlier, and it clearly repeats in many ways the vision of Ahmedabad's Friday Mosque, honouring its dynastic ancestor. Accidents of taste, fashion, and fame have raised Agra's Taj Mahal (1634) to global popular consciousness, and left Champaner's Friday Mosque in shadow, but the earlier masterpiece has finer minarets, and more perfect proportions between ensemble and detail; the entrance at Champaner is also far more exquisite than the gate to Taj Mahal, its vast courtyard more austerely impressive. Of the whole area, ninety metres by sixty, a little less than half is occupied by the great sanctuary. The courtyard has a range of shallow arched cloisters giving a perpetually shifting balance of brightness and deep shadow. Attention to the exterior detail shows the mastery of Champaner's artisans; note the western or *qibla* wall facing Makkah, with its elaborate moulded buttresses. The sanctuary's façade is closed except for five pointed archways. Two slim minarets flank the perfectly-harmonised central arch, and within the dark mosque prepare to be overcome by the supreme stone-carving on the flat vault between the central dome and the mihrab. Ten rows of columns lead you to the mihrab and visions of Makkah, but three more

Champaner. Friday Mosque (1523). Gateway

niches on each side of the mihrab, in disappearing perspective, inspire intimations of infinity, interrupted by a mezzanine gallery pierced for women to view the imam's prayers and sermon. Oriel windows offer a faint Andalusian *reja*-like quality of sensuality to the outer walls, while sophistication beyond Ahmedabad's precursor is demonstrated by such elements as vertical recessed chases in the column-shafts. Subjectively, I prefer it to its model because of its solemn silence isolated from urban hubbub; considered in every detail like a late Beethoven string quartet compared with an earlier. Elevation, literally, to two upper storeys can be achieved up a spiral staircase in the hollow minarets: on the first floor you roam amid cupolas like Marco Polo in the palace of Kublai Khan (unlike you he never attained the miracle of Champaner), and on the second floor you circuit a wonderful gallery. Each balcony has stone seats and you can imagine Sufis and other contemplatives circling here or resting lost in thought above comings and goings in the busy hall below. At the same time there is the unmistakable sixth sense of Hinduism vibrating, a sense deriving doubtless from the *shikhara*-space rising three storeys to the sky, a

Champaner. Shahr-ki Masjid

sense of bubbling exuberance which cannot be contained by the ascetic white marble of a plain and simple mosque. A *hauz* or Hindu-style stepped ablution tank is another startling feature.

A similar feeling of Hindu colour and vibrancy affects the nearby Shahr-ki Masjid, with four sets of ornate columns far removed from Arabian precedent, and five niches of which the central mihrab is untypically the *least* ornate. The central dome is flanked by alternate small and larger domes, below which my footfalls reverberated in shadowy silence.

The Archaeological Survey has set a stone plan in English and Hindi to guide you round ancient Champaner on your own, and I picked my way along a sandy path through undergrowth towards the Kevda Mosque, a square sanctuary with open gallery on the upper storey and a dome above that, the whole built up like most historic Gujarati mosques on an artificial stone platform. Its spectacular situation, with awesome views up to Pavagadh, seems heightened nowadays in its strange isolation with respect to its most brilliant epoch, when it would have been surrounded by plebeian dwellings. Its marble facing has been robbed away, and as an inactive mosque, its sanctuary is disturbed only by sparrows.

I returned across the railway line, then struck out away from the Friday Mosque to the Nagina or 'Jewel' Mosque, a later miniature copy with a gracious gateway before it on a brick plinth. A beautifully proportioned arcade within has four columns on each side of a square beneath a central dome; three sides are open but on the fourth, facing the town, a wall extends up to hip-height.

Oriel windows jutting from the mosque's façade add intimacy on a domestic scale, whereas the staircases up to the galleries open on to the infinite sky. There I found two youths reading poetry aloud, for all the world like Iranian boys learning Hafez in Isfahan. They rushed to offer me an escort to Mahmud Beghada's Palace, ruinous now, by the so-called Vad Talao, or Banyan Pond.

As you wander round Champaner, the nagging question arises: 'what happened to all the secular dwellings of the aristocracy and the common people?' Though there is no single, simple answer, in general it can be said that royal, military and religious works would have been made to endure against elements and invaders. Private houses, shops and warehouses of lesser men would have been made of wood, mud, brick easily dismantled, moved, destroyed or even reused elsewhere. Gujarat's sovereigns transferred their capital from Anahilvada Patan to Ahmedabad to Champaner, and back to Ahmedabad, so that any patrician family foolish enough to invest too much in its property would find it worthless when the court left. We have a few foundations of domestic building at Champaner, but we know from contemporary authors that such homes would have been made of cheap materials, usually covered with stucco or paint or plaster to look better. In fact, noblemen appreciated all too well that their rulers would resent any attempt to aggrandize themselves. Specific sumptuary laws regulated the degree of wealth one could demonstrate in garments, and similar if unspoken limits would have been placed in accommodation. Each to his own caste, his own class.

Pavagadh

The great conical hill of Pavagadh protects or menaces Champaner like a sorcerer's hat, casting a long shadow. Some 822 metres high, it offers like Girnar and Shatrunjaya in Saurashtra the promise of redemption, if you only make the arduous ascent. Unlike those, however, a cable-car system enables you to minimise the difficulty of ascent between Manchi village (with its hotel and restaurant) and the final climb. Plenty of pilgrims earn merit by using the rock path for those linking 700 metres of cableway, or

300 metres of altitude. You may take up baggage weighing only 5 kg, so leave rucksacks at Hotel Champaner in Manchi at the foot of the cableway, which runs from 9 to 12.30 and 1.30 to 5, though when I was there the afternoon session did not begin until 2.15, a test of patience which the calm queue passed with great credit in early afternoon heat.

The hill is sacred to Jains, though their ruined shrines are at the far east end of the hill; to Hindus as a centre for Kali worship, and to Muslims who come to pray at the tomb of the Pir Sadan Shah above the temple to Kali. The lower fortifications are impressive, and must have taken a great deal of courage and manpower to overwhelm. Once past these, a succession of narrow gates had to be stormed before the assault on Sadan Shah Gate, hewn through solid rock. You can wander off the pathway to find the granaries cannily constructed by Muslims stockpiling against siege, and a reservoir for drinking water.

If you don't want a full lunch at the restaurant, any number of strange and unusual regional snacks and soft drinks can be sampled from the colourful, many-scented bazaar between the top of the cableway with its Bhadreshwar Jain Temple and the 250-step climb to Kali Temple. I spoke to a Hindu trembling with excitement, his voice nervously hoarse. 'This is the temple of my goddess at last', he said. 'It is a good fortune for me that I have come here today, a blessed day.' A wizened old woman in a garish red sari gathered round her like a twisted rope thrust magic potions into my hand. A bearded snake-charmer in a faded dhoti stretched out on stones beside his snake basket, oblivious to passing feet. Vendors of bird-whistles waved and whistled for customers. Sacred cows shook their ears against intrusive flies. Brooches and bangles were proffered: charms for the goddess, for women, for girls. Incense, garish powders for smearing on hair and body, lime-juice to assuage thirst, plastic helicopters, videos and plastic windmills. I have always been childishly grateful that, no matter where I have wandered off the beaten trail in India's great sprawling subcontinent, there has always been something passable to eat. I am not one who could, like Amundsen, devour his sledge-dogs.

Clutching the unrequested gift of a small *prasad* packet of sugar pieces intended as a gift to Kali, I enter a second Jain temple on the climb – open, empty, dark, silent, and reverberating to the unblinking gaze of an idol encoded by symbol and colour. Like everyone else, I continue uphill to the Kali temple. The sense of panic and pressure heightens as a busy, bored attendant cracks offered coconuts on the stone to see the water run down like spattering rain and makes us keep to the right-hand side with a reiterated CHALO! CHALO! CHALO! (Hurry along! Hurry up! Get along! Keep moving!) and another endless betel-spitting stream of Hindus courses down the left-hand side. Two older women in the left hold up a frenzied saried girl in red waving a rusty dagger (where did she get that?) and foaming like a mad bitch at the mouth, whimpering like a Greek bacchante. Above me the right-hand procession is being delayed by a girl of

Pavagadh. Kali Temple

sixteen who has swooned, weeping, and is being restrained from scratching at her face by her mother and aunt, who have dragged her to a rock like a wounded doe. I glimpsed at first hand how a girl can be gouged from her privacy by the pervasive fantasy of sacred cows, nightmarish black-clawed witch-goddesses masquerading as mother, as earth, as truth, when all that the older generation wishes is to maintain its hold over the younger at any cost: of terror, of insanity.

I wrote for this girl, in an attempt to appease her troubled spirit, the self-identifying poem called 'The Last Flight Up To Kali'.

> On her surge up narrow steps to Kali,
> slow, impatient in the onward crush,
> she faints into the belly of the goddess.

Her entrails afire, she hears a rush-
ing in her head "I am the goddess
is me, Kali Mata, Kali Mata".

Staring bloody eyes,
the red of spearwounds,
hubbub in the womb, shrieks
within tearing to come out,
the constraining sari is too tight,
it must be torn, my heels rock,
my knees sag and my puppet head
begins to wander on my neck. This
is the daughter in the mother, the
mother in the mother, the knife incising
innocent air, the hilt huddled in
the guilty hand: "Kali will kill
and she is mine" and I her vessel.
There is no other one but We.

Outside Kali's temple I remove my athlete's trainers with a spring in
the sole that make possible even the longest, hardest hike, and with naked
feet push forward into the dark interior of the tiny temple where priests
chant praises of Mahakali, now the terrible mother goddess but in Vedic
times the black tongue of the fire-god Agni, for 'Kali' simply means black,
in this sense of horrific, inducing terror, Bhairavi, Chandika, a fury often
shown as black-skinned, fanged, dripping with blood, garlanded with
snakes and skull. 'Putting the fear of god' into somebody is fairly quickly
and conveniently done by invoking the shorthand 'Kali'.

It is reassuring for a rational mind to descend into the blue day, fresh
air, and see the frail but persevering trees sniffing breezes on high rocks.

Dabhoi
You can travel by bus or rail from Baroda to Dabhoi, but an early-morning
taxi to Champaner and Pavagadh will get you round the circuit east of Baroda via Dabhoi and back to Baroda by nightfall. Dabhoi is unaccountably
omitted from *The Forts of India* (1986) by Virginia Fass; it is one of the dozen
greatest forts in India for majesty of execution and brilliance of detail, and
should not be missed by anyone with a feeling for the Solanki dynasty ruling from Anahilvada Patan, those Rajputs who first decided to wall the
town then called Darbhavati in the twelfth century, and for their Waghela
successors who completed the quadruple-gated fort with associated Kali
Temple, in the thirteenth century. Despite occupation by later Muslims,
marauding Marathas, and the British, the fort displays all its old swagger,
opulence and fantasy both in extraordinary broad sweeps of height and
breadth, and in tiny details. We shall see a more ruinous example at Jhin-

jhuwada, on the edge of the Little Rann of Kutch, and a lesser gate at Ghumli in Saurashtra, but the apex of Hindu military architecture in Gujarat belongs to Dabhoi.

These crowded, narrow streets could be anywhere from Dakor to Patan, with piglets whiffling around a vegetable stall piled high with cauliflowers, fruit stalls loaded with pyramidal oranges and limes, and bruised yellow banana hands so cheap as to be almost free. Half-naked children duck between donkey-carts, chasing each other in a mediaeval never-never land of innocence. Coming from Champaner, you come to the greatest of the four massive gateways: the Hira Bhagol or Diamond Gate named for its legendary builder, Hira, accused by the king of appropriating men and materials to build a decorative *talao* or lake for his mistress. He was walled up with only a secret gap for food and drink to be brought by his distraught lady, and finally released only when the king learned that he alone knew the craft of completing the archway. The story goes in Dabhoi that the king apparently gave way and released Hira to finish the gateway, then immured him again and sealed up the gap. But since this tale is told in most countries of most buildings (and in Bulgaria and Turkey even about bridges), the reader can assess its likely truth. Hira Bhagol, as the main entrance to Dabhoi, has a twelve-foot wide clearance and a length of thirty-six feet. At each side there is a Hindu temple, the one to the north being dedicated to Kali, the goddess worshipped locally at Pavagadh and throughout much of eastern Gujarat, sometimes as the fierce consort of Shiva, but usually in a conflation of all these ideas: where monotheistic religions temperamentally divide and separate divine attributes, Hinduism synthesizes, accretes, and tends to the all-embracing, universalised view: everything is merely an aspect of itself, of something else, or of the whole. You can perceive such a tendency, rare in Christianity, in the Trinity as three-in-one and one-in-three, or in the view of Mary as Virgin, Mother of Jesus, and *mater misericordiae*.

As well as the Kali temple there are stout guard-rooms for sentries and watchmen, but the most staggering creation, which will never be repeated in the following centuries of Islamic military architecture in Gujarat, is the decoration of the inner side of the gate, a riot of complex projections and bays, and ostentatious balconies bursting out on voluted struts, with canopied niches and windows in a fantasy of light, mass and figurative invention. As the Victorian antiquarian James Burgess pointed out: Dabhoi's stone gateway 'is a framework mortised and tenoned together, exerting bending and tensile strains, for which stone is ill adapted ... In woodwork, this would be perfectly legitimate ... and it is evident that the construction of these gateways was actually copied in stone from similar structures in wood then existing.' The Hindu iconography can easily be identified – Hanuman the monkey god, Rama, Krishna, Arjuna, apsaras, yakshas, elephants – but from this superabundance of individuals animal, human, mythological and divine one is inspired to conceive the Hindu world-view as a unity – a great mountain called Meru in the navel of the earth, above which is Swarga, Indra's heaven, and stretching out from it the four insular continents or Dwipas, spread like lotus leaves. Five rows of broken architectonic and sculptured fragments have been laid on the ground.

The Hira Gate is on the east, and you can now explore with the aid of eager local lads the fort area, and then the western or Baroda Gate, locked and with the sign 'protected monument'. I skipped over the metal restraining barrier at an encouraging wink from the leading boy and we climbed up to the top of the gate. There you overlook the rail station's mesmeric intertwining of destinies, a row of slum-dwellings by a mosquito-infested stagnant stream, and a slow-running waste dump mound ransacked by persistent pigs and anxious hens. Though not as extravagant in its creativity as Hira Gate, Baroda Gate possesses its own treasures, such as incarnations of Vishnu and nymphs with fabulous *makaras*, Capricorn in the Hindu zodiac, with the head and forelegs of an antelope and the body and tail of a fish. On this vehicle rides Varuna, who will re-emerge in Greece as Poseidon, and throughout the Roman Empire as Neptune.

The southern or Nadori Gate has, like Baroda Gate, six carved brackets on left and right, but pigeons prefer this gate for roosting, and fluttered in some agitation as I climbed up from one toehold to the next for a closer look. A minor gate close by with four carved brackets is in a damaged state and urgently needs restoration by the Archaeological Survey: perhaps a charitable Hindu organisation like the Bochasanwasi Swaminarayan Sanstha might finance maintenance for this great Hindu fort. The northern or Mori Gate is situated near the former royal palace. Part of a projecting parapet survives overhanging the six carved brackets on each side so their state of preservation is far superior to that of the Nadori Bhagol brackets. Here too there is a lateral minor stone gate with four brackets at each side: here one of the wooden doors (not studded against elephants as elsewhere) remains in place. A donkey stands uncomplaining in the lengthening evening shadow as pigeons cuckle and cluster before sleep. The silent Kali temple on the left reminds one of the cries and hubbub high on Pavagadh just a few hours before. Soon blackness will cast its merciful cloak over the town, and stars will be seen again, mystery out of mystery.

Surat

On the way to Surat the Ambassador car in which I was travelling met a lorry coming very fast in the wrong direction on the wrong side of the dual carriageway at great speed. This event, which could have meant sudden death for all concerned, drew no comment from my driver, insane while sober, who continued to press on the accelerator as though he was trying to push it through the floor of the car to the road beneath. But then, the highway code is interpreted differently on the highways of India.

1. Never look where you are going.
2. You always have absolute priority, until dead.
3. If you can't make yourself heard with your horn, shout a lot as often as possible.
4. Remove your hands from the steering-wheel as often as you can.
5. A so-called 'one-way street' is intended for traffic travelling up, down and sideways.
6. Park wherever you want.

Surat is by no means a beautiful city, but its historical importance is such that no visitor to Gujarat should pass it by incuriously. Its position on the Tapti river is 24 km from the sea, though only 19 km as the crow flies. Neither does the navigable length of the Tapti rival that of the Narmada farther north, allowing Broach to capture the bulk of the riverborne traffic in competition with Cambay. The subject has been authoritatively covered by V.A. Janaki in *Some Aspects of the Historical Geography of Surat* (Baroda, 1974). Classical authors indicate that Broach remained superior to Surat right up to late mediaeval times, when Cambay had silted up. During the Sultanate, Surat became the favoured port for the vast region between Delhi and Golconda, and in spite of the Portuguese invasions from Goa, in 1512, 1530 and 1531, it was the British who ensured the long-term prosperity of Surat and at the same time the future success of the Raj, by a policy of changing alliances, opportune treaties, long-term friendships, and farsighted conciliation. In 1608 Emperor Jahangir awarded a firman to the British to establish their factory in Surat; within four years it became operational. In 1620 the Dutch set up their trading post, abandoned but reopened in 1642; in 1664 the French arrived; and the Portuguese and Persians too had factories.

We know from the *Rasmala* that Suryapur (City of the Sun-God) existed as early as 990 A.D. and Duarte Barbosa affirms that it had become a great trading city by 1514. The Friday Mosque of 1335 was erected on the site of a Jain temple to Chintamani Parshvanatha.

Surat's situation high on the left bank of the Tapti was intended to protect the inhabitants from flash flood, yet floods in 1822 destroyed the northeastern wall of 1717-19, and those of 1837 and 1843 demolished much of the south and south-western walls.

Independent Nawabs ruled Surat between 1733 and 1759, but only as marionettes of the British who controlled trade and from 1759 abandoned the pretence of operating subserviently to the Nawabs and ruled quite openly, gradually transferring trade to their new entrepôt at Bombay, where shipping could more easily and safely anchor.

In 1762 the Nawab of Surat besieged the Dutch in their factory and forced them to shift base to the west, to 'Walanda Bandar' (Dutch Wharf). The Dutch Commodore's Bungalow overlooking the river is now a private residence. Surat's population dwindled to 157,000 in 1825 and to 124,000 in 1835. A great fire in 1837 destroyed not only the congested city within the walls, but even some of the many outer suburbs, and those who survived the fire thought about trying their fortune in Bombay to the south or Ahmedabad to the north. Surat revived like a parched plant after the coming of the rail link in 1858, when fresh industries and factories arose to employ not only Gujaratis but increasingly also immigrants from Punjab, Uttar Pradesh, Madhya Pradesh, Maharashtra and Andhra Pradesh. From 98,936 in 1931, the population shot up dizzily with each passing decade: 171,443 in 1941; 223,182 in 1951; 288,026 in 1961; 471,656 in 1971; 776, 876 in 1981; and 1,505,872 in 1991, vertiginously exceeding the growth-rate in either Ahmedabad or the third city of Gujarat, Baroda.

Today, immigrants from other states comprise more than 70% of the population. Recession in the late 1980s and early 1990s cut into virtually every sector of the industrial base, from textiles to diamond-cutting and -polishing. The modern Textile Market on Ring Road, topped by the landmark revolving restaurant of the Tex Palazzo Hotel, has a theatre and more than a thousand shops in its precincts.

Surat Castle (1540-6) was built by Sultan Khudawand of Gujarat on the site of Ferozeshah Tughlaq's castle on the left bank of the Tapti and was moated with a drawbridge; the moat was filled in as recently as 1959. There are few ruins of the Sultanate period: just Khwajah Diwan Sahib's mosque of 1530 and the Marjan Shami mausoleum of 1540 in Mulla Chakla or quarter. The old city is divided into *chakla*s and the suburbs into *pura*s, many by caste-cum-occupation categories. Thus, Mulla Chakla, with access to the river, was occupied mainly by rich Muslim traders, and Asurbeg Chakla mainly by labourers and poorer fisherfolk.

During the Mughal period, dating from Akbar's conquest of Gujarat in 1573, Surat became the Mughal Empire's major port for merchandise and pilgrims to Jiddah and the Holy Places in Arabia. It proved greatly to the advantage of the English that they cemented good relations with the Mughal Governor of Surat, Prince Khurram, for he ascended the imperial throne in 1628, ten years after the permanent English factory of Surat had been established, incorporating part of the provisional buildings on a site near the present municipal buildings in the heart of the old town. The 'factory' was a small self-contained village where the factors or merchants lived, worked and had their warehouses for storing imported goods and those intended for export. Fortified against attack in 1642, the English factory was 'built of Stone and excellent Timber with good carvings without Representations, very strong for each Floor is Half a yard thick at least, of the very best cement, very weighty ... with upper and lower Galleries or Terras Walks. The President had spacious Lodgings with noble Rooms for Counsel and Entertainment'. The accommodation for up to forty merchants looked out on a fine garden with palms, fruit trees and shrubs, cellars below stacked with fine wines. The factory's access to the river was through Hanumanji Gate. The President, employing his own interpreter, chaplain, mint-master and physician, was protected by a bodyguard carrying silver staves who accompanied him wherever he went and slept outside his bedroom. At the Presidential entry into the dining-chamber, trumpets blew and during the meals fiddlers played sweet music to aid his digestion. The English devoured kebabs, chicken boiled in butter and stuffed with raisins and almonds. On Sundays, dinner might consist of deer, antelope, peacock, hare, partridge, pistachios, plums, apricots and cherries. Of course pork was prohibited in Muslim lands, and beef in Hindu lands, so mutton, chicken, game and wildfowl had to suffice. The ordinary factors were rough and ready, often in trouble at home, and subject to a barracks-style discipline, having to return to the factory before sundown or forfeit five week's wages, attend compulsory prayers (fine for absence on Sundays: five shillings), and pay a shilling for every swear-word dropped.

The Mughal caravanserai built close by in 1634 offered non-European travellers and merchants the facilities that the Dutch, Portuguese, English and French enjoyed in their own insulated factories, but with charpoys (rope beds) instead of European-style beds, and local-style meals. The original Dutch factory was in Mulla Chakla but in 1712 they transferred to Hibr Khan's mansion in Badeh Khan Chakla behind Desaipol.

Competition between the Europeans extended even unto death. The Dutch tombs were surpassed in grandeur by the ostentatious tombs of Gerald Aungier, 'President of Surat and Governor of Bombay, d.1677' and of Sir George Oxinden, 'Anglorum in India, Persia, Arabia Praeses, Insulae Bombayensis Gubernator', whose epitaph of 1669 concludes portentously 'Heus, lector! Ex magno hoc viro vel mortuo aliquid proficias' (Reader! May you benefit from the example of this great man even in death.) I had leapt over the wall of the English Cemetery, since I found its only gate locked, and wandered among a crowd of youngsters who had also scrambled into this hallowed precinct, who eagerly pointed out one tomb after another. Susanna Cantrell died in 1821 at the age of 43, and her husband William in 1832 at the age of 60, 'leaving five children and a large circle of friends'. The pathetic grave of Margaret, wife of Thomas Sanders, bears the inscription: 'D. 1844, age 20 years 8 months. She was a faithful and loving wife, a tender mother, an affectionate sister, and a friend in need. There is nothing true but Heaven'. A caretaker now came up and offered to unlock the newly painted mausoleum of 'Mary, wife of Brabazon Ellis, Chief of the English factory in Surat. She died 1756'. With barely a glimmer of a smile, the caretaker accompanied me to the gate, and unlocked to render my departure more seemly than my arrival. At the back of the English Cemetery lies another for Christian Indians. The Dutch Cemetery is situated some 600 metres towards the city (note the huge mausoleum of Baron Adriaan van Reede, who died in 1691) and next to that is the Armenian Cemetery.

The monumental square outside the Castle compound dates from after

*Surat. English Cemetery. Aungier Mausoleum (left) and in the foreground Oxinden Mauso-
leum (right)*

the fire of 1872. One side is dominated by the English High School (1872) which according to its plaque 'was erected for the benefit of the inhabitants of Surat' and is now the Sorabji Jamsetjee Jeejeebhoy Training College. At right angles looms the impressive Jhaverchand Naginchand Hall (1907), home to the Andrews Public Library named for a retired magistrate. The Library was first accommodated in the Abdullah Beg building where the Gujarati-language paper *Gujarat Mitra* ('Friend of Gujarat') is now. It then moved to the Daria Mahal before transfer to its grandiose purpose-built premises. The former Winchester Museum (1890) in Chowk Bazaar is now called Sardar Sangrahalaya, and has a planetarium next door.

Northeast of the castle I found the Victoria Garden with a zoo and Christ Church (1824), Chowk Bazaar, an Anglican Church consecrated by the missionary Reginald Heber and now the property of the Church of North India. It is a woefully dull and dismal building, in need of a coat of cream distemper, enlivened by a fierce goat mercifully tethered fast, peafowl and noisy crows in the sandy churchyard. 'English Service at 6.30' says the notice, but of course between those weekly occasions the place is forlorn, unlike a colourful Hindu temple or a crowded mosque. What a wonderful difference 'Mad' Mant would have made to this uninteresting church!

The English Factory is illustrated by an old etching in Ovington's splendid *Voyage to Surat* (Oxford, 1929). Ovington stayed at the English factory from 1689 to 1692. It can be found between the castle and Kataragama Gate. The Portuguese Factory, Persian Factory and French Lodge (the last abandoned in 1725) are also close to hand, but the old Portuguese Church no longer survives even as a ruin.

Of the four main mosques in Surat City, the most interesting is Khwaja Diwan Sahib's (1530), but don't miss the Khudawand Mosque, built in 1540 by the ruler responsible for the castle, the Nav Sa'id Mosque at the site of Gopi Talao; or the Sayyid Idris Mosque (1639) with its tapering minaret.

Surat is a Jain centre, the most interesting temple being the 15th-century Chintamani with wooden carvings and pictures of the Solanki king, King Kumarapala and Acharya Hemchandra; and a Parsi centre, though as elsewhere it is forbidden to enter the fire temple of 1823.

Across the Tapti, the industrial suburb of Rander possesses a historic Friday Mosque which as usual reuses components from the Jain temple demolished to make room. Access to Rander is across Hope Bridge (1874), named for the then Collector.

Seagoing vessels too large to berth at Surat used to anchor 20 km away at Suwali, written 'Swally' in English travel books. Thévenot, in his *Voyage*, notes how at Swally he would count masts of several hundred ships, only a minority of them European; Arab dhows with red sails, Mughal vessels carrying pilgrims to Jiddah, and Chinese junks. Of course you would expect many burials here, and the village of Rajgari boasts the splendid domed mausoleum of Deputy Governor of Bombay Vaux and his wife, who both drowned in the river Tapti in 1697.

The Tapti runs west of the original walled city; east of the city is the railway line; the southwest district called Nanpura beyond Mecca Creek was the site of the Dutch Wharf built here in 1729 and the Dutch Commodore's Bungalow, the Sidi Wharf, the English Wharf, the courthouse and the jail. East of this is Sangrampura settled chiefly by Anhavils, Gopi Talao, and Rustampura, originally occupied by weavers but later on by the Parsi community, who settled the quarter in the early 19th century, acted as brokers to all the factories, and built their fire temple and fine houses. Most chose to migrate to Bombay after the fire of 1872, and then poorer weavers working at home resettled here.

The greatest of these Parsi families of Surat was that of Rustamji Manakji, due to his close and profitable connections with the English East India Company. His opulent walled garden and two-storey arcaded house are reproduced in an anonymous painting of about 1800 (*Artibus Asiae* XL, 4). The neat flower-beds arranged in symmetrical rows are clearly of European inspiration, and the painting exudes a fantastic mock-European air, with strange lapses of intended perspective, animal cages, and vines on wooden stakes: it is altogether one of the strangest paintings by a Kutchi artist, like 'The Rao's Procession Outside Anjar', the Rao in question being Godji II (1762-78).

Navapura incorporates the Muslim Bohra quarter called Jhampa, with the Palace of the sect's Mullah, his mosque, and two Bohra mausolea.

Sanjan

The homeland of Zoroastrianism is in Iran, but successive waves of Islamic fundamentalism have resulted in the emigration of Zoroastrians or Parsis (from 'Pars', Persia) to other countries, and in particular to India, North America, and England, though we also have evidence of Iranian Zoroastrians in seventh-century China. Their connection with Gujarat begins with landfall at Sanjan: according to one account in 721 and according to another in 785, after nineteen years on the island of Div, or Diu as the Portuguese pronounced it.

As the Parsi gateway to India, Sanjan has a special place in the hearts of all Parsis. I was lucky enough to be shown round by Mr Dara Patel, who retired from the Central Bank of India in 1991 and since then has been giving community service. The commemorative column in Sanjan set up in 1920 reads:

Homage to Thee, O Ahura Mazda!
This column has been erected by the Parsis of India in pious memory of their good Iranian ancestors who, after the downfall of their empire under their last monarch Yazdazard Shahriyar, for the sake of

their religion dearer than life, left their native land and suffering innumerable hardships at length landed at this once famous part of Sanjan and settled under the protection of its kind Hindu ruler Jadi Rana. "We worship the good, strong beneficent Fravashis of the holy".

Sanjan (the name echoes the Iranian town Rafsanjan) nowadays lies 2 km from the sea, but it retains its emotional appeal to all Parsis and I noted new residential districts marked out for retired Parsis: Bulsara Estate and Irani Park. Mazdalease Apartments are rented by Parsis to Parsis. Sanjan Dharamshala or resthouse was founded in 1919 for Parsi pilgrims exclusively: it is in dormitory style with 5 cots on one side and 4 on the other rented at Rs 12 a night, and Rs 20-25 per meal. Smoking is strictly prohibited. There is a planned Zoroastrian College in Sanjan on land donated by a Bombay Parsi, but when I visited it with Dara Patel the library was locked, and there was no sign of anyone but a caretaker who had (in Mr Patel's picturesque phrase) 'gone for cloak'. Its governing body is the Mazdayasnie Monasterie (Zoroastrian College), All-India Shah Behram Baug Society, Mustafa Building, 2nd floor, Sir Pherozeshah Mehta Road, Bombay 400 001.

I realised that, like the fanatic Christian Crusaders on their martial way to Jerusalem, or like the infantry of pilgrims footslogging it to Santiago de Compostela, I was – almost accidentally – participating in religious tourism, or *yatra* as the phenomenon is widely known in India. The slow and steady march of the body which at one level typifies our short and brutish life on earth but at another symbolises the spiritual yearning for a way to a disembodied divinity, whether through the late Osho in Pune, Mother Meera once of Pondicherry and now in Dornburg-Thalheim in Germany, or the innumerable temples and shrines that cover India from Rameshwaram in the south to the holy Himalaya in the farthest north.

The Parsi way is the most mysterious because, far from proselytising, Zoroastrianism does not permit the possibility of conversion. One is not allowed to look inside a dukhma, or tower of silence, much less into a fire temple. So the enquiry is by reading, travel to the holy places, meditation, and discussion with a Dasturji, or Zoroastrian priest. Luckily, there are first-rate sympathetic accounts written by Western authors such as R.C. Zaehner's *The Dawn and Twilight of Zoroastrianism* (1961). It is hardly surprising that, as an Indo-Aryan myself, I should find the religion more appealing (as did Nietzsche, among others) than such Semitic religions as Judaism, Christianity and Islam. Zoroaster (628-551 B.C.) founded a religion which was intended to reform the existing religion of his polytheistic people and replace it with the worship of his one true god, Ahura Mazda. If we align ourselves with the Holy Spirit aspect of Ahura Mazda, Spenta Mainyu against the Evil Spirit or Angra Mainyu, we all influence our destiny on earth and, more significantly, for all eternity. Thus, instead of the tablets of Moses or the Ten Commandments of Christianity, we find that at every moment of every day we are confronted by decisions that are both literally and metaphorically right or wrong, and we must always choose the right. Luckily, King Vishtaspa of Chorasmia (Khwarizm, that is Iranian Khurasan, west Afghanistan, and much of Turkmenia in the former U.S.S.R.) supported Zoroaster and became a convert. Furthermore, his descendants remained loyal adherents until the Islamic invasions of the seventh century A.D. and forcible conversion by the sword. Some pockets of covert worshippers loyal to the old faith remain in Iran, but most fled in waves from the eighth century, beginning with the so-called Shahinshahis, who calculate the calendar from the death of the last Sassanian king, Yazdegard III. The Qadimis (*qadim*, ancient) founded in Bombay in 1780 claim that their calculation is the more venerable and correct. A third sect, the Fasalis, calculate the calendar according to the *fasal* or season, and observe 21 March as Nowruz, or New Year. However, this chronological schism does not deter opponents from intermarriage.

The sacred fire brought from Iran must never be extinguished, so is protected by the high priest: its romantic wanderings mirror those of the Parsis in search of peace and tolerance, ending in South Gujarat. From Iran the flames were carried to Kohistan in Khurasan for a century, then to the Persian Gulf port of Hormuz for fifteen years, then to Diu for nineteen years, then to Sanjan. Some time after the destruction of Champaner and Sanjan in 1484 but before 1496, the holy fire was carried to the Bahrot Hills for twelve years, then to Bansda for fourteen years, and eventually it found protection in Navsari at the hands of the Dahewad or Desai, revenue collector, Changashah. Changashah ruled that only the priests from Sanjan who had brought the sacred fire from Bansda might tend it, while only native Navsari priests might officiate at future ceremonies, such injunctions to be passed on to succeeding generations. Complications meant that the Sanjan priests left Navsari for good in 1742, taking the sacred fire first to Bulsar and then to Udvada where it has remained to this day, in the *atash behram* there. Another seven principal fire temples in India exist at Navsari, Surat (two) and Bombay (four). I visited the priest of Sanjan, Dasturji Nushirvan Dastur, who can speak only Gujarati, with Dara Patel to interpret. His new fire temples opened as recently as 1990, and he says the prayers for only three or four Parsi houses at present, but those retiring from Bombay will come to this peaceful village and expand the congregation, open only to men. The whole world community of Parsi amounts to fewer than 130,000, yet their influence has been colossal, in the realms of industry (J.N. Tata), philanthropy (too many names to list), music (Kaikhosru Sorabji and Zubin Mehta), science (Homi Bhabha), politics (Dadabhai Naoroji), theology (Dasturji Feroze Kotwal), poetry (Keki Daruwalla), fiction (Rohinton Mistry), cricket (Contractor and Engineer), law (Sir Dinshah Mulla) and many more.

Zoroastrians do not worship the Prophet Zoroaster any more than Mus-

Sanjan. Parsi High Priest

lims worship the Prophet Muhammad: for both religions are monotheistic. According to Zoroaster, Ahura Mazda first created Wisdom or 'Good Mind' in the spiritual world, and subsequently the material world, protected by *fireshte*s or guardian angels. Neither are they in the common parlance 'fire-worshippers', because fire is only one of the phenomena loved by 'the best man', that by the man who loves 'fire, water and animals', presided over by the angels of Righteousness, Health and Good Mind. Fires in fire temples are merely sparks of the infinite light of Ahura Mazda, replete with the divine presence. The protecting angels who come at night to perform ceremonies in the temples speak Avestan, the language of the *Gathas* and the *Vendidad*, those noble hymns and discourses which can be read in James Darmesteter's translation of the *Zend Avesta* (2 vols., "Sacred Books of the East", Oxford, 1880-3; reprinted by Motilal Banarsidass, Delhi, 1965).

Udvada

It is a relief from Vapi's stench of industrial pollution to turn off the 9 km to the 'Vatican City' of the Parsi, Udvada, past venerable banyan trees and towards the sun over the approaching horizon (oh, Ahura Mazda!)

I found a middle-aged gentleman with a ring showing Zoroaster on it, and of course immediately identified him as one of the 160 or so Parsis resident in Udvada. 'We are all of the Shahinshahis here', he told me, 'and we welcome Parsis to our dharamshala.' The fire temple is of course closed to non-Parsis, but he took me to see the walled and gated compound, with the plaque 'The Sacred Iranshaw Fire Temple' at the entrance, and a smaller building labelled D.M. Petit, 1891. The shuttered white building gives away no secrets, and that is perhaps part of its ineffable delight: I should always prefer to imagine the Pope's private apartments rather than to join a conducted tour after gazing up at the Sistine ceiling. Opposite stands a tall three-storey house of 19th-century date: the Din Dastur House.

Navsari

The palm-fringed fire temple in Navsari looks much more impressive, but then I felt I already knew the town from Boman Desai's evocative first novel, *The Memory of Elephants* (1988). I had been invited, for example, into the high priest's guest lounge, and immediately recognised as Desai relates, that 'for every chair there were at least five photographs on the walls, each bordered by an elaborate wooden frame, of *all* our relatives (which meant *all* the Parsis in Navsari; all Parsis in Navsari have photographs on their walls of all the Parsis in Navsari), single portraits, duos, trios, larger groups, at navjotes, weddings, standing like schoolchildren in single file along stoops, seated like prophets on the chairs lining the walls in the sitting-room, arranged in studios with dramatic jungle backdrops, ruin backdrops, the men wearing white ceremonial dress with high collars (satin daglas, cotton daglis) and ceremonial headgear (paghris, fehntas), the women covering their heads with their saris, gazing into the distance as if they had weightier matters to consider than photographs, the children with large, round eyes as if they had something to hide.'

Boman Desai tells me that he believes that Parsis, like most smaller societies, are insular because they fear being misunderstood and, ironically, their resistance to penetration by outsiders only multiplies misunderstandings in the minds of outsiders. This is true, but I find Parsis are particularly resistant to a well-wisher's involvement, presumably because of their decreasing numbers and the threat of ultimate extinction. Such a loss would bereave the world more than the extinction of the whale or Asiatic lion because Parsis have given much more to the world than they have taken.

Navsari has become much more industrialised nowadays, specialising in the cutting of diamonds and rubies, but you can still the see the *talao* full of lotuses like a floating pink and white garden, and streets less congested than other southern towns with a smaller Parsi minority.

Dusk came crowding in like a great shadow over the sky as I sat on a bench in the walled garden of the Parsis at the edge of Navsari town. I nodded at a grave elder at the other end of the bench and we passed several minutes in silent communion before he spoke. 'You are an American', he told me, rather inaccurately, 'and you can tell me this. I have often wondered why you need to laugh so much, so often, Roseanne, those Golden Girls, those Happy Days, I mean. They are making jokes all the time, laughing, trying so hard that others should laugh. I too have a sense

Navsari. Parsi garden

of humour but with my friends I do not always laugh, but discuss many things which may be serious, in a serious way. Is this now old-fashioned in your country?' 'I suppose it is', I answered, assuming the required guise, as I have accepted the title of Estonian in Finland and Dutchman in Indonesia, 'and in my country too.'

I shared his regret at the whittling away of a sense of decorum inculcated in Western Europe by a classical education since the end of the Middle Ages and the beginning of the Renaissance, the earnestness which induced Sir Thomas More to write his *Utopia* and Guicciardini his history of Florence. Later on, Kipling would provide his stylish prejudices, and Churchill would illustrate the differences between Them and Us. Decorum pervades Indian religion and morality from the Laws of Manu to the injunctions of the Qur'an, from the exhortations of Swami Narayan in Gujarat to Catholic missions in Kerala. The cult of seriousness and high morality was stressed in India by imperial civil servants of the Raj acting in the interests of Queen Victoria and her native subjects. The East India Company came to trade, the missionaries came with disastrous lack of success to convert, but the Governor, the Resident, the Collector, all came to view themselves as the purveyors of order in essentially chaotic communities without adequate communications, adequate law enforcement, and adequate application to the job in hand. Nobody said: 'By the way, chaps, we have come to steal your land, profit from your labour, and ship home the goods and money we have seized', and some were actually convinced that Indians would be better off speaking English, 'playing the game', and dressing in western clothes. Certainly, there was a propensity on the part of the caste-ridden English (sorry, that is 'class-ridden') to ally themselves with 'reasonable Indians' such as westernised Parsis, Jains, and princes willing to collaborate against the exploited Hindu and Muslim masses. All of this would have been undermined by a keen sense of humour of the *Goons* or *Monty Python* genre, but the Raj was never noted for an ability to poke fun at its own institutions. Indeed, many of these institutions are still lovingly maintained five decades after Independence, as we shall see at Rajkumar College in Rajkot, or at exclusive clubs in Bombay or Delhi.

Bansda National Park

If you have your own taxi or four-wheel drive vehicle, you can stop at the Forestry Office headquarters near Bansda town to request permission to visit the national park, between 7 a.m. and 6 p.m. every day. I made the mistake of calling first at the park gate 6 km away, where the gatekeeper kindly sent a colleague back in the taxi to pick up the Superintendent Mr H.T. Rana (himself a native of Bansda or Vansda), while I sat in the shade of a banyan, hoping that local leopards would keep their distance. I crashed with spectacular results over one of the banyan's baroquely gnarled root-clusters and toppled heavily into a foot of thick dust, raising the kind of uncomplicated laughter from three urchins that I recall from Oliver Hardy's best pratfalls.

'Very few tourists are coming', said Mr Rana, and though the park is only seven square km in area, it seems a shame that more visitors on their way from Surat up to Saputara do not explore this wilderness, next to lands still owned by His Highness Digvendra Singhji the former Prince of Bansda, who spends most of his time in Bombay. You can stay for a nominal charge (Rs 10) at Waghai Forest Rest House or the PWD but the former has no cook. Bamboo groves always remind me of Japanese ink paintings, and as the sun disappeared behind the forest depths, vertical trunks and slanting branches silhouetted black against a myriad shades of green. High whooshes and screeches above the treetops signalled the return home at dusk of giant fruit bats, so I crept through the bush towards their communal roosts: they looked like squirming black fruit, hanging upside down and swaying quickly, as if in gusts. November to February is the best time for Bansda, which protects seven leopards, as well as their prey such as sambar, antelope and wild pig. Mr Rana is adamant that there are no tigers hereabouts, asserting that the last was seen in Ahwa district seven years ago, but that conflicts with what I was told at Saputara. I saw a colony of monkeys, a distant green-eyed hyena, inquisitive spotted deer in groups of twenty or so, elaborate anthills, and wailing wild peacocks ungainly and alarmed in the undergrowth. Great bridal veils of cobwebs covered holes in banks. Eighty-nine bird species are recorded in the national park precinct, which is inhabited only by *adivasis*, mainly Bhils.

Climbing past the village of Navtad, you soon cross the Ambika river again, and arrive in Waghai, which has a delightful Botanical Garden run by the Forestry Department.

Saputara

As you ascend the Sahyadri range of hills from Bansda, the air becomes clearer and lowland forests give way to teak, bamboo and pine. Just before Waghai, the district changes from Valsad to Dangs: as your bus chugs uphill, criss-crossing the Ambika river's crystal waters, you have left all the congestion of Gujarati towns and cities far below you and enter the spirit world of the tribal people, or *adivasis*, of Dangs. Luckily, we have a first-rate book, *Tribal Art of Dangs* (Baroda Museum, 1971) by D.H. Koppar, director of the Lady Wilson Museum at Dharampur, in Central Valsad. Dangs' population is 90% tribal: most speak as their first language Dangi, a mixture of Marathi, Gujarati and Rajasthani. Barely 10% of the population speak Marathi, and less than 5% have Gujarati as their first language. By far the greatest number of the tribals in the district's 312 small villages belong to the Kunbi (40%) and Bhil confederation (33%), though there is a good number of Warli and a fair number of Gamit. Half of the villages have a population of under a hundred, so they tend to be close-knit and compact. Their totem animal is the tiger, though their pantheon includes the snake,

100

Dangs. Adivasi festivities

sun and crescent. They are subsistence farmers, hunters, food-gatherers and pastoralists like their forebears who probably came from the plain after being turned out from better lands by successive waves of invaders from the coast. In the adjacent districts of Surat and Valsad the percentage of tribals is 46%, in Panchmahals 40%, 17% in Baroda, 10% in Sabarkantha and 5% in Banaskantha, dropping to negligible numbers in the more fertile Saurashtra peninsula.

Encroachment by modern society, with its cinema, radio and television, has taken its toll in Dangs, but luckily every year there is a tribal arts festival at the administrative centre of Dangs, Ahwa, to the north of Saputara; in Saputara itself a fascinating museum opens daily from 10.20 to 6 p.m., except for Wednesday, the 2nd and 4th Saturday of each month, and the usual public holidays, which are regrettably numerous. Saputara Tribal Art Museum provides a good introduction to past and present arts, and a proof that decadence and commercialism are at last catching up even with the remote Dangs. Major forms of expression include the stone funerary column, ornaments of grass such as bangles and necklaces, woodcarving, clay ritual objects, tattooing of the body, and masks used in dance-dramas.

Dance-dramas, performed at Holi, at marriages and at other festivals, draw from local epics with reminiscences from the Ramayana and Mahabharata, while pure dance is enjoyed by the whole community, men and women linking arms in a circle not unlike the Greek *horos*. Female ornament is not so extravagant as among the Hindus: Dangi women of some standing will often wear a double-chained silver necklace called a *bor-ganthi* and a gold nose-ring called a *nath*, an ornate silver armlet called an *eliya* and head and ear ornaments called *saravani*. Close identification with trees, animals and the turning seasons made the Dangi tribes animists and pagans, and to a great extent they still are at heart, even if there is an occasional Hindu shrine, notably to Hanuman, the monkey-god. They are patrilocal and patrilineal, believing in ancestor worship and sorcery. The tribes do not have much to do with each other, because of a certain traditional mistrust and as a result of long distances and difficult terrain. Few good roads exist in the district: apart from the two interstate highways going to Maharashtra most are poor tracks or single-lane roads.

The native cult of the mother goddess is connected with the worship of Kanasri-Mata, goddess of plenty and prosperity, the Dangi Ceres with her sheaf of corn. Prowling tigers have always represented strength and power to the Dangis, and Wagh Dev ('Tiger-God') is ever-present in their minds and their sculptural art both in wood and stone. The rearing or pouncing tiger is often accompanied by the symbols of day and night, the sun, and moon, and by a coiled serpent.

It was at Saputara Museum that I met the genial Surya Goswamy, a sculptor who has been in Saputara for ten years and participates in the local artists' village of seven professionals, with courses for practitioners and a permanent gallery of changing crafts. He comes from Ahmedabad, but trained at the celebrated Baroda University Faculty of Fine Arts, like his colleague the painter Chandrakant Parmar from Nadiad. Surya's wife Pranjil is a painter and yet another painter, J.T. Dave, is now in England. The colony performs an external function as catalyst to tribal creativity as well as obeying its own personal impulses, and the meeting of contemporary individualism with collective animism enables sparks to fly every day. Here is a Warli painting with its colours made of rice powder; there a papier-maché mask, beyond a fruit basket of bamboo. In his Land Rover Surya took me to the local cliff edge to see *vadbari*: tribal idols coloured orange or vermilion, roughly in the shape of gravestones, and set in the earth prominently. On one stone a man with a sword will be an ancestor figure; on a second stone a man and a woman will be a funerary monument; on a third wooden post a horse-god, sun and moon are carved above a coiled *sapu*, or snake. The effect at dawn, or at sunset, is remarkably moving: I felt swiftly transported, a new Icarus, to a skybowl beyond time, place and triviality. A track runs up to Sunrise Point, and the jeep climbs to Echo Point. You find a natural amphitheatre in the mountain-face which lends itself to an echo, past a stone altar with three human figures. I picked up a local quartz pebble, the mica fragments glinting like burnished silver. On the empty road a man came round the corner pushing a cart with a Singer sewing machine of 1910 vintage slipping from side to side in slow motion.

Malegaon, near Saputara. Pagan idols

103

At the Toran Holiday Home I had struck up acquaintance with an *adivasi* called Chintamani from the nearby village of Malegaon; he willingly assented to accompany me, giving 'safe passage' as it were, to the *adivasi* village which has no facilities for visitors and frankly doesn't want its life interrupted. Taking the Bansda road downhill, after nearly 3 km we turned left, short of the forest checkpoint, and parked short of Malegaon, continuing on foot. A mixed-economy village, it grows grain, fruit and vegetables, and grazes cattle and bullocks. The Hanuman Shrine stood open, and inside the idol of Hanumanji stood covered from head to foot in thick orange paint. Wooden and stone idols in front of the tile-roofed brick-built Hindu shrine look excluded: they are local fetish images of tiger and crescent-moon, peacock and serpent. I identified a communal threshing-floor, and a white-painted school, but felt unwelcome, with nobody coming to greet me and left with Chintamani for the more sociable world of Saputara above.

I took lunch at the Kerala restaurant beside the boating lake, which organises rowboats for visitors between 9-12 and 4-6 (Rs 5 for 15 minutes) and four-seater paddle boats (Rs 60 for 30 minutes). Nearby a branch of the official Gurjari Emporium offered Assam trays, and bamboo lamp-baskets for Rs 135. In Chacha's Emporium. the Sikh owner spread his arms around the huge variety of knick-knacks. 'Have you anything from Dangs?' I enquired. He shrugged so theatrically that even a blind man could have understood it. 'Everything today is international', he smiled. 'I was born in Amritsar, but I come from Karachi. For forty years I have been in Mount Abu, Rajasthan. My whole family is in New York, Mister.' I took his point. 'We have matches, daggers, flashlights, dolls, tape recorders, toy pistols, thermos, what you want?' 'A Fujica film and a Mars bar', I replied, guiltily. With *my* figure I should keep off Mars bars.

Up the hill, above the lake, I found that the original Snake Temple no longer existed, replaced by a Shiva temple called Nageshwar (only the black stone lingam and white marble yoni were still in place under a temporary corrugated iron canopy) while women labourers sweated with brickloads under a foreman's vulpine gaze.

I bought two jars of honey (Rs 25 each for 500 grams) from Rajubhai Madhuwala (his 'surname' means Honey Fellow!) at the Honey Centre's five hives, and joined Surya Goswami for a ride over the Maharashtra border to Shivaji's Maratha castle called Hatgadh. 'This is wild territory', he murmured. 'The *adivasis* report that we currently have in the surrounding hills two hyenas, seven tigers, and no fewer than eighty-five leopards.' Hatgadh, an eagle's flight above the wide open roads, is only one of Shivaji's western strongholds where his Maratha cavalry would overnight before descending on their enemies of the time, whether Nawabs or British. Shivaji had another castle at Galkun, 20 km away, and another important fort called Songadh, away to the north in Surat district. The Gaekwad dynasty of Baroda had their origins at Songadh, which commands the main

Saputara. Panorama from Hotel Chimney

road east from Surat to Dhule, Bhusawal, Akola and Nagpur.

It was at the artists' village in Saputara that I first found (and bought) a horse-god of the kind celebrated in Haku Shah's charming *Votive Terracottas of Gujarat* (Mapin, Ahmedabad, 1991). Potters can be found among the *adivasis* of all Gujarat's eastern frontiers; those in the north and centre (as at Lambadia on the Gujarat-Rajasthan border, and Chhota Udaipur, due east of Baroda) where the terracottas are hollow, as well as in the south, where the commonest terracottas are solid. In the north, you can visit Tubraj Hill, 10 km from Lambadia, where live goats and votive terracotta horses are sacrificed to the pagan god Tubraj, after whom the hill was named. At Goli Gadh, seventy km from Surat, on the full moon day in March, just before the Holi Spring festival, the Dublas, Dhodias and Chaudhuris celebrate their own animistic festival by sacrificing solid clay horses. 'I should love to buy one of these horse terracottas you brought from Ambaji: how much are they?' 'Well, we often sell them for three or four rupees each' (ten American cents), 'but for that price it's hardly worth it, so we'd like you to accept one with our compliments.' It stands on my desk now: a horse-spirit raw brick red bearing two ridges for a saddle and a proud curved neck rising to a short stubby head and tiny ears.

105

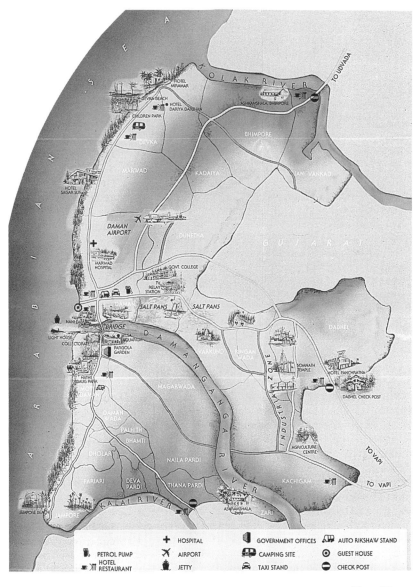

Map of Daman

III: DAMAN

Why is there a Union Territory of Daman and Diu today, forming two enclaves in Gujarat? We cannot understand the 21st century without understanding the 16th, because it was then that the Portuguese gained first Daman (which they spell Damão) and then Diu (known historically in India as Div), the former in 1531, and the latter in 1539. They will be treated separately here because they are so widely separated geographically, but they form part of the same culture that gave us Goa (see my *South India: Tamil Nadu, Kerala, Goa*) and Bassein (the Portuguese Baçaim) and Chaul (see my *Western India: Bombay, Maharashtra, Karnataka*).

Though Daman covers only 72 square km, the territory of Daman, Dadra and Nagar Haveli, beyond the Maharashtra border to the south, covers a total of 385 square km.

If the great age of the Portuguese Empire in India was the 17th century, we must not fall into the Eurocentric trap of believing that Daman had 'no history' before the Portuguese: in fact it shared in the common history of Gujarat until that time. Daman came successively under the sway of the Mauryan kings, the Sungas, Satavahanas, Kshatrapas and Chalukyas, Yadavas, the Rajput ruler Ramashah (evading the Mughal attacks on Rajasthan) settling around the year 1263.

Well established in Goa from 1510, the Portuguese sought maritime advantage along the coasts of Gujarat and skirmished in the area for many years before landing at Daman in 1531 without opposition.

The Portuguese were driven out again, but the Sultan of Gujarat agreed to cede Daman to the Governor of Goa in return for half the customs revenues in Diu. The Sidi (Abyssinian) captain of Daman refused to obey the commands from the Sultan and prepared to dig in against the Portuguese, who returned for a final onslaught in 1558-9 under the Governor of Goa , Dom Constantino de Bragança. He brought nearly three thousand men on more than a hundred ships with enough provisions for a long siege. The Gujarat forces entrenched themselves for a siege intended to endure until monsoon conditions forced the Portuguese to retire, but the overwhelming superiority of the Portuguese arms and fighting spirit caused Daman to fall without the loss of a single Portuguese life, and Dom Diogo de Noronha was left as Commander of Daman, which would remain Portuguese until 1961.

The main industries of Daman have historically been fisheries (undertaken by the Koli community centred in Nani Daman), opium (in the two decades between 1817 and 1837, when the British captured Sind and stopped the valuable trade with China), trade both reputable (with East Africa) and smuggling, which came to a head in the 1970s and is now under control after the introduction of airborne coastguards. Nowadays the main industries are liquor distilleries and the retail outlets connected with them, and tourism, not altogether unconnected with the effects of legal consumption adjacent to a prohibition zone.

Moti Daman

The logical place to begin exploring Daman is 'Great' or 'Moti' Daman, accessible by ferry and bridge across the Damanganga river from 'Little' or 'Nani' Daman. It is dominated by a huge fort, breached through the centre by a public road still named Rua Martim Afonso, whom I take to be the Governor of Portuguese India from 1542 to 1545 Martim Afonso de Sousa. A notice on the iron-studded wooden gate proclaims 'esta porta foi feita aos 8 de Agosto de 1690' (or could it be 1699?), and a plaque explains how the great fort replaced a small Muslim citadel. Construction started soon after the conquest in 1559 and was not completed till the end of the century, covering an area of 30,000 square metres, with ten bastions on the great walls, and only two gateways, the whole protected by the Damanganga on the north, the sea on the west, and a moat on the other sides. Polygonal in form, the fort has projections at roughly 500 foot intervals, carrying splayed angular bastions. The walls are battered and plain up to cornice level, where there is beaded moulding. The parapet wall above has loopholes, but no merlons. Terraces close to the top of the walls are connected to the inner ground surfaces by open flights of steps at many places, a technique practised also at the much smaller Fort of St Jerome on the northern side of the river. Barracks for defenders were established at various points. An inscription above the southern or landward gate notes that it and its bastion were completed in 1581 after the Mughal invasion during Akbar's reign. The northern gate records 1593 as the northern wall's completion date. You can still explore traditional buildings in the administrative area, which boasted a Governor's Palace, hospital, and two churches. The Collectorate and related offices still function within these precincts, and the ruins of old monasteries convey that magic which is provided by the Albanian community in Italy, or the Portuguese Marrano society in Amsterdam, say: a gift of the unexpected, even of the surreal. For the Badrapore district of Moti Daman is full of winding lanes and small houses where a kind of Portuguese can be heard that has been musically Indianised. I recall the amazement of an Italian landing in Malta (where the language is mostly Semitic with Italian borrowings) after having been reassured that the Maltese and their language would seem fraternal to him: 'Ma che fratelli sono questi?' A Portuguese might well ask, 'What kind of brothers are these?', and the answer would be that many are not only descendants of Portuguese settlers, but also Roman Catholics. They celebrate Easter with pro-

Moti Daman. Original Portuguese gateway

cessions, Christmas with trees festooned with lights, and they attend mass with the ardent faith of converts in a territory still surrounded by a majority of Hindus and a minority of Muslims.

Moti Daman has a Yogeshwar Temple and Dholar a Friday Mosque, but the dominant faith in the fort area is Roman Catholicism. Father Manuel Rodrigues from Goa serves the 3,500 Catholics at the daily evening mass in Portuguese and English in the Church of the Infant Jesus (or Bom Jesus in the more picturesque Portuguese). Morning mass is held daily in Our Lady of the Remedies, Moti Daman, and Our Lady of the Sea, Nani Daman, where the parish priest is Father Joseph Dias from Silvassa, a town in Dadra and Nagar Haveli, a part of the Union Territory. Though much more populous than its neighbour across the river, Nani Daman has only 1,000 Catholics these days.

Father Manuel showed me with immense pride over 'his' Infant Jesus, a plain name startlingly at odds with the sumptuous interior, its lofty ceiling, and gilded carved and florid baroque altar, embellished with lifesize statues of six saints and the Infant Jesus, all so much in the style of Goanese churches that we can safely assume that every craftsman came from the sister possession down south. The high altar assumes the pretensions of overlordship in its grandeur and extravagance: we are invited to agree that such an investment – in a carved world, painted red, green and gold, represented a certainty of everlasting power, both spiritual and temporal. 'Have you made converts in recent years, Father?' He smiled with the patience of a misunderstood government leader voted out of power by a misled electorate. 'No,' he responded quietly, 'not one.'

On the left wall a plaque commemorates Constancio Roque da Costa, Secretario Geral da Prefeitura do Estado da India Portugueza, 1784-1836, 'nesta cidade e praça de Damão'.

The Archaeological Survey of India took over the conservation of Bom Jesus in 1983, and Father Manuel has appealed to the authorities for better lighting. The church is said in many books to date from 1606, but Father Manuel showed me sources which affirmed a completion date three years

Moti Daman. Church

110

Moti Daman. Chapel of Our Lady of the Rosary. Adoration of the Magi, in gilded relief

earlier. The Chapel of Our Lady of the Rosary (1623) stands in the grounds of Bom Jesus, as – rather incongruously – does a circular public library I found accommodating five men deep in daily newspapers. Externally simple, Our Lady of the Rosary proves internally to be as ornate as its mother church across the children's playground in the park. Indeed, the altar is perhaps the most exuberantly animated of all the carved and gilded churches of Portuguese India.

Biblical stories are told on sculpted side walls of the apse in the form of episodes corresponding to fresco cycles like (but far inferior to) those of Luca Signorelli in Orvieto or Masaccio in S. Maria del Carmine, Florence. I particularly enjoyed the Adoration of the Magi, the gilt adding to the ingenuous appeal of the gifts: gold, frankincense and myrrh. Strings of rose petals descended in pious homage from the ceiling, just as similar garlands would be acquired by Hindus outside temples to drape around the holy images within.

A young man called Leroy Machado offered to show me around his native Moti Daman. 'I lived here for only three years before I left for Bombay; I've come back after studying and have been working in hotels and as a telephone operator for international calls.'

We left the fort area to find the exotic Church of Our Lady of the Remedies, built in 1607 by Ruy de Mello de Sampayo, Governor and Captain of Daman. Every inch of the pulpit, painted blue and gold, teems with flowers and scrolls and the whole gives the (false) appearance of being held up by two bearded caryatids like ships' figureheads and a third armless figure who is a well-endowed lady in a bra. Sturdy angels in triple columns flank the open door where the priest will appear from a hole in the wall, not so much a deus ex machina as a jack in the box.

Moti Daman advertises the Hilsa Aquarium as an attraction, but a large echoing hangar is a pale shadow of what it could be, with a few seashells labelled in Latin, yet no labels on the aquarium cases which have some tiger loach, gurami, angelfish and other tropical varieties; nothing rare or systematic.

Just inside the fort gate a plaque marks the spot where a great Portuguese poet once lived, but does not hint at the sensation. Manuel Maria l'Hédois d'Bocage (1765-1805), impelled by the model of his beloved Camões to set sail for Goa, spent 28 months there in the Navy, and was promoted to infantry lieutenant at Daman, arriving there on 6 April 1789. Within a matter of two days he had deserted with a companion, and fled to Macao. He returned to Portugal in August 1790, having lost part of his manuscripts (others would be stolen later from him at Santarém), only to find that his beloved Gertrúria had abandoned him for his brother Gil, who had just graduated in Law from Coimbra. At death's door through fever, he never forgave Goa for its pretensions to become another Lisbon, and wrote satires against the now decadent Portuguese Empire, beginning a satirical sonnet:

Das terras a pior tu és, ó Goa,
Tu pareces mais ermo, que cidade;
Mas alojas em ti maior vaidade
Que Londres, que Paris ou que Lisboa.

[Goa, you are the worst hole in the world:
You're more rank wilderness than city,
Yet dare to think of yourself greater
Than Paris, London, than Lisbon more pretty]

Moti Daman has a Portuguese war memorial built in 1949 to commemorate the dead of 'Damão, Terra Portuguesa', as it says, 'aos que morreram per Damão nos sec. XVI, XVII e XVIII', and those who died included many of the old families of De Souza and Vasconcellos, in search of the colonial dream: wealth, power, and missionary triumph for the Church Catholic. One tombstone removed to this memorial is dated 1600, another 1621.

The Superintendent of the Public Works Department works in an old Portuguese office, and I was greeted thereabouts by 'bom dia' more generally than 'namaskar'.

A few minutes' ride in an auto-rickshaw brings you from Moti Daman south to Jampore Beach, beyond which the Arabian Sea swallows the Kalai river. The soft sands are cleaned regularly and Hotel China Town offers a comfortable refuge from the overcrowding of Bombay, and the pollution of nearby Vapi. Palms and eucalyptus stabilise the sand and give shade throughout the day. Swimming is safe, but do remember sunscreen if sunbathing; wear a hat and sunglasses.

Tourism is generally less well developed than in Diu: there is no museum, zoo, art gallery, botanic garden or cultural centre, and the main leisure interest is eating out at the many restaurants, and socialising at Devka Beach in the north of Daman, beyond which the Kolak river meets the sea. An explosion of hotel building at Devka in recent years has led to intense competition between enterprises such as Hotel Miramar, run by the Tandel brothers, and the newer Sandy Resort owned by Nitin Rathode.

I enjoyed every drop of Moti Daman's variety, from a cricket match between Moti Daman and Bhimpore on the browny-green grass of a football pitch just inside the fort gateway that looks just like a military parade-ground become civilian, to a gorgeous Hindu wedding procession escorted by a vociferous brass band along Rua Martim Afonso, the bride stunningly beautiful front centre, in a sari of red and gold, glittering with golden ornaments on hair, nose, neck, arms and feet. Indeed, I could think of little more intriguing than browsing among the 83 volumes of unpublished correspondence and administrative regulations covering Daman between 1592 and 1885 in the Goa Archives at Panaji. (If you think that would take some time to sift through, I should add that there are 165 volumes on Diu there.)

Nani Daman. Hindu procession

Nani Daman

As night fell I was attracted to a patient queue of cinemagoers, though India is a nation now equally addicted to videos hired to watch at home. The movie being shown was the Gujarati-language *Navrang Chundri* (1979) set in a spick-and-span fairytale village with a wicked mother-in-law, a flawless hero and a flirtatious, sentimental heroine whose path is strewn with tragedy and madness before her sudden recovery in the last seconds of the film. Love songs and dances mercifully interrupted the jaded plot, and the uncomfortable realities of dirt, noise, traffic and poverty were omitted as in the popular *Dallas* and *Dynasty*. I yearned for Satyajit Ray's compassion, sensibility, and eye for detail. The Gujarati film industry began with Nanubhai Vakil's *Narsinh Mehta* (1932), starring Mohanlal, but has never achieved greatness despite some worthy efforts such as the historical *Ranakdevi* (1946), Ratibhai Punatar's *Gunsundari* (1948) with Nirupa Roy and Manohar Desai. Even a good actor such as Sanjiv Kumar finds himself playing a two-dimensional character in *Mare Javun Pele Par* and *Kalapi*. The directors blame the distributors, who blame the public for wanting the same old tired formulaic movies: love as flirtation, battles as silly acrobatics, and a simplistic plot of white against black devoid of any psychological development or real-life issues.

Dawn sounds at Hotel Sukhsagar in Nani Daman included revving motor-bikes, men laughing in the street, cockerels announcing the day in nearby gardens, and a muaddin calling Muslims to witness from a local mosque.

For breakfast I bought a melon to eat in the privacy of my darkened hotel room, away from the sun glaring as piercingly as a cat's yowl, but before I cut it open I allowed my fingers to roam its bottle-green globe, like Harish in Anita Desai's haunting story 'Surface Textures' in *Games at Twilight* (1978), who 'ran his fingers up and down the green streaks that divided it into even quarters as by green silk threads, so tenderly'.

Nani Daman's Portuguese-built covered vegetable market of 1879, enlarged in 1937, has since changed to accommodate textile vendors and stalls for spices and stationery. It is organised formally into rows, each uniform and making no concession to the fact that some goods (like radios) take up much more space than others (such as pens): it is regimentation based on control, like the two facing forts across the river, whereas if left to their own devices, Indians will bring their own carts piled in their own way, in the open air, separated and in the sunshine, protecting themselves with a ring of coolness under a black umbrella. Vegetables are now sold *outside* the vegetable market in Nani Daman.

I chatted to a Bengali from Calcutta sent by his Bombay firm to supervise a site in Daman, where he speaks Hindi to the local people, who cannot understand English or Bengali, and indeed have very basic Hindi. I found a country liquor store run by Mrs Purshottam, a Parsi lady, and a telephone stand being operated by a man called Quraish, the family name of the Prophet Muhammad (s.A.a.w.s.) indicating – as at Diu – that Muslim immigrants from the Arabian Peninsula had found trading conditions profitable in Portuguese India.

The monumental heart of Nani Daman is the Fort of São Jerónimo with its main gate facing the Damanganga river and the Fort of Damão Grande on the other bank. The twentieth Viceroy, Don Jerónimo de Acevedo, who named the redoubt for his own name saint, started construction of the fort in 1614, but it was not completed until the viceroyalty of D. Francisco da Gama in 1627. Roughly square, it encloses an area of 12,250 square metres, and has three bastions, a monumental gateway, a minor gate landward, the Church of Our Lady of the Sea (1901; restored in 1966), and the Stella Maris Pre-Primary School. The most piquant reminder of the Portuguese centuries, however, is a little walled cemetery dominated by a little white chapel with the memento mori HODIE MIHI CRAS TIBI ('Today for me, Tomorrow for you') humblingly prominent. Most of these families still remain in Daman: Colimão, Mascarenhas, Pereira; Coello, Machado, Furtado; Fernandes, d'Souza, Rosario. The 'Jazigo da familia Hipólito Albuquerque' (will India never be allowed to forget that name?) accepts the deceased Hermógenes Manuel de Albuquerque, b. 1918, d. 1983, just as if the centuries flipped past as casually as a shuffling of cards.

Taking the steps two at a time to elude the grasp of death, I soon reached the parapet walk extending nearly all the way around the castle

115

Nani Daman. Entrance to the fort

walls, spying down on the activities below. At the shore, women poised head burdens amid noisy altercations, some friendly, others distinctly taunty. The sun lit up the rolling river like a tide of diamonds. Beached boats yawned and fell asleep until nightfall. The old wooden doors of Fort St Jerome have been left in place, as has a recent hoarding proclaiming 'Remove Dowry System. It is a shame on our society'.

I wandered along the shore, and found the public library open (books available 8-11, 3-5, Monday closed) opposite Hotel Sun 'n Sea. The lady librarian immersed herself deep in a magazine while three men monopolised the morning papers. A prominent poster listed holidays and festivals in Daman during 1993: 26 January, 19 February, 8 and 25 March, 5 and 9 April, 6 May, 1 June, 1 July, 11, 15 and 31 August, 2 and 22 October, 13 and 29 November, 19 December (Liberation Day of Daman and Diu) and Christmas Day.

IV: NORTH GUJARAT

From Ahmedabad my Ambassador taxi took the trunk road to Abu Road, Ajmer, Jaipur and Delhi. For most of its length this, like many other Indian highways, is planted with trees on both sides to shelter pedestrians and pack animals such as donkeys, yoked oxen and camels from the heat of the day. We overtook a camel pulling a concrete mixer and women elegant in red and green saris bringing home round baskets of animal fodder on their head, deportment a matter of grace, economy of effort, natural balance and pride. A goatherd waving a stick exhorted his straying animals to keep left. A peacock spurted across the road in alarm at our noisy horn. Traffic diminished in intensity as soon as we turned left at Mehsana (spelt 'Mahesana' on some maps) and headed due west for the Sun Temple (ask for 'Surya Mandir') near the village of Modhera.

Modhera
To set this sublime temple in its context, we must think back to the Solanki dynasty of the 10th-13th centuries. From their capital of Anahilvada Patan, which would be devastated by Muslim raiders in the late 12th century, they commissioned lavish temples of extreme beauty. Many of these suffered despoliation by waves of Muslim iconoclasts, and further damage by the terrible earthquake in the early 19th century, but some remain in reasonably good condition: of these, Modhera's Surya Mandir is the major example. Roughly contemporary with it are the Someshwara Temple at Gorad, the Shiva Temple at Sander, the Mata Temple at Dhinoj, and the Limboji Mata Temple at Delmal. Later are Sunak's Nilakantha Mahadeva Temple, and the Rudramala Temple to Shiva at Siddhapur, one of the later Somnath temples (before heavy restorations), and the Navlakha Temples at Ghumli and Sejakpur in Saurashtra. The Hindu Solanki rulers, and I think particularly of Siddharaja Jayasimha (1094-1143) and Kumarapala (1143-1172), were advised by ministers who were as shrewd as they were tolerant, many of them Jains. We know from their works something of these extraordinary men, and in particular about two merchant brothers Tejapala and Vastupala who emerged into prominence in the early 13th century, and spent much of their great wealth – as successful Jains have repeatedly done – in building great temples, both Hindu and Jain. Indeed, we shall see Vastupala's immortal triple-shrined temple to Adinatha on Girnar Hill, and those lucky enough to have visited Mount Abu will have seen Tejapala and Vastupala's Neminatha Temple (1230) and portrait sculptures in the entrance porch showing not only the two donors, but also their wives.

Modhera. Sun Temple. Original archway

119

But of course it would be misleading to imply that a European Renaiss-ance-style individualism characterised the Solanki dynasty's masterpieces, such as the Adinatha Temple (1032) at Dilwara financed by the Jain Vi-mala, a minister of the Solanki King Bhima I. What we see at Modhera and elsewhere is a well-recognised structural archetype, enlivened by sculptu-ral fantasies and stereotyped friezes. Every member of the community contributed to the temples in kind, so that for instance, 'in the market-place the shopkeepers were to give a spoonful of every kind of grain that was sold, while of cotton each shop was to give as much as a man could hold in his hand and the reapers of betel-plants were required to make a contribution when they reap, and so forth, the ministers of the king being ordered to recognise these imposts'.

The building of Modhera and all other temples was entrusted to the guild of masons, or *silavat*s. The guild or *sena* would be governed by mas-ter-masons who operated without blueprints or models, but could chant the rules of the craft, some esoteric or astronomical to govern the orienta-tion of the building and various auspicious and inauspicious factors not dissimilar from Chinese rules of *feng shui*. The depiction of gods, men, ani-mals and angels would be deeply ingrained in the infallibly prolonged tradition, as in French Gothic cathedrals of the Middle Ages. Further, these masons would maintain hereditary lines to keep the craft both secret and constant. And because the artisans were not priests, when in the four-teenth century and beyond the new Islamic rulers decreed that mosques were to replace temples, it was clear to rulers and artisans alike that there could be no clean break in architectonic features, which is why the early mosques of Ahmedabad, Mehmedabad, Champaner, and coastal cities such as Cambay, Broach and Surat were endowed with Friday Mosques of such elaborate Hinduising ornamentation.

Modhera Sun Temple exemplifies the western Indian Solanki style: a shrine with *cella*, approached from a *mandapa* or pillared open-plan hall. The proportions and details of each component would vary as flexibly as in an Italian Latin-cross church. Most earlier temples, like Modhera's, would unite the two components, though there is an additional *sabha-man-dapa*, or detached hypostyle hall, at Modhera. Most later temples, such as that of Somnath at Prabhas Patan, would possess two rectangular compo-nents joined diagonally. The two types uniformly interrupt their sides by regular projecting and recessing chases to form angles cleverly arranged to produce strong vertical contrasts of light and shade throughout the day. Most temples consist of three stories: a basement, a wall up to cornice-level, and a *shikhara* or spire. At Modhera, regrettably, the *shikhara* is miss-ing. The *pitha* or basement upper surface forms the floor of the temple. The outer decoration of its string-courses has repeating motifs fixed by con-vention from the foot: *garaspatti* or horned heads; a *gajapitha* or elephant frieze here at Modhera badly eroded; an *asvathara* or horse frieze; and a *na-rathara*, or human frieze.

Above the *pitha* level of conventional reliefs comes the *mandovara*, the main area for artistic expression, not only on the wall face, but in niches with a range of deities and their vehicles, associated angels, maidens, animals and holy men in a range from high to low relief. In other temples, where the *shikhara* is present, it often takes the form of a main spire encircled by diminutive replicas seen as turrets or *urusringa*s.

Carry a torch with you for the dark interior of Surya Mandir, and you will be amazed by the elaborate sculptural detail, far removed from the plainness of the Indo-Aryan style in Orissan temples, and much more exuberant than the more celebrated Khajuraho interiors. Here at Modhera, it is as if the theological antipathy to figural representation near the sanctum has been overcome by inspiration from the carving fraternity. The enclosed hall or *gudha-mandapa* has an octagonal arrangement of tall pillars with torana arches across axial pairs of pillars. The walls are plain except for niches with images of the twelve *aditya*s, that is to say the various transformations of the sun in each of the twelve months of the year. *Aditi* means eternity, and we must see behind their names and their personifications the one eternal celestial light, in which the *aditya*s dwell and which forms their essence. They are in fact no more genuinely represented in three dimensions than the figure of Ahura Mazda is genuinely represented in Zoroastrianism, and for the same theological and esoteric reason. In the *Rigveda* Aditi is a mother goddess, Deva Matri, implored by Hindus 'for blessings on children and cattle, for protection and forgiveness'. In both Mahabharata and Ramayana, Vishnu is called the son of Aditi, whereas the *Yajurveda* knows her as his wife.

The shrine-chamber is a simple square cell surrounded by an ambulatory or processional passage scantily decorated: the images are confined mainly to the *cella* entrance.

Windows at intervals enhance a tension between extreme brightness and extreme darkness within. The east-facing temple is so aligned that the rising sun at equinoxes gleams like a golden rod all the way through, to alight on the sacred image at the shrine's heart. Modhera's ethereal aura still defies desecration, earthquakes, and the heavy hand of the restorer, who added his own two-rupees' worth as recently as 1974. A Nandi shrine outside makes a vain attempt to claim the holy ground for Shiva, but this is demonstrably Surya's domain, as Konarak is, erotic scenes vivifying the internal columns.

Modhera's Sun Temple is not an active temple so you do not have to remove your shoes, but a bent-backed war veteran had taken off his chappals in veneration, and surely he was right. Only one of the original four *torana*s survives, but from this you can envisage the original whole. Round solar symbols are carved on ceilings, and round solar capitals convey the eternal passage of the planets; the columns are round, and the round-breasted women sumptuous in their blatant sexuality show what the world lost with the puritanical iconoclasms of Judaism, Christianity and

123

Modhera. Tank (11th century)

Islam. As dusk falls, staff place mats across the floors of the *sabha-mandapa* to receive pigeon-droppings.

Interestingly, a vast rectangular stepped tank with niches all around it situated to the east of the temple almost eclipses the temple in its scale. Dry during my winter visit, the tank will glint with energy during the monsoon season. Architectonic and sculptural fragments are arranged in rows near the tank. A word too for the glorious gardens which the Archaeological Survey of India maintains as a suitable frame for this jewel of a temple. An 11th-century step-well can be found west of the village. You can take snacks at the Toran Cafeteria run by the Tourism Corporation of Gujarat, but the nearest places to stay are the district capital of Mehsana, or the historically significant Anahilvada Patan, nowadays just known as the 'city', or Patan.

Patan
Night had fallen before my taxi-driver had located Aram Graha, the Government Rest House which lets private visitors stay for Rs 60 (non a/c) or Rs 100 (a/c), except that half charges are payable for a stay less than twelve hours. I recommend this rest house for a quiet night because the Neerav Hotel on Station Road suffers from perennial traffic noise and an amplified Bollywood racket from the Kohinoor Cinema next door. The rates here are Rs 200 single a/c and Rs 50 non a/c.

As the Aram Graha offers no meals, I returned to the Neerav's open restaurant for dum alu, Kashmiri pulau, roasted papadum and tea; with free onions and limes and free parathas the bill came to less than Rs 60, or £1.20 sterling in a strange restaurant designed something like a secular Jain temple with a column in the middle of an octagonal room.

Anahilvada Patan owes its geographical importance to its position near the Saraswati river and its tributary the Chandrabagha, and its historical importance to a succession of dynasties beginning in the 8th century and culminating in the 11th-12th centuries with the Solankis. It became a leading Jain centre for study, teaching, pilgrimage and temple-building, with important Hindu buildings, a great reservoir or tank, probably the greatest step-well to be seen anywhere, as well as the stubborn survival of the *patolu* tradition in textiles, and a variety of courtyard houses or havelis worth several hours in the buzzing bazaar. For all its beauty and significance, Patan still looks like a country town undisturbed by tourism. Ahmed Shah I transferred his capital from Patan to Ahmedabad in the 15th century, and Patan's status never recovered, though it has been allocated North Gujarat University as a tribute to its reputation for learning and culture. A new city was founded in 1796 by Zalim Singh, whose royal palace can be glimpsed through the gates opening through a high stone wall in the cantonment 6 km from the city centre. Patan was the capital of the princely state of Jhalawar before accession to the Union.

We first explore the ancient city of Anahilvada Patan, 2 km northwest of the modern town.

The queen's step-well, or Rani-ki Vav, is an even more spectacular example of the monumental well-type we have seen at Adalaj near Ahmedabad. It draws attention to the crucial importance of water in an agricultural land at the mercy of the monsoon, and subject to long and often fatal droughts. If the crops failed, and the animals died, whole communities would be wiped out, so the farsighted prince would dig deep until he found water, and would protect the best springs with permanent stone structures. Whereas the wells in Roman cities would be simple stone cylinders, their rims bitten by invisible centuries of tugged ropes, a Gujarati *vav* can be an architectural treasure of religious iconography in friezes and niches to teach Hindu myth, legend and history. In later Muslim times the *vav* would develop from this rectangular open-plan prototype into a complex of shady underground chambers and courts where neighbours could meet in the cool of the evening, or seek refuge during the heat of noon.

Rani-ki Vav is named for Udaimati, Queen of Bhim Deva (1022-63), son of Mularaja, founder of the Solanki dynasty. It dates from 1050, but has been admirably restored (1982-8) to allow us a clear view of a great Hindu *vav*. One pillar survives from the 11th century as proof of elegant design, but the great well had been silted up for centuries before rescue work by the Archaeological Survey of India cleared out débris and pieced together its fragments. Little remained except for a few rows of sculptured panels

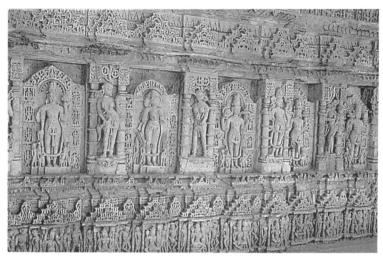

Patan. Rani-ki Vav. Sculptures

in the circular part of the well, and part of the wall which revealed that all
the walls had been made of brick and faced with stone. Pairs of brackets
projecting from the walls supported galleries of the well-shaft proper. Of
course in a majestic setting such as Rani-ki Vav, the sense of incomplete-
ness lends flight to vision. Column-bases can be visualised in riots of fili-
gree sculpture from the precious pillar surviving. Bearded Brahma with
his arm round full-bosomed Saraswati (goddess and river, consort and
mother) sits on his throne with one leg crossed in front of him and the
other hovering just above the ground. I squatted in wonder before a standing Rama in a left-hand niche, then pursued the incarnations of Vishnu,
here as Varaha the boar, there as Narasimha the half-lion, yon as Vamana
the dwarf. Rani-ki Vav bristles with Vishnu's avatars like prickles on a
porcupine. How strange that sculpture can also be considered frozen
music (though that too is true) when here in ancient Anahilvada sculpture
is a lively dance of the universe, with all the gods temporally glimpsed as
they glide and discourse through the quickening centuries. A sign at the
entrance warns 'ALERT FOR BIG HONEY BEE' and now I found them,
swollen dark hanging nests below the top ceiling ahead, on the fifth level.
Make no sudden movements, and if these inquisitive monsters land on
you, stay still as Vishnu enthroned. On the fourth level, the left-hand
panel on the right-hand side shows Ganesha (his trunk snapped off) amid
a bevy of round-breasted, full-bodied maidens of heavenly beauty. Solar
discs in the ceilings throughout hint at the persistence of sun-worship by
assimilation with the Hindu god Surya, but Vishnu reclining emerges into

126

central focus on three separate horizontal friezes ahead, in the circular heart of the well. Another hanging hive hums overhead, and pigeons wooloowooloo'd invisibly around, protected by high niches in shadow.

Not to be outdone by Queen Udaimati, King Siddharaja Jayasimha (1094-1144) of the Solanki dynasty and his learned Jain minister Hemachandra created the 'Thousand Linga Tank' or Sahasralinga Talao. This is clearly no ordinary reservoir: like so many of its type it has temples annexed, elaborate sculpted figures of divinities and semi-divinities, dancing maidens in friezes, and impressive ranks of columns to support ceilings (long vanished) which protected the priests and people of Patan from hot sun. Numerous little temples (the term 'thousand' is a pious convention of the 'Thousand Nights and a Night' tradition) each with a little phallus on a vulva to represent Shiva's generative spirit and the fecundity of Parvati stood on the banks of the reservoir, but were dismantled during raids by the Muslim iconoclast Mahmud of Ghazni on his way to Prabhas Patan to destroy Somnath Temple in 1024, and attacked again by the Mughal Alaf Khan, brother of Ala ud-din Khilji, in 1306. A large octagonal *rauza* or mausoleum was raised on its ruins and, near the middle of the eastern embankment, archaeologists have unearthed remains of a Shiva Temple comprising a basement of pavilions with a colonnade of forty-eight pillars. This had been left undamaged by successive Muslim rulers until the 16th century when it was demolished in retaliation for the murder in Patan of Akbar's tutor, Bairam Khan, resting there on his way to perform the Hajj.

As only one extended family in Patan now makes the celebrated *patolu*, the silk wedding sari that can take six months to produce, it may be difficult for you to find one in Patan, so the best way to survey Patan *patola* is in the Calico Museum of Textiles of Ahmedabad. What you cannot see in Ahmedabad (though it has its own fascinating haveli tradition) is the variety of Hindu and Muslim *haveli*s or courtyard houses that have grown up in this area of North Gujarat. Of course one cannot walk into places where women may still be in *purdah*, but most *haveli*s possess superb exteriors which are well worth finding. And in crowded bazaars, you will always come across fabulous scents of spices and perfumes, sights of bullocks and camel-carts, tribesmen in from the country for the day with their womenfolk.

Walk around the Muslim quarters of Raktavad and Panchpada, and see how the houses are separate, often larger, and less densely populated than in the Hindu quarters. Upper floors will be screened from public view and occupied by the women, who can observe comings and goings through wooden panelling. Fine carvings show the tasteful wealth of the family commissioning the *haveli*, whether it be Yusufbhai Kakawala or Abdulghani Nurwali of Raktavad or Ahmad Patwa in Panchpada. Patan Muslims are mainly Sunni Bohras, rich merchants, with a minority of Sodagars who were encouraged to come from the Arabian Peninsula in Mughal times and maintain strict *purdah*. Some of these flat-roofed Muslim homes

127

were equipped with a wind-tower known in Persian as *bad-gir*, a type known throughout the Arabian Gulf and Sind. Muslim houses in Patan differ from those in the rest of Gujarat by having a *sojala*, or women's mezzanine, constructed between the ground floor and the less-utilised first floor: some Sodagar houses even had separate access stairs to the *sojala*, we learn from V.S. Pramar's invaluable *Haveli* (Mapin, Ahmedabad, 1989).

A Hindu family's *haveli* in Khada Kotado quarter, that of the Patnis, has the characteristic curved wooden balustrade with every square inch covered with floral and geometric patterns, and tiers of delicate overhanging droplets like tassels which replace the elephant heads found elsewhere because of the Muslim influence against representation of living animals.

I was invited to view the abandoned Golsiri Haveli, near the clocktower called Tran Darwaza or Triple Gate on M.G. Road (as Gujarat's thoroughfares named for Mahatma Gandhi are universally abbreviated). From the fruit stalls and auto-rickshaw stand in front of Golsiri Haveli, the mansion is regrettably obscured by rusting signs and garish new hoardings, but go inside the building, with its ground floor a godown for garlic in gunny bags and piles of coconuts, and the plan emerges. A central well netted against pigeons allows natural light to penetrate all the peripheral rooms, and wooden columns, wooden doors, give an airy lightness to the length of the two floors. I ascended to the flat roof, protected by a relatively recent pattern of sloping corrugated iron roofing. From this, steps lead up to a fourth, even cooler level and it needs little imagination to recreate an extended family still in occupation.

Ask your auto-rickshaw driver in Patan to take you to the 12th-century Maheshwara Temple and to other great historic Hindu temples, such as Kali-ka Mataji and Panchmukhi Hanuman. Any one of the many Jain temples will give you some inkling of the glory of this snow-white architectural tradition which you may know from Ranakpur or Dilwara in Rajasthan. Gujarat is the heartland of India's Parsis and of India's Jains and of India's Swaminarayan Hindus. I know nothing at once more relaxing and more elevating and exciting than to sit crosslegged in a Jain temple of Patan such as Doshiwar Mandir and close my eyes. White marble floors and columns gleam brilliantly in the light; padlocked shrines of the tirthankars keep their jewels and their secrets safe, their names lettered in graceful Gujarati script above each door. Crows drop in arrogantly for a while then rise in a whish of angry black for their next peregrination. Striped palm squirrels lollop around, still as lizards if they sense a threat. Pigeons fuss and rush among the cross-legged worshippers fingering beads while a dhoti-clad priest intones prayers. 'Open on three sides', I noted. You can see the first, second and third, but the fourth is always closed. I looked up and the superb carved ceilings spun like starry skies around my dizzy brain. The same old story: India had taken me out of my own life, and transported into another of its own invention.

If you have never seen a Jain haveli temple before ask your auto-rickshaw driver to take you to Kapur Mahetano Pado, where the stone temple has a wooden interior based on the domestic shrine called *ghar derasar;* such a shrine might focus on a tirthankar image or on a *mangala chinha,* or auspicious sign. Wealthy Jains would have every architectonic feature of wood carved with fantastic detail, even down to *jalis* or screens and brackets which might have been structural or purely decorative. Brilliant colours, almost too bright for any single feature to stand out, are used to pick out processional carts and pilgrims, flowers, fruit in bowls and arabesques in two and three dimensions. Even the temples on Shatrunjaya were once, like the Patan haveli temple at Kapur Mahetano Pado, made of wood until, the story goes, the master-builder Uda Mehta once saw a mouse carrying a burning candle in its mouth. Mehta saw at once that one mishap would demolish the work of years, and so from then on insisted that all Jain temples should be created in stone.

Siddhapur

Twenty-seven km east of Patan, on the Arjuni tributary to the Saraswati, the town named for the Solanki ruler Siddharaja Jayasimha (1094-1144) has become a sleepy town aroused only during festivals and rites for maternal funerals, which give the town the name of Matrigaya. This follows the tradition that Lord Parshuram performed these *shradha* rites for his mother at Lake Bindu in Siddhapur. Unfortunately, Lake Bindu could do with its own purification, and Rudramala, the magnificent twelfth-century temple to Shiva, stands in dejected ruin with barbed wire to repel intruders, and a fierce caretaker with a stick dedicated to the laudable pursuit of keeping out anyone not furnished with an even more forceful letter from the Archaeological Survey of India, permitting entrance to this overgrown jungle in the heart of town. During Ala ud-Din's iconoclastic ravagings across Gujarat, Rudramala was attacked in 1297 and what we see now are its sorry remains. How marvellous if some Hindu Maecenas would spend some of his riches on restoring this magnificent temple of Shiva, recreating its several storeys, its eleven subsidiary shrines to the eleven Rudras of the Brihadaranyaka Upanishad (ten *pranas,* or breaths of life, and the *manas* or heart). In the Vedas, Rudra is a deity liable to confuse all those who mistake the scriptures literally: stormbringer and destroyer by fire, yet healer and provider. Rudramala Temple covers an area of more than ninety metres by seventy, and you should begin by studying the proportions of the main sanctuary, with torana arches, great architraves and huge columns that could only have been commissioned by a royal patron.

The bristling caretaker, obviously agitated by years of chasing truant lads from his archaeological preserve, finally settled down beside me on the ancient stones and – still watchfully – began to chat. 'Rudramala used to have golden domes,' he lamented, 'and it was the pride of all Gujarat. It was begun by King Mularajadeo of the Solankis, the architect being Kaladhar Prandhar. But the soothsayers had to be consulted about the exact location, and the stone had to be quarried in distant parts and brought here by oxen and bullocks. It all took many years, and only one storey had been finished by the time that King Mularaja died. He cried on his deathbed "Jai Rudra! Jai Rudra!" (Glory to Rudra!) and exhorted his successors to complete Rudramala. But they all ignored him: Bhimdeo, Karnadeo and Minaldevi, they all preferred to glorify instead Anahilvada Patan, their capital, and forget the god. At last Siddharaja came to the throne of Patan, and he was reminded of the dying wish of Mularajadeo. So he enquired for skilled craftsmen and learned that Kaladhar Prandhar's grandson Gangadhar survived, an old man, in distant Champaner. He summoned Gangadhar and his son Hiradhar, and the astrologer Markand came from Malwa and at a certain auspicious moment and at a certain place on the ground Markand called for a golden peg to be struck into the ground. "Now Rudramala will be secured for all eternity". The King asked him to explain. Markand answered: "The peg has entered the head of Sheshnag who bears the world on his head. So Rudramala is eternal, because time is at a stop". Siddharaja laughed, saying that all things created must have an end: how can the infinite be just a few inches below the ground? The astrologer would not be gainsaid, however, until the King demanded ocular proof. Eventually, despite the astrologer's pleadings, the King ordered the gold peg to be slightly dislodged, and to the horror of all onlookers blood spurted out of the ground and flecked the royal robes with blood, before the peg could be replaced. The dismayed king tried to rub the blood from his garments, but Markand told him: "You have spoilt the eternal life of Rudramala, and it is now destined to lie in ruins before long".'

A ballad in Gujarati recalls the glory of Siddhapur's Rudramala in terms more resonant than an archaeological report or scholarly reconstruction:

> "For Rudra the Great eleven shrines were erected,
> Showered with gold like the peaks of Mount Meru,
> Sixteen hundred columns forested the place,
> Delicate screens and pierced windows shielded the images
> Every shrine chamber door was set with precious jewels,
> With emeralds, diamonds and rubies the glory of the gold illuminated the
> heart
> And the Glittering Ones stood garlanded with pearls."

The caretaker, moved by his retelling of the old legend, sat silent among the stones. A lizard winked at me across the rubble, and a crow settled expectantly on a ledge above a torana arch. I moved towards a tall gateway with two complex tapering columns and capitals, and a looping torana arch. The Burhani mosque on the edge of the temple compound is clearly

Siddhapur. Wooden doors, windows and balcony opposite Burhani Mosque

much later, and I found the doorway open between the noon and dusk prayer. The place was empty, silent and odd, for several of its columns and ceilings belong to the Hindu temple's structure: they have just been enclosed by conquering Muslims, at a stroke reducing the temple's grandeur and increasing the mosque's. From the outside, the Burhani Mosque on its raised platform looks like a house, but its Arabic inscription white on blue proclaims it to all who can read the religious language of al-Qur'an al-Karim. Opposite is a Muslim mansion with an elegant carved wooden covered balcony, and at right angles to this, opposite Nafisa Manzil, stands another three-storey Muslim haveli with splendid, though restrained carving. The *Bohrvad* district of Siddhapur had many decorative balconies, but many more have succumbed to time and neglect. Like Kapadvanj, east of Ahmedabad, Siddhapur was colonised by Muslim merchants of the Bohra caste: converted Hindus who created mansions influenced by European architecture of Bombay and Surat, with their Renaissance-style inspiration. This implies that if you spend time wandering the streets of old Siddhapur you will encounter beautiful examples of woodcarving, and even gates to districts usually known as a *pol* in Gujarat but here known as a *vad*, where a community could isolate itself a night by locking its gates. Such a gate can indeed still be seen near Rudramala itself. Whereas a Hindu *pol* would be a winding, higgledy-piggledy settlement, a Muslim *vad* generally enjoyed regular street planning at right angles, and houses have regular aligned plots. Furthermore, at Siddhapur you will find long narrow plots more typical of South Gujarat, which proves the influence of Daudi Bohras having their headquarters at Surat. I found Siddhapur evocative of mediaeval Gujarat in its leisurely pace, creaking carts drawn by chewing camels, brick walls splatted with dark brown round dung-cakes drying in the sun, and covered women glimpsed tantalisingly round a corner then lost forever.

Palanpur and Vadnagar

North of Siddhapur you can head for Palanpur on the way to Mount Abu. Palanpur is the capital of Banaskantha district with a great percentage cf tribals. Palanpur, known for perfume and diamonds, was the headquarters of a local Nawab whose palace is still extant, as is the baroque carved *haveli* of Mahendrabhai Gafurbhai in Patha Sarak. We stopped for lunch at the pure vegetarian Hotel and Guest House Savera, in view of the R.T.O. Checkpost, Ambaji Road, outside Palanpur. A zephyr riffled inquisitively through the extensive menu of Punjabi foods such as Nargis kofta, Jain dishes such as channa masala, and Madrasi cuisine such as idli sambhar and masala dosa. I sat at an open-air table with my Jadeja Rajput driver Ishwar Singh, surrounded by gossiping sunflowers. Delicious vegetable cutlets and Kashmiri pulao came to Rs 26, and I added a half-kg jar of locally-produced orange marmalade for Rs 28 to spread on my forthcoming breakfast bread slices.

East from Siddhapur take a right turn short of Kheralu to Vadnagar for the important Jain temple dedicated to Adinatha said to date from the tenth century. You are shown notional parts of the original but in all major features this Solanki foundation is later, from the *shikhara* in clusters to the pavilion or *mandapa* and surrounding shrines. Siddharaja's Temple has two superlative torana columns reminiscent of his Rudramala at Siddhapur: tapering, bracketed, superbly carved, such columns exemplify the Indian propensity for colour, form, and decoration as opposed to the slender, simple, austere forms of classical Greece with which Europeans and New Englanders are brought up. Regrettably, these columns are all that marauding Muslims left of the magnificent Hindu temple. It is possible that these torana arches, like those at the entrance to Siddhapur's Rudramala, were intended as *kirti-stambha*s or monumental entrances for the *hindola* ceremony of swinging the image of the god, and for other practices such as the ritual weighing of the ruler against a steadily accumulating pile of gold which, when evenly balanced with the preferably portly king, would be distributed to the deserving poor.

Like nearby Visnagar, Vadnagar is a stronghold of the Nagar Brahmins, a community which arrived in Gujarat in the 3rd century from the northwest and achieved distinction in education, administration, and diplomacy, and count among their number the distinguished poets Dayaram and Narsinh Mehta, the novelist Govardhanram, and the musician Kaumudi Munshi. Vadnagar is credited by some scholars as the home of the Devanagari script used for Sanskrit and now Hindi, and the sisters Tana and Riri have an annual music festival named for them in Vadnagar because of a tale you can hear in any gathering. The Mughal Emperor's favourite musician, the virtuoso Tansen once sang raga Dipak so ardently that his recital affected him with a terrible fever. He told the Emperor that only by hearing pure singing in raga Meghmalhar could he be restored to health and, on reaching Vadnagar, he was told that Tana and Riri of the Nagar community were gifted in this raga. He prevailed upon them to sing for him and was cured of his fever. On hearing this at court, Akbar summoned the girls, but their Brahmin caste laws prohibited their showing themselves before a Muslim court of Akbar and, rather than refuse or obey, they committed suicide. You can see their memorial at Vadnagar, as well as a 17th-century Vaishnavite temple, the Hatkeshwar Mahadev, several times restored. Other souvenirs of the past include four gates in the walls erected by the Solanki king Kumarapala, and an artificial lake.

Taranga

It's half an hour's run from here up into the Taranga hills, mostly barren, on a good wide road with sparse traffic, crossing the Saraswati river, and crossing the Dhamani river into a fertile agricultural district shortly before reaching the village of Taranga, blessed by groups of sacred monkeys. On the way I passed a striding ascetic of the Jain sect which performs no *puja*, and wears while travelling a cotton gauze mask called *maupati* to protect flying insects and any other living things which might otherwise be swallowed or injured. I wrote for him

On the Way to Taranga

The Jain pilgrim
all in white
barefoot, masked mouth,
walks into the window
of Mahavira's beckoning

there is no backward, forward
depth, or breadth

no mirror to reflect his breath
(please will you answer when I call:
This night will have no end at all)

his eyes tread on
although his feet are blind
now there never will become horizon; never
death

Like other hills in Gujarat, Taranga is sacred to Jains, and one can understand their passion for clear air, the immanent holiness of the cool place far from pollution by traffic or business. A Jain pilgrim greeted me politely, with a transistor radio on a white stone wall beside him: 'Do you know that Ahmedabad is burning?' He referred to riots in the crowded *pols* of the Gujarati capital which had induced the local authorities to declare curfew the night before in an attempt to curb communal violence. 'You are welcome to the peace of Ajitanatha', murmured the white-garbed Jain, and opened his palm in the direction of the Jain shrine's gateway.

The secular walls of Vadnagar proved one of the lasting achievements of the Solanki King Kumarapala (1145-72): another is Taranga's colossal temple to the second Jain tirthankar: Ajitanatha, whose emblem is the elephant. The temple, dated by O.P. Tandon to 1165, is massive as befits its mountainous surroundings and is surrounded by several smaller, more recent temples. On the peaks above it you can glimpse diminutive white *chhatris* and a little shrine to Devi Taranamata from whom the village derives its name. Jains come here on special pilgrimage during the full moons at Kartika and Chaiba, the first and sixth months of the samvat year, which is calculated between new moons. Reservoirs of the purest spring- and rainwater have been built to ensure a permanent supply.

The temple measures 150 feet long and 100 feet across, and is one of the least-restored and best preserved of the great Solanki series which includes masterpieces on Mount Abu, Girnar and Shatrunjaya. Though Taranga and Kumbharia are architectural treasures of international importance, on a level with the temples of much more celebrated temples of Konarak and Khajuraho, they still lie far beyond the well-worn tourist paths, and I was the only foreigner during my day there. Indeed, so unusual did I look to the temple attendant that he took the step of graciously allowing me with authentic Jain pilgrims to enter and take photographs within the precinct and mandir, a gesture which I did not abuse by acceptance. The central hall has eight octagonal columns surmounted by round lotus capitals, and beautiful, sinuous maidens on sixteen brackets.

A Jain father, mother and three daughters prayed amid ravishing birdsong, then the four women chanted in practised unison. The Ajitanatha image, more than five metres tall, is not of course to be viewed as a Westerner would view a Western sculpture such as a Luca della Robbia ceramic Virgin and Child. We are not strictly speaking talking of a iconographic tradition at all, for if the *tirthankars* existed at all, as Jain accounts insist they did, the imagemakers have no directive to differentiate their features. So that whereas Western art historians trace a complicated line of descent in religious iconography from Byzantine stasis to Gothic expressiveness and Renaissance humanism, Jains have no such sequence: their images are differentiated only by emblems and attributes, *yakshas* and *yakshis*. Jains do not desire to make the image in some way sympathetic, living or breathing like ourselves, because they do not believe that their line

Taranga. Ajitanatha Jain Temple

of *tirthankars* are within the reach of prayer or assistance to mankind. The saviours exist beyond our universe of accident, time and space, inhabiting a high and luminous place without action or suffering. They are at peace, and these images are wrought to give the worshipper a glimpse of that Quiet beyond our understanding.

Taranga's Ajitanatha image in alabaster has the usual inlaid jewel eyes and, as the worshipping family made its offering in the donation chest and turned away, the attendant gently closed the sanctuary door and extinguished a massive chandelier brightening the centre of the interior. Outside, I studied the fantastic, almost overpowering friezes of dancing maidens, gods and goddesses in frenzied motion, their arms and legs in such a delirium that I could not help contrasting them with the almost absent gaze of the great idol within. These women, with their costume so lovingly detailed that one could compile a history of 12th-century Gujarati fashion from this pattern-book in stone, enliven the Jain temple in a vibrant denial of Jain austerities. If you thought that Jainism would be too intellectual to appeal to you, let this riot of sculptural delights overwhelm you. Revel in the integration of tiny details with the architectural ensemble of sanctuary and columned mandapa, and a superstructure comprising a clustered *shikhara* above the sanctuary, and dense finial tiers above the mandapa. The warm reddish-brown sandstone is easy to carve and to replace; the depth of the carving allows different colours of light and shade to play across the several surface levels at different times of day.

Buses are available from Mehsana, and trains run from Mehsana (10.40-14.05, returning 14.35-17.40; and 18.20-21.00, returning 4.25-7.28), taking over three hours for the 57 km, stressing that the journey, not the arrival, matters.

Ambaji and Kumbharia

But the railway line stops at Taranga Hill, and you make the journey towards the Rajasthani border by bus or taxi: it's about 45 km, and the scenery is spectacular, with the possibility of sighting leopard, jackal, wolf and fox.

Ambaji, on Arasur Hill, has a life of pilgrimage centred on the temple to Shakti, the female aspect of Shiva, though as well as religious tourism the local people mine copper, quarry marble, and sell forest products such as timber, honey and wax. The best time to come to Ambaji is during the full moon day and night every month and during Navratri, when you can see folk dancing and folk drama performed in the temple courtyard.

Near Ambaji is the sacred Jain site of Kumbharia, with five dated marble temples varying in size and complexity, but they have common features in that they stand with surrounding shrines in protective walled courtyards entered by imposing porched gateways. From north to south, they are dedicated to Sambhavanatha, Neminatha, Shantinatha, Mahavira and Parshvanatha. I discuss them in chronological order following Tandon's *Jaina Shrines in India* (1986). The common pattern is that of a sanctum, closed hall, pillared portico, and an assembly hall enclosed on three sides, with shrine-cells sheltered by colonnaded corridors. The sanctuary is surmounted by a *shikhara* with clustered turrets and *amala-sara*s. The grandiose assembly hall usually has an octagonal pillar arrangement, and within, the main circular ceiling comprises seven concentric rings with a huge central pendant. Normally, transept-bay ceilings are flat with abundant narrative friezes executed with a superb sense of overall harmony and lively invention.

Vardhamana Mahavira ('Great Soul') is the twenty-fourth and last *tirthankar*, a contemporary of Gautama Buddha, and it is to him that the earliest of the Kumbharia sequence was dedicated in 1062, thirty years after one of the earliest examples of Jain temples in northwest India, the Vimala Vasahi Temple to Adinatha on neighbouring Mount Abu, over the border in Rajasthan. The octagonal mandapa has a beautiful ceiling with pendant lobes and friezes portraying lives of Jain heroes and *tirthankar*s, musicians, dancers, angels and horsemen. The sanctuary's tower is topped by concentric ribbed circles collectively known as the *amala-sara* beneath a *kalasha* or pot-like finial surmounted by a *bijapuraka*, a slender form like a light-bulb. The interior is possibly the finest at Kumbharia, with fantastic corbelled ceilings alive with a myriad animals and anthropoid figures in an eternal dance.

Just to the northeast is the Shantinatha Temple of around 1082 dedicated to the 16th *tirthankar* whose emblem is the deer. Clearly modelled on the Mahavira Temple, and presumably created by the same guild of craftsmen to similar specifications, it nevertheless has its own appeal, with teaching *tirthankar*s arrested at the point of spreading the doctrines of nonviolence, nirvana, and *anekantavada* or non-absolutism. If you wish to discover more about these teachings, the *Jaina Sutras* translated from the Prakrit (2 vols.) by Hermann Jacobi appeared in the monumental *Sacred Books of the East* series (1884-95) and have been reprinted by Dover (New York, 1968) and in India by Motilal Banarsidass.

The southernmost temple (1105) is dedicated to Parshvanatha, the 23rd *tirthankar*, said by the Jains to have preceded Mahavira by 250 years, that is between 877 and 777 B.C. Though larger than the previous two at Kumbharia, the general plan is comparable, and the decoration continues the great Solanki tradition of exquisite proportions and fine attention to sculptural detail on doors, ceilings, lintels and columns.

The temple to the 22nd *tirthankar*, Neminatha, stands back from its three predecessors and has been dated to 1134, though much of the upper parts are restored. Like the Parshvanatha, it stems from the reign of Siddharaja Jayasimha, but its pillar ornamentation owes more to the Vimala Temple on Mount Abu. The northernmost temple, to the third *tirthankar*, Shambhavanatha, whose emblem is a horse, is dated 1231 and stands far removed from the Solanki style, belonging to the Chalukyan sequence, without subsidiary shrines.

Roda and Shamalaji

If you are taking the main road from Ahmedabad to Jaipur, try to make time for detours to Roda and Shamalaji, the latter being fairly close to the main road. Roda, more isolated and northeast of Himmatnagar has seven temples which constitute one of the earliest surviving Hindu religious complexes in Gujarat. One is demolished but for the plinth. Characteristically, they stress beautiful doorways and carved columns in the porch at the expense of plain sanctuaries. Some of the dark-green sculptures from Roda, like those from Shamalaji and other parts of the former Idar princely state (roughly the new Sabarkantha district) are to be found in the Baroda Museum and U.P. Shah's monograph on them is still in print.

The *shikharas* (pyramidiform temple towers) are reminiscent of Rajasthani temples at Osian and Badoli, and of such Gujarati temples as Ghumli. Their sculptures and ornamental features must be contemporary with similar elements in other temples in North India firmly attributed to a 7th-9th century date. Shah suggests that they are probably of late Maitraka date, the first half of the eighth century.

Shamalaji is a hilly site which will always have been sacred due to its delimitation on three sides by the river Meshvo, and indeed there are signs of a substantial ancient city. The present Vaishnavite shrine of Shamalaji dates from the late 15th century, but there are two major temples much earlier in date, probably around the 9th century: the Ranchhodaji and the Harishchandrani Chori, as well as two more mutilated shrines and abandoned temple platforms. The two Gupta-age bulls of the 6th century from Shamalaji's Shaivite temples have been moved for safe keeping: the finer to Prince of Wales Museum in Bombay, and the less beautiful to Baroda Museum. Other sculptures there come from Shamalaji's Trilokinatha temple, at the end of Khak Chowk, opposite the main shrine. An ancient Surya temple is situated north-east of Khak Chowk.

V: SAURASHTRA

Saurashtra is the belly of Gujarat, pregnant with historic cities, pilgrimage sites, ancient temples and sacred mountains. Indeed, anyone having to visit Gujarat very briefly might limit a sojourn to Saurashtra: Palitana with Shatrunjaya, Junagadh with Girnar, the lion sanctuary of Sasangir, and princely cities such as Jamnagar, Rajkot and Wankaner.

The overriding disadvantage of this plan is that it omits so much that is characteristic of Saurashtra, formerly known as the Kathiawar Peninsula, such as the desertic Rann of Kutch with its extraordinary herds of wild asses near Dasara, Halvad's waterside palace, Lothal's prehistoric town and the atmospheric Hindu pilgrimage centres of Somnath and Dwarka. It is like visiting Beijing and Shanghai, then pretending you have seen China for, as in China, the real people and landscapes are in the countryside.

Dasara
To explore the wildlife sanctuary of the Little Rann of Kutch, which has no exact boundaries and hence no proper delimitation or protection, one of the best places to stay is the village of Dasara, with a population 60% Hindu, 40% Muslim.

The Little Rann is a salt desert wilderness where the Asiatic Onager, or Indian Wild Ass, has its home, but you may also glimpse the Indian wolf, common or Indian fox, red or desert fox, desert cat, desert hare, chinkara gazelle and blue bull or *nilgai*. Among the most attractive birds are the rare *hubara* or Great Indian bustard, once hunted to virtual extinction but recovering now it's fully protected; the common and painted sandgrouse, the flamingo, Sarus Crane, pelican and gray francolin.

By car, Dasara can be reached in 1½ hours, and by hourly public bus in 2½ hours from Ahmedabad. By rail, you can take the Saurashtra Mail sleeper at 9 p.m from Bombay, arriving about 7 a.m. next day at Viramgam, from which around 15 buses daily link with Dasara. The Kutch Express leaves Ahmedabad at 2 a.m. reaching Viramgam at 3 a.m. The Saurashtra Express also out of Bombay leaves Ahmedabad at 9 p.m. and arrives Viramgam at 10.45 p.m.

I arrived late at night in Dasara, and found a room at the Government Resthouse for a few pence. Without light or adequate netting against mosquitoes and other prowlers, my room proved amply large, and the bed hard enough for me to lie luxuriously flat after the rigours of a boneshaking four-hour car journey from the north. I should have stayed by prior arrangement at Fatima Manzil, the home of the lord of the manor, Sarfraz

Malik, whose family once ruled the village of 7,000 inhabitants but is reduced now to the rôle of landlord and hotelier, tour guide and restaurateur, because of the late Indira Gandhi's move to end the Privy Purse by changing India's Constitution. Like most former princes, he has weathered the changes with a smile, ingenuity and hard work and provides three meals a day and accommodation in the many rooms in his small palace on request.

Sarfraz Malik's ancestors came originally from Iraq, stayed for some time in Multan (now Pakistan) and on their way to embark at Cambay for the Holy Places of Islam they camped by the lake at Dasara. For food they killed a blue bull sacred to the Hindus, so their leader was challenged to a duel. The Malik ancestor overcame the Hindu, and the Muslim king of Gujarat encouraged the Muslim pilgrims to settle in the area with their tribesfolk. While besieging Pavagadh, Mahmud Beghada enjoyed great loyalty from the Malik general and after subduing the fort above royal Champaner he gave the Maliks twenty-one villages in *jagir*, that is a hereditary assignment of land with its rents in perpetuity. Sarfraz himself had three brothers: a chemical engineer, an emigré now in California, and another, younger, who died of a heart attack. You could never imagine this slim, quickly-spoken, silent desert stalker relinquishing the Little Rann of Kutch permanently for the deserts of California. His beautiful eldest daughter Shamana attends Unkur School in Ahmedabad, his second daughter is in third-grade, and his third child is a son. Sarfraz himself studied at Rajkumar College in Rajkot. 'Grandmother rules the house', he whispered mischievously, 'and she has said she would like to meet the English writer. Please wait in the drawing-room until she has made herself pretty.' Grandmother had summoned Shamana back from the dangers of Ahmedabad, because of rioting and violence. Sarfraz shook his head over the recent communal disturbances. 'In Surat a Muslim father, mother and daughter were bound together with wire by a group of Hindu *goondas* who poured kerosene on them, then set them alight. Whenever two mobs face each other, the police fire bullets in the Muslim crowd, but against the Hindus they do only lathi charges or lob tear gas only.' We sat in the comfortable *majlis* which has rugs, carpets and pillows in the centre, but four easy chairs and three sofas around the walls in western style. A stuffed eagle, antelope horns and swords dot the walls, and a ceiling fan revolved lethargically, its arms flailing to push away the air which hangs heavy, and floats in warm gusts.

'Falconry is not legal in India', said Sarfraz, 'so I learned the skills in America, and practise it overseas whenever I can.' The windows were kept open, maximising the breeze but offering hospitality to mosquitoes, gnats and midges. 'I tire out a peregrine by keeping it awake all night. I show videos for only one rupee at night, and the villagers who come gladly keep the peregrine falcon awake. After the video, I show Star Plus satellite television and they stay here to watch the fitness exercises because

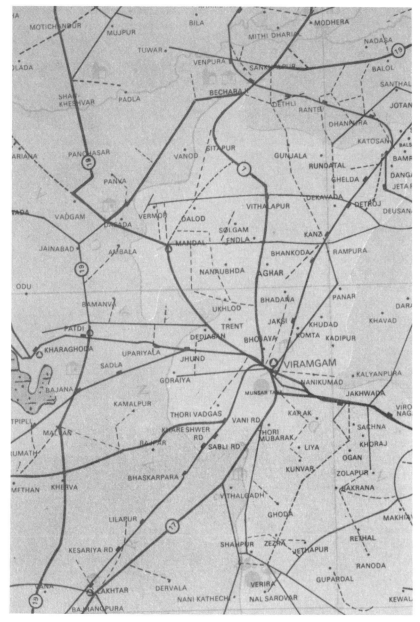

Map of North-Eastern Saurashtra

Western women wear bikinis, which these people never see, of course. The falcon is so accustomed to human company that, after it makes a kill, you can go right up to it without startling it.'

Next morning I took breakfast of bread and tea at the silent rest-house, in that expectant hour before dawn, when the desert shakes off its chill and begins to breathe deeply once more. A car came to take me to Fatima Manzil, where I saw the courtyard menagerie: hedgehogs and white mice, fantails and Indian field mice. Primary experiences like this – with the pink dawn expanding to gold and red – are the stuff of life in India: the rest of the year we read, plan and yearn for such moments so that when they arrive they strike us like bolts of bliss, Joycean epiphanies. Sarfraz drove me in his jeep from Dasara to Patdi, a walled city crumbling from neglect: the dirt road there is maintained by the district, while the highway to Ahmedabad is looked after by the State of Gujarat. Near the filling station, the tank at Patdi screeched and boomed with migrant snipe, locally migrant stint, avocet and bittern.

In eight km we came to India's salt capital, Kharagodha, accounting for 80% of national salt production. Common cranes flew in from the desert to feed in the fields until dusk, and flights of hundreds of pelicans whooshed overhead in V-formation, as if the three leaders had pulled six fishing lines splayed out behind them on which pelicans were regularly caught, equidistant. They were winging purposefully towards the village fish

Kharagodha. Bandstand and camel-drivers at dawn

142

farm owned by Ilyash Malik, who in desperation has to fire shotgun pellets (no rifles being allowed) from his muzzle-loader to deter these flying brigands. Kharagodha was a cantonment area, with British-style houses and shops where up to 1947 you could buy English chocolate. I even discovered a British red-tiled cricket pavilion with a boundary still marked in white and the signs PLAY WITH THE SPIRIT OF PLAY, EVER ONWARDS and FRIENDSHIP FRATERNITY FOR EVER. Camels munched philosophically among the bungalows and in the shade of the bandstand. Green Alexandrine parakeets swooped among the cottonfields. Women carried salt-baskets on their heads like caryatids on the Athenian Acropolis. Salt has been so vastly over-produced that prices have dipped to an almost suicidal level; one bag weighing a quintal (a tenth of a metric tonne) fetching Rs 25-27 in 1991 had two years later fallen to Rs 14, despite the fact that this crystalline land salt is far preferable to marine salt for bleaching, dyeing, leatherwork and food. Over the same period the price of cotton has fallen only marginally from about Rs 150 for a 20-kg bag in 1991 to Rs 140 in 1993.

We looked out for *nilgai* and wild asses sitting in the thornbushes for their cover before roaming to forage in the wheatfields on the edge of the desert but saw nothing but a marsh harrier rising from its roost in alarm. Then suddenly Sarfraz stopped the jeep, and beckoned me to get out and follow him. The official census notes 2,000 Asiatic Onagers but Sarfraz, who is in daily contact with the animals and those who look after them, estimates the total no higher than 1,000. This last surviving descendant of the wild horse was hunted virtually to extinction during pre-conservation days, though their flesh and hide is of no use, and compared with lion or tiger it makes a humble enough trophy. Disease struck herds early in the century until only a few hundred survived, and most of these gradually recovering stocks are confined to the salt flats of Gujarat, where they are increasingly threatened by the spread of human activity. The normal group comprises fifteen to twenty animals, mainly female, who follow the lead of a dominant male. He, shrewdly protective, can be relied upon to distract threats like our jeep by falling behind the herd and veering away at a distance, rejoining the group later when the danger is past. The bodies are pale to reddish-brown, but the neck and legs are usually white. The nervous scattering as they trot away is due to the herd's experience of jeep-driven hunters, but if one stalks them on foot it is possible to see them at close quarters. If you miss a sighting in Dasara, you can see onagers in captivity at Ahmedabad Zoo. A group of eight *nilgai* grazed in the distance as we stopped for a quick breakfast of bread, hardboiled eggs, tea from a flask, oranges and apples. A kestrel swooped past, and a Sarus crane skimmed overhead. I found a dead monitor lizard (*varanus bengalensis*), locally known as *gho*, which is mashed and eaten by local tribespeople. The spiny-tailed lizard or *sandha* in Gujarati is not quite so common.

143

Dasada. Sarfraz Malik with a monitor lizard

South from Kharagodha lies Bajana, with a creek that runs with water most of the year offering a migratory home to fleets of pink flamingo and diving, rummaging pelican. Cranes came in like gracious angels, while spoonbills raked through the water in search of food, amid the sandpipers and the faithful male ruff and smaller female reeve (*Philomachus pugnax*). Ruffs ready to mate capture a few square inches of ground and threaten others with tilts and leaps until their macho behaviour attracts the reeves

144

to visit their chosen male for mating. Shovellers and pintails jostled for territory and food.

The road north from Bajuna to Patdi continues to Zainabad, where a desert camp run by Desert Coursers comprises a sequence of small self-contained huts ideal as a base for exploring the Little Rann.

Jhinjhuwada

Westward, on the Rann's fringe, lies the extraordinary walled city of Jhinjhuwada ('Zinzuwada' on the map) but as always the journey gave us unimagined excitement, from a female kestrel wafting on the current above us to a jackal ambling across the road, an astonished sandgrouse, or desert wheatears zipping up at the jeep's approach then dropping back into anonymous thornbush. The danger to tyres across the cracked and parched desert is not the jagged earth, which crumbles undertyre like salt in pinched fingers, but the tearing, pricking thorns on bushes, some of which seem to crouch low as if in ambush.

We flush out larks, as you might back home in Candleford, but also majestic bustard, native to this thick shrub country where cover can be found throughout the long, panting day. Jhinjhuwada ('wada' means enclosure) has four stunning stone gates, as at Dabhoi far to the east, and these too date back to the 12th century. Much of the walls are derelict, and even the gateways seem to slip ever faster into the anguish of oblivion, so take the next chance you have to note in your travel diary the name of Jhinjhuwada, with its British houses and its customs line faithfully brushed by

Jhinjhuwada. City wall and bastion

145

peons every day so that smugglers could be identified, tracked and prosecuted. Nowadays sacred cows wander along the sandy tracks, infants point open-mouthed at strangers. Around the outstanding 12th-century *vav*, crows settle like village elders at their irritable deliberations. Jhinjhuwada, once a princely outpost, has become a forgotten oasis recognisable by readers of Dino Buzzati's classic *Deserto dei Tartari*. What if the Tartars came in the night, passed, and never noticed us? What if we *were* the Tartars?

Shankeshwar

North from Dasara on the state highway 18 towards Sami and Radhanpur (where you should stop for the Nawab's Palace), I stopped at Shankeshwar, a famous old Jain pilgrimage site, where frantic building activities show that plenty of pious cash is still being raised, though the ancient temple has long since completely disappeared. A fine Jain temple of 1811-12 replaces a temple said to have been demolished in the 18th century, but the image of the main *tirthankar* Parshvanatha in the new temple is dated Samvat 1666, corresponding to 1609-10, while the cell inscriptions I found are dated Samvat 1656-86, or A.D. 1596-1630. The cell-shrines are built of brick, like the temple of Sarotra, and their bricks are moulded and not cut to shape; even the small brackets are of brick, though disguised by a coating of fine plaster.

I was invited into the main shrine, where worshippers with fly-whisks chanted towards a cross-legged image across a silver-covered altar cum cash-box. I gazed up at the intricately carved circular ceiling and dreamed in a wisp of incense provoking anticipation of eternity. Again, as in most of Saurashtra, I was the only foreign visitor. The usual frenzy of chipping and smoothing, carving and cleaning that characterises all Jain temples made concentration difficult outside the main shrine. One of the most pious deeds that any Jain can perform is to contribute towards temple-building, and this provides generations of *sompuras*, the guild of temple craftsmen, with skilled work. I spoke to one *sompura*, Rabindra Kumar Lalshankar, who had been employed continuously at Shankeshwar for the past eight years and expects to remain here until he chooses to leave. As a Hindu by religion, Brahmin by caste, Rabindra finds no theological difficulty in creating Jain buildings. 'The Jains say that the foetus of their *tirthankar* Mahavira was born at first in the womb of a Brahmin lady but the gods wanted him born among the Kshatriya caste, so his foetus was moved to the womb of Trisala. If he was a Brahmin, why should I not glorify his temples? If he was a Kshatriya, that too is Hindu, no? These Jains, they are just part of our great Hindu community, just like Buddhists and all. These gurus, all, like Swami Brahmachari, like Swami Satchidananda, they are all Hindus. Whether we see one cloud or another, it is all the same sky.'

Shankeshwar. Jain Temple with image of Parshwanatha

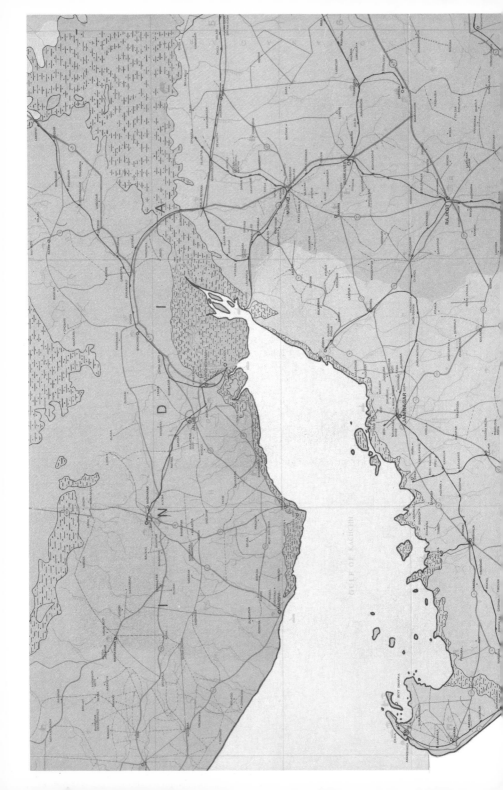

Map of Western Saurashtra

Halvad and Morvi

Exploring the belly of Saurashtra is a matter of multiple choice. From Dasara you can reach Rajkot via Saurashtra, but I wanted to reach Wankaner via Halvad and Morvi, touching Dhrangadhra, another of those small princely feudal states that characterise the uniqueness of Saurashtra. His Highness Maharana Sriraj Meghrajji III, born in 1923, assumed the government of Jhalawar state in 1943 and was educated at Haileybury, St. Joseph's Academy at Dehra Dun and Shivaji Military School at Pune. He spent 1952-8 at Christ Church Oxford, and has taken a prominent part in Indian public life, including service as M.P. for Jhalawar from 1967. He resides at Ajit Niwas Palace in Dhrangadhra, with other homes in Pune and New Delhi, and he continues to act as President of Rajkumar College, Rajkot.

His Highness, called Mayurdhvasinhji, is also the ruler of Halvad (some might say 'former ruler' but these titles are used even today). The Wild Ass sanctuary of 4950 square km which we have explored from Dasara can also be explored from the Government Circuit House or Rest House in Dhrangadhra (best time October to March), or from the rest house in Halvad, where you can arrive by train.

Halvad's dilapidated 17th-century lake palace may be visited by appointment, which is more readily obtained from the Wankaner Palace if you are coming from the south. Give the chowkidar Rs 10 and he will show you the magnificent wooden carvings, the *pallias* or funeral stones and the *chhatris* or mauseola.

Morvi is an enchanting little town on the river Machhu which the road follows from Mali Miyana on the edge of the Little Rann down to its bifurcation at Wankaner. The state of Morvi was one of the 230-odd small feudal states of Saurashtra in a complex condition of peace, war and suspended animation. The British tried to crystallise the molten materials in 1807, solidifying 220 or more, though some of these were barely half a square mile in area. Morvi at last enjoyed stability under its enlightened ruler Thakur Sahib Waghaji (1879-1948), who commissioned two totally different palaces, each irresistible in its own right. Mani Mandir (1880-2), approached across a witty suspension bridge, takes inspiration from European Gothic, Venetian palaces, Rajput arches, Islamic domes and classical columns. The ensemble should be indigestible, but the effect is dazzling, and virtually unrepeatable one would imagine, if one had not seen similar *stravaganze* at Wankaner or Jamnagar. And then you find the Art Deco New Palace (1931-44), which outclasses Miami Beach's Art Deco district despite its modest height of two storeys and its rather odd local granite facing. If you are lucky enough to be granted access to its six dining-rooms and six drawing-rooms, beg to be shown the fourteen bedrooms, one of which can be reached by a lift: you enter Neptune's realm (a bathroom covered in seashells) and a subterranean or even subaqueous bedroom with mural conducive to amour.

Morvi (also spelt Morbi) has a Museum of Dramatic Art founded in

1965 and open daily except Sundays and government holidays from 9-12 and 3-6; it specialises in manuscripts and texts of drama in all languages and all periods.

Wander round the many clockmakers of Morvi, the potters, the Green Market, and find the town gates and quaint tower.

Wankaner

Wankaner's population these days fluctuates around 40,000. At the heart of town stands the modest former Royal Palace of three storeys, opposite the

Wankaner. Gateway into the city

Wankaner. Old City Palace

courthouse. Next to the Palace, Nirmala Convent School opened in 1992; on the other side flows the river Machhu. The Playhouse Cinema on the right of the gateway is a royal initiative.

Call me an old softie, as Dame Edna Everage might, or a capitalist feudal running-dog, as Lenin might have, but I found the hilltop Royal Palace stupendous in its almost tangible nostalgia, less of a whiff, more a typhoon of it. Once beyond the gate bearing the motto IN GOD IS MY TRUST, a Tuscan church with a rose-window turns out to be a garage for the 1921 Silver Ghost, a Rolls Royce raised by jacks to protect its antique tyres. Its number-plate, white lettered on a red background, reads simply WANKANER-1. Antique-car connoisseurs will salivate at the sight of a 1931 Buick (WANKANER-10), a 1941 Ford Mercury Eight (GJY 3903), a 1948 Ford Super De Luxe (GJY 3907), a 1948 Buick Eight (GJY 3908), and a 1951 Ford Custom (GJY 8128), supplemented by a fleet of Mahindra Jeeps and Ambassadors. A driver-mechanic parped a horn at me encouragingly, hoping for an outing, but I shook my head. 'Do they all still run?' He nodded with the vigour of a servant out to make the best possible impression, somewhat negating his enthusiasm by adding 'You can't get the parts, you know'.

I was offered a sumptuous breakfast by His Highness the Crown Prince Digvijaysinh, who tucked into scrambled eggs and toast while we chatted in the great dining-room adorned with tiger trophies on the wall dated 1965 Burhanpur and 1969 Mandla. Digvijaysinhji was a member of Parliament for ten years, and Deputy Minister of the Environment and Ecology during Indira Gandhi's time. Like his father, he graduated from Clare College, Cambridge. The Crown Prince is violently opposed to transforming royal palaces into hotels. 'It is important to make the distinction that we take paying guests: five rooms in the guest-house and twelve in the other quarters by the swimming-pool, but that we live in our own palace and invite our guests for meals. We benefit from the income, and the guests benefit from spending time in these beautiful surroundings, safeguarding our heritage. Let me tell you about it. Princely India accounted for 30% of India's population and 40% of the surface area, but in Gujarat the figures were quite different: here princely India comprised 65% of the population and 80% of the area. The United States of Saurashtra had their capital at Rajkot, and the Union Territory of Kutch was an independent 'Part B' state. After 1971, privy purses were abolished because of Indira Gandhi's constitutional changes and a recent court case to restore our rights was rejected by the Supreme Court. This was unjust and had a number of catastrophic effects which I shall itemise. One, we lost our revenues. Two, the existing long-term Rajput primogeniture system lost its importance, leading to interminable and bitter family disputes. Three, if you had no male heir, you could previously adopt a Jhala Rajput as a son but after 1971 six lines of the forty salute states became extinct in the absence of a male heir. Four, emigration arose with the deprivation of rights here, so that Porbandar for example left for London to become a lawyer. Very few princely families can now afford to maintain their palaces properly; few are not in dispute; few have not sold or converted their properties; few have a genuine interest in living there and protecting their heritage. We have nothing like your remarkable National Trust or invaluable English Heritage. We Jhalas are one of the 36 major Rajput clans; we governed five salute and five non-salute states in northern Saurashtra. Our forefathers established themselves first in Patdi, then in 1487 the capital of the Jhalas moved to Halvad. In 1605 the two Jhala brothers fought: one took Dhrangadhra and the other, Sartanji, came to Wankaner. He was killed in battle, after which his wife committed *sati* in the heroic Rajput manner and their joint monument can be seen in the town centre. Eventually, in 1917, the feud was settled by the Ruler of Porbandar, who set the two men together on the beach and told them to make up their quarrel before they left the beach: a summary, sensible and oddly impressive way to make peace among rivals. At that time the best princely state for simplicity, efficiency and progress was Gondal. The Ruler had absolutely no sense of humour, so he spent all his money on his people: schools, sewerage, hospitals, roads, he had no sense of fun at all.'

'My greatgrandfather Banesinhji ruled from 1861-81 from the old palace in the middle of the town, where we had ruled for 13 generations. Gandhiji's father worked for him from 1878-80, and Mohandas lived here for some time as a child. When Banesinhji died, my grandfather was only 3 years old, so by the Walker Settlement of 1807, an heir under 20 would be substituted by a British administrator called a Resident: five such men effectively controlled Wankaner between 1881 and 1899. The Residency was the right wing of the palace built in 1882; the left wing dates from 1895. My grandfather's then Resident, Colonel Hancock, took him to England in the summer of 1898, and three years later my grandfather became Maharaja. I am now going to develop the old Residency wing into a colonial-style guesthouse with furnishings of the period for the eight bedrooms and two public rooms: old Burma teak, four-poster beds, you know, that style of thing, planters' chairs. The estate will be transformed into a nature reserve called Sylvan Valley, and replenished with original flora, instead of these thousands of terrible thornbushes brought here from Africa. We have checklists of flora compiled in 1839 and 1867 and we are combing Saurashtra to bring back grasses, shrubs and trees before we reintroduce herbivorous fauna: gazelle, deer, and antelope. The Kathiawari breed of horses, recognised as recently as 1970, will be bred here.'

Yuviraj Digvijaysinhji took me on a tour of the first floor, from which his grandfather ruled Wankaner State for 49 years, from 1899 to 1948, with a view of a third of the whole principality visible from his bathroom window. A hundred species of hunting trophies fill the walls and floors: as rich a collection as I saw anywhere in India. Down a spiral staircase we came to the silent treasury, much as Howard Carter would have encountered at last the Tomb of Tutankhamun, not so dusty, not so newsworthy, but still an astonishing revelation; pigsticking spears, a linen chest called *majus* in Gujarati, caparisons for horses and elephants, three English swords presented at the Delhi Darbar, duelling pistols made by E.M. Reilly, thrones for the Ruler and princes, silver-plated howdahs, silver made

Wankaner. Royal Palace

at Wankaner but not, the Crown Prince conceded, as fine as Kutchi silver from Bhuj, the royal ensign, emblem, standards, a throne from Banaras, a *pichchwai* from Nathdwara (Rajasthan), and a memorable array of Indian swords and daggers. At the foot of the steps a striped palm squirrel lay lifeless, a victim of suffocation: it had found its way in but then the door had shut...

We drove down from the hilltop palace to the guesthouse below, with its Art Deco swimming pool and enclosed step-well where music could be played over the sound of plashing fountains on hot dry summer nights.

Tarnetar

Just as you will head for Pushkar in Rajasthan at the time of the great annual fair in mid-November, so if in Gujarat around mid-September you will time your arrival at Tarnetar, near Wankaner, for the three days corresponding to 4-6 Bhadrapad Sud, the first half of the eleventh month of the Hindu calendar. You can stay in tented accommodation organised by the Tourist Corporation of Gujarat, who will arrange a one-day, two-day or three-day package from Ahmedabad (HK House, off Ashram Road, tel. 449683 or 449172). To get there by train, take the line from Bombay to Baroda, Ahmedabad, Viramgam and Surendranagar for Wankaner, alighting half an hour before Wankaner at Than, which is only 9 km from Tarnetar. The nearest airport to Tarnetar is Rajkot (76 km).

'Tarnetar' is the local formed of 'trinetra', 'three-eyed', referring to Lord Shiva, but the modern Trinetreshwar Temple was built by Rao Lakhpat Karansinhji as recently as 1902, on the site of much earlier shrines.

Legend says that Arjuna killed a swimming fish with bow and arrow here, judging by its refraction in the water, and thus won the hand of Princess Draupadi. Ever since, Hindu girls may select their own future husbands at Tarnetar in a so-called *swayamvar* ceremony. Young men preening themselves to await choice sit under embroidered umbrellas and wear attractive embroidered jackets (as peacocks might fan out their tails).

The fair opens when pilgrims take a dip or *papnashu* (sinwashing) in the kund or reservoir, equivalent so they say to a dip in the Ganges itself. Sadhus and rishis pass among the visitors. The usually deserted area quickly fills with fairground stalls and attractions: big wheels and merry-go-rounds. Folk dances and songs can be seen and heard at some locations; at others, *bhavai* groups perform the traditional dance-music-dramas of Saurashtra. Maidens approach boys of their choice and then retire, for the families to arrange marriage if suitable at a later date. Every *adivasi* girl dresses in her brightest sari to show off her beauty, talking and laughing loudly, and flashing her eyes, flaunting her gold-ringed hands and flicking her shawl across her face, provocatively sensual.

Rajkot

Rajkot was founded in the 16th century by the Rajput chief Kanwar Vib-huji, and Jadeja Rajputs ruled the small city until it merged with the Union of Saurashtra after Independence. Gandhi spent some of his early years here, and his father's home has become a permanent Gandhi Memorial (ask for Kaba Gandhino Delo). Rajkot is linked by rail and bus to Gir, Bhavnagar, Porbandar, Veraval, Junagadh, Ahmedabad and Baroda. The airport serves Bombay.

Rajkot is world-famous for its Rajkumar College, an Indian equivalent of Harrow School in status, with a town-centre position similar to that of Sherborne School. Founded in 1868 by the Rulers of Kathiawar (now Saurashtra), the first of the former Chiefs' Colleges was the first to become a public school, in 1938. If it just lacks the cachet of the 'Eton of India', Ajmer's Mayo College (founded in 1875), Rajkumar College can nevertheless claim to have educated hundreds of the royal and aristocratic sons of Bharat. Founded by Col. R.H. Keatinge, V.C., it has enjoyed a succession of notable headmasters, but is now headed by a very experienced Parsi lady, Ratanbai Framroz Cooper, who has been at the school for 35 years. She spoke to me in her soft, measured, cultured English in her office crowded with papers, books and memorabilia of the school and its old boys. The first term runs from July to October (depending on Diwali's occurrence); after a six-week vacation, the second term runs to April. The aims of the College are to 'combine emphasis on academic and intellectual development with the personal and physical development of its students and to foster abilities and qualities along with the cultural background and to develop a sense of service and civic concern to enable pupils to give of their best as citizens to their motherland.' I caught a sense of zeal for learning and dedication to the all-round burgeoning of a complete human being lacking in the west where standards are notoriously slipping in curriculum and behaviour. I was impressed to learn that anyone earning fewer than 40% of exam marks would have his name put up on a notice-board: a powerful incentive to do well. The ratio of staff to boys is 84:700; 46 of the staff are teachers. The age-range of pupils is 7-17; they should be fluent in speaking English after one, and in writing English after two terms. Most boys are boarders, and they come from all over the world. They begin Hindi at eight, and at 10 or 11 choose between Gujarati (the regional language) and Sanskrit (the classical language). At the moment no second European language is available, though anyone who wishes to do French can visit the Belgian nuns. 'Finding staff of the right calibre is our biggest headache', confessed Miss Cooper, 'their salary is the same as government salaries, and when they do come they to tend to stay all their careers long, but of course our standards of syllabus, discipline and general involvement with the work of the school is much more demanding than teachers find in other Indian schools.' No corporal punishment of any kind is permitted, but high levels of good behaviour persist.

The gardens are palatial, and the quadrangle distinctly majestic, with an impressive statue to J.W. Coryton Mayne, M.A., C.I.E., Principal from 1903 to 1923. Mayne looks more like a general than a headmaster, and well he might, for many of his pupils would a play a key part in India's armed forces, as well as Parliament, the civil service, and all the professions. It is fashionable in England to pour scorn on public schools, their elitist image, and the discrepancy between their vision and the often disappointing realities. The argument is that the top echelon of society is self-serving, and should be weakened, if not abolished. But the collapse of communism has shown that a headless proletariat cannot produce wealth, security, fairness or even equality: corrupt bosses will emerge. So one message is that there should always remain a place of top-quality education for the wealthy, brilliant, and gifted, and parental income is not the only criterion for admission at Rajkumar: the College accepts Government of India merit scholars and Indian Public Schools' Conference Trust merit scholars, as well as its own merit-cum-income-based part-scholarships. It recognises that in a united India of many languages other than Hindi, English must always remain the language of instruction, however that might disappoint linguistic nationalists.

On leaving Rajkumar College, every boy is handed a card bearing on the front 'Happiness & Success in the life before you' and within it the full text of Rudyard Kipling's 'If–':...

'If you can meet with Triumph and Disaster
And treat those two impostors just the same ...

'Yours is the Earth and everything that's in it,
And – which is more – you'll be a Man, my son!'

On entering the school, the boy receives a similar card, with the Sanskrit text from the opening invocation in the Katha Upanishad, 'it' denoting the cosmic power of being, and the three *shantih*s comprising internal, surrounding and universal peace:

Om! Saha navavatu!	*Om! May it move us together!*
Saha nau bhunaktu!	*May it possess us together!*
Saha viryam karavavahai!	*May we achieve greatness together!*
Tejasvi navadhitamastu!	*May our intellects shine together!*
Ma vidvisavahai!	*May we never clash together!*
Om! Shantih! Shantih! Shantih!	*Om! Peace! Peace! Peace!*

The word *aum*, commonly transliterated *om*, is stated in the Upanishads, where it apparently originates in textual form, to possess a mystic or cosmic power and to merit long meditation. Later on, scholars assigned the letter *a* to Vishnu, *u* to Shiva and *m* to Brahma to indicate the monosyllable's meaning as a unification of the Hindu divine trinity, but this has no

Vedic authority. The last line has entered the permanent treasury of English literature by its inclusion in T.S. Eliot's *The Waste Land*. As Ezra Pound wrote to Eliot in a letter on Christmas Eve 1921, 'The POEM ends with the Shantih, shantih, shantih', and there is no grander homage that can be paid to the nobility of Sanskrit.

Wandering around Rajkumar College's 25-acre estate in the centre of Rajkot is an extraordinary experience, not unlike exploring Harvard's campus in Boston for variety, colour and vivacity, were it not for the spirited laughter of young lads visible through open windows in freshly laundered white shirts and the polite greetings, 'Good afternoon, Sir!' that take you back to the era of Mr Chips. The Assembly Hall, shiny brown, was given by the Queen Mother of Jamnagar: that is presumably why a portrait of Ranjitsinji the immortal cricketer is flanked by those of George V and Queen Mary, an unlikely alliance but one that seems natural in Rajkot.

Rajkot is flat as a pancake, consequently ideal for walking, cycling or auto-rickshaws. The people seem quieter than elsewhere, the roads wider, the traffic less demented. A genial Sikh cashier in the Havmor restaurant confirmed this impression: 'Everywhere is peaceful in this town. I don't want to go back to Punjab.' Opposite the Havmor, the former Alfred High School (1875) has been renamed for its most prestigious pupil, one Mohandas Karamchand Gandhi, Father of the Nation, no less.

Next to the flamboyant Jubilee Gardens I found an Islamic cemetery; on the way in I drank refreshing sugar-cane juice from a vendor grinding cane through an iron mangle. Boys with kites left over from the spring celebrations scurried along walls and paths like shrieking squirrels.

The Lang Library established in 1856 is a great decaying stone barn open only 9-10.50 and 5-6.50, with English-language books bound in a uniform red: Erle Stanley Gardner, Harold Robbins, Donne and Shakespeare, but everyone without exception (including the staff) was reading the day's Gujarati newspapers. An attendant refused permission for me to take a photograph of the spiderwebbed building, which could have been used for the set of a Hammer horror movie with Vincent Price, and would have certainly inspired another set of etchings from Piranesi to equal his *Carceri*. A plaque commemorated 'Lt. Harry Laurence Gordon of 2nd Bombay Lancers, Duffedar Mahomad Shakir and Naik Naji Sajan of Kathiawar Agency Police killed while attacking dacoits in Malia 19.12.92', that is of course 1892.

Farther along Jawahar Road we come to the main reason for visiting Rajkot: the Watson Museum, named for Col. John W. Watson, Political Agent of Kathiawar (as Saurashtra was known up to 1947) from 1886-1893.

Conveying the flavour of that time is a grandiose and virtually immovable monument to Queen Victoria (1899) by Alfred Gilbert, the sculptor responsible for Eros (properly Anteros) in Piccadilly Circus. Solemn loyal

Rajkot. Watson Museum

portraits surround her: from left to right, an unnamed officer, Lord Harris (Governor of Bombay), His Highness Mahabat Khanji II, Nawab Saheb of Junagadh, and H.R.H. the Duke of Clarence and Avondale, who visited Kathiawar in 1890. The centre of the ground floor is a celebration in good portraits of the Rulers of Kathiawar, with captions in both English and Gujarati (though the museum's guidebook is out of print in both languages with no prospects of a reprint). Opening hours are 9-12.30 and 2.30-6 daily except Wednesdays, holidays, and the 2nd and 4th Saturdays of each month. Harappan relics from around 2,000 B.C. have been unearthed over many stretches of Gujarat, not only in the best-recorded locality, Lothal, but also at Deshalpur, Rojdi, Rangpur, and at Prabhas Patan. If we ask what features of life are common to the Aryans who came to develop the great Indus Civilisation of Mohenjo Daro and Harappa (in modern Pakistan) and the linked Lothal in India on the one hand, and the later civilisations on the same land mass, we could point to the worship of the mother-goddess, the three-faced deity, the lingam and yoni as male-female symbols, and the swastika; the use of stone or rough pottery for vessels, the use of bangles, nose ornaments, ivory combs, and kohl for the eyes.

If you have just come from Jhinjhuwada you will enjoy finding objects rescued from that deserted site: a Dig-Palika or protectress, Shiva, Indrani, Kalabhairav and a Maheshwari of the early 12th century. Other highlights

159

include a marble Vishnu from Siddhapur and a Jain *tirthankar* in white marble from Dharmdev. We shall see Ghumli beyond Jamnagar, so the Ghumli columns at the Watson dated 900-1300 are of great interest. Look for fine MSS and book covers of the 15th-16th centuries, particularly the Jain examples like those at the Indology Museum in Ahmedabad; and 18th-century miniatures, the most exquisite being a delicate group of singing worshippers in the Mughal style. Rare inscriptions on copper and textiles are outclassed by a series of fine bronzes, including a Rajput-style attendant used as a lamp-holder. The upper floor should be explored for dioramas of life among the tribals: Ahirs, Mehrs and Rabaris, with embroidery, silver betel boxes, musical instruments and woodcarvings. To acquire or just investigate contemporary handicrafts in Rajkot, see the State Handicrafts Development Corporation shop called Manjul at 4 Sardarnagar (West). The National School of Weaving would be happy to show you around: ask for Rashtriya Shala Educational Institute (Gandhiji's primary school), where *patola* and other weaves are being systematically revived. Rajkot has become an industrial city since Independence, with a ring road to ease traffic congestion. The river Aji runs through the town, and the Kaisar-i Hind bridge of 1910, designed by the influential and prolific R.B. Booth, was financed by the then Ruler of Bhavnagar.

A pleasant picnic spot can be found about five km from Rajkot, at Lal Pari Lake, and another by the Aji Dam, 10 km out of the town. For a nature education sanctuary, you can visit the 7 sq. km Hingolgadh Reserve, hill country that once provided the local royal family with game. Nilgai, spotted deer and gazelle are protected here, and you might see jackal, jungle cats and hares in the gentle hillscapes; down by the marshes a twitcher could see many waders, ibis and crane. You can stay in the forest castle for Rs 1000-1500 per person, including all meals, guides and transfers from Rajkot airport or station. However, if you have limited time in Gujarat, you should select Sasan Gir as the premier sanctuary.

Jamnagar

For me, highlights of Saurashtra were Shatrunjaya above Palitana, Girnar above Junagadh, the Sasangir Lion Reserve, but perhaps above all the astonishment of Jamnagar, for nothing in the travel yarns I had so assiduously studied prepared me for the flood of revelations in this marvellous city, from the cricket picture-gallery to the stunning lake city, from the complex Jain community studied with enthusiastic sympathy by Martin Banks in his excellent *Organizing Jainism* to the magnificent stonecarving on the historic City Palace, from the Sir Peter Scott Nature Reserve to the imposing Willingdon Crescent.

It is said that one of Krishna's sons mocked the sage Vishwamitra, who cursed the whole of the Yadava race to which Krishna belonged. When the Yadava nobles reached Prabhas Patan they got drunk and killed each other, except that the mortally wounded Krishna was rescued by a

Jamnagar. Old City Palace

heavenly chariot, and a tidal wave covered their home, Dwarka. Bardic chronicles tell how Krishna's grandson Anirudha escaped the slaughter, returned to Dwarka, built the original temple to Krishna there, and emigrated to Sind. Overthrown by the Arab invasion of Sind, the Yadavas nevertheless reasserted their control when Arab defences weakened, and spread their authority to Kutch, where their leader at one time was Jadoji, a Rajput who gave his name to the whole Jadeja branch. Jam Rawal of the Jadejas left Kutch for Kathiawar in 1535 and in 1540 established his line at Jamnagar. He called his city on the rivers Rangmati and Nagmati 'Nawanagar', 'New Town', a name no longer commonly used. The second ruler was Jam Rawal's second son Vibhaji (1562-9) and the third Jam Vibhaji's eldest son Sataji (1569-1608) during whose rule the Mughals invaded Gujarat. Threatened by the Mughal Viceroy, Amin Khan Ghori of Junagadh wrote an appeal to Jam Sataji:

> "High Prince, the common danger we must face:
> Close on my fall will follow your disgrace"

Sataji sent his wazir, Jaso Ladak, with thirty thousand men, and together, Junagadh and Nawanagar repulsed the Mughal advance. Rival members of the dynasty disputed their claims to rule until the accession of Jam Ranmalji, an adopted son of Jam Jasoji's widow, son of the Jadeja lord

161

of Sarodar. The monsoon failed in 1834, 1839 and 1846, and Jam Ranmalji established works such as the Jamsarovar Lake and the Lakhota Palace to look after his people, to make sure they had enough to eat and drink. He was followed in 1852 by Jam Vibhaji, who opened schools, hospitals, and the railway line to Rajkot.

Vibhaji's son Kalubha grew up to become a savage and violent youth and was exiled from the state and barred from succession in 1877; his second son Jaswantsinhji was born in 1882, a matter of a few months after he had begun his adoption of Ranjitsinhji, but left it incomplete. The British tried to influence Vibhaji in favour of Ranjitsinhji, a promising lad, as opposed to an infant who would be brought up in the *zenana* like Kalubha, but Vibhaji was not to be moved, and agreed only that Ranji, to become the greatest cricketer that India has ever seen, should be given an allowance, educated at Rajkumar College under the care of the Resident, and given a village (Khilos, near Rajkot). Macnaghten, Principal of Rajkumar, took Ranji to Cambridge University, sailing in 1888, and the rest is history, yellowing in the pages of *Wisden* perhaps, but brought vividly to life in Simon Wilde's authoritative *Ranji: a genius rich and strange* (1990).

Ranjitsinhji, ('Victorious Lion'), in 1899 became the first batsman ever to score 3,000 runs in a single season. On a single day in a single match he scored two double centuries against Yorkshire. Not only did he reap a valuable harvest of runs for Sussex and England, but his nephew Duleepsinhji also represented England.

To the Lion's regret, Jaswantsinhji was enthroned as Jam Sahib in 1903 but died of typhoid without a male heir three years later and Ranji was finally installed in 1907. He found Jamnagar dirty, indebted, poor, corrupt, and virtually without commercial contacts with the outside world. He replaced filthy slums with modern housing, instituted drains and a new city dispensary near the mosque, electrified the town in the 1920s, and provided free primary education from 1911 and free secondary education from 1916. Pariah dogs roamed free because the large Jain population absolutely refused to take any form of life, even that of a rabid dog. The Jam simply told the Jains that if the dogs were removed by a certain date he would refrain from shooting them. Within a matter of days every ownerless dog had disappeared off the streets and to this day they have not reappeared. He built Bedi harbour and the vital railway to Okhamandal via Dwarka, with financial support from Baroda. He also built the charming Kileshwar palace as a summer retreat in the Barda Hills. Without a son, Ranji adopted as heir his nephew Digvijaysinhji, the last ruling prince of Jamnagar and father of the present Jam.

'My father Digvijaysinhji was India's delegate to the Imperial War Conference. In 1942 a Polish ship escaped from German invasion with 1200 children and 20 women on board. The Government of Bombay would not let them land but only gave them fuel, food and water. When they reached our coast, my father sailed out from Bedi port to take off the children, put

162

them in tents, and in six months he had built a Polish camp at Balachari, at a personal cost of 10 lakhs, and maintained the camp until the end of the war.

A few years ago the Vice-President of Poland paid a special courtesy visit to the Balachari area, now a beach resort with a golf course, to thank the Jam Sahib for his father's generosity of spirit which protected so many Polish women and children during the darkest period of the War. The Balachari Palace is now a military school. In 1948, Digvijaysinhji became Rajpramukh or Prince President of Saurashtra until the area was absorbed into first Bombay State (1956) and then Gujarat (1960).

Shatrushalyasinhji succeeded to the title of Jam Sahib of Nawanagar in 1966, and has inherited all the vigour, enthusiasm and capacity for hard work of his eminent predecessor. When I called on him at his palace Pratap Vilas (motto: Nil Desperandum), a caretaker pointed round to the back, and a passer-by showed me the modest bungalow where he lives and works today. Pratap Vilas has a garden overgrown and untended, echoing to the scream of peacocks, but the Jam Singh's view from his bungalow is one of the best in the town, even though the last monsoon caused extensive damage to the palace by cyclonic storms.

Pratap Vilas was started in 1907 and finished in 1915 in a flamboyant Italianate marble and orientalising vein, with Belgian tiles and Austrian heat-resistant glass.

Jamnagar. Pratap Vilas

163

In the palace, Jam Sahib showed me the Picture Gallery with an Edward Burne-Jones (two others having been sold), a double portrait of W.G. Grace and Ranji, English landscapes by Stuart Lloyd, and a storm-damaged 'Parable of the Sower' by E. Long. A spectacular view down reveals the Darbar Hall, where no darbar was ever actually held: it was used mainly as a badminton court, ballroom for dances and banqueting hall. When the boys of Hurstpierpoint School come to play cricket the boys are entertained here.

The zenana wing of the royal palace was used until 1966, when Jam Sahib's mother moved to Bombay.

In 1968 Jam Singh began to modify his palace grounds into a nature park, and live specimens were acquired, such as blue bulls, blackbuck, monitor lizards, wild hares, antelope, partridge and porcupines. Between 1968 and 1972 he spent Rs 3 million on the nature park but when the Privy Purse was unconstitutionally withdrawn at the instigation of Indira Gandhi, the project had to be abandoned, so the public are at present not allowed in, because the facilities are not complete. Jam Singh drove me through his reserve, and I saw at close quarters some of the 22 *nilgai* bulls and 35 cows currently resident. Only the herd bull covers a female and the normal litter is one or two. Snake-catchers come to remove snakes back over the walls, but they return into the sanctuary. Crocodiles have been rescued from drought, and the West African species of Crowned Crane is being bred here. Only a small effort by central or state government would bring the project to fruition, and gifts or pledges should be directed to: The Sir Peter Scott Institute for Nature, Jamnagar. The aims are to complete the zoological and botanical park in the existing 3 million square feet of palace grounds; to create a breeding facility for endangered species on Rozi Island for the Great Indian Bustard and the pangolin. Ajar Island should become a bird sanctuary, with wardens to monitor the sandbanks northwest of Ajar used by turtles for egglaying.

The centre of Jamnagar could be considered the small circular fort of Lakhota on the island in the middle of Ranmal lake. You reach the fort along a causeway protected by the Bhirbhunjan Gate, outside which is a temple commissioned by one of the wives of Jam Vibhaji by whom the immortal cricketer Ranjitsinghji was adopted. You emerge into the fort by steps through a guardroom hung with swords, powder-flasks and muskets. A large circular platform is surrounded by a wall whose interior forms a colonnade and whose double loopholes for muskets and embrasures for guns display the state's martial readiness. The outer edge of the Lakhota has a higher structure used since 1946 as a museum, open 9-12 and 3-6 daily except for Wednesdays and government holidays, with sections devoted to painting, rather better sculptures, folk art, natural history, and coins. Before guesthouses existed in Jamnagar, political officers and state visitors overnighted in those rooms, which must have seemed to the more uneasily imaginative like cells intended for Counts of Monte Cristo.

Jamnagar. Lakhota on Lake Ranmalji

An interesting series of frescoes in need of restoration portrays Jam Ranmalji (who died in 1852) firing on horseback at a lion which has seized one of his African (Sidi) followers; another shows a pig-sticking safari; a third shows the Jam carousing with his court; and a fourth takes for its theme women bathing in a pond at Dwarka, surrounded by ash-smeared worshippers who gaze at them in rapt meditaticn.

From the top storey of the fortress you can see many attractions ot Jamnagar: the tall square Darbargadh or Old Palace, a white Jain temple, the grey Baldavil Temple, and the massive walls and twin minarets of the Friday Mosque, its sandalwood doors inlaid with mother-of-pearl. On the banks of Jamsarovar Lake, also called Lakhota Talao, rears the Bhujia Kotha, a bastion reached by stone steps (the sign reads KOTHO) from which a child solemnly informed me one can see Bhuj. I equally solemnly agreed, and if one takes Bhuj to mean the coastline of Kutch, on a clear day he might well have a point, though as usual I doubt it.

Another centre of Jamnagar is the monumental Willingdon Crescent, in the sense that when the cholera-choked, malarial slums of old Jamnagar were demolished to make way for the well-planned modern town, the Crescent and the hygienic Chelmsford Market formed the nexus of a wide road system with clean pavements, lighting and sewers.

Jam Sahib asked his driver Rajmamad to accompany me to the City Palace, founded by Jam Rawal in the 1540s and a joyous festival of spirited

Jamnagar. Willingdon Crescent

stone carving. We passed through a gate marked Gaibansha Pir's Dargah (10-11 a.m., 5-7 eves, Sunday, Thursday and Friday), where a Muslim saint is worshipped by the faithful. Only pigeons now flap around the superb City Palace, which could become a marvellous museum if only the revenues were available.

We saw the Hanuman Temple, the Ram Temple, and a florist called Majid Khan gave me roses on a stick in a touching gesture.

Industries in modern Jamnagar include marble-quarrying in Bhawad and Kandorna districts, copper-mining in Khambalia district, silk and gold embroidery and dyeing.

Khijadia Bird Sanctuary has already been declared a bird sanctuary by the State Government of Gujarat in a scheme to reclaim fertile cultivable land from the sea, a scheme started in 1920s and completed in the 1930s. Unfortunately this has been undermined because local cultivators have been allowed to pump water for their fields, so an area which should remain flooded throughout the year now becomes dry for up to six months every year, and salination has returned. The pumping-out of water must be stopped in the interests of the birds, of land reclamation, and of the farmers themselves, whose water in artesian wells will soon become too brackish for agricultural use. The Barda Hills Wildlife Sanctuary must be guarded against poaching and deforestation, and its road network maintained. The Kileshwar summer palace given to the State Education Department by the late Jam Sahib for pupils to benefit from outdoor nature study has become ruinous through disuse, and should be returned to the Sir Peter Scott Trust. The Barda Hills form a habitat for mongoose, python, tortoise, civet, wild boar, chital, sambar, nilgai, panthers and wolves and the botanical resources, equally rich, are in danger of disappearing.

Marine Sanctuary

In Jamnagar you can arrange with an agent such as Dodhia of Mahavir Kutir, Mahilla College Road, Jamnagar, to obtain the permits and fulfil other formalities to visit India's first marine nature reserve, comprising 42 tropical islands and the southern coast of Kutch, with habitats ranging from coral reef and rocky outcrops to lagoons and mangrove forest. Expect to spend about 2-2½ hours sailing from Rozi port to the coral reefs. The naval base nearby rents its lands from the Jam Sahib at Rs 1 per annum! Beginning from Jamnagar, you can take a boat from Rozi nearby to Pisketan Island, Mundera Island, Nara Island, and land at the tip of the peninsula at Okha, a railhead from Bombay. At Okha you can also hire boats.

Birds you will expect to see on these islands include dunlin and whimbrel, sanderling and sandpipers, curlews and black-winged stilt. Diving from coral reefs, you will find octopus, sea anemones, puffer-fish, and schools of dolphin. The sanctuary extends for 458 sq km, of which the national park covers 163 km.

Gop, Ghumli, Morpurgadh, Bileshwar

We took the road saying 'Porbandar 120 km' out of Jamnagar, then after 5 km left the coastal road to Okha; it took 50 minutes to reach the village of Lalpur, where we stopped for tea. Like my driver Ishwar Singh I poured the sweet, scalding milky tea into my saucer and we slurped it from the sides in a duet for thirsty two-legged vacuum-cleaners. Shortly we came into view of the high sanctuary on a bare brown hillside above us where the Maitraka-period temple of Gop rises like broken teeth on a bruised jaw. The sparseness of the remains should not deter you: we are in the presence of the greatest sixth-century architectural triumph of Valabhi, a capital and a culture which has all but disappeared. It is as if all ancient Athens had vanished but for the Acropolis, and indeed this location is almost as spectacular, for the temple is raised on a podium or *jagati* and its elevation dominating the surrounding plain for many miles gives it an awesome presence not lost on the original builders. Sculptures include a frieze of *gana*s, the mischievous dwarves who follow Shiva, a Rama, a Skanda, Vishnu and two guardians, but most have been robbed away because there is no effective supervision at Gop. So we are left with the design and achievement of the temple with an inner shrine surrounded by an internal ambulatorium. The splendid superstructure may be unique: the roof is the first known example in India of a wedge-shaped or *phamsana* roof which comprises two

167

sloping rectilinear roofs, the lower one with two great arches on each side of the kind known as *chaitya*s in Buddhist architecture, or *gavaksa*s here, corresponding to the ogee arch in European Gothic. The upper roof has one such arch to a side, and the whole is surmounted not by the customary notched ring stone called an *amalaka* but by a bell-shaped finial known as a *ghanta*. Stylistically, Gop is of course a puzzle still. The *phamsana* roof style vanished from Gujarat and is found only in the far north, around Kashmir; the sculptural style seems to fit in loosely with Early Western Chalukya figures; the semicircular moonstone effects at the foot of the east-oriented temple's double staircases is not known at this period outside Sri Lanka and Andhra Pradesh. But these historical difficulties, seemingly insoluble, lose significance for an imaginative wanderer footloose in Gujarat; we conjure up worshippers prostrate at these windy heights, and bearded ascetics unimpressed by the apparent passage of time.

Ghumli is another of those remote sites for which a local guide will be essential, but it contrasts totally with dry, eagle-eyried Gop because this village in the fertile Barda Hills has been populated continuously for many centuries, with a step-well considered to date back to the 12th century, though a flourishing community probably existed three hundred years earlier. Also of the 12th-century is a Jain temple dedicated to Parshvanatha, though only the mandapa or columned hall remains, indicating that an anti-Jain iconoclast may have destroyed the sanctuary.

The great step-well is abandoned nowadays, and urchins dive flamboyantly with screeches of joy from a ladder into a new tank beyond.

There is a sign (but only in Gujarati) from the path to *Navlakha* ('Nine-Lakh') temple, that boastful adjective indicative not so much of the actual cost as the generous intentions of the builder who started from a stupendous stone platform. It has to be said – and Jam Sahib has said it – that the apparently Shaivite temple has been so heavily restored internally that most evidence of its original destiny as a temple to the Sun, like that of Modhera, has been carefully erased. Only the outer base of the *shikhara* or curved temple steeple gives some idea of what the Shaivite reformers intended, though the usual elephant frieze repeats an obsessive image with Ganesha as son of Shiva-Parvati and royal mount. The two-storey mandapa has its own dignity, but I (the only visitor) preferred to consider Surya's sublime green setting here, and his appearance at the equinox from the carefully-oriented façade to a rectangular stone window at the rear, where the image of the God might be placed to receive his own rays in natural homage at awestruck moments as the laity experienced the magic of the priesthood. Intricately-carved sculptures at several levels lap the rear and sides like waves of exuberant stone. In the shade of a great banyan a folk Ganesha painted orange at the left and a Shiva in the centre on a modern low plinth insisted on the reshaping of Hindu thought from a pagan-based evocation to the sun and his works to a Shaivite theology. If you spend more time at Ghumli, the local people will escort you to the

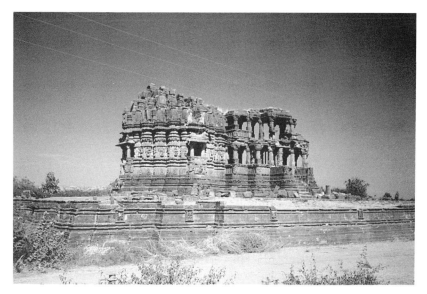

Ghumli. Sun Temple

Gate of Rama, small temples, ponds and ruins spread over such a wide area as to leave no doubt of Ghumli's historic significance.

Between Ghumli and Bileshwar the road bends below a massive castle which, like all else in the former State of Nawanagar, belonged to Jam Sahib. It reminded me of Shivaji's forts on hilltops throughout Maharashtra, with their superb views over surrounding valleys, on a clear day as far as the next hillfort. Just beside the road there is a series of four rows of *pallias*, those equestrian funerary markers in low relief that we should call headstones if they were placed above a corpse in a graveyard. Here at Morpurgadh the four commemorations in the front row, twenty in the second, twenty-two in the third, and twenty-one in the fourth seem to have been juxtaposed by the hand of a museum curator, though they stand erect, in various stages of erosion, most with triangular summits like protecting roofs. Such heroic *pallias* can be found in little clumps in many places round Gujarat, near the site of battles – and which district of Gujarat has not seen its share of battles?

Bileshwar village centres on a 7th-century temple created during the Maitraka dynasty which is thus coeval with Gop. Like every other place name ending 'eshwar', Bileshwar is now devoted to Shiva, but the old temple dates back to sun-worship times, when it was dedicated to Surya. The Nandi in front is a much later addition. Oleanders blushing pink in the forecourt gushed three inquisitive striped palm squirrels, emerging

169

like squeezed toothpaste from a tube, one after the bright-eyed others. A protected monument, the Shiva temple is also active with worshippers. Narendra Giri, its voluble whitegarbed priest, handed me *prasad*, a flower, and a welcoming Limca. He placed a rush mat down inside the temple for me to take crosslegged rest. The white-painted lingam in the shrine has been painted with a head facing out: a Rajput moustache and short round beard occupied the yoni, behind lockable blue wooden gates. I asked Narendra for a key to ascend the ancient Surya temple, and we picked our way barefoot through encrusted pigeon guano on stairs and roof. Pigeons still colonise every available square inch of the niches of the five-storeyed pyramidal roof, nesting, roosting, burbling, ruffling, flapping in white light and resting above the dark simplicities below.

Dwarka

India's seven sacred cities, to visit which the Hindu will obtain eternal happiness, are Ayodhya, Benares and Mathura (all in Uttar Pradesh), Gaya (Bihar), Kanchipuram (Tamil Nadu), Ujjain (Madhya Pradesh), and of course Dwaravati, nowadays known as Dwarka. 'Dvara' or 'dwara' means door, and 'dvarika' (here Dwarka) is a small gateway or doorway; the port is thus considered relatively minor, and indeed Dwarka has no great natural harbour, just a silted-up mouth of the river Gomti.

For the sake of an easy life I ignore the scholarly controversies about legend v. myth v. history, and hope to summarise one of the many stories about Lord Krishna. He is said to be the eighth incarnation of the god Vishnu, though in the Mahabharata he appears as an epic hero of mystical tendencies. In the later Bhagavadgita, now regularly interpolated into the massive Mahabharata, he already occurs as 'the Divine One' and develops his divine characteristics in the Harivansa and the Bhagavata and other Puranas. Unlike most other religious figures, Krishna entered the folk mind for his human qualities: a boy who steals buttermilk, a youth who chases girls, and a man who steals other men's women – as in the case of Sisupala's betrothed, and suggests cheating – as in the case of Yudhisthira's lie to defeat the prowess of Drona, and Bhima's foul blow which broke the thigh of Duryodhana.

Krishna is said to have come with the rest of the Yadava clan from the city of Mathura to build the fortified city of Dwarka, after which he eloped with Rukmini, daughter of the Raja of Vidarbha and the betrothed of Sisupala. A small temple to Rukmini north of the bus stand – I was assured by a priest – may be more 1500 years old, but its domed mandapa and stepped sanctuary cannot be older than the 12th century in its present form. But pilgrims crowd here for the Dwarkadhish temple to Lord Krishna, open from 6 to 12.30 and 5 to 9 p.m. Theoretically closed to non-Hindus, the temple may allow entry, if one makes the right request to the right people with the required quantity of tactful persistence at an appro-

Dwarka. 19th century engraving

priate time, and with a non-aggressive posture and a gentle tone of voice. If a conducted tour is offered, I suggest you agree, because if a Hindu queries your rights in Gujarati, the appropriate response is from another Hindu, also in Gujarati.

The lower part of Dwarkadhish temple is of 16th-century date, and the rapidly soaring honeycomb-effect steeple of the 19th century, with its numerous clusters of small towers. The mandapa before it is also many-storeyed. Internally, the sixty-pillared sanctuary is a hive of voices, colours, incense and sculptural voluptuousness. The West has never managed to compete with Indian sculptural creativity, its daring eroticism, many-layered mythic intensity, and extraordinary continuity.

Even in the Middle Ages our European sculptors remained pious and dutiful, inhibited and puritanical – if one excludes the lewd shiela-na-gig on rural churches, or the Gothic gargoyles intended to remain apart from all principal iconographic features. Here at Dwarka, and again at Somnath we can admire the natural exuberance of the anonymous guild-sculptors patronised by rulers and nobles, merchants and ministers.

If you cannot enter a given Hindu temple, content yourself with the knowledge that the exterior is probably of greater interest to you than the hectic interior. And many of Dwarka's festivals (not to mention the beaches) can be enjoyed by anyone. Numerous minor festivals occur be-

171

tween the major festivals, which are the Maha Shivaratri dedicated to Shiva at his Bhadkeshwar temple on the seashore (February-March), the Fuldol (March-April), the Bhima Ekadashi at Dwarkadhish (June), the Hindola Festival lasting 15 days in August-September, the Monday fair every week of Shravana at the Shiva temple (August-September), the birthday of Lord Krishna or Janmashtami (August-September) and the Navratri or Nine-day festival (October-November), in addition to the annual Holi and Divali celebrated throughout India.

A cycle rickshaw can take you round to the Hanuman tank, the Sun temple at Vasai (about 10 km), the ancient Maitraka capital called Kankavati, the museum of Shardapith Math, and the Mahadev Temple at Nageshwar (about 13 km). Tongas are available for shorter distances.

I confidently recommend the five-hour conducted tour bookable from either the Tourist Bureau or the Panchayat. You can often find an English-speaking courier who can point out the Ved Bhavan (school for Vedic teaching) and other temples not easily identified on this Gujarati-speaking coast, such as Bhadrakali, Savitri Devi and Siddharath. It is worth asking to look around the Hindu monastic establishment or 'math' founded in the eighth century by the revered teacher Shankaracharya (788-820), whose sect is headed in Kanchipuram by His Holiness Jayendra Saraswati. A vibrant disputant and eager traveller, Shankara took Dwarka to represent the west of India (ask for the Shri Jagatguru Shankaracharya Math) and envisaged his Vedic message reaching out towards the Occident, just as his math at Kanchi was intended to proselytise Asia from the south.

If you have your own transport you may wish to visit the site of Pindara (on the Gulf of Kutch) which is reached (72 km from Dwarka) by taking a left along the road to Jamnagar, or by bus from the rail station at Bhatiya. Yadava-dynasty monuments at Pindara include a great Surya temple and Purvasa ashram where Hindus perform the Shraddha ceremony.

Along the coast the railhead ends at Okha, an all-weather harbour from which Bet Dwarka (Dwarka Island) can be visited. Buses can also transport you the 32 km from Dwarka or Okha: again, as at Dwarka, the temples of Bet Dwarka have seen constant renovation and restoration, so they are an archaeological and artistic muddle. Yet they too offer that insight into the stillness within hubbub, the core of sudden enlightenment within hot, sweaty, dreary noisy humanity that may make a whole five-thousand-mile journey worthwhile for the rest of one's life. Or not, depending on mood, temperament, and character. I found an Australian on Bet Dwarka who wished profoundly that he had never come, yet after the unsolicited gift of a Sprite drink from a complete stranger became a different man, less haunted by his own temporary, minor problems and more attuned to the flow of the sea that lapped around our feet. 'Just stay here five minutes longer than you ever intended', I thought, 'and the flickering light will burn brighter'.

It seems an interminable coastal drive, from Dwarka to Porbandar. But no matter where else you may be tempted you stop for tea, don't fail to make a halt at the temple of Harisiddh Mata. Folklore says that on seeing the deity appear at the top of the hill the ships sank, so her temple was transferred to the foot of the hill, where it would no longer disturb mariners. The truth was explained by Jam Sahib of Jamnagar, who administers the temple. A cross-current catches vessels unawares when the tide flows: water rushes into a coastal lagoon and either strands or sinks incautious navigators. The temple on the top of the hill is on an ancient Shaivite foundation; the modern temple is a Shakti dedication, that is, to the female energy of Shiva. Mahmud of Ghazni, the Muslim invader, cut off Harisiddh Mata's golden dome when he bore down on the southern coast of Kathiawar in 1024. He seized gold and jewels presented over the centuries to the temple, removed the idol of the deity and threw it away. In fact, the dominant Hindu communities of the region simply replaced the idol, regilded a new dome, and donated enough gold and jewels to substitute what had been desecrated. In trying to understand the depth of R.S.S., V.H.P. and B.J.P. feelings about the Muslim minority, it is historically necessary to bear in mind such ravages as those of Mahmud of Ghazni here, Mahmud Beghada to the east, or Mughal-appointed viceroys throughout Gujarat.

Porbandar

Porbandar, in the words of Charles Freer Andrews, a British disciple of Gandhiji, 'becomes a vision of glory at sunrise and sunset when the slanting rays beat upon it, turning its turrets and pinnacles into gold'. The glittering Arabian Sea beyond compensates for the cacophony in the crowded, dirty bazaar.

The town will always be associated with the Gandhi family: Bapuji's grandfather Uttamchand Gandhi had served as prime minister to the Maharaja of Porbandar's Jethwa Rajput state and this position was inherited by Gandhiji's father Karamchand, who passed it to his brother Tulsidas on assuming a similar position in Rajkot, and later Wankaner.

The mid-18th century Gandhi family home, open daily from 8 to 7, is situated close to the Makanji family home near Manek Chowk. Gokuldas Makanji's daughter Kasturbai was married to the young Mohandas Gandhi when they were both thirteen: arranged marriages often go wrong but the Gandhis stayed married for sixty-two years. Though Gandhi came to hate 'the cruel custom of child marriage', he always felt guilty that he treated Kasturbai lustfully. 'If my affection had been absolutely untainted with lust', he later confessed, 'she would be a learned lady today', yet she could barely read and write simple Gujarati.

Gandhiji was born here in 1869, and the three-storey home remains un-

173

spoilt by and large except for neon lighting and green paint, its 17 rooms indicating the prosperity of the extended family. Off the actual room of Gandhi's birth you can see the kitchen of his grandmother, Lakshmibai. A wooden shrine in a wall has a hole excavated below, where cash or jewels could be left as if it were a safe-deposit. The persistent attendant, Ramesh Bardh, proffered *Bhalepadharia* ('Welcome') in Gujarati and constantly referred to his high caste. 'These flowers,' he waved, 'these are not in your country?'. 'Oleanders are found all over the Mediterranean,' I had to declare. From the balcony I watched boys flying kites on yellow flat roofs. Kirti Mandir has been complemented by a photographic display in the memorial building, similar to that you can see in Ahmedabad at the Sabarmati Ashram and Bhavnagar's Gandhi Smrti.

As usual, the place to watch passers-by is the bazaar, close to Kirti Mandir. A serious-looking housekeeper fingered limes from which the ingenious vendor was squeezing the juice as 'limbu pani', literally lime-water, but actually fresh juice. Beside pyramidal coconut stalls I found bananas – a vital standby if you are eating at wayside shacks which never offer dessert – and paid Rs 4 for a hand of twelve.

Kirti Mandir is a benefaction of the industrialist Nanjibhai Kalidas, who also endowed a women's college, a science college, Tara Mandir in memory of Nehru, and Bharat Mandir in memory of the illustrious heroes of myth, legend and religion whose figures are painted in a comic-strip style popular in India, and in the same general mode as the Shamsan Bagh in Jamnagar. The idea is to let the people disport themselves in a pleasant garden environment, but remind them of their past as a spur to spiritual endeavour in the future.

Across the main road from Bharat Mandir, out beyond Jubilee Bridge, stands the Nehru Planetarium: I attended a sparsely filled showing one afternoon with a comfortable pan-chewing Bombay wallah on one side and a peanut-chewing family on the other. During the winter, flamingoes turn the Jubilee Creek white and rosy pink with their startling entrances by the flock, rising and settling like curved eiderdowns.

Every so often an auto-rickshaw driver in India will take it upon himself to deviate from what you want, and my advice is to accept the change like a swing of the pendulum: you will return to an established pattern soon enough. My proud smiling driver in Porbandar had quickly realised that I wanted to see everything, not just what I had happened to prepare for in advance, so we swung into the shade below an ancient banyan, and he fell asleep in the passenger-seat like a twisted doll. I had come to another shrine of the monkey-god, Shri Rukaria Hanuman Mandir, which wore a sign in English almost certainly borrowed from a Christian wayside pulpit: 'Blessed are pure. They can see the light of the Lord'. I have never forgotten a wayside pulpit I once saw in Wimbledon: 'Go as far as you can see, then see how far you can go', or possibly 'See how far you can go, then go as far as you can see'. I have tried to put this into practice my whole life long without having the faintest idea what it means. Two priests sat between a low white-tiled wall and the green-doored sanctuary inside which a standing reddish-brown Hanuman gazed out in sempiternal vigilance. Above the shrine a painting showed Hanuman kneeling before Rama with Sita his wife and Lakshman his brother. A worshipper came to ring the bell, alerting the god to his wishes, and a priest came out to offer me *prasad* in a screw of newspaper, in exchange for which I placed coins on a table.

My driver stood up, apparently snapping from deep sleep to instant awakening, and roared off with me on the second bridge back to Porbandar, on the other side of the railway line from Jubilee Bridge. 'Omid', screamed a mystery hoarding, 'don't ENVY it, BUY it!' and below the exhortation a row of little boys sat by newly-fashioned cricket bats for the forthcoming season.

My appointment at the Maharana's Hazur Palace was with the gentle, bespectacled Mr Pota, seventy-eight years old. 'Today is Makar Sankranti', he explained, 'that is Kite Day, so only the lower rooms are visible.' Seeing that I seemed to be straining to comprehend the connection, he added, 'the women cleaning and attending palace have their day off, so there is no-one upstairs to show.' Mr Pota kindly offered to take me round. 'Kumar Sahib, that is to say His Highness, actually practises criminal law in London itself, and returns to Porbandar three or four times a year. Generally, he stays eight to ten days only, but he says his next stay at the end of January will be for twenty days. I am his personal assistant, and I stay here 9-1 and 3-6 every day.'

Though built in the late 19th century by Maharana Bhavsinhji, Hazur Palace is dominated by Kumar Sahib's father Natwarsinhji, who died in 1983. The drawing-room shows him in a photograph taken at a Gir lion shoot, and another in state attire. The downstairs dining-hall is a melancholy place full of shadows overpowering light and absences populating the long table like a silent shrine to Miss Havisham. In the hallway a Gir lion, stuffed like a lifesize toy, no longer utters even a whispered threat. Italian coloured tiles decorate the empty sitting-room. The Library has died too, its collected works of Galsworthy and Hood forever trapped shut. In the billiard-room I found two marine paintings by Juan Couver and another reference to Hanumanji, the monkey god, and Mr Pota stated soberly that His Highness was descended from Hanuman, to which there is no known response. The most attractive room in Hazur Palace is the Fountain Room, with a marble fountain inset in the floor, and attractive paintings such as a portrait of a young woman by J.D. Gondhalekar, and cool-looking white columns. In the zenana wing, the silver banqueting room glows pallidly, as encroaching sunlight penetrates seaborne haze. Natwarsinhji was himself an architect, and composed music in the European style. Guests of the former royal family in Porbandar stayed in the guesthouse called Lal Mahal, or Red Palace, but that is shut up at present.

Maharana Bhavsinji was responsible for many other public buildings, such as the town hall and public library which, like virtually all Indian public libraries, is run down and needs a major injection of capital, adequate annual budgets, and staff training for expertise and motivation.

Porbandar's colourful dhow-building yard and fishing port are situated at the opposite end of the town from Hazur Palace: a drive along the seafront gives you the chance to appreciate the fine promenade houses which benefit from offshore winds, and the modest lighthouse. Magnificent dhows are still being assembled by master craftsmen and apprentices here at Porbandar as at Mandvi, Veraval, and elsewhere along the coasts of Gujarat. Gobind showed me three dhows at different stages of completion and, as in Oman or Bahrain, I marvelled at skills which enable masters to turn piles of wood into durable seagoing vessels. More humble craft, filled with nets, floats and gunny sacks, propped themselves on the beach as if gazing inwards to the peaceful lagoon. A fifty-footer bearing the Indian flag on bamboo poles fore and aft puttered softly from its berth into friendly, calm waters before rounding the harbour spit and into the treacherous open seas.

My auto-rickshaw driver finally after asking seven bemused passers-by brought me to Maharana Sartanji's pleasant summer pavilion (ask for 'Rana-no Choro') which could be dated to around 1782, twenty-five years before the English East India Company agreed to protect the port town's ruling family from predatory neighbours. The pavilion is three-storeyed to benefit from sea breezes in its double cusp-arched top pavilion and its slender columned middle storey. Its ground floor repeats on all four sides

Porbandar. A dhow half completed

the cusp-arched Islamic lightness of the top storey, creating the same effect by longer columns which seem to be of wood like the interior columns but are actually of stone, though as feminine as a veil of gauze.

Porbandar's strategic position as the principal port between Veraval and Kutch had always been envied: it is the natural seaward outlet for all those Saurashtran towns and cities from Rajkot and Gondal to Jetpur, Upleta and Junagadh. Its hardwearing golden-cream stone can be seen today in the major public works of such great cities as Bombay and Karachi. And its links with East Africa and the Gulf can be seen in the streets even now, as negroes who came as slaves or servants over many centuries of trade.

Mr Pota of Hazur Mahal had telephoned ahead to the summer palace in the Barda Hills called Anut Niwas, so that I could look around, but I was not prepared for the superb views over Khambalia Dam, half an hour north from Porbandar town. An old wooden board left off the main road bears the barely-visible legend 'Private Property', and you wind uphill through dam-irrigated fields to the summit, where a magic gate opens and a marble staircase leads to two cupids on a dolphin. Though now owned by His Highness Kumar Sahib, Anut Niwas was built in 1927 by Maharana Natwarsinhji, and it bears all the hallmarks of Art Nouveau accelerating into Art Deco, perfect in its period, and unspoilt as if transfixed in amber. Not only is Anut Niwas conceived in the perfect place for a summer retreat, catching every breeze, long and low to afford ample shelter from the menacing sun, but it provides the perfect antidote to the grime, sweat and noise of city life. The first thing you see is a neatly-folded umbrella in a stand, and then glass and ceramic Art Deco objects in a case lead on to period furniture all bought and installed at the same time, even to a wind-up H.M.V. gramophone, and charming minor European landscape paintings. From the drawing-room one moves into an office, then to a bedroom, and a morning tea-room co-ordinated pink like the Maharani's bathroom and toilet. Down a wooden spiral staircase I found two safes by Godrej and massive cupboards. Upstairs again, the Maharana's bathroom is co-ordinated lilac, and the library stocked with John Buchan, Georgette Heyer, Edgar Wallace and half a shelf of Denise Robins. A curious form of Roman tile impluvium nine inches deep in the heart of the house leads to an amply-supplied kitchen and the Art Deco dining-room, its chairs fitted with slots in the arms for cigarettes and matches. Dinner-plates are monogrammed 'M.N.'. A guest-bedroom and -bathroom decorated in orange takes one back to Dornford Yates and Sapper. You expect Jeeves to shimmer imperturbably out of the woodwork, and there she was in a glass-fronted bookcase, precisely as I had predicted: *Jill the Reckless*, in original dustwrapper.

Anut Niwas in the Barda Hills, above Khambalia Dam

Kutiyana

From Porbandar the roads to Rajkot and Junagadh diverge in the small but bustling town of Kutiyana, crammed with stalls for fruit and vegetables, a filling-station with a stench of petrol, oil and diesel overpowering senses beyond smell: a sense of optimism suffocated by fatalism, a sense of drive smothered by passivity, a sense of buoyancy overcome by apprehensiveness: a lit match and we'd all explode. My taxi-driver always knew as if by telepathy which restaurant to avoid and which to patronise, though outwardly they would seem identical to me, equally smirched by grease and oil. We passed a brown shack and entered a green shack resembling a garden shed, furnished with rickety off-white tables, matching benches, and a ceiling fan spasmodically astonishing flies that drifted into its orbit like sputtering helicopters out of control. It was difficult to imagine a hotter day, so I didn't. A dingy wash-basin bore on its rim something that might once have been soap. The kitchen is luckily obscured from view by a blackened curtain which might have been used to dampen down coal-fires in a sequence of emergencies. I am sorry to say, oh disapproving advocate of starched linen napkins, that I loved this shack and its good-humoured customers more than any pompous five-star hotel run for the benefit of absent shareholders. Clients and 'servants' dovetail here in an efficient slice of popular capitalism: for under a dollar I lunched off *thalis* with rice, chapatis, papads and two steaming bowls of refreshing tea while all around me came the satisfied chomping of workers eating plain food then paying a reasonable price.

Junagadh
Ashoka's Edicts, the Caves and Uparkot
Though for some incomprehensible reason excluded by most major travel companies from their Indian itineraries, Junagadh and its neighbouring Girnar Hill must be one of the most exciting and historically vibrant cities in the subcontinent.

When the Mauryan emperor Ashoka ruled much of the northern subcontinent between 273 and 236 B.C. from Pataliputra (the modern Patna) he set up a series of Buddhist edicts on pillars and rocks in the Brahmi alphabet (from which current scripts of India, Sri Lanka, Java, Tibet and Burma derive) using the Prakrit dialect which bears the same relation to Sanskrit as Italian does to Latin. In the ninth year of his reign, Ashoka won a great victory in 261 over Kalinga, nowadays known as the Telugu coast of the Bay of Bengal, that is the eastern coastline between the Godavari and Mahanadi.

Sickened by the slaughter of a hundred thousand in Kalinga lands and the capture of 150,000 prisoners, he determined from then that military conquest (Digvijaya) would be replaced by the ethical conquest (Dharmavijaya) of Buddhist law. He regarded all men as his equally-beloved children and, in the manner of the Persian sovereign Darius he created inscriptions and monuments to proclaim the law of love and justice. It was he who founded Srinagar in Kashmir, he who built Deo-Patan in Nepal, replaced wooden buildings by stone palaces in Pataliputra and established hospitals and dispensaries for the sick throughout his territories. He prescribed active toleration of all groups, whether Zoroastrian, Buddhist, Brahman or Jain. To quote these wonderful edicts at Junagadh, which can be found protected in a modern building on the road from the city to Girnar Hill, "to foster one's sect, depreciating the others out of affection for one's own, to exalt its merit, is to do the worst harm to one's own sect."

Ashoka preaches "mastery of the senses, purity of thought, gratitude, and steadfastness in devotion" (Edict VII) and "the least possible impiety, as many good deeds as possible, kindness, liberality, truthfulness, and purity of thought" (Edict II). Edict I inveighs against the slaughter of living beings for sacrifice and ostentatious feasting. At one time, he recalls, the royal kitchens slaughtered millions of animals for food, whereas nowadays only two peacocks and one deer are the daily quota, and those too will disappear in future from the menu. Edict II deals with medical treatment for human and animal patients throughout his kingdom, the digging of wells and the planting of trees along main highways. Edict III prescribes quinquennial tours of city throughout his realm by all governors, district officers, and sub-district officers. Edict IV exhorts all his subjects to practise the dharma, with special reference to kindness to all living things and purity in one's private life. Edict V establishes the corps of officials known as Dharma Mahamatras whose task is to spread the Emperor's message of love, tolerance, compassion and non-violence to all castes and all sects. Edict VI guarantees that anyone bringing him state business to transact will have access at all times of the day and night, wherever he may be. Edict VII urges self-control, devotion, gratitude and purity of thought. Edict VIII proclaims royal dharma tours of the empire, beginning at Bodh Gaya and visiting ascetics, monks, the aged and infirm. Edict IX gently criticises superstitious rites and suggests replacing them with actions of reverence to elders, courtesy to servants, liberality to monks, and restraint in action to those not of the same religious persuasion. Edict X is devoted to the rejection of glory and fame in this life and submission to Dharma, which involves abjuring corruption. Edict XI emphasises kindly acts towards friend, relative and stranger alike. Edict XII urges restraint in speech, neither honouring one's own beliefs nor attacking anyone else's: instead, Mahamatras should promote knowledge about all religions in the empire. Edict XIII apologises for his conduct of war during the Kalinga wars mentioned above: the only true conquest, of the mind and spirit by Buddhist Dharma, should be voluntary. Edict XIV summarises the previous thirteen.

These beautiful rock inscriptions on a rounded granite boulder are now protected by a caretaker who sells an English-language book on Junagadh for Rs 5 only if you buy 12 postcards of Badoli for another Rs 5. Opening hours are 8.30-11 and 2-6 except for Wednesdays and public holidays.

From the Ashokan Edicts, you can relive the Buddhist monastic life and times of early Junagadh by skirting the ancient lake of Sudarshan and then the northern edge of Uparkot (literally 'Upper Fort') to discover the atmospheric Khapara Khodia Caves, cut into living rock but severely damaged by mediaeval and later quarrying, so that all the upper storey has disappeared. Yet we still have a fascinating hermitage surrounded by earthworks, provided with watertanks in the western wing, and based on an L-shaped eastern wing for monastic cells with access by modern steps. James Burgess felt that this was the palace apartment of the Chudasama ruler Rao Khengar, but his views have been rendered obsolete by the discovery of pre-mediaeval inscriptions, the identification of common features in the so-called 'Buddhist Caves' on Uparkot, and the absence of supporting evidence. So we take the Khapara Khodia Caves to be the earliest monastic settlement, abandoned because excavation had cracked rocks which allowed rainwater to seep in and made life too unpleasant for the monks, who consequently left before making decorations visible in similar Buddhist caves in Maharashtra.

Much more interesting are the three-storeyed 'Baba Pyara' Caves so called by reference to the nearby religious school of one Baba Pyara. This Buddhist monastery is a thirteen-cell establishment on the opposite side of

Junagadh. Uparkot. Khapara Kodia Caves

181

Uparkot, 150 feet high, cut into the rock and decorated with Buddhist symbols such as the fish, *triratna*, *swastika* and *ankusa*. The three-storey form follows the terraced rock strata, has one large cell (for an abbot?) and three smaller cells; the central group has a great apsidal *chaitya* hall to the west and across a great courtyard cell groups to the north, east and south; the southernmost group is aligned west-north-west, and comprises five caves now numbered 9 to 13 running east-west, of which is second (numbered 10) has an inner hall with a capital related to those in caves at Nasik, Maharashtra. The date of these caves cannot be later than the 2nd century A.D. and may well be much earlier.

The third cave-group is the 'Buddhist Caves' on the Uparkot citadel close to the Adi Chadi step-well, and these too are on three storeys cut from bare rock. These may be the latest of the cave-groups, datable by delectable pillar-carvings to the 2nd century A.D., though the excavations themselves may have been much earlier; the style is Satavahana, influenced by Scythian and Graeco-Roman elements.

Uparkot was established by the Mauryan dynasty of the 4th-2nd Centuries B.C., strengthened when Junagadh became capital of the region in the 2nd-4th centuries A.D. under the Kshatrapa dynasty and remained significant until after the fall of the Gupta empire in the 5th century, but from the 7th to the 10th centuries it lay wild and overgrown, until its military importance was again perceived and it was reinforced by Sultan Mahmud Beghada (who seized it in 1472), then later in 1683 and 1880.

Uparkot lost its value when the capital of the Kathiawar peninsula moved from Junagadh to Valabhi (the modern village of Vala, 21° 52'N, 71° 57'E, in Bhavnagar district) as headquarters of the Maitraka empire founded by Bhatarka *c.* 470 A.D., an event possibly triggered by a natural disaster such as the Sudarshan lake's bursting its banks. The Maitrakas remained fervent patrons of Buddhism in the 6th century A.D.

The Chudasama dynasty settled around Junagadh from 875, and it was their ruler Graharipu I (*d.* 982) who hacked the citadel free from the jungle, while Navghan II transferred the Chudasama capital from Vamanasthali (now Vanthali, near Girnar) to Uparkot in 1098. In Uparkot the spectacular Navghan step-well is named for Navghan I (*c.* 1060): a ten-foot wide passage spirals down seven flights to steps nearly 120 feet. The cistern must have held huge quantities of sweet water enabling defenders to withstand long sieges, and a great granary fitted with grids provided food for the besieged. No guards pester, no beggars swarm, and nobody tries to sell you anything at Uparkot. Another (also presumably 11th-century) Chudasama step-well is known as Adi Chadi. Now dry in the winter, like Adalaj near Ahmedabad it has a circular head, but its form is actually semi-circular like an apse.

Most interesting of all, perhaps, is the Friday Mosque begun by Mahmud Beghada of the Ahmadshahi dynasty when he defeated the Hindu princes of Kathiawar in 1470.

Junagadh. Uparkot. Friday Mosque

He chose to utilise an existing Chudasama royal palace on Uparkot, but even then he did not finish his mosque. The palace is known locally as Ranak Devi Mahal after the consort of Rao Khengar II, the king who attacked Anahilvada Patan, the capital of the Solanki empire of Siddharaja Jayasimha and eloped with Siddharaja's bride-to-be Ranak Devi, whom he married at Uparkot. Siddharaja then followed him south to Junagadh with revenge in mind, and succeeding in slaying Rao Khengar but Ranak Devi refused him, preferring to commit *sati* in the historic Rajput manner. All this happened in the 12th century: the last of the Chudasamas was Rao Mandalika, the victim of Mahmud Beghada who forced the Hindu to embrace Islam as Khan Jehan, and gave Junagadh the name Mustafabad, a name no longer current. But the historic fortification of lower Junagadh date from the late 15th century, and Muslim sovereignty over Junagadh remained intact until Independence, when only the rulers of Junagadh, Jammu and Kashmir, and Hyderabad continued to hold out.

You can make sense of the riotous Hinduistic carving of the mihrab and the almost incredibly rich flanking mihrabs only by relating this splendid incomplete mosque (its domes graciously open to birdsong and leaping striped palm squirrels) to its pre-Islamic origin. The fortress-like structure rises four-square on a stolid brick platform, with four slim round columns (in no sense minaretlike) at the corners. A small Muslim cemetery in front of the mosque makes its anonymous presence jagged, like a fading but insistent memory. In front of the mosque, an evangelist was selling Hindu devotional texts at Rs 4 each, while parakeets cackled as they outpaced our movements. Though the mosque is no longer active, I felt uncomfortable not removing my shoes.

A young lad took me to see the great Ottoman guns. The Nilam cannon bears a bronze inscription in Arabic dating its casting in Egypt to 1531. It is at present pointing *towards* Junagadh, as if the enemy of the Muslims resided there... The second, much smaller, was also left by the Ottoman admiral Sulaiman Pasha defending Diu, to aid the Sultan against besieging Portuguese and when Diu was lost the cannon were brought here.

Later Junagadh
The Hindu Chudasama Kings of Junagadh ruled from 875 to 1472, followed by Tatarkhan Zafar (1472-5) and other Muslim rulers until 1492, and Muslim Governors or Fuzdars of Sorath (that is, Saurashtra) from 1692-1748. In 1748 Muhammad Sher Khan or Bahadur Khanji called himself the first independent Nawab of Junagadh: he became the first of nine so-called Babi rulers, the others being Mahabat Khanji I (1758-74), Hamed Khanji I (1774-1811), Bahadur Khanji II (1811-40), Hamed Khanji II (1840-51), Mahabat Khanji II (1851-82), Bahadur Khanji III (1882-92), Rasul Khanji (1892-1911), and Mahabat Khanji III (1911-47).

The Hindu majority numbering 80% demanded the Nawab's signature to the Instrument of Accession to India in 1947, but the Diwan, Sir Shah Nawaz Bhutto, father of Zulfiqar Ali Bhutto, announced Junagadh's accession to Pakistan on behalf of the Nawab on 15 August 1947, trusting for support to sea links between Junagadh State and the seaports for Pakistan. But at the end of October 1947 the Nawab left for Karachi from Keshod Airport, and the Diwan fled to Pakistan on 8 November. Possession passed to the Regional Commissioner at Rajkot on behalf of the Government of India in 1947, then in the referendum of February 1948, the total voting for accession to India was 190,870, while the numbers voting for accession to Pakistan totalled a mere 911. Administration of Junagadh passed to the Union of Saurashtra in 1949, to Bombay State in 1956, and since 1960 it has been a district in Gujarat State.

The modern city we see today dates largely from the second half of the 19th century, when Nawab Mahabat Khan II in partnership with the British Political Agency decided to modernise Junagadh, and in keeping with the spirit of Victorian England built or expanded public institutions such as bazaars, a clock-tower, gateways, schools, hospitals, a district court and jail, a public library and the Bahauddin College. The preferred style of Venetian Gothic involved very thick wall to keep out strong sun and monsoon rains, a profusion of delicate surface ornamentation, a preference for horizontal cornices over vertical lines, and elegant columns in preference to continuous wall surfaces. Wall paintings stirred the spirit, and dec-

184

orated false ceilings in stucco (Sardar Baug Palace) or canvas (Rang Mahal) gave an atmosphere of play to otherwise overpowering halls. The Great Hall of Bahauddin College measuring a hundred feet by sixty has a timber-trussed roof below which a gallery in wood is supported on brackets at the upper-floor level.

As I wandered around the campus of Bahauddin College, a shy bespectacled youth of nineteen advanced. 'Your country's name?' he enquired. Conscientiously, 'The United Kingdom of Great Britain and Northern Ireland'. 'Ah', he said, 'Ireland. Capital of your country is Dubbling. Are you knowing English?'

'Enough for all practical purposes.'

'Then you can be helping me with one thing?'

'Possibly.'

'Mister and Mistress I am knowing, but which is Mistess?'

'I'm not sure yet: can you give it me in a sentence?'

'I have it written in my note. "A Mistess is a police between two walls".'

I scrabbled desperately in the junkyard of my Indish like a deoxygenating treasure-seeker on a wrecked ship. 'Could it be, "An armistice is a peace between two wars"?'

His face cleared into a relieved beam. 'Thank you, sir'. I had passed my viva voce, and the milling crowd of three and a half thousand which had already congregated around us began to melt away, leaving only my interlocutor: 'But, sir, what is 'A Mistess is a piece between two *walls*?'

To this day my dreams are haunted by an androgynous mistess, uniformed and helmeted, twirling a truncheon like Chaplin's stick, patrolling between two walls or indeed wars in the mind of a beleaguered Indian, himself caught inextricably between the scaleable, comfortable wall of Gujarati and the threatening heights of English, an opportunity to escape for many, but a barrier to the vast majority.

Opposite the Civil Courthouse (1949) stands a complex of monumental Nawabi mausolea begun in 1878 by Mahabat Khanji II and completed in 1892 by his successor Bahadur Khanji III. The eighth Nawab Rasul Khanji is also buried here, but the ninth in line, who departed for Pakistan, died in his adopted homeland and has been buried there. Dilawar Khanji, the last in the line, died in 1992.

Hafez Muhammad Faruq, *katib* of the Friday Mosque next door, kindly welcomed me into his mosque before evening prayers; beyond the varicoloured columns like those of a Tuscan church I found a cool marble minbar. The *hafez* (a courtesy title revealing that a man can recite the Qur'an al-Karim by heart) explained that he earns Rs 60 per month (less than £1.50) for switching on the mausolea floodlighting at 6 p.m. every day and switching it off again at 9 p.m.. The Friday Mosque dates to 1886-97, and the madrasah or religious school from 1887-88.

Of all these mausolea, the most extraordinary is the pirouetting, funfairish, spiral-staircased tomb of Rasul Khanji's chief minister Bahauddin, known here by his Urdu title as Vazir-e-Azm, or Great Minister. He constructed the Bahauddin Building in the town, and the stunningly magnificently Bahauddin College. Behind silver-plated gates one can see silver-plated inscriptions above the graves. The immense double-storeyed crescent with domes and minarets is called the Reay Gate after a Political Agent. Don't miss the New Bazaar, which also dates from the rule of Mahabat Khanji II.

These new mausolea were built here because the previous graveyard in the city centre at Chittakhana Chowk (close to the Relief Hotel) had become too congested. If the latter cemetery is closed, just ask near the entrance for Karimbai, and if he isn't there, someone will run to fetch the key. Regrettably, the place is falling to rack and ruin for lack of proper maintenance, unlike the much more ostentatious series we have just seen dating from the 19th century. But these 18th-century tombs show more humility in size, their proportions are more fitting, and their play of vertical columns, delicate arches, horizontal cornices and variously-dimensioned domes produces a dazzling effect which could only be enhanced by cleaning. By the main gate is the mausoleum of the first Nawab of Junagadh, Sher Khanji called Bahadur Khanji, and his wife Ratanbai. Other tombs commemorated his successors Mahabat Khanji I, Hamed Khanji I, and Bahadur Khanji II. Overgrown, and as silent as the Chittakhana

Junagadh. Royal Mausolea opposite Relief Hotel

Chowk beyond is noisy, the graveyard is a treasury of great stonecarving: the only other occupant during my visit was a kestrel perched in a mossy dome – no sulking rat would elude his beady eye and sharp talons.

The Darbar Hall Museum at Diwan Chowk in the city centre opposite the Collector's Office reopened in its present form in 1977. A sign in Gujarati indicates its existence outside, and another in English can be found at the top of the stairs, with a notice 'SMOKING AND SPITTING STRICTLY PROHIBITED'. Hours are 9-12.15 and 3-6 daily except Wednesdays, the 2nd and 4th Saturdays in the month, and public holidays. Photography is prohibited, which is a pity because the only postcards I could find depicted exhibits in the Baroda Museum.

The greatest attraction is the Darbar Hall itself, rearranged to evoke the atmosphere of Babi Junagadh during the zenith of their influence in the second half of the 19th century. Furniture and fittings seem mostly appropriate to the period, but garish neon lighting detracts from the effect: how much more atmospheric to hang illuminated chandeliers! On fine carpets lustrous silver-plated thrones, lovingly polished till they glitter, bring back those more spacious days when time could be cajoled to slip more slowly down the hourglass. A department of palanquins and howdahs reinforces this palatial impression: a sumptuously carved silver-plated howdah depicts four round-hatted silver servant-mermaids at the corners, and a ferocious silver tiger beside the velvet seat. The textiles must not be missed: some carpets are lavishly gold-embroidered; another red silk carpet is edged with diamonds like bright stars in a scarlet sky. In the arms and armour room, turtle-shell shields and Gurkha kukris consort with rifles, mediaeval armour and daggers captioned 'javelins'. Royal portraits and historic photographs dominate the Picture Gallery. Don't miss the patrician exterior of the City Palace, now for the most part disused, the upper storeys blackened and distraught.

Another museum in Junagadh can be found off the Rajkot road in Sakkar Baug, which daily teems with visitors mainly heading for the Zoopark. Ambiguously known as 'the Junagadh Museum', it was founded in 1901 and opens daily except Wednesdays and government holidays from 9 to 12 and 3 to 6. Photography is allowed for a nominal charge. Look for wonderful prehistoric and protohistoric stone and bone implements, stone sculptures including a standing Vishnu of the late 9th century, bronzes, miniatures though not of the first rank, manuscripts, stone and copper inscriptions, silverware, glass, porcelain, woodcarvings, textiles and folk art.

Sakkar Baug Zoopark, established in 1863, is the third oldest in India and specialises in the breeding of the Asiatic lion in captivity. This is necessary because poaching in Gir Forest Sanctuary will never be eradicated, and naturally-occurring epidemics might decimate lions in the wild. Yes, of course, caged lions droop and sag, gazing through mists of nostalgia at a forest they may never see again, but the alternative is extinction, a thought even more atrocious. Between 1969 and 1989 fifty males and 78 females were born at Sakkar Baug Zoo, and many have either returned to the wild or departed for other zoos by exchange. The present census in Gir Sanctuary is 284 roaming free, while a further 100 Asiatic lions (found naturally nowhere else in the world) are confined in zoos. The struggle to keep the species alive is being won: the census for wild lions has risen steadily from 180 in 1974 to 205 in 1979 and 239 in 1985. Tigers and leopards, less cliffhangingly threatened, can be found here patrolling stone floors and narrow ledges with scarcely curbed ferocity. Sakkar Baug Zoo also specialises in blackbuck, blue bull, Himalayan black bears, horned antelopes, gazelle, sloth bears, spotted deer, hyenas, wild asses, and birds. Monkeys are of course a common sight in India, but many villagers coming from desert areas have never seen such marsh crocodiles, the three companionable narrow-jawed Indian gavials (*Gavialis gangeticus*), found also in the Indus and Brahmaputra, each with more than a hundred teeth, or the large Indian porcupine. It almost seems redundant to lock up birds, when even a short trip beyond Junagadh will reveal fifty species in season, but here are Greater Flamingo, White-Necked Stork and Rosy Pelicans displaying their extraordinary features. Alert dogs and busy crows cannot tell the difference: which is the zoo? In the playground children grin and chatter, while their more sedate relations gather round in a circle on the grass, unwrapping picnic cloths and canisters, slicing fruit and opening flasks of tea, while vendors with lethal machetes slash coconuts at the top and insert straws for you to drink the refreshing milk – three rupees. Pi-dogs sniffing and circling fearfully outside the garden seem not to have been blessed with the peace of mind that non-violence may bring.

At Junagadh Rail Station I enquired about trains to Sasangir for the Lion Sanctuary on the line to Delvada. The one-way single fare is Rs 88 first-class and Rs 13 second-class. The bookstall offered books, magazines and newspapers exclusively in Gujarati. Paintings in the station booking-hall depict Gandhiji as I expected, but also Saint Narsinh Mehta, that major Hindu religious poet of 1414-1480 whose works are recited today, never having gone out of fashion, unlike the religious poems of Herbert and Milton, say, which no longer form part of the cultural baggage of the average Englishman.

Girnar

The Buddhist, Hindu and Muslim dimensions of Junagadh give way in the cool, fresh heights of nearby Girnar to the Jain dimension: again, if you appreciate the mind of the pilgrim, you will approach their elevation of mind, their multi-faceted excitement and their ardent dedication to the climb. You start as early as possible, then rest and meditate in the heat of the day. Wear a hat, use ample sunblocking cream, take mineral water in a light plastic bottle, and carry the absolute minimum. Invalids and the aged can be car-

188

ried up on *doli*s carried by coolies.

Hot drinks are available in the dark of six a.m. at any of the many little cafés at the foot of Girnar, near Damodar Kund (Damodar being another name for Krishna). I sipped boiling sweet tea among pleading pi-dogs, and shared a packet of biscuits with a bitch and her anxious puppies. The shadows of avid drinkers reared and fell as oil-lanterns swung on ropes to splash the dark: such a scene could have been watched by Rudyard Kipling a hundred years ago.

If you are here on the day of Shivratri, the 13th of the sixth month of the Hindu calendar, you can visit the temple of Bhavnath (Bhav is another name of Shiva) where a night festival honouring Shiva attracts Ahirs, Mehrs and tens of thousands of worshippers to an area usually occupied only by Rabaris. Among the *sadhu*s and laymen from all over Gujarat you will see naked monks known as *nagabawa*s, mendicants singing *bhajan*s or fervent hymns to Lord Shiva. Massive tents accommodate up to 350 pilgrims each; food is provided free of charge. Vendors set up stalls for trinkets and souvenirs, and there are fairground attractions such as snake-charmers, jugglers, story-tellers, and those little versions of the Ferris Wheel that spring up all over India at the least excuse to the utter delight of small children and their screaming mothers. Bhavnath Festival continues for some days.

Girnar pilgrimage lasts the year round, however. One may limit one's ascent to the first 4,000 steps, paid for by a lottery and built between 1889 and 1908, so that any able-bodied individual will be able to visit the Jain temples. At 6.55 I began the easy roam through scrubland – broad steps followed by level stretches. 'Rs 1,400 to carry you up, sahib!' urged a doli-walla, showing me his two bamboo poles, with a canvas seat slung between. I strode on, unimpressed by the outrageous overcharging, and determined to conquer unaided the cone of the extinct volcano that is Girnar. Because Saurashtra is predominantly flat, the few 'hills' that exist are given fanciful legendary explanations, such as a common belief that a giant was travelling south carrying a fragment of the Himalayas and dropped it here (Girnar Hill is 3660 feet high at Gorak Nath) or at Palitana, where Shatrunjaya Hill is 1978 feet above sea level. These and other such basaltic extrusions have a less picturesque explanation in volcanic history.

At eight-fifteen dawn had broken, and I turned back to see the expanse below me, the Sonarekha river glinting on her way to the white roofs of Junagadh, while monkeys sat in hopeful groups on the step-wall and a kestrel shrivelled up into a speck ever higher. I offered to carry a stone from the head-cushion of a pretty labourer, but she giggled with her friends before wiggling flirtatiously as she sped ahead, her deportment elegant as a swan's.

A rabbit scampered away down a hill. Lizards slid or sat, silent as green idols. A wild peacock fluttered in a scream of loss. Two squirrels pattered up a wall following the direction of the stripes on their back. Vendors of yellowish water (mainly little girls or old women) offered their overflowing terra cotta pots, but I declined with a smile, taking draughts of my own bottled water when out of their view and feeling guilt for refusing their private enterprise. It had taken me 2 hours and 20 minutes of slow walking, often resting and turning to look back, to climb the 4,000 steps up to Deva Kota, a fortified enclosure associated with Rao Khengar I of Kutch (1548-185). Here I caught up with a Bombay hydraulics specialist called Kiran Parekh. a Jain who not only visits the Jain temples of Girnar two or three times every year, but continues up a further 800 steps to the Hindu temple of Amba Mata.

Deva Kota enclosure is so densely packed with temples that one might assume that its builders felt permanently threatened, and with some justification, for Shatrunjaya in particular suffered disastrously at the hands of Muslim attackers in the 14th and 15th centuries.

Before examining the cluster of temples on the left, enter first the granite temple constructed at the command of Rao Bhojraj of Kutch (1632-45), and then the greater temple sponsored by Vastupala, who like his brother Tejapala devoted much of the family's colossal wealth to the creation of temples here and (from about 1230) at Dilwara on Mount Abu. Vastupala was Diwan, or Prime Minister, to Viradhwaja Waghela (1214-43) yet his brother made no lesser contribution to the founding of new *derasars* or temples. Nowadays, the main channel for funding renovation and maintenance of Jain temples in Gujarat is a foundation known as Anandji Kalyanji which I found in Palitana.

The main complex of Jain temples on Girnar Hill is situated 600 feet (and 800 steps) below the summit. The largest is the roughly rectangular temple to Neminatha, begun in the reign of Dandanayaka Sajjana (1128) and completed in 1159. Inside, an injunction reads 'Please leave your camera, radio and luggage here' though anyone with the fortitude to bring luggage this far up Girnar must rank with Superman. You can best judge the plan of Neminatha from the steps up to Amba Mata: a great courtyard is surrounding by a colonnade with images of the *tirthankars* of the Jain religion, 'ford-makers' allowing us to cross to liberation, or *moksha*, after the wearing-off of karma-bondage and the attainment of *kevala* or omniscience. Jainism has many similarities with other Indian religions, but its idea of the soul's having an inherent upward motion of its own is unique. The way to *moksha* is divided into fourteen stages, of which a layman can achieve the first five, but only an ascetic is capable of passing through the last nine.

I sat crosslegged at a discreet distance from the main image of Neminatha, 22nd *tirthankar*, whose colour is black and whose symbol is the conchshell. His jewelled left eye seemed to be fitted in his head slightly higher than his right. Jain ladies came and went, chanting Jain sutras in an incantatory continuo that will not have altered over the centuries, being passed from grandmother to mother to daughter. Mr Parekh, advancing towards

190

the idol with a grandson at each hand, chanted the Navakar Mantra to allow his sin and miseries to disappear.

Namo Arihantanam
Namo Siddhanam
Namo Ayariyanam
Namo Uvaiihaynam
Namo Loe Savvasahunam
Eso Panch Namukkaro
Savva Pavappanasano
Mangalanam Cha Savvesim
Padhamam Havai Mangalam

By the power of this mantra, Mr Parekh explained, fire was transformed into a throne for Shri Amarakumar. When we emerged from the dark interior, a stupendous view from the stone balcony spread dotted with birds: crows, an eagle, a vulture. I heard on all sides the more comfortable cooing and fluttering of pigeons nesting all round, in temple niches, domes and rock clefts. In the outer hall Mr Parekh pointed out indications on yellow stone intended to represent 2452 feet belonging to the first Jain disciples. Interestingly, the temple had to be restored three times within a century after its construction, and even today maintenance continues. 'I am a Vaishnavite from Kheda', smiled a pilgrim, introducing himself to me as I stood entranced by the clear air over Girnar, 'but I came here to pay respects' and indeed the majority of visitors are not Jains at all. Once alone I shouted with joy at the exhilaration of life lived to the plenitude, like a moon become full, or a woman's giving birth to a perfect child. A woman with a superhuman headload of gunny-sacks rested for a moment by the wall, then gingerly repositioned her burden for the next stage of her journey. A notice read: 'Ambaji 800 steps, Anand Gufa 140 steps, Mahakal Gufa 150 steps, Savadas 150 steps, Bhartvan Sashavan 1400', indicating a new way to the foot of Girnar hewn out in the 1980s.

Other temples on Girnar pale into triviality compared with Neminatha's, but the beautiful Mallinatha temple (1231) owed to Vastupala and Tejapala should be seen. A double-domed rectangular mandapa forms the structure's nucleus, from which three shrines open – one in each direction, the fourth opening being the entrance. As usual, the eastern shrine is the main one, here devoted to the 19th century *tirthankar*, Mallinatha, whose colour is blue and symbol an urn. The two lateral shrines have other Jain symbols: the northern has a square-based monument called Sumeru, in Hindu myth the centre of the earth, on which Indra's heaven lies, and the abode of deities corresponding to Olympus in western myth; the southern has a circular-based monument representing the Jain pilgrimage temple-hill of Parshvanatha in Bihar, the alleged birthplace of the 23rd *tirthankar* whose colour is blue and emblem a cobra. Ceilings are carved with flying figures and heavenly damsels that you will see elsewhere, deliberately

Girnar. Jain temples, from Ambaji

stylised of course to avoid any hint that one might see human individual traces in these delightful symbols. It is hard for me, as a stranger, to grasp how a Jain ascetic's religious fervour could be deepened by these amply-bosomed females with rounded arms and legs, tapering fingers, and come-hither faces, but I am sure one could argue that they might correspond to the 'temptations of St Anthony' courtesans familiar in western iconography. Corbelling of the domes is a feature of the Solanki dynasty, but little else from the 13th century survives, beyond the niches, eaves and basement mouldings. Dates merge and disappear with the persistence of renovation and repair: thus, Samprati Raja's temple may have been erected in 1158, but the clustered tower almost certainly dates from the restoration of 1453.

Three temples lie to the left of Neminatha's. The southernmost is dedicated to the first *tirthankar* Rishabhadeva, and contains a huge idol to him like the Bhim Padam on Shatrunjaya. His colour is gold and his emblem the bull. The idol's throne has figures of all 24 *tirthankars* carved in 1442. Opposite this temple is a modern temple known as Panchabai's, and west of this is one called Merakvasi, dedicated in the 15th century to Parshvanatha. Another to Parshvanatha, dated 1803, has a large marble image protected by his emblem, a cobra. The last temple to the north is Kumarapala's, named for the local king (1145-72) who built as many Jain as Hindu temples all over Gujarat, including Shatrunjaya and Diu, Mount Abu and Cambay, Mangrol and Idar. The long portico on the west side was restored in 1824.

I took tea with a cha-walla crouching over his charcoal with single-minded concentration. He protected his head with a wide brown scarf and his body with a flowing white dhoti. Hot sweet milky tea came flowing out of the high fountain of his jug into a tiny cup three feet below in his other hand without a drop spilled.

All the rocks on the way up were marked with the names of thousands of egotists, to the point where enterprising vendors now sell chalks for this purpose: I suppose it must be marginally less offensive than carving your name on stone with a chisel. Adrenalin removed all the tiredness from my legs and body: I appeared to be climbing the last eight hundred steps on air. I bought a cheap, garish oleograph of Girnar Hill wrapped in cellophane with a piece of string for me to nail it on the wall. I light incense now before the picture of the Sonarekha winding below god-cluttered heights.

Mr Parekh said, 'Though I come from Bombay, I was born in Junagadh, and I revere not only all Jain *tirthankars*, but also the mother goddess of this temple.' The present shrine to Amba Mata is believed, following an inscription in the Neminatha temple below, to date from the same time, that is 1159, but these peaks will have been worshipped as energy-giving sources of the earth goddess from the dawn of man's religious sense. Young Hindu couples bashfully offered fruit and flowers to the silent image of the draped mother goddess beyond silver doors. A white-bearded guru all in pink told me, through Kiran Parekh, the valley's legend full of gods and holy cows, the upshot being that all the shakti or psychic energy of the whole of Saurashtra emerges at Amba Mata, a neat parable for dormant vulcanism. Amba Mata's vehicle is the lion, which explains why a lion image sits in the intimate little temple, so different in its noise and bustle from the more solemn Jain sanctuaries below. Bapu, the white-bearded guru, introduced me to the younger guru, who also possesses the powers to bless and cure: Mahantshri Tansukhgiri explained that Amba Mata is another name for Shiva's consort Parvati. 'She can travel by lion from her home in the Himalaya here to our temple in one second, like (and he twiddled his fingers for the simile), like a television

193

Girnar. Ambaji Temple. Interior

picture'. I tried to give the gurus a donation for the offered *prasad*, but Kiran diverted me from the path: 'allow me to gain the merit for giving this offering' he begged, and of course I acceded. The guru proffered another sweet rice-cake. 'You are not tired', said the guru, his eyes fixed on mine deeply.

'No,' I answered, 'but how did you know?'

'I did not know', he chuckled, 'but *Parvati* knew.'

Another thousand steps first down, then up again, brings you to the highest peak of Girnar (3660 feet), with a sheer drop on both sides. On a windless day the route is safe, because the steps are walled, and the views in all directions are outrageously magnificent. 'What have I done to deserve this splendour?' I asked myself, and nobody answered. The Shaivite temple to Goraknath has its own windswept fascination: *sadhus* come from all over Gujarat and celebrate their high distinction together with weary travellers and pilgrims. One *sadhu* will rubber-stamp your t-shirt with the trident of Shiva; another will offer you *prasad* for a small donation; another will regale you with tales of the pilgrim Gorakhnathji whose footprints are said to be present here.

A further two thousand steps down, then even more steeply back up in the same direction brings you to the hill of Guru Dattatreya, whose footprints are equally revered. Or as Mohanlal Meghji Desai has it, in his *Gir-*

194

Girnar. Across the ridge from Ambaji to Goraknath and (in the distance) Guru Dattatreya

nar-Junagadh Guide as immortally rendered by V.D. Savalia: 'There are feet of Guru Dattatreya on the mountain people touch the feet and alms-giving by the recitation worship people become free from many births'. Jains know the peak as Neminatha peak. After this you can visit the Kamandal temple and the Kalika peak.

It was nightfall by the time I trudged gamely back down to the cafés where I had begun the day. I drank seven cups of tea and a bottle of Bisleri mineral water and agreed a price with an auto-rickshaw wallah for the quick ride back to Hotel Girnar, where an omelette and chip awaited.

Tomorrow I should see not the mythical lions of Parvati, but the real Asiatic lions of Gir Forest.

Sasan Gir Lion Sanctuary

Sasan Gir is on bus routes and the railway between Veraval (45 km to the south) and Junagadh (60 km to the north). Lions provided excellent big-game hunting during the Raj, and the Nawab of Junagadh maintained a hunting lodge which you can stay in today. Following the terrible famine of 1899-1900, the Nawab began to protect the Asiatic lion, which today numbers only about 400 specimens worldwide. The census of 1974 showed only 180 animals, that of 1979 an encouraging 205, rising to 239 in 1985 then 284 in 1990. Some are kept in captivity at Junagadh Zoopark and a litter of two cubs were born at London Zoo in 1993. Leopards have also recovered steadily, from 155 in 1974 to 212 in 1990.

The habitat varies from arid to semi-arid because the southwest monsoon misses Saurashtra once on average every three years. Grasslands, scrub, savannah and dry deciduous forests are intersected by several hill and river systems. The soils tend to be shallow, making agriculture unprofitable, so pastoralism is more popular these days, and the cattle-owning Maldhari tribes in the area impoverish the forest by removing groundwater and cutting trees and branches for fuel. Gir forest covers 1412 sq km, of which 1154 sq km has been designated a wildlife sanctuary (opened by Nehru in 1956) and a nucleus of 258 sq km the National Park. The sanctuary is closed to visitors during the monsoon season, from 16 June to 15 October or 15 November, depending on the rains. The cool dry season lasts from November to early March, followed by three months of hot dry weather. Most rainfall falls in July and August, if the monsoon visits at all. Of seven rivers running through Gir, only the Shingoda, Jataradi and Hiran are permanent watercourses. Of the vegetation, 70% of the forest cover is teak, which at the far east is replaced by dhavda (*Anogeisus latifolia*). Other habitats include babul forest, dry savannah, and tropical thorn forest degenerating into thorn scrubland. The dominant colours are sandy, tawny, dusty: in short, lion-coloured, and the most successful denizens of Gir are those which most closely reproduce the hues of their environment, such as spotted deer, gazelle, Hanuman langur, and the lazy wandering lions (99), lionesses (122) and cubs (63).

On arrival at Sasan Gir, you register at the reception centre, which opens at sunrise and closes at sunset: night visits are prohibited. You pay a modest entrance fee per person, camera fee, vehicle (an Ambassador copes perfectly well with sanctuary trails) or wait for an available vehicle. A jeep fare is Rs 2.50 per km, shared by up to 6 passengers. Keep silent in the sanctuary and wear inconspicuous clothing, if possible light brown. Gir lions are wild but not vicious, so if you stay in your vehicle at all times and keep your voice down you are in no danger. If your vehicle breaks down, stay in it until another comes along: several rangers patrol all familiar tracks.

I started off by studying the photographs and scientific data in the Orientation Centre, then found the Crocodile Rearing Centre, where a one-year-old marsh crocodile was gurgitating meat brought in from Junagadh, while a keeper threw fish for little croclets. At the age of five or so, the crocodiles are released into Kamleshwar Dam. Visitors are invited to see feeding, at 5.30p.m. on alternate days. Staff take eggs from the artificial dam and rear them here in basins to ensure their conservation in an alien environment. Apart from Sasan Gir there are only two other crocodile-rearing centres in India: at Calcutta and Hyderabad.

India has a management programme for crocodiles considered among the best in the world, with those of Australia, Papua New Guinea, the U.S.A., Venezuela and Zimbabwe.

This contrasts with deplorable *shikari* expeditions for crocodiles documented in a myriad Indian sporting memoirs, such as Hornaday's *Two Years in the Jungle* (1885), which is an account of taking adult gharial from the Yamuna River. Then there is W.H. Shortt's 'A Few Hints on Crocodile Shooting' in the *Journal of the Bombay Natural History Society* (1921). Tribes of hunter-gatherers (most of whom still practise some form of hunting) were directly responsible for much of the decimation of India's crocodile population, earning cash since the 19th century to supplement their subsistence economy by hunting on behalf of middlemen acquiring skins for processing centres such as Kanpur and Calcutta in the north, and Hyderabad, Mysore and Madras in the south. The total of adult gharials known from India, Pakistan, Bangladesh and Nepal in 1983 was about 300, so these long overdue management programmes need to be vigorously supported and strengthened.

If Gir had not been established as a lion sanctuary, its fame would have spread as a bird sanctuary, for 310 avifauna species have been recorded, and a record card with a list of locally identified species can be requested on site. Be sure you ask for a bird guide and take with you Martin Woodcock's *Birds of the Indian Sub-Continent* (Collins, 1980), profusely illustrated throughout in colour. You might not see many reptiles, but of the twenty-three species recorded, you will almost certainly see a marsh crocodile or mugger at Kamleshwar, turtles, tortoises, geckoes, chameleons, lizards, and skinks. Less common are Indian python, common Indian Krait, Russell's Viper, Indian cobra, and the dhaman, or common rat-snake.

Though I should have felt disappointed without a lion-sighting, the pleasures of Gir include many other intriguing mammals: a proliferation of spotted deer, the larger blue bull, sambar, four-horned antelope or chausinga, Indian pangolin, honey badger, Indian foxes, striped hyena, jackals, Indian gazelle, crested porcupine, pale hedgehog, and three kinds of mongoose. The Superintendent, Mr Kataria, had spent five years at Bansda National Park in the hilly east of Bulsar district: he sorted absently through an inventory of fodder which a lorry had just been dumped outside his office while the driver stood to meek attention at an instinctive distance: near enough to be summoned; far enough to avoid interrupting. 'We used to lay bait for a 'lion show' up to 1987, then we stopped this method of entertaining tourists, and when I came in 1990 I continued the 'wild' policy of taking the visitors to the lions instead of bringing the lions to the visitors. I lean to the concept of protecting the animals from too much exposure and restricting the entertainment angle. We employ 16 trackers to patrol different corners of the sanctuary, monitoring all animals, not just the lions. We take all our sick animals to the zoo in Junagadh. In the last four years three fatal incidents have occurred, all to Maldharis, whom we are gradually shifting outside the sanctuary. They are given compensation when they move and if their livestock happens to be attacked. Our policy is to limit the roads and trails that humans and vehicles can use. You know that 2 trains a day pass through the sanctuary on their way to Delvada and Veraval. Many times travellers have spotted lions, and the train has actually killed three lions. We have around 500 staff for the whole sanctuary. In October-June 1991-2, the number of visitors rose to nearly 45,000 from only around 15,000 five years back, because we are very keen to pursue environmental education to high school students, especially to those living close to Gir. We divide the whole sanctuary into small blocks and carry out a policy of controlled burning to minimise the dangers of large-scale fires. Most of our deciduous forest and scrubland is tinder-dry and a forest fire would otherwise destroy all mammals and reptiles with a few hours.'

A trip lasting around three hours can be taken at any time, but the best chance of sightings is shortly after dawn, and shortly before dusk. My first trip took me via Kamleshwar Dam towards Kankai, including half-an-hour in the watchtower above the dam, and another half-hour as the guest of a Muslim Maldhari in his *nes* or compound fenced with wooden palings and brushwood. Ishmal Bapu is the elder of five families, a number usual in a Maldhari *nes*, and herds 25 to 30 buffalo. His courtyard, thick with buffalo dung, is scavenged by chickens. I was invited to drink buttermilk offered by a bespectacled lady, her head covered by a white shawl. The wattle-and-daub home with a tiled sloping roof against monsoon rains shelters three sons and daughters of Ishmal. The family lived first in

Haripur, but moved here despite the threat from lions because the water and grazing are far superior. Ishmal's daughter Muni held a *kuhari* (an iron chopper) used for cutting branches to allow buffalo to penetrate the undergrowth for pasture. A peacock flew down into the compound with an exhibitionistic squawk which we all ignored as we sipped tea which Muni handed round in little glasses and tin saucers. Just as camels occupy most of the waking thoughts of the Tuareg of Algeria, so buffalo remain the abiding interest of Maldhari pastoralists. Their value in the market depends chiefly on their milk, so a buffalo's price may range from Rs 5,000 up to Rs 10,000. As the paterfamilias, Ishmal leaves the grazing of his herd to younger folk, but you can tell from his restless eyes and his tapping fingers that he feels his place is in the forest.

Kamleshwar Dam checks the river Hiran, and a two-storeyed white building nearby acts as an Irrigation Department rest-house and an observation post to watch marsh crocodiles sunning themselves on the dam slopes, and to note animals that come to drink at the water's edge, such as a group of spotted deer and a family of five Hanuman langur monkeys (there are no rhesus monkeys in the Gir), then a bold stag dipped his head into the shining waters, using his antlers as a set of bumpers against snapping muggers. On our way we saw no lions, but examined trees attacked by white ants, which often live in symbiosis with snakes, and by a river a yellow cumulus cloud became on closer inspection millions of tiny yellow butterflies milling like a little universe. The guide Jitu picked for me a three-leaved *beliputra* specimen, collected by devotees of Lord Shiva to decorate the lingam during the holy month of Sravan.

I took a Gujarati thali lunch at the Forest Lodge amid swooping green parakeets cracking their jokes on the balcony in squeaky voices above grumbling crows in the garden. In the river below, a woman rubbed soapy clothes against a boulder with fierce determination: no mother-in-law could stand a chance, in theory. Storks fished with their thrusting sudden beaks, and striped palm squirrels skipped about on the balcony ledge with the chirpy self-confidence I connect with London sparrows. Pink and blue hydrangeas coloured the gardens, which otherwise maintained their stubborn winter brown.

In the afternoon, we headed south towards the Shingoda river and its dam on the route called Raydhi-Dedakiri. We traversed a village of 85 Sidi families, Muslim negroes originally from Africa who settled here centuries ago, in a self-contained community. Spotted deer barked warnings of our approach and another group melted into the undergrowth, having been surprised at a river, where a common kingfisher streaked past in a blur of iridescence. A Little Green Heron stalked prey at the water's edge, then we emerged into the dusty teak forest, with limp brown teak leaves the size of elephant-ears. A team of rangers was burning brush and beating it down into a great blackened circle with leafy branches.

A jeep met us with a ranger pointing eagerly backwards: 'a lioness has

199

been seen just to the right a hundred yards back', and we continued as quietly as our snorting engine would allow. Wild peacocks brushed through dry bracken and a frightened sambar ran swiftly away. We stopped, waited and listened. The only eyes I saw belonged to alert spotted deer, 20,000 of which roam Gir: there are more than 1,200 sambar and 500 chinkara. A common kite sank down with a relaxing gust while a kestrel circled, hinting at a possible kill in the vicinity. A Hindu Maldhari wearing a white cape and trousers passed along the track, guiding his fourteen buffalo attentively. Lions will attack a buffalo when sufficiently famished, though they prefer small prey. Each buffalo carried its attendant *bagalo*, or crane, feeding on the ticks and other noxious insects troubling the lumbering beast. A dozen spotted deer just beside the road made so much noise as they trampled through the brittle fallen teak leaves that in theory a lion would merely have to crouch long enough for them to pass his way, detecting them from afar by sound, but in practice their sense of smell is so acute that they can detect a lion's presence very early. But no sightings of a lion today! After a thali meal, I sat on the verandah to watch the sunset and at 7.30 heard a muaddin calling the faithful to prayer across the river.

At 6.10 a.m. I looked for breakfast. 'Have you tea?' 'Yes, we have only tea.' 'Oh, no bread-butter?' 'No, we have only bread-butter'. This was getting better all the time, But I forbore to ask for porridge, in case he didn't have only porridge.

We left at 7 a.m. and by 7.20 we had met our first wild peacocks of the day, and seen our first wide-eyed spotted deer. In ten minutes, the guide begged the driver to stop the car. And there was 'my' first Asiatic lion in

Sasangir. In the Lion Sanctuary, early morning

the wild – a massive eight-year-old male few yards behind a sleek seven-year-old female, neither showing any fear of the car or of us. The male pounded on the ground with both hind paws, first facing her, then with his back to her. She sat down, feigning lack of interest, so he matched this by wandering off down the dusty road, tail high, then suddenly sitting in the centre of the track, behind the car. If she continued on her way, she would have to pass him. She considered this ploy, then turned and (green eyes illuminating the dawn) padded away into tree-cover, and found a gap in a wall. The male, still stirred by the mating season, decided to abandon his pose and padded after her, at the same pace or slightly quicker, vanishing through the same gap. On the other side of the trail, a male and female chital, alert for each other, stood immobile below a keswo tree. Teak forest gave way to wheatfields, one of which parted like a curtain to reveal a splendiferous peacock in full wedding finery, displaying in front of a peahen.

We now came to the Sidi village of Shirwan, with a population of some five hundred in forty houses, mostly farmers, with working bullocks rather than buffaloes. 'Don't try going into Shirwan', warned the guide, 'the Sidis don't welcome strangers here, or at Sidibachcha or Jambulsulvar'. The road is closed to visitors by a sign near a mighty sacred banyan at the Devadunga river, some way before the village of Jamwala. A little red-tiled school shone white in the morning sun. An old Sidi came down the track with a load of wood cut for domestic use as fuel, and he let me shake hands with his inquisitive grandson, black-eyed and bonny. A yellow-wattled lapwing skimmed overhead, and a jackal slunk past into the shade. Nobody guarantees sight of a pride of lions at Gir, but my own experience of seeing a lion and lioness during three three-hour safaris, I am assured, is not at all unusual.

Chorwad

My driver crashed my hired Ambassador car just outside Chorwad, luckily just outside the Palace Beach Resort. Chorwad itself is a fishing village, timeless in its observance of tides and currents. The late Nawab of Junagadh built his summer palace here in 1928, with a private beach now cleaned by the Tourism Corporation of Gujarat. I couldn't stay in the palace itself, because the porch had collapsed a few months earlier, luckily with no loss of life, and the palace has been declared unsafe, so the charming manager, Krishna Dev Singh Thakur, son of the Victoria Cross recipient Santram Singh Thakur, found me a comfortable room in the palace annexe with a shower, two twin beds beneath typical Gujarat mirror-style embroidered hangings, a rattan sofa, expensive wardrobes, easy chairs and coffee table. On the beach I found a Rajasthani cameleer charging Rs 10 for a twenty-minute ride. He is allowed the camel franchise from 9 a.m. to 5 p.m. as long as he cleans up the beach after the camel; let's say the hotel has

Chorwad. Summer Palace (1928)

kept its half of the bargain. Lifeguards protect swimmers, but the current's undertow is considered too dangerous for children, who are provided with a sea-water swimming-pool. A light suddenly flickered on at dusk in the Shiva temple to the right and I passed a sign 'Swimming is Dangerous in the Sea'. This is surely mistaken. Swimming is perfectly safe; *drowning* is dangerous.

Laughing girls on holiday swathed in bright saris passed a coconut-seller: they were clearly amused at my funny panama hat and heavy build, so much less attractive than their own. Dusk slid over the sea like silent smooth shutters, and I headed towards the Seaview Restaurant, opening to the evening breeze. (Mosquitoes are no hazard at Chorwad until April.) As usual, breakfast can be taken any time from 7 to 10, lunch from 12.30 to 2.30, snacks from 4 to 6, and dinner from 7.30 to 10. Unlike England, India possesses restaurants where the customers' convenience is consulted rather than the staffs'. I ordered a full litre of Bisleri water (leaving some for the night and morning), chicken and sweetcorn soup, locally-caught fresh fish and the best *nan* I have ever tasted, even in Gujarat where bread is taken seriously by all communities. After service coffee I left the restaurant to pad out like a tall cat into the warm velvet night, where the sea breeze soughed like Echo in Strauss's *Ariadne auf Naxos*.

Veraval

Not long ago, in Bahrain Gold Suq, I was speaking to a Gujarati jeweller, who told me he came from Veraval, the first consonant and the third lingering between 'v' and 'w', the second between 'd' and 'r' and the last pronounced as far back as the tongue can rise and strike the palate. The first vowel hovers between the 'e' of 'then' and the 'e' of 'the', the second is an 'ah' produced for a doctor's inspection, and the third shuts up submissively before the closing consonant. It sounds totally magical, like a name out of *Sindibad* or *Ali Baba*: I longed to visit the place, which derives its modern name from the ancient Velakula, also stressed on the second syllable. Civilisation has been dated hereabouts to the Chalcolithic, and if we accept Pargiter's opinion that the principal war recorded in the Mahabharata occurred around 950 B.C., the Yadavas came from Dwarka to Prabhas Patan (now Somnath) about that epoch, and would have used Veraval's harbour facilities. Lord Krishna's later life is connected with the Kathiawar peninsula, and it is said that here he was shot by the Bhil, Jara. Records show that seafarers traded with the Arabian Gulf, the Red Sea, and the coast of East Africa from antiquity, and it was only with the rise of Surat that Veraval surrendered its premier position as the port of embarkation for Muslim pilgrims from western India to the Holy Places.

Because it is so closely linked with Somnath, you won't stay in Veraval itself, not because the accommodation is inadequate (it is better than anything you will find in Somnath) but because the stench of fish will drive out even the hardiest traveller. If you have no sense of smell, there is nothing to stop you staying in Veraval, and watching the construction of dhows on a stretch of beach opposite the fishing-harbour (one just finished had been sold for Rs 35,000) or wandering among the hundreds of fishing-boats. The old summer palace of the Nawab of Junagadh was

Veraval. Fishing port

203

utilised as Somnath College until replaced by the modern building close by. It is a gracious two-storey Venetian-Gothic pile with a breeze-pavilion on the roof, now sadly vacant and incongruously overlooked by a prosperous modern Birla Rayon Factory.

Prabhas Patan (Somnath)

In the *Shivapurana* and the *Nandi Upapurana*, Shiva is reported to have stated 'I am omnipresent, but I am especially in twelve forms and places', which are in order this present Gujarati city; Srisailam, Andhra Pradesh; Mahakaleshwara at Ujjain, Madhya Pradesh; Omkara, either at Ujjain, or possibly the Mahadeva shrine at Omkara Mandhatta on the Narmada; Amareshwara at Ujjain; Vaidyanatha at Deogarh; Rameshwaram, Tamil Nadu; Bhima Shankara, probably identifiable with Bhimeshwara at Dracharam, near Rajamahendri, Andhra Pradesh; Visheshwara at Benares; Triambaka ('Three-Eyed') on the banks of the Gomati; Gautamesha, of uncertain location; and Kedarnath, Uttar Pradesh.

The place itself was originally dedicated to Soma, the deified juice of the climbing plant *Asclepias acida*, a drink described in great detail and praised in the *Rigveda*. The Brahmans drank it and thought of it as a panacea, giver of riches and superhuman powers, enlightener and enlivener, hallucinogen and magic worker exactly as in the case of Bacchus in Western pagan religion: one can observe its effects in *The Bacchae* by Euripides. In Puranic mythology later on, Soma became identified with the moon; another significant myth says that as the result of a quarrel Soma's body was cut in half by Shiva's trident, an episode presumably illustrating the victory at a certain point of Shiva's adherents over the old shamans. And just as Somanatha proclaims by its very name a pre-Shaivite cult of the moon-god, so the Surya Mandir close by, housing the Prabhas Patan Archaeological Museum, unveils the pre-Shaivite dominance of the sun-god, Surya, whose temple here dates to the 10th century in its present form, but presumably pre-existent temples (of wood) were burned or cleared away to allow construction of this massive enterprise.

As to the great place of pilgrimage, Somanatha temple itself, legend says that its first incarnation in gold was due to Somraj, the moon-god; its second in silver was created by Ravana, possibly a faulty rendering of Ravi, another name for Surya or Suraj, the sun-god; its third in wood by Shri Krishna; and its fourth in stone by Bhimdeva. Whatever its real ancestry, in historic times it is recorded first in the 10th century, enriched beyond measure by pious donations, and sacked in the third decade of the 11th century by Mahmud of Ghazni (998-1030), the Sunni Muslim iconoclast, who returned to Ghazna in eastern Afghanistan with the temple treasures, including the famed silver gate of Somnath. Kumarapala, ruler of Anahilvada Patan in northern Gujarat, paid for the restoration of the temple in 1169 and its wealth again grew as pilgrims returned. In 1297 Ala ud-Din Muhammad Shah of the Khilji dynasty reconquered Somnath for

Prabhas Patan. Somnath Temple

Islam, and Islam retained the coastal belt with governors responsible to the Mughal Empire from the time of Muhammad bin Tughlaq in 1325 to the annexation of Somnath by the Nawab of Junagadh's Diwan Amarji in 1770. Thus, as Spuler has written, Mahmud of Ghazni 'created for Islam an extensive territory in India, and laid the foundation for the religious division of this area, the latest effect of which has been the creation of the independent state of Pakistan'. (And incidentally, the subsequent rise of the R.S.S. and B.J.P. trading on popular fears of Pakistan exacerbated by Hindu nationalists themselves.)

Several other waves of destruction engulfed Somnath and its temples, the last being Aurangzeb's in 1706, so it is with some surprise that we see the modern building recreated as if it were a Solanki-period temple in the manner of Modhera's Sun temple, due to the efforts of Sardar Vallabhai Patel whose statue stands outside. The massive mandapa and the main shrine smaller in area but taller in gentle pyramidal stages loom in a vast courtyard which has the effect of minimising by optical illusion the number and importance of visitors. Opening hours are 6 a.m. to 9.30 p.m., and major *puja* times are 7 a.m., noon and 7 p.m. A red sign right of the entrance proclaims 'Shri Ram' (Lord Rama). Already the modern temple seems to have acquired a timeless air of decay, neglect and rotting fish permeates the courtyard from the beach below, where children are transformed instantly from pilgrims to paddlers. Left is Ganesha, right is Hanuman. Nandi faces the image of Shiva with the legend 'Secret offering is the best offering in the eye of God'. The silver-plated wooden gate stood open at 12.55 and I watched a blind Hindu being led among the columns,

205

feeling each in turn, by his dhotied companion. Photography is prohibited, so I eagerly 'learned' the scene by heart: a temple attendant passed leaves and a polythene-packed prasad, possibly sugar nuggets, to an unending chain of the devout, who pressed their brown foreheads against the dirty stones, chanting 'Ram, Shiva, Ram, Shiva' incessantly, as if their continued existence depended on the unbroken incantation. Through the left-hand door I saw the sea shimmering invitingly, entrancing the glittering-saried women resting on the balcony as if on a ship's balustrade, as if on a steady garden swing.

From here, between 8.30 and 12.15, and 2.30-6.15, you can visit the Prabhas Patan Museum, identifiable some 250 metres along the main street north from the temple by that familiar blue enamel plaque reading 'Protected Monument'. The museum is far more interesting than the modern temple, because it preserves art treasures (mainly sculptures) from most periods. Two attendants inside the cool porch were playing the traditional game of navkokri, but one was so superior in tactics that within a few minutes his victim had cried 'mercy' with a rueful grin of resignation. The collection ranges from the first-rate (a superb 11th-century dancing maiden) to the meaningless (a fragment of a plain stone pillar): the problem is as usual that of scarcity of documentation, for there are no guidebooks, catalogues, postcards, and even the few very captions that exist have not been translated out of Gujarati into Hindi or English. But all time spent here is supremely worth the journey for the cool ambience of a Temple to the Sun, with the remains of the ancient shrine reconstructed by the Chalukyan Maharaja Shri Mularaja Deva Solanki of Anahilvada Patan. Beneath five great domes an amorous couple, a *maithuna*, have been rapt in each other's gaze since the 10th century; an 11th-century masterpiece depicts Agni, God of Fire, who presides over the earth as Indra the air and Surya the sky; a fine Vishnu; a magnificent Uma Maheshwara of the 11th century, near contemporary dancing girls wuith instruments; the great 11th-century Shiva Nataraja displayed in the centre of the five domes as if in 'the still centre of the turning world'.

Don't miss sections of the torana of the 12th-century temple rebuilt by Kumarapala (1169) with goddess and dancing-girl, or the equestrian Bhairava of the same age, or a Parvati disfigured in the breasts by the raiding armies of Muhammad bin Tughlaq.

Outside a dog foamed at the mouth and moved its limbs epileptically in a manner I recalled from veterinarian textbooks. Little girls pointed in amusement at the animal's quivering agonies, but I glided in fear beside a wall until I had left the rabid beast far behind. The dog I had eluded reminded me of the outrage that surrounded Gandhiji in his 'silent' year, 1926, when he defended the Ahmedabadi mill-owner Ambalal Sarabhai, who had incensed Hindus by rounding up and destroying sixty stray dogs which infested his properties. 'What else could be done?' argued Gandhiji, though his beloved Hinduism forbids the taking of life of any

Prabhas Patan. Sun Temple

living being. Gandhi wrote to his critics in *Young India*, citing 1,117 cases of hydrophobia during 1925 in one Ahmedabad hospital alone. 'The ideal of humanity in the West is perhaps lower,' he wrote, 'but their practice of it is very much more thorough than ours. We rest content with a lofty ideal and are slow and lazy in its practice. We are wrapped in deep darkness, as is evident from our paupers, cattle and other animals'.

I decided to hire a tonga for the afternoon, because Prabhas Patan possesses many sights, signposted (if at all) only in Gujarati, spread out over a wide area reflecting the former significance of this holy city, which has existed on this site no earlier than the 1st century A.D. according to the Department of Archaeology's report *Somnath 1956* by J.M. Nanavati, R.N. Mehta and S.N. Chowdhary. The tongawallahs and auto-rickshaw-wallahs have a little printed card in Gujarati headed 'Somnath-ki Akasan', listing eleven of the sights of the town, and you can simply ask the driver to call these out and answer 'ji' or 'nahi' ('yes' or 'no') according to your preferences and time available.

Lunch is limited to Gujarati thalis, and if you decide to eat at a little restaurant opposite the bus station, the world of Somnath and its pilgrims unfolds before you like a slow-moving feature-film. My only companions turned out to be a gloomy, tense Gujarati family of five who, having packed all their bags, trunks, blankets and suitcases, were tucking into their last lunch in Somnath before embarking on their longest adventure, via the teeming, daunting city of Bombay for the cold, colourless, drab and silent cities of midland and northern England, where men are said to wear grey and women brown. In Leicester, they would seek out fellow-Gujaratis, their local temple, cassettes of film music and videos of the latest movies in Hindi and Gujarati, trying to reproduce in their neon-lit kitchens the succulent tastes and heady, spicy aromas of their native town. But without the whir of ceiling fans, zephyrs from the deep blue sea, munching cows, red saris, gold earrings, green saris, pungent incense and laconic tongawallahs drowsing behind their ponies, the crowds of pilgrims and the piped music eternally celebrating human love – what could ever be the same?

Behind the tonga stand I found the cream dome of the Ahalya Bai Mandir named for the Maratha queen of the Holkar dynasty (1765-95) who paid for its construction in 1783. Within, a Shiva lingam on yoni with a naga is protected underground in a domed chamber with an electric fan to keep the priests tolerably cool and an image of Parvati opposite her consort's emblem. Multi-coloured flags strung beside four neon bulbs gave a party-feeling to the occasion undermined when a white-robed ascetic first touched the lingam, then abased his forehead to touch the cold stone yoni. Silver gates barred the way to the upper shrine.

My tonga clip-clopped through the flat, silent streets of Prabhas Patan to a Surya Mandir which a priest informed me sagely would be 2,000 years old next week, but in fact anyone can see that most of it cannot date beyond Solanki times, and as for its ultimate origin, only prohibited excavations could prove what is underneath. Ugly concrete homes desecrate the sanctity of the place, which has a picture of Swami Vivekananda within. Very close to the right I found an underground cave with a Shiva lingam, above it a Ganesha painted bright orange, a Nandi bull opposite, and modern mosaic tiling of appalling vulgarity. In the distance, towards the sea, a neat cemetery has squat anonymous forms on square stone bases.

Next stop for the tonga was the complex of shrines and bathing ghats known as Tribeni Tirth: the meeting of the Hiran, Saraswati and Kapil rivers at the sea, always a particularly holy spot in Hinduism, where all rivers are sacred, and three triply so. The Queen's Temple, or Raniji Mandir, has a shrine with an idol bedecked in bright red clothes, and a tiny little modern enclosure. A row of temples faces the confluence: Shri Satyanarayan Mandir, Shri Radhakrishna Mandir, and Mankeshwar Mahadeva Mandir, and visible from them, again very close to the shoreline, rises the Lakshminarayan Mandir. Pilgrims recline on stone benches in the heat of the day, contemplating the palm-fringed oasis town, the gentle crystalline-white-blue of the seafoam, and the Lord of the Meeting of the Rivers. Lakshminarayan's great columned hall, used for meetings, echoed emptily to the conversation of two priests near the door; a sweeper prodded invisible dust, leaves and insects from one side of the hall to the other across the modern marble floor, and I resisted the temptation to buy necklaces of shells like those on Bombay's Juhu Beach from a vendor of souvenirs. The only guidebook in Somnath (indeed the only book I saw there at all) is a dreadful mishmash called *Jay Somnath* by Jashvantlal M. Panchal, translated unluckily by Mukundrai P. Vyas: "Somdev (Moon God) came on Prabhash Tirth with his beloving wife Rohini for prayer & after 4,000 years penace God Shiva became pleased on "Somdev" & in Sukla Paksh more and more improvement & lighting came day by day". One aspect of the profound duality of the Hindu attitude to books and learning is unthinking reverence towards any kind of set text or scripture, so that learning something by heart is much more common than viewing it critically; the other aspect is an antipathy to reading anything more substantial or demanding than the morning paper. Most Hindus may be linguistically so sophisticated that they may comfortably speak five languages; but to judge from publishing sales figures they do not choose to read much in any of them. The result is that in Gujarat libraries remain poorly funded and administered and bookshops cater to the schoolbook and comics market almost exclusively in Gujarati, with very little in other Indian languages and even less in European tongues.

Mahuva – Talaja – Gopnath
A tea-stop at the Hotel Ruby in Mahuva gave the chance to see the bazaar in its customary frenzy of gaudy colours and hubbub of noise – shouting,

209

Map of South-Eastern Saurashtra

roaring of cargo trucks, hooting of national-permit lorries, grinding of gears as buses lurch among the cattle and people. The town used to be a port called Madhumavati and Madhupuri, but silting on the Gulf of Cambay has forced construction of a new harbour to the south. Nowadays Mahuva is best known for its crafts in wood for building, furniture and children's toys, brightly-coloured and on offer for a few rupees, such as little horses and carts.

Near Mahuva a local man will point out the way to Khatpur, the ancient Kanakavati, capital of Kanaksen Chavada, alleged founder of the Chavada rulers. You can still identify brick remains of Kanakavati, in another of those revelations that spring upon you everywhere in India, at even the most unexpected moments. And I did not expect to find an island (called Shiyal) close by Kanakavati almost completely covered with the remains of yet another Jain-administered civilisation, called Shrilingapura once, a name with strong Shaivite associations. Great fortifications protected a palace, step-wells, and a fresh-water reservoir. Jain marble images have been rescued. Local tales relate how one of the Chavada kings, called Meghananda, and his son Abhiraja took prisoner the ruler of Kalyan near Bidar, Karnataka and thirty-six Rajput princes, whom he imprisoned in a wooden cage in a jail whose remains are gleefully pointed out by a local whitebeard. The story goes that they were rescued by Ugoji, the Rajput Wala chieftain of Bhadrod, who inadvertently kicked Kawat of Junagadh when hurriedly breaking the wooden palings of the cage. Kawat, his honour attacked by the kick, is said to have killed his deliverer in revenge later on. This incident is dated to the 12th century.

The coastal road is still commandeered by farmers with oxen, villagers with cows and bullocks, and an occasional stately camel pulling a creaking cart with a drowsy man propped up on rice-sacks. Women pick cotton in the fields until dusk, and flocks of sheep spread and dash across the road, failing to obey the shouts and flails of the few shepherds. The landscape is pancake-flat until Talaja is glimpsed in the distance, another volcanic cone now extinct, some 350 feet above a tributary to the Shatrunjaya, north of Talaja town.

A local boy will show you the Buddhist caves on the northwest face of Talaja hill. Many of them, dated around the first century A.D., have been demolished to make easier passage up to the Jain temples or their antecedents. The so-called Ebhal Mandapa, a cave 75 feet by 68 feet and 17 feet high, received its name much later, from one of the Rajput Wala chieftains who came here from Mewar. It is said that the first in the line was called Ebhal, and the sixth in the line, also called Ebhal, seized Talaja from the local Koli people (the same race who originally populated Bombay) around the 12th century A.D. Ebhal Mandapa has four octagonal pillars in front, but none inside; neither has it the usual wall separating verandah from inner hall that we find in Kanheri or Nasik caves (see my *Western India*) but we can identify its Buddhist origin by a rail-pattern above the front of the cave, while another cave to the west presents a ruined dagoba of a simple, early type, with only the base intact. A large cave has been adopted by local Hindus for the worship of Khodia Devi, and others near the foot of the hill are still to be excavated. A steeper climb to the crown of Talaja hill leads up to two Jain temples white of walls and domes, achieving a sense of spiritual intensity almost equal to that of the distant Shatrunjaya temples they face northward.

If you have time to spare, take the road south from Talaja to the temple of Shiva at Gopnath near the Gulf of Cambay, which corresponds in sanctity to its companion-shrine of Bhimnath north of Bhavnagar. Nearby Jhanjhmer has a fine fort said to have been built by the Rajput Wala chieftain Jhanjharasi.

Palitana

Though it may at first sight seem like 'any other Indian town', which in fact hardly any of them do, Palitana can be considered a *temenos,* an antechamber to the possibly illusory wholeness of all reality which to an agnostic seems to comprise nothing other than the Void. Like Junagadh at the foot of Girnar Hill, Palitana is a cluster of homes, shops, offices and services, with a rail terminus via Sihor to Bhavnagar eastward, Botad and eventually Ahmedabad northward, and Jetpur-Porbandar westward. There is a rail line parallel with the coastline of Saurashtra, but to reach it near Talaja you have to travel via Bhavnagar by rail, so everyone goes direct by bus.

Almost as old as the hills, Palitana became a petty state when founded by Shahji, a Gohel Rajput of the same background as the rulers of nearby Bhavnagar. The Rajput sovereigns protected the Jain monuments, including the sacred hill of Shatrunjaya, from which the river of the same name runs down and through the town. If you take the Willingdon Market on the north side of the bridge as your point of origin, the bus stand, rail station and Western-style Hotel Sumeru lie in the direction of Bhavnagar, and the main mosque opposite a Jain temple is on the way to Taleti Road and the steps up to Shatrunjaya. I refer the reader to details of staying in Jain dharamshalas on Taleti Road in the accommodation section of the Useful Information chapter. Don't ignore Palitana because of the extraordinary significance of the mountain above it, but give yourself another day to mingle in the bazaars and talk to Jain pilgrims who will be delighted to discuss their elevated faith and principles, and to share with you their joy at being able to visit this stupendous temple city, whose nearest Christian equivalent would be Vatican City if it were spread out on a magic hill in pure air with a distant view of another city (Bhavnagar), the Gulf of Cambay and the world spread out like a baby's view of a quilt from the middle.

The most interesting place in Palitana valley is aptly enough a new museum devoted to Jain life and art: the Shri Vishal Jain Kala Sansthan on

Taleti Road, the main thoroughfare leading from Palitana town to the steps to Shatrunjaya. The initiative for the museum came from the archaeologist and art-historian Acharya Bhagwant Shri Vishalsensurishwarji (Virat) Maharaj Saheb; the architect of the attractive two-storey museum is B.L. Suthar. Opening hours are 10-12 and 3-8, and because of the large number of religious objects in the museum it is treated as a shrine and you remove your footwear before entering and paying the token fee of Rs 2. No postcards are on sale, but a small illustrated album captioned in English is available against a small donation. Regrettably, few of the items are dated, and captions are almost exclusively in Gujarati. Many of the pieces are very fine, some are very beautiful and others are not, the best department covers arts of the book, with miniatures and palm-leaf books such as a tenth-century Sanskrit Tatvartha Sutra written in Kannada script. Dates given in the Vikramaditya calendar beginning from 57 B.C. are preceded by 'Samvat', meaning 'year', so that a lovely Kalpa Sutra in Magadhi and Padimatra script is dated Sam. 1547 and a prayer written by the calligrapher Shri Shobhan Muni with symmetrical designs for empty spaces within the text is dated Sam. 1489. A magnifying glass reveals Jain sutras written in a microscopic Pali on ivory.

Exquisite paintings on ivory are outclassed by great ivory carvings such as a miraculously cool, classical Parshvanatha (the 23rd *tirthankar*), flanked by Dharandra and Padmavati and a serene Adinatha (the 1st *tirthankar*) also measuring 10" high x 5" wide. Images of the *tirthankars* are in white jade and black jade, serpentine, coral, malachite, serpentine, sandalwood, opal, sapphire, ruby and emerald.

A sequence of paintings reminiscent perhaps of naive Ethiopian religious panels depicts moments in the life of Prince Vardhaman before attaining omniscience while absorbed in the highest stage of meditation. In these works – and in many others I have seen in Jain murals – it is extraordinary that the prince who will become the 24th *tirthankar* as Shri Mahavira Swami is endowed with the palest countenance and a red-lipped, almost androgynous grace, like a Madonna in a Florentine Gothic altarpiece. Parallels between Mahavira and his contemporary Gautama Buddha are irresistibly powerful: on the one hand, a handful of scholars have suggested that Jainism and Buddhist separated doctrinally shortly after the sixth century B.C. but worship the same figure; on the other, most Jains and Buddhists themselves explain the coincidence by referring to an upsurge of religious intensity at the time, possibly as a rebellion against Brahmanic formalism, and possibly because of migration from other parts of Asia. The upper floor balcony is fitted with hundreds of figures showing scenes from the life of Mahavira on the lines of the Neapolitan presepio or crib. A Jain ascetic sat cross-legged, reading the *Bombay Samochar* and vaguely blessing those who came to sit at his feet.

A little way along Taleti Road I stopped to admire a range of colourful embroideries, absurdly cheap at anything from Rs 100 down to Rs 40.

Next door I found a cassette of Jain religious music for Rs 22, which I am playing as I write.

I met Mr R.D. Shah, manager of Sheth Anandji Kalyanji, the Jain charitable public trust responsible for looking after everything throughout India from pilgrims to temples, as regards the Svetambar Jains, the sect predominant in Gujarat, Rajasthan and Maharashtra. The 'sky-clad' or naked Jains called Digambar are more numerous in Madhya Pradesh, Punjab, Haryana, Delhi, Uttar Pradesh, and Bihar.

Mr Shah explained that one need not be born a Jain, but could convert by accepting the disciplines and creeds. 'The main criterion is non-violence: if all the world turned Jain tomorrow, we should have no more war, no battles, no ethnic cleansing or whatever name they give to genocide these days. Then of course we must visit the temple, and follow the rites in that connection. Then we are more than vegetarian: we don't even take vegetables such as potatoes which grow underground.'

'I have been a Jain all my life', I confided to Mr Shah, 'except for my unforgivable weakness: I couldn't give up potatoes any more than I could give up breathing.'

His polite gaze reminded me that I was lying: if potatoes did not exist, I could survive perfectly well. 'You see, there are good Jains who are not perfect. We may not take food after nightfall, but if man has been travelling for a long time and couldn't find anything to eat all day, it would not be a mortal sin if he ate after nightfall. There are degrees of austerity in Jains: some monks and nuns travel for months at a time, and they may not be given a lift but what if they fall ill? They must not knowingly tread on or ingest any living thing, but of course we know that unwittingly we kill microbes every time we breath in or let our feet touch the ground. What to do? Just live as plainly, simply and austerely as we can while not interfering with our neighbours. You will see cows roaming on our sacred hill and defecating there. Hindus take them up for grazing and we disapprove, but we do not speak or act violently towards our Hindu neighbours.

Shatrunjaya

The name Shatrunjaya is derived from the words 'jaya' (victory) and 'shatru' (enemies), the enemies in question being defined as *dwesh* (hatred) and *raga* (attachment to worldly things). The hill is not only the most sacred Jain *tirtha*, or place of salvation through pilgrimage, in Gujarat, but in the whole of India.

The Muslim rulers of Mughal India gave a series of imperial *firman*s or grants to the Jain merchant Shantidas Jawahari (*c.* 1590-*c.*1658), which had the effect of protecting Palitana town and its sacred hill from desecration by non-Jain interference across the centuries. Shantidas travelled extensively on religious pilgrimage throughout India and for professional reasons as both jeweller and financier.

But to begin at the beginning. I drank the rest of my bedside mineral water, spread two pieces of bread from my travelling jampot, emerged into the fresh air of dark Palitana at 6 a.m. and in a few minutes reached a café at the foot of the steps. There I stopped for an invigorating cup of hot sweet tea and a packet of Parle G biscuits which I shared with a tiny mongrel puppy; vendors offered walking-sticks at Rs 5, and doliwallas suggested Rs 200 to carry me up the steps and back down, a reasonable figure which I gently refused.

The red, softly breathing dawn escorted two Jain ladies in white carrying sticks and a procession of Hindu-owned cows up the steps below a crescent moon: a prelude to one of my greatest adventures. I stopped to close my eyes in bliss and an elderly gentleman of quiet peaceful authority interrupted his ascent to ask if I felt all right. 'If I have ever felt better', I admitted, 'I cannot recall the occasion'. He smiled.

'It is good you are making the pilgrimage'.

'Don't you mind if a non-Jain makes it?'

'No: we are not like the Muslims who stop you seeing Makkah and Madinah, or the Parsis who prevent you entering a fire temple. All our temples are open', and he explained how etiquette when visiting a Jain temple on Shatrunjaya or anywhere else can be reduced to a few essentials. Shorts are disrespectful, and women should not wear tight dresses or leave the head uncovered. Take your shoes off and leave outside anything to eat or drink including pills and medicines. No belt, handbag, or anything else made of leather should be taken inside, neither should you smoke, laugh, or talk or photograph, sit down, lie down or lean against the walls. When approaching the sanctum sanctorum, or *garbhagriha*, men should stand at the image's right hand, and women on the left. If these points sound severe, I should add that foreigners who infringe these models of behaviour are tolerated with great charm and grace by worshippers and priests, but if you have questions, it is polite to ask them once prayers are finished and the Jains return outside the temple. Most Jains are well-educated, speaking at least Hindi and English as well as Gujarati.

The Jain sage introduced himself as Muni Chandrasekhar Vijayji and gave his postal address as the Kamal Prakashan Trust, Zaveriwad, Ahmedabad, though he is always wandering. Twenty years ago he retired from his business in Akola, Maharashtra, giving up house, family ties, property and money. He has been living at a dharamshala in Palitana for the last twelve months, presumably as a non-paying guest. At the foot of the hill he showed me how to take a ticket for a free meal on the way down, later in the day, and explained that as a Jain living saint he doesn't touch women at all, taking out a notepad and writing on it for me a "Gift from India" which he tore out and presented to me: "Don't make bed with wife on Monday throughout life. Tell this to all". I asked him why Mondays would be especially perilous and he whispered "Monday is when females have much wish for making bed", a revelation that I have not been able to confirm from subsequent enquiries.

Jains should fast and refrain from sexual intercourse on five days of every month: the fifth, eighth and fourteen of the first half of the month or Sud, and the eighth and fourteenth of the second or Vad.

As he pointed out the enormous new temple in the plain called 108 Samvasaran Mandir from the number of images around it, he explained various dietary laws: breakfast may be taken 48 minutes after sunrise, but not before; lunch may be taken at any time, but dinner must be finished before sunset. Betel-chewing, smoking and all kinds of alcohol and drugs are forbidden to Jains, as are root crops such as potatoes, ginger, onions, carrots, and brinjal because it has a large number of seeds. Intermarriage is allowed. The caste system and untouchability form no part of Jainism. There are various sects, of course, as in other religions, including some who frown on the later practice of worshipping idols, which of course also marks the evolution from early Buddhist practice to later. Sthanakvasis denounce visiting temples and worshipping images there as idolatrous, but both Svetambars and Digambars concur in temple-visiting. Digambars reject the authenticity of the corpus of scriptures published by the Svetambars, and assert that Mahavira never married, that images of Mahavira must be nude, that Jains must adopt nudity, and that liberation can be attained only by one born a male. Jains state that the Mauryan Emperor Chandragupta abdicated his throne and travelled as a Jain monk to South India where he died, in emulation of Mahavira's own abdication of the world at the age of thirty and his dedication to teaching asceticism, repentance and non-violence.

You can mentally notch your progress up the steps and into the sky from the numbering of every hundredth step: youngsters race up, and old ladies alight from their covered *doli*s at intervals to rearrange themselves. At a Hindu shrine to Hinglai Devi Mata a Jain from Rajkot accompanied by his wife and daughter nodded to me, and said he made the pilgrimage three times a year. 'Luckily we live very close to the sacred hill'. Unlike Girnar, which possesses a sacred temple compound, the *whole* of Shatrunjaya is sacred, so no Jain is allowed to sleep there (and by implication soil the precinct) or eat there. However, as a practical measure to safeguard temple treasures, some sixty non-Jain security guards stay on Shatrunjaya throughout the night.

Though I counted about 3,500 steps up to the temples, much of the early and middle sections of the climb are interspersed with long flat stretches, completely without shade or shelter, so wear a hat and use sunblocking cream, long-sleeved shirts or blouses and long trousers or skirts or dresses as modesty requires.

The ecumenical emperor Akbar in the 16th century issued a *sanad* or imperial charter granting the hill of Samet Shikhar, now known as Mount Parshvanatha, in Bihar to Hira Vijaya Shri Acharya, then pontiff of the Svetambar Jain sect, and also granted Arbuda (Mount Abu) in Rajasthan,

216

Chandragiri in the Himalaya, with Girnar and Shatrunjaya in Saurashtra. Akbar gave them in perpetuity, and a clause prohibits the killing of animals either on, at the foot of, or around, these hills.

The earliest Jain temples are believed to have been erected in the year 882 Virata, equivalent to 313 A.D. and James Burgess suggests that the first probably arose on Girnar.

Jains say that the first *tirthankar*, Adinatha, visited Shatrunjaya, that his son Bharata erected the first temple here and that his disciple Pundarika attained *moksha* here. It might well be that shrines were erected here very early, because the hill lends itself to all kinds of awe. Muslim incursions in the 14th and 15th centuries destroyed evidence of early Jain and Hindu temples and it was only in the 16th century, given the security afforded by Akbar's *sanad*, that the great *tuks* or fortified temple compounds that we see today arose in all their extraordinary splendour. Some writers perpetuate the absurd legend that there are 863 temples on Shatrunjaya, exaggerating by a factor of seven or so. Many temples date in the present form from the 18th and even 19th centuries, and as you wander around you will see bamboo scaffolding, wheelbarrows, and other evidence that Jains still regard temple-building as second only to personal devotion, and have no false modesty about appending their names to trusts, charities and temples, so that while a legion of artists, sculptors and masons remain anonymous, wealthy patrons are immortalised in the names of their *tuks* and temples. This temple-city, just like Girnar, looks all the more impressive for its situation 2,000 feet above the valley, and for aggregating one shrine near the others, producing an effect like a crown of brilliant white pearls. Two ridges some 1140 feet long run nearly exactly east-west, and between them a slight dip is also filled with temples. Battlemented walls surround the holy places, and all gates are carefully closed at sundown.

After roughly 3,200 steps up to the temples, you reach a bifurcation near the summit: a right-hand path leads to Adinatha Temple in Khartavarasi Tuk, whereas a left-hand brings you to the lower-level Motishah Tuk in the centre before the last ascent to Adishvara Temple in Vimalavasi Tuk, which as the climax should be left to the end. This has the practical disadvantage that photography permits are to be bought only at the entrance to the South Ridge, where the following notice is posted:

'It is advisable not to climb on holy hill before sunrise and come down before sunset. Most valuable ornament, cash, etc. should not be with them. Gaurds staying on ach rest venue as two gaurds are ever concurrent in foot moblic duty to relax from arised trouble. Thanking you'.

There is no charge for admission anywhere on the mountain. The North Ridge's series of minor temples leads inevitably to the six

217

major *tuks*, of which the first you reach is also the largest and most striking. It is the so-called Chaumukhi ('Facing Four Ways') Temple of 1618, created on the foundations of an earlier temple, dedicated to a quadruple-faced idol of Adinatha, here given his other name of Shri Rishabdev Bhagwan, the first *tirthankar*, whose colour is gold and emblem the bull. Each cross-legged figure backs on to the square column below the dome, their hands folded tidily as we were taught in primary school, their staring inlaid white eyes with black inset round pupils. A carved elephant faces the image seen on entering. Two green parakeets pecked greedily into water at a little well where little girls called Modhi and Bannai were giggling and selling water to thirsty pilgrims. Around the massive wall, rows of small-scale *tirthankars* are sheltered from the wrath of nature in deep niches with overhanging cornices. At each change in the sunlight, the beautifully-sculpted capitals seem to glow like ice, or gold.

Behind the Adinatha Temple is a much smaller tuk with a fine frieze of three full-length figures and several miniatures.

Sakarachand Premchand's tuk again gleams cream in the sun's warmth scattered with shrieking green Alexandrine parakeets, whereas one's recollection of the ensemble remains misleadingly, insistently, white. It is built up on a platform above a steep slope. Two Jain pilgrims were chanting before the image of Parshvanatha under a white dome carved with eight voluptuous maidens dancing and playing. I sat and closed my eyes in the quiet shadow, grateful for the absence of touts, guides, vendors: Shatrunjaya is a primaeval experience harking back to the days before Thomas Cook transformed travel into tourism. The chanting continued, as in a Tibetan monastery (*Om* is one path, *Hare Krishna* another, by which the rational, logical modern mind is battered into submission before the numinous, the conscious before the subconscious, so that spaces around one may be filled by mystery, Zen riddles, or what I have called 'dislogic', Dada 'nonsense', or the shaman's senseless gabble).

Next to the left is the 16th-century *tuk* of Ujambi Hemabhai, sister of Sheth Hemabhai Vakatachand whose *tuk* can be found immediately behind. The latter is dominated by a fine temple with perforated stone screen walls and numerous altars making a cross comprising five squares. A much large *tuk* behind these at the western edge of the ridge was founded by an Ahmedabadi Jain called Lalachand Modi Premchand. In purely formal terms, its main sanctuary must be considered one of the most harmonious and best-proportioned of the yellow sandstone shrines on Shatrunjaya. The pair of carved stone chowkidars or temple guardians carry a parrot on their raised hands, and of course one sees as many rose-ringed and Alexandrine parakeets nowadays as did the original sculptor of these masterpieces. If you hear a more musical green parrot, it will be the rather smaller blossom-headed parakeet, very swift in flight: the male with a reddish-purple head, or the female with an off-white head.

Within, a Jain attendant in yellow moved solemnly below a curious

Shatrunjaya. Vallabhai Temple (centre background) behind Motishah Tuk

painted cupola: the lower part portrays a procession of all mankind and the animal kingdom coming to pay reverence, then a frieze of fifteen dancing girls, then painted panels showing sacred places of the Jains, such as Pawapuri in Bihar, Abu in Rajasthan, and Girnar.

Descending the slope to the two *tuk*s between the high ridges, I came first to the more westerly, built at the expense of the Vallabhai family in the 19th century. Shrines do not completely line the four inner walls, but the impression is unexpectedly defensive, even military, as though like European mediaeval Crusaders the Jains contemplated trouble from the surrounding plains. Spiritually as well as physically, this is a retreat from the potentially hostile Hindu majority, Muslim minority, and from violent criminals such as bands of dacoits who once roamed the countryside unchecked. The main temple has been netted to protect it from falling rocks and contamination by birds flying overhead. The dome has been damaged and attendants were sweeping dust away into tin oilcans and scraping up birdshit with the tin lids.

A great deal of maintenance is also continuously in progress at the Motishah *tuk* which dominates the depression between north and south ridge. The main temple funded by a business family from Bombay in 1836 is surrounded with inexplicable asymmetry by a number of minor temples and tiny shrines. Wealth is ostentatiously demonstrated by silver-painted wooden doors at the entrance and silver-plated gates to the main shrine. The idols have one palm on the other, both upraised. Each corner of the *tuk* is sumptuously rounded by towers from which the white paint has again begun to peel away. Complex wooden scaffolding allows teams of restorers access to the pyramidal spires.

And now we arrive at the South Ridge, its jagged spires gradually ascending from east to west up the slope, as we have seen from the North Ridge. Within the compounds, the atmosphere is domestic, friendly, and colourful; the view from the walls could hardly contrast more: remote, fantastic, in some cloudy moods threateningly stormy, gray-white hazy, with all the familiar edges of Indian clarity lost in mazy distances.

Entering the complex of the South Ridge you first see on the right the 18th-century Bhulavani, called 'labyrinth' because of the many small domed cells surrounding the central shrine from which an image in a basement can be seen, illuminated. Next on the left is the Hirachand temple, followed by a series of minor shrines, the Elephant Gate or Hathipol (19th century) and the Kumarapala Temple, recently restored. The atmosphere among the Jain pilgrims in this Vimalavasi Tuk heightens, though their intensity appears more their eyes and stiffening posture than in any gaiety or suppressed delight at reaching the summit after a two-hour climb. A Bombay Jain whispered to me, 'It is said that Adinatha, our first *tirthankar*, visited this place ninety-nine times' and I nodded in polite admiration. Worshippers were lining up in a canopied metal framework, having carried out their ablutions and changed their clothes, to enter the temple of 1530 dedicated to Shri Adishvara for puja at 12.00 noon. The previous temple on this site dates back to 960, and it is said that one or more existed before that, but no archaeologists will ever be permitted to excavate. The black and white square paving seems clinical when compared with the lavish stone-carving in soft cream sandstone. I hurried to explore the temple before puja, from the darker *cella* to the branching balconies of the upper storey, providing fabulous views on every side. Semi-circular arches are cusped and braced with the typical Jain convoluted strut-system. Carved dragons on the ridges might remind you of a Chinese temple if they only were fiery red. From the octagonal gallery I looked down to the *cella* and out on three sides. The front has a colossal *chaumukh* (four-faced idol of Shri Rishabhadev) on a round unpleasantly wedding-cakeish plinth of three tiers. I closed my eyes and stood in a non-existent place at a non-existent time, outside history and geography, with

Shatrunjaya. Adishvara Temple. Preparations for Jain puja

my heart beating outside heat and cold, calm and tempest. At such moments you live so abundantly that if you were to die then they could mark your grave: HE DIED AFTER ACHIEVING FULLNESS. The rest is just chatter.

It was in this daze that I tiptoed around the temples of Simundur Swami and Ranaji Gandharia, the latter a 16th-century masterpiece and thus contemporary with the great temple nearby.

At the foot of the mountain, just before the pilgrim canteen closed for the day at six p.m., I presented my numbered blue pass and was presented with my refreshing snack of *ghantiya* made of channa and gram with oil, *bundi* (pure ghee, or clarified butter), water in a tin glass, and tea. The average number of pilgrims using the canteen daily is a thousand, though roughly 1,500 slips are distributed on the hill.

On returning to my room that evening, I discovered that ingenious brown ants had climbed my bedside table and were deep into devouring a loaf of sliced bread in the packet, and a chain-gang, a deliberate procession like individual cells in a giant brain, continued the transfer of my hoard to a nest behind the wall. In Jain territory I felt suitably non-violent and picked up the swarming bread to release my table from its mobs, placing the polythene pack near a hole in the wall to enable my fellow-animals to proceed with their foodgathering unhindered.

Bhavnagar

Bhavnagar was founded in 1723 by Bhavsinhji, a Gohil Rajput, whose Old Palace or Darbargadh in the city centre is now a bank. The present royal family of Dr. Virbhadra Sinhji lives in separate accommodation in the Nilambag Palace grounds, having converted the palace itself into a hotel.

Even if you are not staying there, take lunch or dinner at the Nilambag ('Turquoise Garden') Palace built for the then Maharaja in 1894-5 by the highly distinguished William Emerson, who was responsible also for the Takhatsinhji Hospital (1879-83). Later to become Sir William and President of the Royal Institute of British Architects, Emerson, born in 1843, found himself dispatched to Bombay at the age of 23 to work on his master William Burges' designs for a Bombay School of Art, but this never came to fruition. Instead, he worked on the superb Crawford Market in Bombay

Bhavnagar. Takhatsinjhi Hospital (1879-83)

(1865-71) before his masterpieces in Allahabad: All Saints' Cathedral (1869-93) and Muir College (1872-8). He then moved to Bhavnagar, before ending his career with the triumph of Calcutta's Victoria Memorial Hall (1905-21).

Like Gondal, Bhavnagar could be considered a progressive state as far as women were concerned, because the royal palace had no zenana, or women's wing. After Takhatsinhji's reign (1876-96), Bhavnagar became one of the eight richest of the 282 princely states of Saurashtra, the others being Jamnagar (called Nawanagar in some books), Junagadh, Morvi, Gondal, Dhrangadhra, Porbandar and Idar. Their total annual revenue came to £4 million, four times that of all the other states put together. Credit for much of the administrative energy in the state must be given to two Nagar Brahmin families who between them supplied all the Diwans, or Chief Ministers, between 1845 and 1947. The chief income for the state derived from customs duties levied not only on goods arriving at deep-water harbours such as that at Bhavnagar itself, but also on goods carried by rail on its 400 miles of track. One saloon on the state railway carriage furnished for the maharaja typified the 'palaces on wheels' so common throughout India during the Raj, with a bedroom, sitting room and kitchen, so that while he was travelling the maharaja never had to use a local hotel.

The reputation of chief administrators in Bhavnagar reached such a peak in the 1920s and 1930s that promising young men would be sent there to learn efficient practices such as swift decision-making, good housekeeping, and the evaluation of priorities.

Regrettably, civic institutions have been allowed to decline since the time of the Barton Library. Colonel Barton collected the books and laid the foundation stone in 1882. Roosting pigeons nowadays cause a perpetual mess, tiles have fallen to the imminent peril of the five staff and half a dozen readers, and the rickety tables and chairs need to be replaced, in the view of K.C. Vasudeva, writing in *The Times of India* in 1993. Of the 69,000 volumes, most lie unread and out of date. The annual grant is a meagre Rs 15,000, though the Library derives an additional Rs 15,000 a year by renting out five shops on the ground floor. The atmosphere is dark and forbidding, remote from the modern public library service that a progressive secular state should offer its citizens.

The Barton Museum (1895) was another well-meaning enterprise by the good Colonel, housing his collections and those of subsequent donors such as Mr Oza. Opening from 8.30 to noon and 2.30 to 6, the museum excels in farming tools (other Gujarati museums except the Kutch Museum at Bhuj and the Utensils Museums in Ahmedabad are weak on rural life), beadwork, woodcarving, arms and armour, stuffed animals, and musical instruments. The upper floor, occupied by the Gandhi Smrti, has an expertly displayed collection on the life of the Father of the Nation, with the results of his Matriculation Exam of November 1887 at the Samaldas College in Bhavnagar. He attained 89% in English, 45½% for his second language (Gujarati), 59% for Maths and 54% for General Knowledge, coming joint 404th.

Amba Chowk bustles with all manner of shops, including the textiles for which Gujarat is famed throughout India. In a shop there I bought my wife an attractive cloth print from Jaipur in Rajasthan for Rs 83 less 40% discount (offered, not negotiated), but there is no need to enter a shop: you can find ample choice from pavement stalls mounted on bicycle carts, which can just be driven home when the vendor realises his day is over. The clutter on the streets befuddles the mind with colours, shouting in Gujarati, sudden shafts of blinding light on whitewashed walls, and the pell-mell helter-skelter of tooting auto-rickshaws and parping cars. The Friday Mosque can be recognised in Amba Chowk by the white dome astride a square tower, with a tiny white crescent horns up towards circling crows. Darbargadh, the Old City Palace, is now abandoned by the royal family, and the Darbar Hall, now the Town Hall, is named for Krishnakumar Sinhji (1921), who took his place in history as the first ruler to surrender his state to the Indian Union at the behest of Gandhiji.

You can see the Ganga Jalia Temple commissioned by Takhatsinhji for his beloved consort, and on top of an incline the Takhateshwar Temple dedicated to Lord Shiva, of no great artistic or architectural interest, but

Bhavnagar. Old City Palace

224

Bhavnagar. Bus and auto-rickshaw station

picturesquely located for views to the seaport, where hovercraft speed
your passage to Surat, and towards the airport, where regular daily flights
connect the city with Bombay.

One of the countless fascinations of Bhavnagar, apart from Victoria
Park, and the Central Salt and Marine Research Institute near Circuit
House, is the parade of extraordinary buses. From the front, they look like
red lorries, with the number and destination in Gujarati. From the back,
they look like a double-decker bus. From the side they look like the front
third of a bus and the back two thirds of a truck with seats higher at the
front three windows than at the rear. The whole contraption is an ingenious response to the demands of Gujarati travel, where too many people
customarily clamber into too small a space, rendering the old single-
decker coach dangerous by overcrowding. I don't know how many passengers are theoretically permitted on a Bhavnagar bus (and similar vehicles ply the streets of Ahmedabad and other cities), but the numbers are
much less frequently exceeded than used to be the case. The best feature is
that the driver has a compartment to himself, whereas on most Indian
country buses he is crushed into a corner by flour-sacks, overflowing urchins, chickens crammed into bamboo baskets and squealing piglets wres-
tling each other in wicker cages. These majestic urban buses, elephantine
in their ponderous progress, represent yet another ingenious solution to

225

India's critical transportation problem, which employs millions and keeps the precarious economy afloat for business, tourism, industry, and the day-to-day business of survival. Those who have known the rigours of delays in other Asian countries can only shake our heads in wonder at the fact that, wherever you want to be in India, sooner or later you can get there cheaply, and with the minimum of hassle, by road, rail, air and sea.

I was invited by the present maharaja's younger brother, Shiv Bapu, to watch migrant birds on Bor Talao, below his palace Bhav Vilas. Shiv Bapu showed me a pamphlet called *Rulers of Bhavnagar in Historical Rhymes* (1940), an official panegyric and chronology by the state bard, one Jogidar Pingalshibhai, who picked out all the creditable tales.

'Our dynasty came to Saurashtra from Marwar in the 12th century', continued Shiv Bapu, 'and founded our capital at Ghogha, a seaport to the south, but as a result of battles, skirmishes and vicissitudes of victory and defeat we transferred our dynastic headquarters several times, and 350 years ago built the Sihor Palace around 23 kms westward from here. Guests can take lunch there at the Darbargadh, and enjoy the fine gardens.'

Shiv Bapu sat on the verandah with me, sipping tea and gently smiling over the amiable eccentricities of Shri Maharaja Takhatsinhji, who ruled from 1878 to 1896. 'My greatgrandfather chartered a ship when Queen Victoria invited him to England for the investiture of the Prince Consort. He took his own Ganges water on board, and all his own staff, including the court musician Rahim Khan. He took his own buffaloes, which excited some comment on arrival, I can tell you; his Indian cook prepared chapatis and all other food in Indian style, to be eaten from thalis by hand, in the customary manner. He knew how to use a knife and fork, of course, but the story goes that at a banquet in Buckingham Palace, he mistook the finger-bowl for a drinking-vessel and drank the water out of it, whereupon Her Majesty sized up the situation in a flash and quickly drank from her own finger-bowl. Not to show him up, you see. Noblesse oblige. I always liked that story. And of course the one about Cambridge University's giving him an honorary degree, though he didn't know a word of English.'

Shiv Bapu explained that Bhavnagar had become one of the three Indian states which specialised in falconry and cheetah-training. 'My grandfather Bhavsinhji and my father Krishna Kumarsinhji conceived the idea of trying to hunt without wounding, and with rifles to shoot as few birds as possible, not the indiscriminate firing that used to happen elsewhere. My father developed a technique of keeping a falcon in the air, 'waiting on', so as to chase away seagulls and other birds damaging crops. After my father expired in 1965, no more training was undertaken. But I should tell you about the cheetahs and the caracals, trained by Muslims from Punjab who had settled here generations back. The cheetahs came from East Africa, and at one time we possessed 32: the Indian cheetah even then was almost extinct. The leashed cheetah would sit up on an ox-cart with a driver and two trainers. At a certain moment, the trainer would unleash the cheetah against blackbuck, which would either be killed swiftly or survive without being wounded. We had the caracals trained to hunt chinkara deer; against a destructive flock of feeding pigeons they would leap in the air and hit half a dozen at once, bringing them down and scaring the rest. Of course lions always threatened our people and livestock, but wild boar became much more numerous and destructive, and the villagers pleaded with us to tackle this plague, either pigsticking or with rifles. Of course, pigsticking caused a lot of carnage among horses and men, because a wild boar with its massive tusks could go insane if only wounded and a spear would have to find the boar's heart at a single thrust or it could threaten everyone around.'

The present maharaja, who inherited the privy purse as the elder brother, has become a businessman while Shiv Bapu as the younger brother has lived somewhat in the shadows, turning his talents to wildlife conservation as a naturalist on the board of the United Nations Park Project, with special interest in the blackbuck in the Velavadar Sanctuary. His palace, Bhav Vilas, dates from 1939-45 and was built of local stone and Burmese teak. Trophies from earlier hunting expeditions in Bhav Vilas include moose, caribou and Kodiak bear from Alaska, but the special importance of the palace is its situation on the bank of Bor Talao, a tank attracting dozens of waders, as well as birds of prey.

Velavadar Blackbuck National Park

Once the private game reserve of the Maharaja of Bhavnagar, Velavadar is now a sanctuary 34 sq km in area for the beautiful antelope species called blackbuck, here found more numerously than anywhere else in India. Foxes, jungle cats, blue bull, mongoose and desert hare are found in good numbers, and you might also see the Indian grey wolf, which has suffered a terrible decline in recent years. Ornithologists will enjoy the sight of harriers, shikras with their harsh call like a black drongo's, sand grouse, Sarus crane, curlew, hoopoe, Indian reef heron, francolin, blackbreasted quail, pipits, and the running Sirkeer Cuckoo, a weak flier that you might mistake for a mongoose. Among local birds of prey are black-shouldered kite, the ashy-brown Laggar Falcon, and the brown Short-toed Eagle.

In the late 1940s, the blackbuck population exceeded 15,000 throughout the Velavadar-Mithapur grasslands. After Independence, numbers fell to the catastrophic level of two hundred in 1966, as a result of hunting, drought, and the expansion of agriculture. In 1969 an area of 9 sq km was declared a wildlife sanctuary, upgraded in 1976 to National Park status with an enlarged area of 17.8 sq km, then increased in the following year by a further 16.2 sq km. The habitat is a flat coastal grassland of fertile black alluvial soil known as the Bhal region, covering 2600 sq. km.

Velavadar. Blackbuck

Droughts are frequent, and cyclones bring great destruction with rains so heavy that adjacent villages are cut off from the National Park: the cyclone and rains of 1982 drowned 311 blackbucks, a terrible loss mostly accountable for the reduction in numbers from an estimated 1554 in 1977 to 1218 in 1983. The 1989 count came to 2314 blackbuck, a fine result partly attributable to vaccination of local cattle against the foot-and-mouth disease that was killing blackbuck too.

As the park has no perennial source, fresh water has to be piped into artificial water-holes from Malpara village, 15 km distant. If Malpara becomes dry, water tankers bring in emergency supplies.

You cannot easily hire a 4-wheel jeep in Bhavnagar, but if you are staying at the palace in Utelia, by Lothal, you can hire a jeep for half a day, with or without picnic.

You can stay within Velavadar at the central two-storey Forest Lodge, Kaliyar Bhavan, which offers both board and lodging in five double rooms at Rs 60 per room.

The park manager, R.L. Japardia, nominated a guide to accompany my Ambassador car, which negotiated the 16-km perimeter asphalt roads with a certain amount of huffing and coughing. We stopped at intervals but, unlike the Gir Forest tracks, Velavadar is so exposed that many of the animals you would like to see run off in protective company at the first putter of an internal combustion engine, and one is not encouraged to explore the grassland as a tracker outside the vehicle. The only cover that visitors can take is behind clumps of the thornbush *prosopis juliflora*, which provide pods eaten by the blackbuck. As at Bansda and Hingolgadh (near Jasdan, Rajkot district), I was disappointed by the Velavadar Sanctuary as a place to observe Indian wildlife, and greatly prefer the Little Rann of Kutch Wild Ass Sanctuary and the Gir Forest Lion Sanctuary.

228

Sarangpur

I took the road from Velavadar northward to Lothal via Barwala and Rojid to accept a long-standing invitation to visit Sadhu Vishuddhaswarupdas at the Swaminarayan Temple in Sarangpur locally known as the Sarminaran (Four Minaret) Temple. A Hindu revivalist and missionary movement which we have already seen at Akshardham, Gandhinagar, the Swaminarayan runs a two-year course 'to become a saint', as they say, the earliest age being 17, and thus initiation can be complete at 18. The course consists of studying the *Vachanamrit* ('Spoken Nectar') scriptures and devotion in the morning, other texts in the afternoon, and in the evening half-an-hour of hymns, half-an-hour of commented scriptures, and a further half-hour of hymns and texts. I was shown the assembly hall and introduced to many of the white-robed initiates, or parshads, and the orange-clad saints, or sadhus, who study a further 3 or 4 years. Many of their activities are concerned with the concept of *seva* or service, such as ladling out food to pilgrims and the needy. Crosslegged on a plank, I was offered a sufficient vegetarian lunch which I took with my right hand, squeezing up grains of rice into a ball and moistening them in dhali, and taking chapatis, curds and vegetables such as cauliflower pieces from a thali, or compartmented tin tray. Next to me sat a friendly Gujarati accountant, who now teaches English and helps overseas students feel at home, and a retired chemist from Romford who now helps with the business side of the temple.

Devotees normally offer 10% of their income to the movement, but if you wish to become a sadhu (I felt more comfortable with the Hindi word than their preferred translation of 'saint'), you cut all family ties and proffer all possessions, receiving in exchange simply two sets of clothes, including the cylindrical orange hat called pagh worn outside the temple, one to wear and one to wash. They have no personal possessions except perhaps a few books, no money, and must abstain from all worldly pleasures, taking only whatever minimal food is necessary to sustain body and mind. Music is allowed, however: instructors provide tuition on all the Indian instruments, particularly on the sarod and flute, shehnai, tabla, harmonium, sitar and pakawad. The language of the movement is Gujarati, so if youths come out from families in Neasden or Leicester, say, they are taught Gujarati in the first year, and afterwards acquire Sanskrit. They sit in the six classrooms cross-legged in front of small desks for three hours a day.

Exams are held every fortnight, and all the questions are set by computer: the pass-rate fluctuates between 90% and 95% due, I was assured, to high motivation, and the willingness of students to help each other.

Three hours a day are spent on homework, one hour on services, and three hours on assemblies morning, afternoon and evening. Service could include looking after the 145 cows providing milk for 200 sadhus. The accommodation has capacity for up to 2,000 visitors, who generally offer a donation towards food and lodging.

Sarangpur. Swaminarayan Temple. A sadhu among the laundry

The attitude in the temple is one of great friendliness, willingness to please, and a genuine rejection of caste coupled with acceptance of fraternity among all religions. I cannot however quite comprehend why the movement needs to become so rich, when the needs of sadhus are doctrinally restricted.

Lothal

The Chalcolithic inhabitants of the region stretching from modern Baluchistan through Pakistan and Northern India to Punjab – that is the precursors of the Harappan civilization exemplified most notably by the civilizations of Mohenjo Daro in Sind and Harappa in Punjab – dwelt in village cultures of the late fourth and early third millennia B.C. In scale, if not in civilised values, they correspond roughly to the smaller of the Greek settlements we call rather misleadingly 'city states' as if they were comparable at some meaningful level to Athens, and they were separated by much the same topography: hills and distances that cut them off by rivers and hazards of travel that persuaded the inhabitants to stay where they were, and to regard their neighbours as actual or potential enemies.

At Lothal, this local village culture is called the Red Ware Culture from their micaceous pottery. Then from about 2400 B.C. invaders from the north whom we know as Harappans took over to utilise the harbour and develop the beadmaking industry, increasing the material prosperity of the burgeoning town until the Great Flood about 1900 B.C., when the Mature Harappan period gave way to three centuries of decline. In this Late Harappan Period, when the devastated town, like so many of the Harappan sites in the delta regions of Sind, Saurashtra, and South Gujarat, gradually recovered, poor farmers, artisans and fishermen returned to their homes in the hope of starting a new life. Urban life however never full resumed, trade with other centres never reappeared, and the populace lived in poor reed huts and may even have passed into illiteracy. Those few who could write simplified their style by dropping pictorial signs. In time, Lothal silted up, and was excavated between 1955-62, providing the best Harappan-culture site yet found in India, though not on the same scale as Mohenjo Daro near Multan.

Lothal can be visited from sunrise to sunset daily, but the Archaeological Museum is open daily only between 10 and 5 from Saturday to Thursday.

Three museum watchmen nodded briefly in welcome before turning back to stare passionately and open-mouthed at a televised Test match between India and England. One can almost always recognise a museum's nationality from the activity of its attendants: in Italy, uniformed staff yawn over the morning newspaper; in Russia, women knit ferociously for a second income; in England, guards pretend to look at the pictures while beadily ensuring that visitors do not touch anything. I think my favourites are the goggling cricket fans in a semi-circle, ignoring us as we tiptoed past.

A map in the museum shows literally dozens of Harappan and Late Harappan sites throughout Western Gujarat, extending just east of the Sabarmati south of Ahmedabad at Valotri, Changada, Kaneval and Vagha Talao. Harappans also colonised the mouth of the river Kim around Bhagatrav, to exploit forests in the hinterland and agate-bearing mines. Mengam at the mouth of the Narmada is known to have been a port providing agate, jasper, chalcedony and carnelian to Harappan beadmakers.

While examining the site at Lothal, remember that the harbour may lie 20 km from the navigable Sabarmati these days, but its harbour was prosperous for many centuries, and even as recently as 1850 boats could moor at Lothal.

It was in fact the proximity of the sea, the river, and hazards of flooding which prompted the Harappan builders of Lothal to create a boundary wall outside the town, and to build all dwellings on a high platform of sun-dried bricks up to two metres high. (Even as I speak, the BBC World Service reports that 3,000 people have been made homeless as the Sabarmati bursts its banks during current monsoon rains.) The ruler's palace on the acropolis of Lothal was built up on a platform three metres high, and enjoyed access to its own well, drainage, and paved baths.

The lower town comprised a bazaar and residential area, a warehouse on a plinth 3½ metres high, to store merchandise being imported and exported by boat, and a dock to the east of the town, away from the main current to avoid silting.

The most important industry, beadmaking, can be studied in the museum: techniques worked out by Harappan lapidaries have not essentially been improved upon by Cambay craftsmen working four thousand years later. As well as its familiar bead exports, Lothal also specialised in steatite microbeads made by rolling a paste of ground steatite on a length of string, baking it solid, then cutting the resultant roll with a tiny saw. The minute beads would then be strung for necklaces, armlets and even waistbands. The Harappans loved beads of every kind and there is evidence for gold beads, but most of these will have been melted down for other uses at a later date, and have consequently disappeared but we can judge their sophistication by a gold microbead necklace of five strands at each end, then ten strands in the middle: nowhere else can you find microbeads of gold below 0.25 mm in diameter. Finger-rings are made of thin copper wires in double spirals, obviously mimicking gold, while the poorest citizens had to rest content with shell and terracotta ornaments, such as bangles.

Seals played an important documentary part in the Harappan economy: more than 200 have survived at Lothal, many of them masterpieces of glyptic craftsmanship, the animals most often portrayed being the blackbuck (or mythical unicorn?), elephant, mountain goat, short-horned bull, tiger, and the mythical elephant-bull. Seals with a copper ring on the reverse were affixed to cargo, with the ruler's seal to authenticate contents or to validate payment of taxes. The Harappans of Lothal worshipped the fire-god, and the sea-god but there is no trace here of mother-goddess worship; trade with Dilmun-age Bahrain is proved by the discovery of a seal with a dragon and leaping gazelle.

Wonderful large painted jars stand up well to comparison with contemporary ceramics elsewhere: they are strong, consistently fired and realistically painted with animals such as a stag, humped bull, cow, horse, birds on branches, and a fox: Lothal's unique formal contributions to Harappan wares are a small jar with flared rim and a kind of convex bowl, both in the micaceous Red Ware by now easily recognised. These works all date back to Mature Harappa; ceramics decline to trivial gestures on poor wares in Late Harappan Lothal. The same of course is true of terracotta works such as human figurines, or toys such as games-figures comparable to a chess set belonging to the Pharaonic queen Hatsheput. A model of a boat has places for a toy mast with sail, while evidence for land transport consists of toy bullock-carts. Spinning-tops and marbles evoke a childhood not far removed from our own.

Writing and graffiti on terra cotta and seals in Mature Harappan is hieratic, mixing pictographs and phonemes, developing later into a pure cursive style as occurred in Chinese and Egyptian. The museum also displays mirrors of bronze and copper, and a variety of objects made from shells, chert from Sind or Karnataka (including knives) and bone (including pins). An ivory workshop on the acropolis proves the governor's direct involvement with the industry, for which the elephant had probably been domesticated. Metallurgists at Lothal used 99.8% pure copper imported from Oman alloyed with tin to make spearheads, arrowheads, fish-hooks, chisels and ornaments.

Modern science and technology depend on accurate weights, measures and calculation of time and direction: Lothal presents impressive evidence for Harappan expertise in all these spheres, astonishing in view of the enormous area under their control four millennia ago. The Lothal brick measured in the ratio 1:0.5:0.25. A ring-shaped shell with four slits acted as a compass measuring angles on a plane surface in multiples of $40°$ up to $360°$, so that a good millennium before the Greek conceived of an eightfold vision of the sky, such knowledge was available to Harappan sailors and land-travellers. Indus weights of chert and agate are hexahedra for local use, and truncated spheres for foreign trade. Harappans used the decimal system for width, and three different weight systems, beginning with gold discs weighing 50, 100, 200 and up to 3250 mg for precious stones and gold. A second system for daily calculation began with 1.2184 gm and ran up to 10865 gm in ratios of 0.05, 0.1, 0.2, 0.5, 1, 2, 5, 10, 20, 50, 100, 200 and 500. The unit 1 corresponded to 27.584 gm, corresponding almost exactly to the English ounce, which is related to the Greek uncia of

27.2 gm. A third system began at 0.871 gm, continuing in the ratio of 0.05, 0.1, 0.2, 0.5, 1, 2, and 10.

The physical environment of Lothal may disappoint those who want Troy or Jericho to look more dramatic; those for whom 'ruins' are flat and depopulated. But if one views the flood around 1900 B.C. as a personal disaster, wrecking one's own family, home and business as the Mississippi and Missouri floods of 1993 devastated an area of the U.S.A. the size of Britain, then the heart is captured. Those floods swept away Lothal's fragile, brickbuilt homes and factories, leaving only foundations, platforms, fragmented walls, wells, drains, and paved floor. The ovoid town centre (230 metres west-east and 285 metres north-south) has been peripherally covered with earth by the Archaeological Survey of India to protect outlying areas from being washed away by rains and floods. Greater Lothal during the Mature period extended over a wider area, attested by dwellings uncovered 300 metres south of the mound.

The so-called acropolis resembles a Roman inner city with cardo and decumanus more than a Greek hilltop palace complex: its east-west length is 128 m and its north-south dimension 61 m. Twelve baths in a row are connected to the sewer by expertly-crafted runnels and an inspection chamber for solid sewage can be seen. Three roads and two alleys can be traced east-west and two roads north-south, serving houses occupied by the governor and his ministers, presumably with a treasury.

The lower town comprised a bazaar, artisans' workshops for beadmakers, coppersmiths and others, and residential quarters. The later they were built, the more inferior the manufacture, with signs of hurried planning and poor materials, as well as crowding of smaller rooms: mudbricks are no longer used; the Late Harappan arrivals used mud and reeds, and made do without drains.

Harappan engineers had realised that the Gulf of Cambay had the highest tidal width, so that ships could be sluiced through the Sabarmati river estuary by an inlet channel at high tide, and berth in the dock at Lothal. Stone anchors excavated in the basin could be used on sandy and rocky beaches.

The more we study Lothal – and contemporary Harappan sites such as Dholavira in northern Kutch – the more we understand the superb levels of knowledge and communication familiar in the Indus Valley region four thousand years ago, a fact I pondered as I returned to my accommodation in Utelia Palace close by.

VI: DIU

We have seen how the Portuguese prised Daman from local control in 1531. Eight years later, the Portuguese had achieved a secure hold on Diu, an island off south Saurashtra with the inestimable advantage of a harbour clear of the dangerous tides which were to impoverish Cambay, on the eastern side of the Gulf.

Diu island, seen from the Gujarati shoreline near the beach resort of Ahmedpur Mandvi, appears long, low and hazy, reclining in the shallow seas like a surfacing submarine.

An excise checkpost at Ghoghla-Diu is manned by immigration officials who ask you to write your passport and visa details in a register, but there is no customs inspection for alcohol, whereas I had expected no passport check and a search for intoxicants. Diu and Daman, unlike the State of Gujarat, have no legal prohibition of alcohol, which means that they benefit very largely from what one might call liquor tourism. Indeed a so-called tourism office next to the border crossing between Gujarat and Diu could offer no general tourism literature or maps whatsoever, and airily directed me to Diu Town for the main tourism bureau.

Yet Diu's streets are not obnoxious with drunks; on the contrary, bars tend to be more quiet and restrained than one would think, and Diu town is so clean and tidy that the impression is more of a better-class village in Algarve than a Gujarati town.

We first hear of Diu as a stronghold of the Chudasama dynasty in 1298-9, when it was seized by Ala ud-Din Khilji, recovered, then regained by Muhammad bin Tughlaq in 1349.

A century before the Portuguese attacked and took Daman in 1531, Diu had become a wealthy harbour and shipbuilding centre for the Gujarati merchant fleet and for warships; it was taken over in 1510 by Malik Ayaz, Governor of Saurashtra, a Georgian who had converted to Islam in the Ottoman administration. It was this renegade Georgian who built up the prosperity of Diu by creating a fort and harbour defences, and constructing a bridge to the mainland suburb of Ghoghla. After defeat by the forces of the Portuguese Viceroy Francisco d'Almeida and his Mamluk ally Amir Husain in 1509, Malik Ayaz persuaded Sultan Muzaffar II of Gujarat to repudiate his offer of Diu made to Albuquerque in 1513, and it was Malik Ayaz who managed to repel Portuguese onslaughts by sea in 1520 and 1521. Ayaz died in 1522 and was succeeded by his son Malik Ishaq. Ishaq considered defeat by the Portuguese inevitable, so he rebelled against the Sultanate and offered Diu to the invaders. Sultan Bahadur took over the

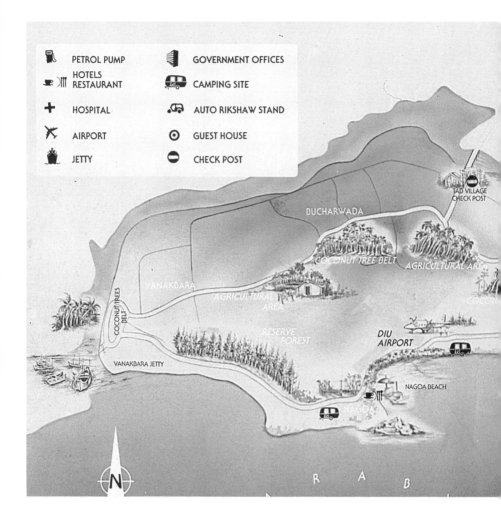

throne of Gujarat in 1526 after conflict with his brothers, and had the rebel Ishaq killed while escaping from him in 1530.

The second son of Malik Ayaz, Malik Tughan, had meantime become governor of Diu and in 1531 overwhelmed the Portuguese under Viceroy Nuno da Cunha, who was surprised by the arrival of Tughan's Ottoman allies Amir Mustafa and Khwaja Safar. Persisting in his desire for Diu, da Cunha was offered the island in 1535 by the Emperor Humayun and his unruly subject Sultan Bahadur. Da Cunha preferred to sign an accord with Bahadur Shah in exchange for military aid. Bahadur now expelled the

236

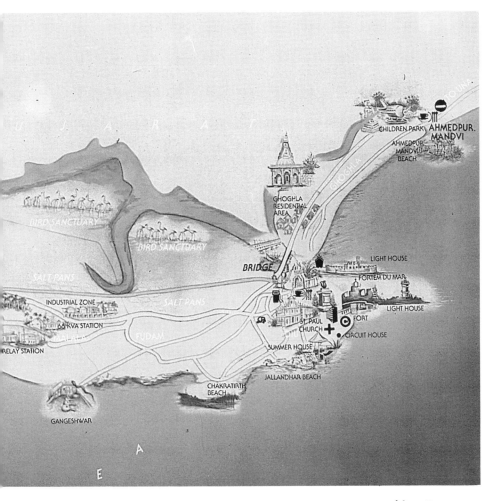

Map of Diu

Mughals from Gujarat and in 1536 returned to Diu, where a messenger invited da Cunha to leave his redoubt. Suspecting treachery, da Cunha refused, but invited Bahadur on to his galleon where the Sultan was mercilessly killed in an incident reflecting no credit whatsoever on the Europeans.

The Portuguese under Nuno da Cunha then seized the arsenal of Diu but, as R.S. Whiteway tells us in *The Rise of Portuguese Power in India, 1497-1550* (1899), 'although Bahadur's palaces were carefully searched, only a very small quantity of treasure was brought to the public exchequer'. The

Sea fort (Panikhot) off Diu, with lighthouse and Chapel of Our Lady of the Sea

following year the Ottomans began a new siege of Diu with the arrival of the fleet of the Greek-born eunuch Sulaiman Pasha, Governor of Egypt. This incompetent general could have swept the Indian seas clean of Portuguese vessels with the seventy-two vessels that set sail from Suez but, instead of taking on single ships at sea or attacking smaller Portuguese coastal possessions, Sulaiman set his sights on the one virtually impregnable Portuguese enclave in the whole of India, so after several months the siege was called off and a truce signed in 1539. Another siege by Khwaja Safar lasted seven months in 1546 before the Muslims were routed by Governor João de Castro, appointed Viceroy in 1548. From then on the Portuguese secured customs duties on all goods from Gujarat through their pass system called *cartaz*, and remained secure there except for devastating Muslim raids in 1668 and 1676, until December 1961.

We cannot begin to understand coastal Gujarat in the 16th century without appreciating the military might of the Portuguese. No Indian ship might sail to East Africa, Indonesia, China or Japan without the Portuguese *cartaz*, or safe-conduct pass; if a ship violated this rule it would be boarded and challenged by the fleet of warships built in Gujarat for this purpose by the Portuguese. Duty had to be paid on all cargo, and certain cargoes were prohibited: among them weapons, spices, timber, iron and copper which might be used for trade or munitions. As the 16th century wore on, the Portuguese enforced a system of convoys for merchant vessels to improve control and taxation. Not only the major settlement of Goa, but Daman and Diu too became influential ports where ships were built and customs duties levied, enriching both Portuguese and indirectly those working for them. Local merchants who did not choose to live in Diu or Daman had to pay taxes and duties at their local port and at Diu or Daman, a factor which caused many to abandon Rander/Surat and Cambay for the less costly Portuguese possessions. In the long term, the local population would be divided into two factions: those who benefited from Portuguese hegemony, such as landlords, merchants, and agents; and on the other hand the landless and tribals, and rival merchants from the interior who could see better times if the Portuguese were removed.

On land, the Portuguese were harassed by local rulers protesting against foreign violation of their homeland in the justifiable belief that taxes and duties levied against them were illegitimate. At sea, piracy became a recognised method of undermining Portuguese self-confidence and regaining cargoes which Gujarati seafarers reasonably considered their own. Then rival European powers began to harry Portuguese vessels and even convoys. Both the English and the Dutch found Bengal more profitable than Gujarat, but strategic reasons led them to open factories, that is to say, trade centres, at Surat in the early 17th century, and later elsewhere, as at Ahmedabad (where the English had a factory from 1616).

Incidentally, most of Diu's Gujarati *banias* or *vanias*, as the merchant class are known, were not local but interlopers unlike the *banias* of Rander to the east, and they had their own 'captains' who acted as agents for all Gujarati merchants in dealings with the Portuguese at Diu, Goa and Hormuz on the eastern Gulf. Indeed, the prosperity of the *banias* and of the Portuguese in Diu was so far interlinked that, when the Dutch and British attacked in the 17th century, Portuguese fortunes collapsed, and with them the luck of the *banias*. Bocarro notes that by the 1630s Surat's trade protected by the British and Dutch had eclipsed that of Diu, and by the 1660s the number of *banias* had declined from an all-time record of 200,000 (most of them wealthy) to around 7,500 (many of them poor). Most of the *bania* families simply moved back to Cambay, the city from which most had originated.

While in Diu I happened to meet two members of the noble Bragança family sympathetic to the plight of the few remaining Indian Catholics on the island (there are no Portuguese left, but some Indian families still speak Portuguese at home) and Dom Duarte told me he had offered to replenish documentation such as printed books and journals on the history of Diu destroyed by termites and high levels of salinity. The beloved novelist R.K. Narayan has paid tribute to the meticulous, all-destroying termite as a hygienic annihilator of paper which sentimental people like me collect or save in the belief that 'it will come in handy', and there is no doubt that the world would be engulfed in paper if we did not take stern action, but the case of Diu and Daman is special. For centuries, the course

Diu Town. Post Office

of their destiny was determined either from Lisbon or from Goa, rather than from Ahmedabad, Bombay or Delhi, so if we want to understand their history, we need documents from outside.

Much of old Diu is worth tramping on foot, particularly early in the morning when old men emerge, or at dusk, when children are summoned to tea by tetchy mothers, in Gujarati. Portuguese has died out as a lingua franca in Diu, and you are more likely to hear Hindi among Indian tourists, or English among foreigners. Compared with Goa, Diu is rustic, unspoilt, and if it lacks the major tourist complexes of its big brother to the south, Diu has lost little or its original charm, and local residents are correspondingly more interested in the latest arrivals. These arrivals are now likely to come by air, as well as bus, car or boat, for Diu Airport (situated just north of Nagoa Beach) receives a Vayudoot flight leaving Bombay at 6.15 and sends reluctant holidaymakers back to the sprawling, sweating metropolis later the same day. The nearest rail station to Diu is Delvada (8 kms; use auto-rickshaws) and from there you can reach Junagadh and Sasangir. If you don't want to hire bikes from the Krishna or Shilpa cycle-hire stores, buses from Diu Town square will take you round the southern road to Vanakbara via Nagoa Beach, and the northern road via Bucharwada: the round trip is quite enchanting. From the same square, state transport buses will take you to Veraval, Junagadh, Rajkot, Palitana and Ahmedabad. I don't recommend the Bombay bus run by Goa

240

Diu Town. Nagar Sheth Haveli

241

Travels leaving at 8.30 daily because it takes more than twenty hours, but it calls at Bhavnagar, Anand and Vapi (alight for Daman) and if you want any of these intermediate destinations it would be correspondingly less exhausting. Shared taxis can be booked to centres throughout Gujarat from the main square, but this is a hit-and-miss alternative, unless you are already travelling in a group with an agreed itinerary, or do not mind where you land up next. Since the new causeway transformed the island into a virtual peninsula permanently linked to the mainland near Ghoghla, the mystique of isolation has given way to the routine convenience of all-day, all-night connections by road. But there is still a regular ferry to Diu: it departs from Kotdhla on the mainland to Vanakbara harbour regularly during daylight hours, with a bus to the town of Kodinar, from which connections are available to Prabhas Patan and Veraval on the coast, or Junagadh and Rajkot to the north.

I asked directions to the Nagar Sheth Haveli, and Bashir M. Kureishi offered to come with me. In Makata Street I came across this extraordinary polychrome mansion, rising all the more dramatically in its narrow lane because of the miniature scale of its surroundings. Monumental stone lions in the round glare balefully at intruders, but this two-hundred-year-old haveli needs little protection against burglars, for it is empty, abandoned thirty years back by the owner, Shantilal Kalyanchand, who is now living in Bombay. The three-storey building has a wide portico at ground level, and broad balconies painted orange, green and blue which look less gaudy than they sound in the brilliant southern light. Stone balconies in patrician mansions close by are more conventionally European in style, with wooden shutters above and below, and plants in pots enlivening the strict horizontals.

The first and most important building of historical significance that the modern visitor to Diu comes across is the fortress, which Martim Afonso de Sousa had built between October 1535 and March 1536. Governor Nuno da Cunha told his then ally Sultan Bahadur that 'the Portuguese fight like heroes and work like forced labourers'. Bahadur had fled from fallen Champaner and needed respite from Emperor Humayun's relentless harrying of his turbulent Gujarati subjects. Bahadur could not put all his trust in the Portuguese, and sought alliance with the Ottomans of Egypt. Interestingly in view of what happened later, the treaty allowing the Portuguese to build the fortress at Diu excluded the King of Portugal from claiming customs receipts, and forbade religious proselytizing.

The fortress was restored and battlements erected in 1834. You enter across a bridge through a daunting gateway with a plaque in Latin for eternity and Portuguese for perpetuity of ownership. Alas for the Portuguese, barely four hundred years later their overseas possessions in India had been taken, at the cost of minimal loss of life, only one church and a few secular buildings. The fort itself is admirably planned and executed, with three sides approachable only by sea, and the fourth by a moat. Cannon and cannonballs lie about in lazy profusion: the threat by sea has long disappeared. Part of the fort is given over to a district jail and a lighthouse. The rest is a quiet, almost melancholy haven of memories, dominated by the beautiful cathedral of 1601 in stunning bridal-gown white, and the Diu Museum in São Tomé. Dedicated to Our Lady of the Immaculate Conception, S. Paulo adjoins the former Jesuit seminary now the Nirmala Mata High School, the only one on the island. Father Mariano from Calangute on Goa is the Principal of the school, and teaches both English and Portuguese. He showed me the cathedral lovingly, like any devotee of lost causes. 'I have taught at the school and officiated in the cathedral for two spells: from 1981 to 1985, and then from 1989 to 1993. Diu once had eleven churches, but in time many have collapsed through lack of maintenance and were never rebuilt. Nowadays we have only 207 practising Catholics in 37 families attending services in five churches throughout the whole island of some thirty thousand souls. I am the only priest in Diu, so I have to say mass in each church in turn: the whole parish moves with me, to keep the churches alive. The best church is São João de Deus in Diu town, the cathedral is the second best, the third is São Paulo which had been restored, the in Fudam we have the imposing church of Nossa Senhora dos Remedios (1767) and in Vanakbara Our Lady of Mercy. S. Paulo was designed by Father Antonio, the same Italian Jesuit responsible for Rachol Seminary of 1580 near Margão in Goa. The marvellous woodcarving is by Goan artisans from Ribandar. I don't have much money for restoration, but I have managed to get some emergency preservation work done on the pulpit. I am leaving on today's flight to Bombay for a fortnight to attend my brother's wedding in Goa.'

'Do you prefer the peace of Diu to the more lively atmosphere in Goa?' Father Mariano put his head warily on one side, like a diplomat before a microphone. 'Goa has the warmth of a natural home: I know everybody, and they think when I leave I am going to a desert island like Robinson Crusoe. But you see I have a mission, and I am needed more here than there, where every village has its own comfortable priest. Imagine, Diu once had great religious collections of paintings and books and sculpture, but everything has gone except for a few items we have managed to collect for the museum. Classes five to ten (ages 11-16) in our high school have three language options: French, Portuguese, and Gujarati, in addition to compulsory English. Do you know what the parents decide? For Portuguese, one per cent, for Gujarati 99% and for French, nobody at all. It is sad that these parents do not understand the meaning of the word 'education', of bringing out from the child his fullest potential. They think only of passing exams with the least exertion and, because they speak Gujarati at home, they think the children should have Gujarati lessons at school. For what?'

São Tomé is a vaulted stone basilica, with a gallery. Its exterior is fortress-like, with a wooden door proportionately too small in a wide façade strangely low in the central arch and looming much taller in the twin lateral towers clearly meant to be seen from the sea. Diu Museum (founded in 1992) opens from 8 a.m. to 10 p.m. seven days a week, and has three members of staff. Ecumenically, it displays not only some of the hundreds of Catholic Goanese and Portuguese artefacts made in or brought to Diu, but includes also Hindu images and inscriptions and fragments of Jain temples, such as those from the excavations below Prince Hotel in Diu Town. A silver table is four hundred years old, and most of the standing images of saints, though undated, can be stylistically attributed to the late sixteenth and seventeenth centuries. In polychrome wood, they are ascribable to local Indian craftsmen from Goa in some cases, and in others to continental masters. There is a tombstone of one Fernando de Castro, who died at 19 in 1549, a figure of Our Lady of the Rosary, a Portuguese chair, two angels, the Dead Christ behind drapery like a mosquito net, Our Lady of the Immaculate Conception; above are Our Lady of Mercy and St Thomas, the church's dedicatee. What I remember best are the tall gilt statues of disciples, three-dimensional presences of the mission overseas, as solidly presumptuous as the figure of Vasco da Gama standing outside the Collector's Office still, if it has not been removed since I last saw it.

I ascended steps to the gallery of São Tomé and met there a softly-spoken Scot called Michael Ledingham, who has a display of his paintings (some for sale) in this improvised art gallery. As an artist he has evolved through surrealist and photorealist phases to his present realistic style, using Indian landscapes, and for preference those of his adopted Diu. 'Daybreak in Varanasi' (Rs 5,000) conjures the atmosphere of the Gangetic pilgrim city. *Lassmi at Nagoa* (Rs 8,000; 'Lassmi' is the local pronunciation of the popular Hindu girl's name Lakshmi) is a serenely sensuous portrait of a woman at once of her surroundings yet clearly her own frank personality. Michael has lived in Diu for 8½ years; within two years he had become completely fluent in Gujarati, unlike most foreigners.

'Nowhere else in India have I found every landscape and every mood in an area under forty square kilometre: quarry and fishing village, forest and bird-sanctuary, desert and farmland, town and beach, church, mosque and temple. Everything but the emphasis on money which dries out the soul in big cities. I live at Nagoa Beach, and come to Diu town if I need to buy anything. I can live off the income from my paintings throughout the year, because my wants are minimal. Yes, I suppose, Gauguin's example did influence me, and Maugham's Strickland, and the 'Sixties hippy lifestyle. But then, having looked at many other lifestyles, I never found anything to match Diu. Have you?'

I confessed that for a painter no more idyllic island could be found, and took my farewell. From the entrance to S. Tomé the battlemented Sea Fort with its own lighthouse gleamed bright in the midday sun, its gray-brown walls almost golden in the warm light.

St Paul's Church (1610) has a beautifully-proportioned façade in three

Diu. St Paul's Church

storeys of white marble surmounted by a cross. Its central doorway is tall and arched; the two flanking doors shorter and rectangular. The vast interior is basilical in form, with a blue and white scheme in the nave and three dark altars contrasting with the flood of bright light entering from above and laterally. The grandiose Jesuit seminary is pierced at first-floor level by eleven arched windows, and don't miss the splendid Lusitanian courtyard with its rounded arches and lush greenery.

St Francis of Assisi's Church nearby (1593) has been converted into a Government Hospital and Primary Health Centre. Its ambulance bore the slogan 'Small Family Happy Family', which derives more from the Indian Government's family planning programme than from Roman Catholic

Diu. The former St Francis of Assisi Church, now a primary health centre

doctrine. Yet a woman could be seen still drawing water from the old Portuguese well in the courtyard as if under siege, and clinics for leprosy and filaria (parasitic worms) are active. It must seem uncanny to a Hindu or Muslim, being treated for worms in a Christian church.

It was time to change more travellers' cheques into rupees, so I reluctantly sped down the wide flight of steps creating a majestic platform for St Francis of Assisi and returned to Diu town centre, where tellers at the State Bank of Saurashtra sat in front of mountainous piles of forms. Each teller is confined to a glass cubicle, the safe in the centre has a metal cage, and an armed guard stands by the quarter-open door. I was motioned to fill out a form, signed my cheques and received a numbered brass token for surrendering to the cashier. The day's rate was chalked up at Rs 43.93 = £1. I then queued at the cash desk, and the whole process ended triumphantly in 20 minutes, quicker than I dared hope.

My taxi passed the salt-flats on the way to the landmark Portuguese church at Fudam, then continued down to the shore of the Arabian Sea, to find the Shaivite temple of Gangeshwar. At the entrance a white Nandi bull had been draped in a fetching pink sari and garlanded. Shri Hanumanji, strewn with petals, guards steps down towards the shore, and the roar of the sea makes a dramatic aural background to this primaeval cavern, where five yonis and five lingams are set in a flat mosaic floor, below nineteen steps and a five-headed cobra squirming in blue stone set

246

into the living rock wall, beside a bell to summon the god.

On the inland road to Nagoa Beach, look at the attractive flat-roofed houses with tiny shuttered windows to protect the residents from intense summer heat. Diu has only about 600 cultivable hectares, and an average rainfall of some 70 cm, but the coconut plantations seem to do well, and certainly look romantic to northerners like me. As does the broad expanse of the horseshoe Nagoa Beach, possibly the cleanest in India, in the absence of a town or sewage outlet close by. The unusual palms of the African *hoka* genus are the only examples growing in India. Swimming is safe on Nagoa Beach. Beachlovers can also try Chakratirtha Beach, Jallandar Beach, the old Summer House, and the new Circuit House (some accommodation) much nearer Diu town. In the morning paper at the Circuit House I read that the B.J.P. were winning state by-elections in Gujarat, a four-year-old boy had been killed in Maryland by a falling statue of the Virgin Mary, and in Kerala ownership of a parrot had been adjudicated on the basis of the parrot's knowing and repeating the forenames of the children of one competing family but not those of their rivals, a bizarre psittacine Judgment of Solomon.

The western end of Diu seems even quieter than the eastern side, and Vanakbara village has a fishing port of endless fascination, near both a forested area and a coconut plantation, with a fort and the Church of Our Lady of Mercy. From here you can see the village of Kotdhla on the coast

Diu. A dungcake cart near Vanakbara

of Gujarat, and ferries plying between Kotdhla and Vanakbara at frequent intervals, whenever boats fill up. Officially that means six times a day, taking ten minutes and costing Rs 2. Urchins run and rummage among the fishing smacks, and ducks dash in between incautious feet. Excited women and children spill up on to the jetty from one end of the little boat, and men wait docilely until last. Bars offer beer, spirits and IMFL, or 'Indian-made Foreign Liquor'. Rum is made in a Diu factory. Dung-cakes in great piles await buyers. Goa State Co-operative Bank Ltd still has a branch here, reminding you of the days of the Union Territory of Goa, Daman, and Diu. (Nowadays, Goa has its own Union Territory). Diu is much more attractive than Daman, conserving much more of its Portuguese heritage, so if pressed for time and forced to choose between them, I recommend the island off Saurashtra rather than the enclave in Valsad district.

VII: KUTCH

The metre-gauge railway from Gandhidham to Bhuj was extended in 1990 to Naliya in western Kutch via Sukhpur, Deshalpur, Sukhpura Roha, Sanosara, Mathala Halt, Mothala, Dhavala Wada, Kothara and Naliya Cantonment. The distance between Gandhidham and Bhuj is 59 km and the rail trip takes about 2 hrs 15 mins. From Bhuj to Naliya, the daily 105-km journey takes about 3 hrs 30 mins, departing daily at 10.35 and reaching Naliya around 14.05, leaving again at 14.20 and arriving in Bhuj at 17.49 hrs. The line from Gandhidham to Bhuj serves Gopalpur, Adipur, Anjar, Sapda, Ratnal, Kuka and Madhopur Road, and there are departures from Gandhidham at 0.47, 4.45, 8.15, 10.35, 11.32, 13.51 and 17.12.

Bhuj is also served by buses, and is linked with other cities in Gujarat by air.

Bhuj
Totally different from any other city I have ever seen, Bhuj is a bustling walled city in the depths of Kutch's hostile wastes, boasting an inner citadel, lake, palaces and temples overlooked by a great hill fort. The whole lower city buzzes with streets of shops and residential quarters unexpectedly coalescing as at Moroccan Fez, and quiet sandy corners where you find a grazing goat or wandering cow, as at Rajasthani Jaisalmer.

Unlike most other Gujarati towns and cities, Bhuj has retained its integrity, its historical continuity. Whereas cities throughout the Communist and highly-developed world have torn out their hearts to promote office-buildings, ministries and grandiose projects dedicated to the new (I think of tragic Bucharest and industrial America), Ahmedabad still retains in addition to its great Islamic monuments communities known as *pol*s with great havelis beautifully carved: the Yogesh Shah haveli in Haribhaktini Pol, and Sushila Shah's haveli in Sankdi Sheri.

Bhuj – more isolated, less populous – has retained many other features of the past such as residential areas in the bazaar area, and here you can wander happily for hours, surprised by a cul-de-sac, by a snuffling hog, by chasing infants involved in a game of catch-as-catch-can or running after a rusty bicycle wheel as a hoop. You might find a pile of recently-made kiln-fired pots made from clay collected from local ponds and thrown on traditional potter's wheels, sun-dried, and painted by the women with natural colours, usually white, black and red.

Because it is important to Indians to believe as well as to know, and the two ideas seem often interchangeable, I summarise Mudrika Jani's retell-

Map of Kutch

ing of the Bhujia legend. Once upon a time Kutch was ruled by Naga feudal chieftains; a queen, Sagai of Sheshapattana, rose up against them in the north of Kutch and allied herself with Bheria Kumar to overcome the last Naga chieftain, Bhujang. At a great battle between the two, Bhujang conquered Bheria, and Sagai committed *sati*. From then on the hill where he lived became known as Bhujia, and the town at its foot Bhuj. The people worshipped his power, and he changed from a malevolent despot to a benevolent ruler and after his death came to be worshipped as a god. Local people still revere him and celebrate his festival on the fifth day of Shravana month of the Hindu calendar.

Bhujia hill rises to a height of 160 metres at one end and has a hill fort which has often served in the turbulent past as an outwork defence. Bhuj is most probably the classical Tej and certainly the Sulaimannagar of the Muslim writers. Much earlier it had formed a bridge for Harappan-period colonists moving east from the Indus Valley towards the river Sabarmati, effectively their eastern limit. J.P. Joshi is sure that Harappans crossed Kutch by land (and we do have many Kutchi sites of apparent Harappan age) but S.K. Gupta asserts that the Rann was under at least four metres of water during the Harappan period, a generalisation not borne out by subsequent geomorphological change, which has been quite erratic.

But Bhuj as we see it today is a creation of the Raos of Jadeja race, beginning in 1548-85 with Rao Khengarji I, though the massive walls encircling the town date from the time of Rao Godji I (1715-18), and building continued under Rao Desalji I (1719-52). Kutch was liberated from Mughal control in the reign of Rao Lakhpatji. The heart of the walled city is a cluster of buildings intended to protect the dynasty of Rao Khengarji I Jadeja from outside assault, following the transfer of his capital from nearby Anjar in 1548.

Aina Mahal Palace is the 18th-century creation of the extravagant and ambitious Rao Lakhpatji (1741-60) who seized the throne from his father Rao Desalji at the age of thirty-four. He commissioned Ramsingh Malam to construct Aina Mahal, with its Hall of Mirrors of Venetian glass, much of it brought from Venice by Ramsingh himself. Ramsingh hailed from Saurashtra, but became disillusioned with local princes who did not understand or reward his genius. No: it was in Bhuj that patron and protégé met their match. Lakhpatji paid for Ramsingh to return to Europe to perfect his skills in glassmaking and ironfounding, following which Ramsingh set up a glass factory at Mandvi, and designed the palace there. You cannot understand the ingenious innovations of Aina Mahal without appreciating the genius of Ramsingh and the vision of his patron. Ramsingh turned out cannon from his iron foundry and china tiles from a tile factory, he learned stonecarving in the European style, and clockmaking. As an architect he was also responsible for the *chhatri*s or ceremonial mausolea of the Raos of Kutch on the outskirts of Bhuj slightly damaged in the 1819 earthquake.

The Hall of Mirrors has white marble walls covered with mirrors and gilded ornaments, and the floor is a pleasure-pool lined with Ramsingh's tiles, with a platform above it surrounded by a series of fountains operated by an elaborated systems of pumps below a Venetian chandelier. The heterogeneous nature of the objects and their sources (Hogarth engravings, celestial globes, the finest Kutchi embroidery) proves the internationalist spirit of Bhuj two hundred years back. Lakhpatji was a poet himself and encouraged other poets to come to his court, not to mention the many girls who sang, danced and quite possible satisfied other whims of their prince. By contrast, Lakhpatji's successor Raydhan II (1778-86 and 1801-13) was a cruel despot who converted to Islam, attempted to convert his subjects, went mad, and caused fear and havoc throughout Kutch, arming himself heavily as he understandably trusted nobody.

As well as the small state apartment called the Hira Mahal, and the exhibition of coins, Aina Mahal has an art gallery with rulers' portraits and photographs of Bhuj city, a marriage chamber created in 1884 for Maharao Khengarji III and his bride, and a great Darbar Hall for ceremonial state occasions. The silver-covered throne in the centre is flanked by rows of gilt chairs, with many other exhibits such as weapons, fans, and historical manuscripts. Aina Mahal is open daily (except Thursdays) from 9-12 and 3-6. There are postcards and books on sale, and a guide-service in English and Gujarati.

Next to Aina Mahal is a palace built for Rao Pragmalji II (1860-75) by Italian architects and Kutchi builders. Its Darbar Hall is today a museum of Victorian-Edwardian taste, with tiger-skins and mounted trophies on the walls, stuffed lions and Art Deco figurines. You have to relinquish your camera at the foot of the stairs, and your shoes outside the hall. Recover your shoes and ascend the tower, from which all aspects of Bhuj can be studied on a clear winter's day. From one side, the Italianate *logge* could be in Emilia or Romagna; from another, the ample terrace gives way to a treeline on the horizon casting shadows into the limpid lake; the third side is a jigsaw of red-tiled roofs and trees still deep green months after the monsoon ended; the fourth is a distant perspective of bungalows and offices; while a fifth panorama presents a higgledy-piggledy mass of close-fitting buildings in the bazaar. Opposite the clean, tidy reddish Prag Mahal a generous cornucopia of fantastic carved wooden balconies and window-screens enlivens walls as if hornets' nests had solidified.

Kutch Museum was founded in 1877 by the British Principal of the Arts School established by Rao Khengarji III, and named after Sir James Fergusson, then Governor of Bombay. The present building dates from 1884, but the Museum was opened to the general public only after Independence, having till then been reserved for royal guests.

On two floors, it offers a general conspectus of tribal life through a series of dioramas, coins and currency (including the *kori*, Kutch's own monetary unit from 1617 until Kutch joined the Union), embroidery, a

Bhuj. View from the tower of Prag Mahal

shipping display, arms and armour, paintings, sculpture, embroidery, textile crafts, musical instruments, and gold and silver. The museum opens from 9 to 12 and 3 to 6 daily except Wednesdays and government holidays; at other times you can see an interesting display of stone sculpture in the forecourt, where craftsmen are brought from outlying parts of Kutch to practise their skills: during my visit I met the only surviving bell-maker. If you want to discover more about the neglected paintings of the region, B.N. Goswamy and A.L. Dallapiccola have produced an excellent illustrated monograph called *A Place Apart: Painting in Kutch, 1720-1820* (OUP, Delhi, 1983).

In Kutch Museum I asked to see musical instruments not on display; Jadia Umesh Prabhulal, a musicologist attached to the Museum entrusted with arranging recordings, performances and festivals, showed me all he

254

Bhuj. Kutch Museum. Muslim bell-maker demonstrating his craft

had and then invited me to his home to examine his collection of home-made folk instruments made from simple materials such as bamboo and hollowed nuts. Sidhik Mitha Jat, a man in his sixties now, comes from Ahmedabad and in his spare time plays the surando, a remarkable stringed instrument rested on one knee, bowed with the right hand and plucked with the left. The body of the surando has in its centre a wooden semi-circle like a peacock fan. Other stringed instruments of Kutch include the ektaro, ravanhatho, jantar and the popular sarangi.

One day after taking a thali with Umesh at the Anam Restaurant, I drove out with him to meet the leading flautist Sumarbhai at the port of Mundra. Sumarbhai, son of the noted nagara-player Sulaiman Juma', also plays the nobat and the flute-like sundari, ten inches long and made of sesame wood. We found him at his home near Shah Murad Pir Dargah, and he played melodies for us, crosslegged and serene. He is 73, but gladly makes long journeys to perform at Jain festivals and at Navratri.

While we in the West spectate, at lavish German and Italian opera, the ballet traditions of Russia and France, and plays by Shakespeare, Tennessee Williams or Vaclav Havel, the ever-lively folk arts of Gujarat live on through thousands of amateur practitioners, mostly unknown. Try if you can to see a *bhavai* performance: this is Gujarati folk drama headed by the Darpan Academy of Performing Arts in Ahmedabad and other towns and cities. It is traditional, often coarse, and is dedicated to the mother goddess.

While in Bhuj, visit the cultural centre, called Bharatiya Sanskriti Darshan, and look at the recent reproductions of *Ramalila* frescoes on the walls devoted to scenes from the story of Rama. From the railroad at Naliya it is but a short if bumpy busride to Tera. At Tera Castle Dr Rudrasingh Jadeja and his wife Durgaba kindly allowed me to see original frescoes from which the Bhuj copies were traced. Shri Gagubha, called Hamirji, was the youngest son of Maharao Desalji II (1819-60) and hence not born to rule by the system of primogeniture customary in Kutch. But as Gagubha was a favourite son, Desalji installed him as ruler of Tera and ordered the castle to be renovated so he could live there, and the four walls of one bedroom were painted with the Kutchi story of Rama at the instance of Sumaraji, heir-apparent of Tera, in 1845. But he died without issue and in debt, so his jagir or landlordship passed to the state of Kutch in 1847, and thus by gift from Desalji to Hamirji.

The frieze consists of sixty-four scenes, running anticlockwise from the invocation of the great Creator, Brahma, who is approached by the earth mother in her guise as sacred cow and other gods who implore deliverance from the oppression of the rakshasas or evil spirits assaulting the earth. The plea is answered by the descent of the God Vishnu in his seventh incarnation as the hero Rama, at Ayodhya in northern India. The dominant colours of the sequence are red, yellow, black and green, against a uniform white background which transmutes the scenes from a transient time of day and place, making them of permanent application to spiritual growth. Twenty-three of the scenes have been faithfully reproduced in Ramsinhji Rathod's marvellous study *Kutch and Rama Randh* (Bhuj, 1992). The scenes follow the order of the celebrated *Ramarandh* performances which once took place throughout rural Kutch but have become extinct. A *peda*, or 'fivesome', of male Brahmins from the Charan community would travel from village to village after Diwali, once the harvest was in, and hold their religious entertainment by firelight at night, usually in an open courtyard in the heart of the village. The play would be acted by up to four actors at a time, miming to the narration by the *nayak* to the accompaniment of cymbals and drums. The play would be lengthened or shortened according to the mood and size of the audience. If you want to see a living survival from the *Ramarandh*, the nearest approximation would be folk songs heard in villages such as Ramwada near Koteshwar in westernmost Kutch, or Koli folkdances reviving episodes such as the abduction of Sita in parts of Eastern Kutch.

One of the most colourful sights in Bhuj is the Swami Narayan temple, belonging to the oldest of the three sects of the Hindu cult of the being they call 'the God-Supreme'. Born in Chhapaiya, Uttar Pradesh, in 1781, the young man became a spiritual guru at the age of 21, denouncing the caste system, and surrounding the poor and needy. He wrote the text *Vachanamritam* and his sayings have been collected in a further volume entitle *Shikshapatri*. He settled at Gadhada near Sarangpur in Gujarat, and he

Bhuj. Swaminarayan temple. Upper floor. Sadhu and devotee

has more adherents in Gujarat than in any other state. He taught chastity, poverty, freedom from addictions, knowledge of the Vedas, and in a lifetime of 49 years he inspired the building of six temples, and began several educational centres intended to promote Hinduism through a hierarchy of enlightened gurus, each appointed by his predecessor. The Kalupur Swami Narayan Gadi at Bhuj has as its present head Acharya Tejandraprasad. The second sect, the Vadtal Swami Narayan Gadi, is headed by Acharya Ajandraprasad. The third, and by far the largest and most powerful, is called the 'New Movement', or Akshar Purshottam Swami Narayan Faith, and its current guru is called His Divine Holiness Pramukh Swami Maharaj. It is this latest movement which has created the extraordinary new Akshardham complex we have seen at Gandhinagar.

The Bhuj temple is on two levels: downstairs devotees prostrate themselves, pray and worship before brightly-lit locked and jewelled shrines. An inner courtyard gives way to an upper area where *sadhu*s live, teach, study and meet the faithful. I found the unquestioning faith of the never-ending throng quite remarkable in our sceptical age, and watched as the devotees sought to touch the feet of the *sadhus*, or 'saints' as they refer to themselves, or to touch the hem of their orange robes.

It was in Bhuj that Rao Khengarji I set up a 'great monastery' or Moti Poshal in a special building that has survived from the sixteenth century period of the Jain *sadhu* Manek Mirji. At this monastery royal bards were trained in oral history by the *godji* (guru) who looks after the royal spear given to Khengarji by the *sadhu* and the rock-crystal image of the mother goddess Ambaji which Manek had brought with him. A poshal is a monastery where a Jain stays while carrying out his *posha* vow, one of the four disciplinary Jain vows.

Sharad Baug Palace, open to visitors who can buy plants from its nursery, is the most relaxing and verdant of the royal palaces in Bhuj: as elsewhere the City Palace complex is completely surrounded by other buildings.

The delightful modern palaces, with their clattered furnishings, and airy porticoes letting light but not sun through the many windows, have tiger-skin tugs, tennis trophies and Art Deco ornaments below brilliant chandeliers. The unobtrusive caretaker allowed photographs, though I had to remove my shoes as if these were temples to sovereignty. They are kept immaculate, like the gardens with their high-stepping tame cranes and lavishly-illuminated peacocks which crash through the thick undergrowth as dramatically as any tiger. The palace had no other visitors that morning but a Jain couple from Bombay on a weekend's holiday. 'Think', said the husband, 'if you had such a peaceful refuge in Bombay it would be overcome with visitors like bees round a honeypot'. My sentiments precisely, but even the most persistent Western travellers to India seem to miss Bhuj, which is like missing Key West in Florida because it is – quite literally – out of the way.

I felt incurable melancholy for the great Madansinhji Sawai Bahadur, whom I had met in England shortly before his death in June 1991. A great tennis-player, representing India at Wimbledon between 1934 and 1938, Madansinhji reserved two Centre Court tickets at Wimbledon every year until his death.

Madansinhji, as eldest son of Kumar Shri Vijayarajji, was educated to rule by Professor J.H. Smith, who made Bhuj his home and became known locally as Dinabhandhu, or friend of the lowly. He joined Nehru in the march towards Independence, and refused to show the British monarch's head on coins minted in Kutch, preferring instead his own profile and the inscription *Jai Hind* ('Long Live India'). After the death of Vijayarajji, Madansinhji acceded as Maharao in March 1948, then seceded on 1 June. After Mountbatten suggested that he joined India's nascent foreign service, Madansinhji travelled to London's High Commission, then led by Nehru's sister Mrs Vijayalakshmi Pandit. After several years there, he was appointed Ambassador to Norway in 1957, then to Chile in 1960, retiring two years later to Bhuj. There he ceaselessly promoted relief funds and works to alleviate suffering in drought-prone Kutch, and encouraged tennis and cricket in the area.

The great gardens of Sharad Baug Palace have nurseries for plants, and grass courts to which leading tennis players were regularly invited. You can saunter down leafy paths overhung with hibiscus and waving palms:

Bhuj. Sharad Baug Palace. Detail

migrant birds call from their hideaways, relaxing after their long flight across the deserted Rann of Kutch.

Don't leave Bhuj without visiting the intricate, symmetrical step-well called Ramakund, fifty-six feet square, made of hard red sandstone; it fills with water whenever Hamirsar Lake overflows, which occurs whenever the water-level reaches the elephant relief on Raghunathji no Aro in Ramawadi. Sculptures in high relief on panels and niches around Ramakund depict characters from the *Ramarandh*, notably Rama himself, Lakshman, Sita and the monkey-god Hanuman.

The Rest of Kutch

If you want to explore Kutch in any detail, six coastal towns have a great deal of antiquarian interest: from west to east these are Lakhpat, with a fine fort; Koteshwar, an ancient port and fishing village; Narayan Sarovar, with its important Vaishnavite temple; Jakhau, with straggling houses; the once-magnificent port of Mandvi, which outshone Bhuj; and Mundra's walled town with its shrine of Pir Shah Murad of Bukhara and its walls made from the ruins of the Jain city of Bhadreshwar close by, then finally Bhadreshwar itself.

North of Bhuj are those geomorphological surprises: the 'islands' which remain above the level of the flood-plains when much of the rest of the Rann of Kutch is submerged by monsoon rains: Dholavira of the flamingoes, Dhinodha, Nanama, and Jandharia. In ancient times, the Rann formed a permanent arm of the Arabian Sea and Kutch was a real island, cut off both from Sind (now in Pakistan) and from Kathiawar, now called Saurashtra. Kutch bore the same relation to the rest of Gujarat as the Scottish Highlands to the rest of the British mainland: wild, with inhabitants speaking a dialect different from the rest of the people, and without any major cities.

Inland, there were fewer towns: Anjar was the capital before Bhuj; Bhachau has an impressive hill fort; Kotai has an early Surya temple later adapted for Shiva and Vishnu; Tera has an important fort; and Kera a historic Shiva temple.

In recent times, Kandla was developed as a modern port begun by Maharao Khengarji III (1876-1942) and completed as recently as 1955. Gandhidham north of Kandla is a planned town intended for refugees from Sind.

Other excursions can be made to the Banni grasslands in the north, during the dry season, and to handicraft centres such as Nirona (bells and rogani embroidery), Sumrasar for embroidery (ask for Mr Nathani), and Khavda also for embroidery. Silver is still made in Bhuj, Anjar, Bhachau, Mandvi and Mundra. You can get to Sumrasar, Khavda and the main towns by local buses, but for the villages it is preferable to have your own car.

If you have a car or taxi, take the road north from Bhuj towards Banni, the wide stretch of grasslands before you reach the Pakistani border. On the way, you can stop at the Black Hills, to see the Dattatreya Temple, where the priest can summon up rare white foxes like the ghosts of Japanese myth. Beyond Jamkundaliya is the desert and a lake where thousands of flamingoes come in season. At Hodko and Gorevali stop to look at the handicrafts: embroidery at Hodko, leather at Gorevali, and both at Dhorada.

Mandvi

Southwest from Bhuj, the coastal town of Mandvi once resounded to the bustle of shipyards, where Rao Godji (1760-78) built and maintained a fleet of four hundred oceangoing vessels, including one that sailed to England and back in 1760. Mandvi, as the port for Anjar, Bhuj and the interior, concentrating the communications of Kutch in its fist, waxed with trade westward to Zanzibar and southward to the Malabar coast, then waned as vessels grew in size and rejected Mandvi's harbour as too small, and trading patterns of India changed in favour of Bombay and Surat. The African fleet sailed in October and returned in May, when the wealthy shipowners would anxiously scan the horizon from the so-called Tower of Wagers, near the lighthouse, gambling on whose ships would land first.

Mandvi was founded by Rao Khengarji I in 1574, and its first temple was Sundarwar. Then followed the Friday Mosque (1603) for local Muslim fishermen, Lakshminarayan Temple (1607), a second mosque called the Kajivali (1608) and the Rameshwar Temple (1627) rebuilt after the earthquake of 1819. Rao Lakhpatji (1741-60) ordered Ramsingh Malam to construct him a royal palace, which the europhile had decorated with carvings of bibulous Dutchmen with bottles and drinking-cups as well as tigers and dancing-girls, amusingly at odds with the palace's later function as a girls' college. A new palace, called Vijay Vilas, was built west of the town by Rao Vijayarajji (1942-8). The British Political Agent posted to Bhuj had a summer bungalow at Mandvi, escaping to the sea from Bhuj's stifling summer heat, but the British cemetery to the east of the town tells its many forlorn anecdotes of youthful ensigns and captains lost in the fastnesses of Kutch, their pallid wives who succumbed to the appalling climate, and their children who may have picked up strange diseases for which the local British doctor may have found no cure.

Along the coast eastward you come to the minor port of Mundra: the harbour silts up quickly and treacherously, and only country craft can force their dogged way along the crude canals, bringing fine hauls of fish for markets in the interior. Mundra's magnificent stone wall is religious in origin, for it was dragged block by block from the ruined Jain city of Bhadreshwar.

Bhadreshwar

Ancient Bhadreshwar lies 1 km north of the present coastline; the modern village occupies part of the western area. The unreliable *Bantvijaya Chronicle* reports that Bhadravati was established about 516 B.C. and became a wealthy port. Sir Henry Yule took Ptolemy's Bardaxema to be Porbandar, but W.F. Sinclair and most later scholars believe it to be Bhadravati.

Bhadreshwar is nowadays the major centre of Jain pilgrimage in Kutch, but there are others near Gandhidham, Tera, Naliya, Jakhau, Kothara and Suthari. The temple is said locally to date from 'about 2500 years ago, 45 years after the nirvana of Lord Mahavira, the 24th *tirthankar*' when Shri Kapil Kevali Muni 'installed here the idol of Lord Parshvanath (the 23rd *tirthankar*'). This may be true, but we have no evidence apart from the bald assertion and O.P. Tandon's *Jaina Shrines in India* (Delhi, 1986) observes that Jainism's 'rich cultural heritage...started from about the fourth century B.C.' The first literary record of built temples in Gujarat (as opposed to excavated caves) dates from the 8th century A.D. In 1248, Seth Jagdushah carried out a major renovation, and there are said to have been nine major renovations since, as well as constant maintenance paid for by Jain merchants and businessmen. Indeed, temple-building is a particularly pious activity among the Jains. The modern triple-arched polychrome gateway with numerous slender attached pillars on the four uniform columns would look more at home in a fairground, but the massive ensemble, gleaming white, is as impressive as a snowy pine-forest nestling around a central icy dome, the whole shining under a perpetual blue sky. Within the sanctuary a beady-eyed warder gestured that I should hand him not only my shoes and my hat, but my shoulder bag and camera. No photography, and no note-taking allowed, so I cannot vouch for the possibility that the naive frescoes of the life of Mahavira, the 24th *tirthankar*, were painted by a single artist in the middle of this century. You gaze through the centre to see the principal image, which here is of Lord Mahavira, last of the *tirthankar*s or 'makers of the river-crossing', as one translation as it: the 'ford-creators' who assist living Jains to accede to the supernal zone at the zenith of the universe, beyond the reach of prayer. You can think of these 24 beings as transcendent, without features (which is why their idols are uniform and distinguished only by their individual symbols, colours, trees, *yakshas* and *yakshis*); without time, space, action; omniscient and forever at absolute peace. These idols then should not be viewed as one might view Leonardo's 'St Jerome' or 'Last Judgment', where human characteristics threaten to overturn an image's sanctity. We may 'read' a European painting, but one must empty one's mind before a Jain idol and see only the upper spheres, as in the last few canti of Dante's *Paradiso*:

> E vidi lume in forma di rivera   [And I saw light flow like a stream,
> fulvido di fulgore, intra due rive   shining in splendour, between two banks
> dipinte di mirabil primavera   gleaming with every hue of lovely spring]

Fifty-two small shrines surround the main shrine, and in the deri numbered 25, behind a locked, barred gate, is the idol claimed to be the original idol of Lord Parshvanatha brought here 2500 years ago. A three-day pilgrimage and festival at Bhadreshwar's Jain temple is held on the 3rd-5th days of the month of Phalgun Sudi, during which period you cannot stay at the temple. Non-Jains are not allowed to spend the night within the temple compound, but you can find basic accommodation elsewhere in Bhadreshwar if you don't want to go back to Bhuj.

Mehrdad Shokoohy's *Bhadreśvar: the oldest Islamic monuments in India* (Leiden, 1988) is a brief but fascinating account of what might possibly have been the earliest settlement of Muslim immigrants. To find the building, cross the road south from the great Vasav Jain Temple. One of the two mosques, both dated like the shrine of a certain Ibrahim about 1159-60 possesses most of its original features intact, and shows the kind of simple, austere building plan adopted before the flowering of Islamic monuments exemplified by 15th-century Ahmedabad. The shrine is known locally as Lal Shahbaz, the name of a figure legendary among the Shi'a of Gujarat and Sind, whose dates do not tally with this monument. We know that such early settlements existed, from accounts by Muslim geographers, but it is only recently that this group of buildings, with a

Bhadreshwar. Jain Temple

step-well and many contemporary tombs, definitively proved the arrival in coastal Gujarat of Iranian Isma'ili seafaring traders half a century before the conquest of Delhi across the steppes by land. In this connection, it is interesting to compare the mosque of Abulqasim bin Ali al-Iraji (1286-7), another pre-Sultanate building, in Junagadh. Here at Bhadreshwar – until we locate prior examples – is the earliest example of the incorporation of Indian features in Muslim architecture. Shokoohy proposes the idea that the collaboration was due not to the Muslims using temple spoils in the mosques, nor their exclusive employment of local Hindu craftsmen, but to a genuine rapprochement between the two communities. If this is true, and we shall never be sure, the theory could help to dampen the flames of sectarian violence currently burning Bombay and some cities of Gujarat on account of the destruction of Ayodhya's Babri mosque by Hindu extremists. But it won't.

The larger of the two venerable mosques, called the Solah Khambi, must be dated around 1175, like the step-well called Dudha Vav close by. Shokoohy sees the same workmanship in the smaller or Chhoti Masjid, dated not much later than 1160, as in the Shrine of Ibrahim. Chhoti Masjid stands on a platform 45 cm higher than ground level and measuring 15.2 metres wide by 20.5 metres long, and is also built of large stone blocks, having a courtyard with a double colonnade at the qibla end and a sanctuary chamber. Neither of the two historic mosques is in use today, so I asked a local Muslim called Husain to show me the active mosques. By far the earlier stands much higher above ground than the surrounding houses, and an area has been cleared in front of it. It is small, befitting a rather limited congregation, with a courtyard giving on to a simple pillared sanctuary. A second, at the end of a *cul-de-sac*, has a cloistered, almost secretive quality, with a locked door that has to be opened by a caretaker living close by. Painted bright blue and green on the outside, it is equally bright within, and a twin tiled roof gives it the appearance of a private house until you notice twin minarets peeking above, with loudspeakers pointing in opposite directions for the muaddin's five daily calls to prayer. A *haveli* opposite has two storeys, the lower painted turquoise with elaborate wooden carved door and ground-floor windows beyond a pillared portico, and a balconied upper storey surmounted by a flat roof.

Anjar

Nearby Anjar was made capital of Kutch by Rao Khengarji before he established his permanent capital at Bhuj. The British East India Company's Political Agent, James MacMurdo, had his quarters at Anjar, where he built himself a bungalow on the model of his Scottish home at Dumfries, and had it painted with frescoes in local Kutchi style. Other examples of Kutch mural painting can be seen at Bhuj in Aina Mahal and Kutch Museum, the Bhandara of Doramnath at Moti Rayan, and in the Akhada of Jangi at Dhrang. The Kutchi folk style, wholly anonymous and mostly updated, seems to have developed in the time of Rao Lakhpatji II. The subject matter of these frescoes includes animals and birds, especially elephant and deer, flowers and plants, episodes from the Hindu epics, the Ramayana and Mahabharata, and scenes from everyday life. MacMurdo, promoted to captain in 1817 at the age of 31, died at Warnu, near Adesar in Waghad district on the edge of the Little Rann of Kutch, in 1820 and is buried there.

A clever, resourceful and learned man, MacMurdo mastered the Kutchi language after entering Kutch as a Hindu pilgrim. He would sit and chant Rama's name at the temple of Madhavrai at Anjar. Kutch remained in a divided and lawless state after the death of the great Diwan Fateh Muhammad and the unstable Muslim fanatic Rao Raydhanji II in 1813. Eventually, to quell dacoity and the warring factions the Company sent Colonel East with 4,000 fighting men and troops of the allied Gaekwad, and MacMurdo sent word to enemies of Rao Bharmalji II that the Company meant no harm to the lands or peoples of Kutch and took Anjar and its port called Tuna from its ruler Husain Miyan after a single brief artillery attack had breached its walls on Christmas Day, 1815. The Company's force then moved on Bhuj and compelled Rao Bharmalji II to sign the historic treaty of 1816.

The Rao agreed to make good all losses caused by the dacoits of Waghad; to stop confiscating property shipwrecked on the coast and return it to its rightful owners; to forbid Kutchis to cross from Kutch into neighbouring areas to cause damage and seize booty; to suppress local piracy; to prohibit the engagement of Arab mercenaries, except for his own bodyguard of no more than 400 men; to forbid any but British agents or troops to enter Kutch from any direction; to pay 200,000 *koris* a year and to receive the Company's Resident at the capital; and finally to assign the fort of Anjar with 24 surrounding villages and the port of Tuna to the Company in perpetuity.

In return, the Company promised to obtain the restitution of lands robbed from the Maharao by treacherous subjects; to subdue lawless Waghad to the Rao's control; to ally themselves with the Rao to stop incursions of outsiders into Kutch; and to refrain from killing cows and bullocks in Kutch. This 1816 treaty made Kutch unique as a partner of the Company in Western India; only some forty states out of the five hundred or so throughout Greater India were considered important enough to warrant their own treaty as opposed to an informal agreement or a grant of privilege.

In Anjar, MacMurdo was known as Bhuriya Bawa and greatly admired as a devotee of Rama. His bungalow is still used, now as the Deputy Collector's office, so the paintings he commissioned on his walls are looked after and shown on application. (They say, among themselves, that MacMurdo's spirit still arrives daily to pray at Madhavrai Temple.)

Narayan Sarovar
Narayan Sarovar, southwest of Koteshwar in westernmost Kutch, is considered one of the five sacred lakes of India, with Bindu at Bhubaneshwar in the east, Pushkar in the centre, Pampa in the south and Mansarovar in the north. The religious importance of Narayan Sarovar is connected with the meeting of the Indus and the sea (Ratnakar Sagar). Shri Hanuman is believed to have collected its water, with those of the other four sacred lakes, to mingle with the divine mixture needed for religious rites at Ayodhya during the coronation of Shri Rama. It is still a place of pilgrimage, with white towers like tent-tops jutting above the bastioned walls beside Sangamtirtha.

USEFUL INFORMATION

When to Come

The best months for Daman, Diu and Gujarat coincide with the depths of European winter: November to March. My favourite month is January, after the holiday season running from Christmas to New Year. The Tropic of Cancer passes through the State of Gujarat, which surrounds Daman and Diu, but on the whole Gujarat suffers neither extreme cold nor extreme heat, except in the desertic western region in high summer, which may reach 45° Celsius in May or early June. The southwest monsoon makes life relatively difficult from mid-June till mid-September: the southern region is the wettest, enjoying up to 155 cm of rainfall, while Kutch may receive 30 cm or in some years hardly any rainfall at all.

How to Come

Ahmedabad's new airport, opened in 1979, is one of the most attractive in India, which made me wonder why everything proceeded so slowly. Air India (tel. 42 56 44) connects with Bombay once or twice a week. More frequent flights – often fully booked, so check first on 42 33 11 – by East West Airlines connect with Bombay daily, arriving in Ahmedabad at 7.30 p.m. daily and returning at 8 p.m. to Santa Cruz Airport. Indian Airlines (tel. 35 33 33) is notoriously less dependable, according to the timetable arriving in Ahmedabad at 7.30 a.m. and returning there at 7.50 a.m., but such times are merely indicative and should be checked before departure to the airport.

Bombay and Ahmedabad connect by air with a number of provincial cities: check the current situation with your agent. Airports exist at Daman, Diu, Bhuj, Bhavnagar, Jamnagar, Rajkot, Baroda, Surat, Keshod (for Junagadh) and Porbandar.

For those with a great deal of time, trains are a wonderful way to see Gujarat, providing you stop off where this guidebook recommends. Much more comfortable than the buses, they have toilets, and of course your choice of travelling companions. Ahmedabad connects with Delhi on metre-gauge railway through Rajasthan via Abu Road, Ajmer and Jaipur and takes up to twenty-four hours if (for any reason) you never want to get off. But the Sarvodaya Express (only about 19 hours) takes the broad-gauge line from Delhi via Kota to Baroda, then turns back north to Ahmedabad.

Bombay to Ahmedabad on the broad-gauge line can take anything up to 15 hours, so choose a fast train taking only nine hours. These are really quite comfortable, with meal service on board, and convenient stops at Vapi (for

266

Daman), Bulsar (or Valsad is another variant spelling), Navsari, Surat, Broach (spelt also Bharuch), Baroda (officially Vadodara) and Anand (for Cambay, officially Khambat). Much of the state is accessible by train, but the southern and western side of Saurashtra and the coast of Kutch relies on buses.

Buses remain, as always in India, the most frequent and dependable means of transport: they are cheaper, faster, and cover many more localities. After arrival by bus, you find an auto-rickshaw stand for instant transport within a town or city to hotels. Most hotels very close to bus stands or rail stations tend to be nasty and noisy: get as far away as possible in the time available.

Avoid local buses within city boundaries; their destinations are shown exclusively in Gujarati. Take a taxi or auto-rickshaw in big cities like Ahmedabad, after establishing the fare *first*. Reduce any figure originally demanded. Taxis will be dearer than auto-rickshaws, but even then the chances are that few taxi-drivers will speak more than rudimentary English, so persuade a hotel receptionist to write out your itinerary in Gujarati before you leave the hotel in the morning.

On arrival at your airport or rail station or bus station *always* ignore touts accosting you and join the queue for taxis or auto-rickshaws. India is a country where service is still a proud tradition, and your hotel will normally be able to arrange reconfirmation of onward or return airline bookings, or buy rail tickets at the station: be prepared to tip anyone who saves your time in this or in any other way, because your stay (no matter how long) is always too short to spend in queues.

But the way to explore medium-size and small towns is on foot, for which comfortable shoes are a necessity. I have always found India safe for walking alone, but then I take precautions such as looking for and avoiding potential trouble, such as gangs of rowdy youths, or crowds where pickpockets mingle.

If you feel happier in a group, organised tours are arranged by the Tourism Corporation of Gujarat, Ltd., headquartered at HK House off Ashram Road, Ahmedabad 380 009, tel. 449683, 449172, telex 0121-6549 TCGL IN, with regional offices in Delhi, Calcutta, Madras, Bombay, Baroda, Surat and Rajkot. One five-day tour covers much of Saurashtra and another covers parts of North Gujarat and South Rajasthan including Udaipur, Chittorgarh and Mount Abu. One six-day tour from Baroda and Ahmedabad covers Kutch and another from Ahmedabad and Baroda takes in Saputara with other parts of South Gujarat and West Maharashtra including Ajanta, Ellora and Aurangabad.

Private companies offer different tours. I recommend North West Safaris, 312 G.I.D.C. Estate, Sector 28, Gandhinagar 382 028, tel. 22991, 23729 and 21549, with branches in Ahmedabad and Bombay. Their arrangements by theme include an 11-day Gujarati Handicrafts tour; a 22-day Religion tour beginning in Ahmedabad and ending via Nasik and Aurangabad at Bombay; a 13-day Desert Odyssey beginning in Bhuj and visiting the Great Rann, the Little Rann and Rajasthan's Thar Desert; an Archaeology tour lasting ten days, from Ahmedabad to Lothal, Shatrunjaya, Diu, Junagadh, Bhuj and Dholavira, and Patan with Modhera; and a 13-day Wildlife tour.

Hotels and Restaurants
Accommodation in **Ahmedabad** is surprisingly sparse for a vibrant city of three million. To avoid the heaviest pollution, I stayed at the inexpensive Circuit House Annexe in Shahi Baug, which has the great advantage of being only ten minutes from the airport, and very close to the Calico Museum of Textiles, the city's major gallery. But only Gujarati thalis are served in the basic restaurant, and then only by prior booking. Equally quiet is the de luxe Cama Hotel, facing the Sabarmati river (Rs 575 for a double). I recommend the Goan-owned 18th-century Ritz (Rs 375 a/c double; Rs 225 non a/c double) for its charming rooms and courteous staff, but if this is full try the neighbouring Ambassador (Rs 250 a/c double; Rs 200 non a/c double), in the vicinity of Lal Darwaza for the local bus station. The Rivera (Rs 500 a/c double) near the Cama has equivalent status.

The Hotel Karnavati on the other back of the Sabarmati (Ashram Road) charges a high Rs 800 for an a/c double and, like the Rivera and Cama, has a liquor shop for permit-holders, with a facility for issuing a temporary permit on the spot. It must be pointed out, for foreigners in dire need of alcohol, that the liquor will be expensive because Gujarat, like all prohibition states, will charge a great deal above average for those in pursuit of even a wee dram. A lunch in the Karnavati's Haveli restaurant seemed to me the slowest service I have ever suffered, but the quality was fine. The nearby Nataraj (Rs 500 for a/c double) is categorised four-star.

Two hotels near Relief Cinema are the Kingsway (Rs 280 for a/c double), the Balwas, 6751 Tilak Road (Rs 260 for a/c double) on G.P.O Road and the Capri (Rs 450 for a/c double) on Relief Road. Within 1 km from the modern Railway Station are the Hotel City Palace, opposite the Calico Dome on Relief Road (Rs 230 for a/c double); the Metropole (Rs 290 for a/c double), the Balwas, 6751 Tilak Road (Rs 260 for a/c double) and the cheerful Moti Mahal in Kapasia Bazaar (Rs 260 for a/c double). Really cheap guest houses can be found even closer to the rail station and Lal Darwaza, but if getting a good night's sleep is your priority either miss these out or fit earplugs. The traffic in downtown Ahmedabad *never* stops.

I wish I could enthuse about the tourist complex called Samudra Beach Resort at **Ahmedpur Mandvi**, on the Gujarati side of Ghoghla village. The accommodation is in private bungalows, varying in rates according to occupancy. The food is said to be Chinese, continental and Indian, but the choice during my stay was extremely limited, and the service slow. Twenty-four extra family rooms are said to be in the building stage, but the occupancy of the beach resort has fallen dramatically since the Russians stopped coming here and, compared with neighbouring Diu, I cannot imagine why anyone not an unforgiving teetotaller would choose to stay in Ahmedpur Mandvi when Diu's beaches are within a short drive.

Banaskantha district used to offer little in the way of overnight stays, but now there is a Nawabi palace hotel at **Balaram,** north of Palanpur en route to Abu Road, Rajasthan.

A state-run Toran Picnic Centre near the temple of Balaram Mahadeo offers six single rooms and a dormitory. (Balarama is in the Mahabharata the elder brother of Krishna). If you are travelling between Ahmedabad and Abu Road, Balaram makes a splendid overnight stop, convenient for Jessore Sloth Bear Sanctuary's trails for jeeps and trekking. If you don't see a bear, you may still see nilgai and sambar, jackals and hornbill.

Baroda is the best-equipped city in Gujarat for a wide range of accommodation. The most expensive are the Surya Palace, Rama Inn and the Express hotels. The Surya Palace is situated opposite the Parsi Fire Temple in Sayajigunj, the city's major business and shopping district. Single rates – for comparison with other hotels – are Rs 1100 for a suite, Rs 725 for a de luxe room, Rs 575 for an executive room, and Rs 480 for an economy room; double rates are respectively Rs 1300, Rs 925, Rs 775, and Rs 660. This modern high-rise block built in 1985 has a set meal for as little as Rs 100. Equally central (and therefore noisy in the lower storeys) is the three-star Rama Inn, one of the Best Western chain, which opened on R.C. Dutt Road in 1988. My room 411 was a back room with balcony, twin beds, Western-style toilet, fridge and TV and cost Rs 650. The restaurant is veg and non-veg, with Punjabi, Chinese and Continental cuisine.

The four-star Express Hotel, also on R.C. Dutt Road, was built in 1976 and operates a vegetarian Gujarati restaurant and an excellent multi-choice non-veg restaurant called Bliss. A double room is Rs 750. I must say I prefer its more peacefully-situated cousin, the three-star Express Alkapuri built in 1987 at 18 Alkapuri, where a double is Rs 650. It has only 25 rooms, compared with the Express's 65 and this would be my first choice now in Baroda.

I have stayed at two cheaper hotels in Sayajigunj. The Ambassador has no restaurant, but room service will go out to the Copper Chimney and bring you back pomfret and chips. The tempting Ambassador Sweet Mart is a patisserie on the ground floor. Room 302 is a double room for Rs 200. Across the road is the three-star Hotel Surya, with helpful staff and a good restaurant. A double is Rs 330, but negotiable in off-season. Two hotels in Sayajigunj even cheaper than these are the Vikram (double Rs 144) and the Som Galaxy (double Rs 122). Apart from hotel restaurants, you can eat at the ever-reliable Havmor and Kwality Restaurants, near each other on Tilak Road east of the rail station.

Bhavnagar's leading hotel is the wonderful centrally-located Nilambag ('Turquoise Garden') Palace just off Nilambag Circle. Converted from royal use into a hotel in 1983, it offers 14 rooms and suites on all three floors (there is no lift) for US$40 (double occupancy) or US$30 (single), plus luxury taxes. Room 101, between inner and outer courtyards, has twin beds, TV, desk, dressing-room, ceiling fan, bathtub, shower and western toilet. You might relax in the Roman-style colonnaded swimming-pool, or see a local wedding, because parties are often held in the spacious grounds. Meals are varied and excellent value, enlivened by the presence of waiters in traditional garb, elegant chandeliers, white linen and a glass-fronted armoire with a stuffed peacock, a silver tray, and the packet of cornflakes. The Nilambag is very quiet, like the Circuit House which is situated a long way out, and has no local auto-rickshaw-drivers, so they have to be summoned by phone.

Unfortunately all the other hotels are less quiet, though convenient for businessmen and transport. The Apollo, opposite the bus station, can be ruled out for its perennial disturbances, as visitors crash in and out all night. So the choice of a mid-range hotel rests between two hotels beside Peel Gardens: the Bluehill (a/c double Rs 425), with disinfected western toilet, bathtub with shower, and a delightful Nilgiri veg restaurant offering Chinese and Indian cuisine; and the Jubilee (a/c double Rs 325-375), with very clean western toilet, bathtub with shower, and a first-floor veg restaurant, the Ankur, purveying Indian, Chinese and Continental cuisine.

Cheaper hotels are of course available in the bazaar area and on Station Road if you can take the hubbub and prefer to pay less. Nearest the rail station is Mini Hotel (a/c doubles Rs 150); slightly farther on is Shital Hotel in Amba Chowk (a/c doubles Rs 60).

For a quiet night at **Bhuj** in garden surroundings I stayed at the Umaid Bhavan, the Government Rest House, but I recommend instead the more friendly Hotel Prince on Station Road. Ask for a back room because of the incessant traffic noise, which affects also the nearby Anam. If you have to stop close by the bus station, the Sagar is your nearest lodging, or opposite the rail station you could try the ramshackle Paradise Lodge. For the atmosphere of mediaeval Bhuj, however, old India hands will make for either the Green Hotel or the City Hotel, one on each side of the ebullient Vegetable Market. If your rickshaw wallah cannot understand what you say, tell him to make for Shroff Bazaar, and ask from there.

When it comes to food, the only excellent Western cuisine is in the airconditioned Hotel Prince's restaurant, though most of the desserts were 'off', and service slow. Hotel Anam's airconditioned dining-hall offers only Gujarati thalis, though portions are generous and refills free of charge. In the bazaar area, I recommend the even cheaper Green Hotel.

Broach itself has no tourist hotel yet, but Shuklatirth on the sacred Narmada River has an enchanting Toran Holiday Home, with simple rooms at only Rs 30 for a double: very highly recommended for the atmosphere if you enjoyed Gita Mehta's episodic novel *A River Sutra* (1993).

A convenient night's stop along the coast between Porbandar and Diu would be the Palace Beach Resort at **Chorwad** run by the Tourism Corporation of Gujarat. Built in 1928 as a summer palace by the Nawab of Junagadh, it was allowed to deteriorate after he left for Pakistan in 1947; it became a guest-house in 1956, passed to the Tourism Corporation in 1978, and in 1992 the porch collapsed while the palace was being recorded on video by a French tourist, so he has a unique record of the fall of the Palace. Its twelve double rooms have not been used for accommodation since then, but the rescued royal furnishings now decorate some of the 18 double rooms in the palace annexe. A further sixteen cottages have double accommodation, and Sagar

Awas has a further 24 doubles. The hotel was greatly favoured by Russians until the collapse of the rouble: now average occupancy has dropped to 45%.

Daman has three types of accommodation. Long-stay holidaymakers can rent a villa or bungalow in the completely unspoilt Great Daman (locally known as Moti Daman) on the southern side of the Damanganga river. Sightseers wanting overnight accommodation before a quick visit and continuing back to Vapi (road and rail links) for the rest of their tour of Gujarat may prefer one of the small hotels conveniently situated near the buses and autorickshaw stand in Little Daman (Nani Daman). Weekenders wanting to get away from it all will enjoy the safe swimming, relaxed lifestyle and idyllic quiet of Jampore Beach, where Hotel China Town (a/c double Rs 350; non a/c double Rs 250) is at present my premier recommendation for the whole of Daman. More lively than Jampore Beach in the far south is Devka Beach in the far north, with a large choice of hotels, many of them on the right-hand side of the road, which means away from the beach, due to planning regulations. Swimming is not safe off Devka Beach.

Sagar Sun, the first hotel you will meet on the way from Nani Daman to Devka, is a complex of five rooms (Rs 150, non a/c) and fifteen cottages: five a/c for Rs 350 the night, and ten non a/c for the incredibly good value of Rs 200. Here the clientele is mainly Indians from Bombay and Gujarat, enjoying freedom from liquor prohibition. In Devka proper, the Hotel Ashoka Palace is ideally located for families with young children, opposite the amusement park called Tourist Complex, and offers a non a/c double for Rs 250. The Dariya Darshan Hotel ('View of the Sea'), on the 'wrong' side of the road, has an a/c double for Rs 400-500, and a non a/c double for Rs 300, as well as cottages and an eight-person dormitory. I enjoyed their chicken bullets in the garden restaurant, and found a range of beers and spirits that would satisfy anyone. Hotel Summer House is also equipped with an open-air restaurant; an a/c suite is Rs 350 and a non a/c double is Rs 150. Your choice at Devka is broadened by the Miramar and the marvellous new Sandy Resort (1990). The Sandy Resort has a swimming pool, health club and children's playground. Room 101 on the ground floor is an a/c double for Rs 450, and for Rs 25 more you opt for a more spacious room on the first floor, with TV, western toilet and shower.

The Miramar offers six seafacing cottages (Rs 700) for four, and 41 de luxe rooms with bath and shower (Rs 500 for a/c; Rs 400 for non a/c), with special discounts for package deals. An open-air restaurant provides Continental, Chinese and Indian food. I should mention that not all rooms (for instance no. 205) face the sea.

Apart all these new hotels at Jampore and Devka, there is one traditional Parsi haven: Dossu Olliaji's Duke's Hotel, founded in 1941 and so no longer pristine, but with an atmosphere all its own. If you have never tried Parsi cuisine, this is the place to start. Breakfast might be sweet and sour prawns, a fried egg, chapatis and hot sweet tea; lunch would include local freshly-caught fish or mutton; dinner might include pomfret or another fish followed by chicken sauté with chapatis and dhal.

There is nothing so pleasant in Nani Daman, and indeed the most depressing hotel in the whole district is the Marina, a once aristocratic Portuguese villa rebuilt in 1861 though apparently untouched since, with common toilets that drive one out instantly through the door. Your best bet in Nani Daman is the Sukhsagar, nearly opposite the Marina. When I stayed there the only room available was an a/c double at Rs 250 which I secured for Rs 100 after promising that I wouldn't turn on the airconditioning. It was a cold January night when I arrived, so my promise was easy to keep. If this is full, twin hotels on Seaface Road are worth trying, though the traffic is noisier than at the nearby Sukhsagar. The cheaper is the Sovereign (a/c Rs 275; non a/c Rs 90) and the dearer Gurukripa ('Teacher's Blessing'; double Rs 375; non a/c 175). The Gurukripa has a recommendable a/c restaurant with veg and non-veg Indian and Chinese food, while the Sovereign specialises in veg cuisine from Punjab, South India, and Gujarat. In general, your meals will be taken in hotels, where, unlike hotels in Diu, there is usually no need to order in advance.

In Winter 1993, Sarfraz Malik established at **Dasara** a Safari Camp built for him by the semi-nomadic Bajania tribesfolk from the Rann of Kutch and finger-painted by local women in traditional style. Each hut is an independent double bedroom with a western toilet and bathroom. Evening barbecues are enlivened by folk-dances and songs accompanied by local instruments.

The best birdwatching months in the Ranns are October through February, and reptile and mammal viewing can be recommended in the summer months (March through June). Though the Rann is submerged by the Arabian Sea and river waters during the monsoon, sightseeing can still be arranged from Dasara from July through September.

Accommodation in **Diu** is divided between Diu Town and the beaches. At Nagoa Beach, Ganga Sagar Guest House can be recommended, if you don't want a private bath or hot water. There is a Tourism Department hut at Jallandar Beach. If you want modern facilities, try the Hotel Samrat on Collectorate Road, near the vegetable market. The current rates are Rs 450 for an a/c double room, Rs 250 for a de luxe double, and Rs 200 for a double with bath, and they guarantee a 24-hour hot water supply. The a/c Peacock Restaurant with tinted glass offers Chinese or Punjabi food, but at present no Western cuisine or thalis.

If you prefer to stay in colonial-style rooms, the alternatives are the delightful, quiet Fun Club on Old Fort Road, and the even cheaper and rather less appealing Hotel Mozambique near the vegetable market. Closest to the fort is the unbelievably cheap Public Works Department Rest House, which is of course open to non-official guests if there is room. Should all these fail there are the Apana (Old Fort Road) and in the Fish Market area a Hare Krishna Guest House and Nilesh Guesthouse, the latter with some baths.

Accommodation at **Dwarka** is intended mainly for Hindu pilgrims, as at Somnath, and dharamshalas – some offering rooms for non-Hindus – can be found near Gomti Ghat, Bus Station Road, and Bazar Road. The Tourism Corporation of Gujarat Dormitory comprises twelve rooms, some of four, some of six and some of eight beds, for Rs 20 each. Nearby a Public Works Department rest house called Vishranti Grah can be found 2½ km from the rail station but if you are a rail passenger I suggest a retiring room (again only non a/c is available).

Gondal has a royal palace offering top-priced accommodation (Rs 2000 up to Rs 5000 including all Continental-style meals and excursions). Ask to see the rail saloon car, horse-drawn carriages, and more than thirty vintage cars. The palace has its own swimming pool and squash courts, and guests are also offered trips on a motorboat on lakes, to a colony of block-printers, and to silversmiths. From the Crown Prince's Palace where you stay, you can also see the Royal Palace (Darbargadh). Gondal is recommended as a magnificent overnight stop between Sasangir and Bhuj.

Hingolgadh is a splendid wildlife sanctuary on routes between Rajkot and Palitana or between Lothal and Junagadh. From the fortress you have marvellous views over rolling hills covered by scrub and forest. Seven royally-equipped rooms and a beautiful dining-hall make a stay here the memory of a lifetime. Hingolgadh offers protection to nilgai, Indian gazelle, jungle cats and jackals. Jasdan Palace is noted for the private library of the royal family, a handicrafts collection, and a stud farm for Kathiawari horses. To the west you can visit Gadhada, a site holy to Hindus of the Swaminarayan sect.

Accommodation in **Jamnagar,** a city amazingly not yet on any major tourism itineraries, is excellent and so far not always fully-booked. Hotel President on Teen Batti has 26 double rooms (Rs 480 a/c and Rs 300 non a/c) which can be had for single occupancy at Rs 380 a/c or Rs 200 non a/c; ten more rooms are under construction. The outstanding Seven Seas restaurant offers a wide-ranging menu of Chinese, Continental and Indian dishes. Even more attractive is a garden restaurant at Hotel New Aram, Nand Niwas, Pandit Nehru Road. This is the former mansion of Jam Sahib's jeweller and financier Alibhai Zaveri, who emigrated to Pakistan in 1947. The residence was converted into a hotel and opened in 1970, with a white façade and designs in blue and salmon-pink, about 150 m from Pratap Vilas. Ten de luxe a/c doubles are available at Rs 620, 17 a/c doubles at Rs 500, and 3 non a/c doubles at Rs 320. I was lucky enough to find a much cheaper room at the Government Circuit House on Dwarka Road, in the same compound as the Gymkhana Club and the District Superintendent of Police. The only sound at dawn emerged from the throats of heavenly songbirds in the surrounding trees.

If you want to stay in **Junagadh,** as at Palitana I urge you to stay at a Jain dharamshala or guest-lodge. This is because the experience of climbing Girnar Hill should be taken humbly and sympathetically in the shadow of Jain pilgrims, following their practices and learning their faith as an act of harmony and understanding. It is a great privilege to be able to climb the Jain mountains in their company, and one should take every chance to eat with them, and stay in their lodgings. The costs are low, and if the comforts are slight, then that too is part of the experience the non-Jain should share. Hindus and

Buddhists will be encountered on the path, and if you are a Christian there is much in Dante or Bunyan which will invigorate your ascent, as you recollect their words and the spirit behind those words.

If you prefer not to participate in the Jain way, a degree of modest comfort can be found in the Tourism Corporation's Hotel Girnar near Majwadi Darwaja (Rs 325 double a/c; Rs 100 double non a/c), with a full Gujarati thali meal for Rs 20. They are accustomed to providing very early breakfast for pilgrims and I managed to get before 6 a.m. a cheese sandwich, toast and butter and service tea. Even more friendly is the Relief Hotel managed by Alex Sorathia, whose brother Faiz runs the excellent restaurant, situated at Chittakhana Chowk near the spice market. Double a/c rooms cost Rs 325 and non a/c only Rs 60 with shower and western-style toilet. Faiz offers a packed breakfast at 4 a.m. and you can eat in the restaurant from 5-3 and 6-10, with a choice of Indian, western and Chinese dishes. Faiz has the best biryani in Gujarati, and the helpful staff will book you bus, rail and plane tickets, arrange bike-hire for Rs 20 a day, and a guide for Rs 50-100 a day. If the Relief is full, try the Vaibhav near the S.T. Stand (with a/c restaurant) run by the Vithalani family where a room comes to Rs 120 for an a/c double; or at Kalwa Chowk the more depressing Capital Guesthouse with a non a/c double for Rs 32.

No accommodation even for Jains is available on Girnar Hill itself, so you must descend before nightfall.

Limbdi, a convenient stop on the long drive between Ahmedabad and Rajkot, can offer two double bedrooms in the palace itself, and ten cottages around Ramsagar Lake. Attractions here include boating on the lake, a swimming-pool, horseriding, indoor games, and a museum and library. The former royal family of Limbdi have set up a tourist encampment for birdwatchers on their own land overlooking Nal Sarovar Lake, celebrated for its flamingoes, pelicans, storks, cranes, geese and ducks.

Lothal until recently could offer only two doubles at Rs 50 and two dormitories for students at Rs 15 per bed. Now, only 7 km away from the archaeological zone, you can stay at the magnificent palace of Utelia, still occupied by its owners. Each of the 14 double rooms has attached western toilet and bathroom and meals for up to 32 people can be taken in the dining-room. A double room costs Rs 650, with a reduction of Rs 100 for single occupancy. Western and Indian cuisine are uniformly excellent. Lunch can also be provided for parties on advance reservation to the Estate Manager, Utelia House, 9 Gandhi Bagh, Ahmedabad 380 006, tel. 0272-445770.

To stay at coastal **Okha**, you can book a room at the Government Circuit House in its counterpart at Jamnagar. Otherwise, there is a European guest house in Okha, from whose first-floor balcony you can see dolphins playing.

No accommodation exists on the sacred mountain of Shatrunjaya for religious reasons, so you have to spend the night down in **Palitana**. This is a great pleasure because, despite what some guidebooks assert, you will always be welcome at a Jain dharamshala such as Oswal Yatrik Gruh built in 1978 on Taleti Road, Palitana 364270, tel. 02848-2240. You can write in advance direct to the manager, Mr Bharatkumar Ratilal Sheth, and he will if space permits put you up for a donation of Rs 51 or more at Panch Bangla ('Five Bungalows'), where rooms have toilet and bath, as long as you obey such basic rules as not bringing in non-vegetarian food. Pilgrims may stay free of charge in Hazari Niwas. Most dharamshalas will give you a room without any advance notice but always book in advance if you plan to visit Palitana during the festivals or *melas*. In 1993 the Pagan Sud Tiras Mela held on 6 March attracted 1 lakh of pilgrims (a hundred thousand) and Vaisakh Sud Trij Mela held in May brought around 75,000 worshippers to celebrate Lord Adinatha's breaking of his fast by taking sugarcane juice. Room 21 at the 50-room Oswal dharamshala, with a Western toilet and a geyser providing hot water from 4 to 9 a.m., has a double bed with mosquito nets and a kitchen for cooking your own exclusively vegetarian meals. But be careful not to infringe the Jain prohibition against betel nut and all root vegetables.

Some seventy-five dharamshalas exist in Palitana at present, with others under construction. I have not tried to get a room in the Digambar dharamshala, a large cream building overlooking the river by Willingdon Market.

A Western-style hotel on Station Road, the Sumeru run by the Tourism Corporation of Gujarat, has just 1 a/c double for Rs 200, 13 non a/c doubles for a very reasonable Rs 100, and five dormitory rooms where a bed costs Rs 20. The staff is so helpful that they will lend you their copy of James Burgess' elephant folio *The Temples of Satruñjaya, the Celebrated Jaina Place of Pilgrimage near Palitana in Kathiawad photographed by Sykes and Dwyer* reprinted 'for the celebration of the 2500th Anniversary of Bhagwan Mahavira Nirvan' in 1976 and distributed by Motilal Banarsidass of Bombay. You can obtain limited Western dishes at the Sumeru. In town the noisy Sravak Hotel near the bus station does *not* offer the kind of peace and quiet a pilgrim seeks, but if you relish such a surreal contrast, their Gujarati thalis can be recommended. And there is a cinema nearby.

Champaner has no accommodation for Westerners, but luckily the hill resort of **Pavagadh** nearby has a state-run (if confusingly-named) Hotel Champaner at the village of Manchi and this I strongly recommend: 32 doubles at Rs 100 are cheap enough, but a pre-booking party may use a 15-bed dormitory for only Rs 20 per person.

In **Porbandar** I stayed at the Toran Tourist Bungalow on Chowpatty Beach (Rs 175 double a/c; Rs 100 double non a/c), but I recommend instead the nearby 4-room New Oceanic Hotel (Rs 300 double a/c), which intends to expand because currently it is nearly always overbooked and offers Chinese as well as Indian and Western cuisine. Dinner at the Toran consisted of curry, chapatis, yoghurt, boiled rice, spicy potatoes, and slices of cucumber, onion, carrot and tomato.

Lal Palace was a hotel up to 1991, but now the alternatives in town are the Vaibhav or Flamingo on M.G. Road five minutes from the bus stand, and the Sheetal opposite the G.P.O., two minutes walk from the bus stand. With a rail ticket, you can stay in a station retiring room.

If you find yourself at Ambaji near the Rajasthani border, late in the day, you can find accommodation in the Nawabi-period hotel at **Poshina**, one of the northernmost villages in Sabarkantha district. Seven rooms have recently been renovated, each with a bathroom: the current tariff ranges from Rs 350-500. An attraction of the area is the folklore (Bhils and Garasias), in particular snake-charming, carpet-weaving and native weapons.

Accommodation is available in all price-ranges at **Rajkot**, Saurashtra's British-nominated capital during the Raj. Number 1 is the Galaxy on Jawahar Road (Rs 330-390 for double a/c), for amiable service and spacious, clean rooms, with the great advantage of proximity to a branch of Havmor Restaurants, whose vast choice of Chinese, Indian and European specialities – including fish – makes a high point in any Indian day. During lunch at Havmor a video was being shown of the Palkhi yatra to Pandharpur, described in my *Western India*. The Modha family's Samrat International, 37 Karanpura offers double a/c rooms for Rs 250-300. The Tulsi on Kanak Road (Rs 225-275) can be recommended for its Kanchan Restaurant, while on the same road the rather noisier Ruby (Rs 180) is somewhat too close to the bus stand for comfort. I have not seen the Mohit International, Sir Harilal Gosaliya Marg on Racecourse Road. Cheaper guesthouses for budget travellers can be found near the bus stand: the Ashok (divided into two parts), the Jayshri, Jeel, and farther north the Anand, Intimate, Himalaya and Ashirwad. All these are non a/c, like the Government Circuit House (Rs 66, with vegetarian meals) in the quieter Sardar Bagh, and the Government Rest House (Rs 8) but you don't need airconditioning in Rajkot in December or January, when you should plan your trip to Saurashtra.

A wide choice of accommodation exists in **Saputara**, which is the most pleasant hill resort in Gujarat, at 164 km from Surat, via Bardoli and Bansda.

The best place to stay is Savshanti Lake Resort on Nageshwar Mahadev Road: they also manage the best hotel in Anand district in the Savshanti Anandam Club, Chikhodra and the excellent Savshanti Towers on R.C. Dutt Road, Baroda. For a modest Rs 325 you can enjoy a double-bed with a ceiling fan, a vase of pink roses from the garden, a shower and a western toilet, and the following meals all-inclusive: bed tea, breakfast, lunch, evening tea and dinner. The hotel is beautifully situated to benefit from hill views, the adjacent lake, and an open-air fruit market. The second choice would be one of the two high-altitude places: the Chimney and the Hilltop with the cryptic advertisement 'You think thinly? You come thyself'. The third would be the versatile, rambling Toran Hill Resort (Rs 100 for a double room; Rs 25 for a dormitory bed; Rs 600 for a whole four-bedroom bungalow), and its own cafeteria just up the road run by the enterprising and charming Hemant Upadhyay. Outside it stands a pair of *gora dev* terra cottas representing the tribal horse god of eastern Gujarat.

Staying at **Sasan Gir** within the Sanctuary and National Park you have a straight choice between Sinh Sadan Guest House and the Tourism Corporation of Gujarat's Lion Safari Lodge. The first is the former Nawab of Junagadh's private hunting lodge, with 9 non a/c rooms at Rs 60-80, 3 non a/c VIP rooms at Rs 350 and 8 a/c rooms at Rs 450. The second offers a choice of five four-bedded dormitories at Rs 30 per person, 22 non-a/c doubles at Rs 150, and 2 a/c doubles at Rs 350, and must be recommended for its views over the river, while the Sinh Sadan has only inward-looking views over a rose garden. Both offer modest breakfasts and Gujarati thalis for main meals.

The best place to stay in **Surat** for tranquillity and comfort is currently Dhawalgiri Guest House, opposite the Collector's Bungalow, Athwa Lines (single Rs 350). In the same area is Hotel Soffitel, at Ambika Niketan Bus Stop, Parle Point, Athwa Lines (single Rs 275). As usual cheap hotels cluster near the railway station, the best being Simla Guest House (single Rs 75), and more expensive hotels such as the Dreamland on Sufi Baug (single Rs 141 a/c or Rs 99 non a/c). Not far away is the Oasis on Varaccha Road (single Rs 250 a/c or Rs 175 non a/c) but I have a preference for the Tex Palazzo on the Ring Road (single Rs 270 a/c or Rs 175 non a/c), because of its top-floor revolving restaurant. Occasionally the windows are cleaned and you are rewarded with intriguing views.

With access to a car, I prefer to spend the night out of Surat at the Toran Holiday Home, Hajira, 28 km from Surat on the beach: the four triples come to Rs 100 each, and the six doubles to Rs 75 each, incredibly good value.

The twin-towns of **Veraval-Somnath** offer a rare variety of accommodation. Veraval's Tourist Bungalow on Somnath College Road near the Nawab's Palace seems deserted and decayed but Room 5 (Rs 127.50 for double occupancy; Rs 105 for single) had a sea view, hot shower and western toilet. Even quieter is the Circuit House not far from the lighthouse, with wonderful views over the sea at dusk. If you want to stay near the bus stand for an early start, your best bet is the Satkar Hotel (Rs 200 for an a/c double) but of course it's noisy at most hours. My overall recommendation in Veraval would be the Hotel Park, which opened in 1992 just outside the town off the main road to Chorwad with the best restaurant for miles including Chinese and Continental cuisine. Far from Veraval port's fishy smell of fish, the town centre din, and dingy older rooms, the Park offers fresh air and from the second floor country views including palms and wheatfields. And then my favourite luxury: a bathtub for a long soak.

Six km from Veraval is the Hindu holy town of Somnath, where the Tourism Corporation of Gujarat has only a café: they operate a hotel only in Veraval. So if you want to experience the feeling of the great pilgrim centre, you stay in Somnath at the Shri Somnath Temple Trust guesthouse, which has more than a hundred double rooms at a very low rate. You can find it halfway from the bus stand to the main temple, but you'll have to ask because its signs are in Hindi and Gujarati only. And of course, its meals are vegetarian Gujarati thalis only, so for variety you eat at the Toran café or at one of the restaurants opposite the bus station.

In **Wankaner** the stark choice of accommodation is between a very basic Government Rest House (Rs 40) near Willingdon Hospital in the town or a couple of run-down inns near the bus stand and rail station; and the highly desirable Purna Chandra Bhavan, or Oasis Guesthouse, run by the former royal family (Rs 1,000 for board with 3 meals in the royal palace) which needs to be booked in advance (tel. 02828-324). During my stay the Oasis was taken over by a German party, so I stayed in the town and visited the Palace by appointment.

Railway Retiring Rooms

This quaint designation refers to small hotels attached to rail stations which are normally available only to those with rail tickets. Retiring rooms are very convenient if you arrive at your destination late at night, and the station is small enough to be spared a great deal of late-night through traffic. This effectively rules out Ahmedabad, Surat and Valsad.

I definitely recommend using one such, as an experience, if you expect to be travelling by train, just as I suggest using a dak bungalow at least once, a government rest house a least once, in Palitana a Jain dharamshala or pilgrim's hostel, and at Sarangpur perhaps the Swami Narayan Hindu temple.

Retiring rooms are available at the following stations in Gujarat: Ahmedabad, Anand, Ankleshwar, Bharuch, (Broach), Bhavnagar, Bhuj, Dwarka, Godhra in Panchmahals, Gandhidham, Jamnagar, Junagadh, Morvi (very pleasant), Palanpur, Porbandar, Rajkot, Surat, Surendranagar, Vadodara (Baroda), Valsad, Veraval and Viramgam.

Passports and Visas

Every visitor to India must have a valid passport, with a visa for India (business type is more expensive, or tourism), and special permits for any restricted areas you hope to visit. There are no restricted areas in Daman or Diu, but the Gujarati border with Pakistan may be restricted from time to time. None of the itineraries in this book, however, include restricted area. Allow two weeks for your visa, after obtaining the visa form, and supply (currently) three passport photographs with the appropriate fee: higher if an agent obtains it for you. In the U.S.A. the Embassy is at 2107 Massachusetts Avenue, N.W., Washington, D.C. 20008, and there is a Consul-General at 3 East 64th St., New York, N.Y. 10021. In Britain, send passport, visa, photos and fee to the High Commission for India, India House, Aldwych, London WC2. In France, the Indian Embassy is situated at 15 rue Alfred Dehodencq, 75016 Paris.

To be on the safe side, I take photocopies of the first three pages of my passport and my Indian visa, and keep them in a place distinct from the passport itself.

Customs and Currency

To pay for accommodation, unless you are member of a prepaid group you must pay in rupees obtained by changing currency or travellers' cheques within India. This is simplified by the fact that many of the bigger hotels will change money for you and give you the necessary receipt, enabling you to pay your bill and, even more significant, to change money back on leaving the country. Don't try to change money illegally: it is not worth the risk of getting caught and those who do either get caught by tricksters or find that, at best, they have made a few per cent over the authorised rate. Hotels display the daily rate of exchange in dollars, sterling, Deutschmarks and a few other leading currencies, and anyone who has tried to change money at an Indian bank will know what a boon the hotels' service will be. But not all hotels will change money, and few hotels will change more than a couple of hundred dollars' worth on any one day: you cannot insist. Keep your receipts in different places, so that in case of loss or theft you have at least one receipt to show.

It is prohibited to carry Indian currency into or out of India, so a mixture of cash (small quantities) and travellers' cheques (the bulk) in easily convertible currencies should be carried in a variety of places, such as a waist-belt or neck-pouch. I have a hip-pocket sewn up at the back and opened inside; ladies carry a bag in front of them or sew an inside pocket inside a skirt or jeans. Backpackers should never put money in a backpack, where it is neither visible nor secure. Replenish small change each morning from your hidden store, when you take malaria pills.

The currency throughout India is the rupee, divided into one hundred paise. Coins are minted in denominations of 5, 10, 20, 25 and 50 paise and one and two rupees, and notes are printed in denominations of one rupee, 2, 5, 10, 20, 50, 100 and 500. Take care of the notes, for it is quite common for a shopkeeper or hotel or restaurant cashier to refuse a note if it is torn on one or more edges. Holes caused by staples on the interior of a note are normally not a problem. Tipping in small denominations oils the slow machinery of travel throughout India: few are exempt from this golden rule.

As a rule of thumb, one avoids giving money to beggars, but produces one- or two-rupee notes for services actually rendered, like a small boy showing you to the correct bus in a crowded bus station in Baroda or a station porter finding you a sleeping berth in the train from Bombay to Gandhidham when all hope seemed lost forever.

Small change, I emphasise here, is very hard to come by, and you should take every change to change larger notes into smaller denominations. ALWAYS KEEP IN RESERVE YOUR AIRPORT DEPARTURE TAX, which in 1994 was Rs 300.

Customs searches entering and leaving India have in my experience always been conducted perfunctorily, simply, and scrupulously; you are treated neither like a leper nor a mafioso. As usual, you may bring in 200 cigarettes and spirits (up to 0.95 litres), but remember that many states in India have introduced Prohibition. Gujarat is one, but Daman and Diu are not dry.

Goods to be declared in the red channel on arriving at an international airport in India include any weapons, dutiable goods, high-value articles, or foreign exchange worth in excess of the equivalent of US$1,000.00. You have to fill in a declaration form the description and value of your baggage contents.

The Tourist Baggage Re-Export form should be produced with listed articles at the port of departure, including such items as expensive personal jewellery, cameras, binoculars, radios and tape recorders.

On departure, you may export goods to a maximum value of Rs. 20,000, *except that* gold articles may not exceed Rs. 2,000 in value, silver Rs. 200, and non-gold precious stones and jewellery may not exceed Rs. 15,000. You may not export ivory, animal skins, antiques, and gold items such as ingots, bullion or coins. Moreover, if you have spent more than ninety days in India, you need an income-tax clearance certificate from the foreign section of the Income Tax office in Ahmedabad, Bombay, or your city of departure elsewhere.

Health

Travellers have always experienced trials and tribulations of the digestive system when visiting a new country, and this is as true of India as anywhere else. One therefore takes all sensible precautions to minimise hazards, such as never drinking the water or using it to clean teeth: a wide range of reputable mineral waters in lightweight plastic bottles can be ordered in restaurants and bought in shops and wayside stalls. I am never without a 'sticky bag', with water-bottle and sun-cream, as well as a lightweight clean bag for books, maps, films, notebook, camera and films. Together, these two bags will fit comfortably and unobtrusively in a cheap, tough Indian shopping bag available in any bazaar, which can quickly be replaced if damaged or lost. To sterilize water, some travellers use Sterotabs or a similar preparation in ordinary water, but tablets can never be 100% safe, whereas the mineral water, in my experience, is entirely trustworthy.

Avoid the obvious temptation of 'going native' with food, and keep faith as far as possible with your normal diet. This has become much easier with the spread of international-style hotels in major cities such as Ahmedabad, Baroda, Bhavnagar and Surat. The fact that Gujarat is dominantly vegetarian does *not* mean that one should try unpeeled fruit and vegetables, buffets left in warm temperatures, milk-derived products and over-spiced sauces. Unless you can see that seafood has been boiled for 10 minutes or more, don't be tempted. Where you can get meat, avoid it rare. Never buy fruit juices from street stalls: coconuts slashed open while you wait are of course quite safe.

Just as you avoid the water, you must avoid ice. So what does that leave us? Boiled water, bottled mineral water and fizzy drinks, tea; tinned food; bread freshly-baked; food thoroughly cooked (but not reheated) and served piping hot; and any fruit that can be sliced open in your view, such as peaches, papaya, melons or bananas. An omelette or a boiled egg is a safe standby, freshly-boiled rice is filling and safe even if dull, and potatoes are quite often available now. Most Indian restaurants on the beaten track have become accustomed to the more sensitive Western palate and stomach and often reduce the amount of chili or curry powder when serving foreigners. If in doubt, make your wishes clear to the waiter: 'no chili!' and though he may not be able to carry out your wishes to the letter, the dose may be reduced by a sympathetic cook. Buffets are often divided into Western-style and Indian-style counters, and if you are not accustomed to routine Indian dishes at home, play safe and choose from the Western varieties.

It is virtually impossible to prevent all stomach problems, because your digestive system rebels against innovations, wherever you go. So take as little alcohol as possible, eat in moderation and by all means carry out here and now that slimming plan you were considering. Take pills such as Streptotriad unless you are sensitive to sulphonamides. I find that Imodium clears up diarrhoea quickly, and never travel anywhere without a good supply. After an attack of vomiting or diarrhoea, avoid eating anything for up to twenty-four hours, rest as much as you can, and to avoid dehydration take plenty of weak tea without milk or sugar, or bottled mineral water.

Toilets exist everywhere tourists are expected, such as major sights, palaces, forts and museums. You may have to use a squat-type toilet, and you will usually be expected to bring your own toilet paper, which I keep in convenient rolls of thirty sheets or so, rubber-banded, to save space. Gujarat is by and large not so well provided with Western toilets as neighbouring Rajasthan or Maharashtra, because tourism is still slightly less well developed, but as tourism continues to spread geographically, and upwards into the de luxe category, more lavatories are being adapted for Western use. You do not have to stay in a given hotel, or dine in a given restaurant, to use their facilities.

Injections needed for India vary from time to time and must be checked at least a month before departure with your local doctor to allow time for the full courses prescribed. Foreign nationals over the age of 18 staying more than one year (except diplomats and previously accredited journalists) are required to undergo HIV testing within a month of arrival, unless you can show a certificate from a WHO collaborating laboratory issued within a month before arrival. Immunisation against Japanese encephalitis is recommended if travelling between August-December and March-May, and against meningococcal meningitis if visiting New Delhi from November to May. Children should be immunised against TB; adults are less at risk. You should have been immunised against polio and tetanus within the last ten years. Against typhoid there are three types of immunisation to select: injectable Vi (single dose) and the two-dose vaccine both last three years, while the oral capsules need an annual booster. Hepatitis 'A' is a significant risk if the antibody is negative; hepatitis 'B' can be communicated through contacts with sex or contaminated blood, needles and syringes: vaccines are available, but take with you a standard medical pack with syringes and needles available at chemists. Cholera immunisation is now not normally recommended for India, with only 26 deaths to date, but again it is vital to ensure strict food and water hygiene. Yellow fever is no danger. Rabies vaccine should be considered if you intend to travel in rural areas or outside standard package tours: you can take two doses a month apart, which gives you several days to reach a doctor, if attacked, for another course of two doses. If you are attacked without preventative doses, you must reach a qualified doctor in the course of a few hours, and take six doses.

Malaria is endemic throughout India in all seasons, and the London School of Hygiene and Tropical Medicine suggests two Proguanil tablets daily (in a trade name such as Paludrine) and two Chloroquine tablets weekly (in trade names such as Nivaquine or Avloclor) taken in a single dose with or after food beginning one week before entering a malarial area and ending four weeks after leaving a malarial area. If a fever reaches 38°C or higher seven days or more after arriving in a malarial region, obtain medical help or self-treat with either Halfan, or quinine with Fansidar and then find a doctor. As malaria is transmitted by mosquito bites, try to leave rural areas before dusk, cover as much exposed skin as possible after dusk and use a rub-on or spray repellent on the rest of your hands and face and exposed legs and feet; try to sleep in a screened room or under a bed net tucked in and checked for holes, having sprayed inside beforehand. Buzzers are useless against mosquitoes, but coils, vapour pads and air conditioning have some deterrent effect.

Always consult your local doctor or British Airways travel clinic to check on current conditions. You know from experience how far you are affected by sunstroke and exposure, exhaustion by trekking or dehydration, but always err on the cautious side by covering your head and arms, and using your favourite sun-screen lotions systematically. After taking a shower or bath, rub or spray with insect-repellent on exposed areas. In a hot, tropical and often humid climate even a minor cut can turn septic quickly, so keep at hand antiseptic cream and a choice of three or four dressings to stop minor accidents becoming major. I always pack a tiny pair of folding scissors, and a roll of soft toilet paper can help to rub down mud or dirt in the absence of running water. A bath-plug of the standard variety is a great boon in all but five-star hotels, but *do* remember to take it away with you when you dry yourself. If you have no plug, or leave it behind, a wodge of saturated toilet-paper stuffed into the hole will retain water for a period. I always take to India my own shampoo sachets, toothpaste and shaving-kit, handtowel and soap in a soapdish. Most guesthouses will provide a towel and soap if asked but if you arrive on a slow train after midnight you may not want to wait for them.

Clothing

Take as little as possible, but remember that nights in hill stations such as Saputara can be cold in winter and, if you intend to travel in buses or trains by night, an anorak can double as a pillow. Increased pollution makes a face-mask desirable on long road journeys and within Ahmedabad. On any long journeys by car, bus or train I wear an airfilled cushion (obtainable at major airports before departure) on my shoulders to take the weight off my head, and reduce wear and tear on my neck muscles (and bruising) caused by bumping, braking and jerking.

Speaking the Languages

Readers familiar with my previous travel guides may recall my opinion that learning one or more of the local languages will repay the effort in proportion to the effort. Sadly, the huge effort required in learning Gujarati would not be worth the time spent because most educated Indians in the State, as well as Daman and Diu, speak English and would regard an effort to speak in pidgin Gujarati as offensive to them and faintly embarrassing. In country areas, it is harder to find an English-speaker immediately, but the younger generation will gladly display its knowledge. Portuguese, once current in Daman and Diu, is now fast dying out, to be replaced by English as the foreign lingua franca, as elsewhere in India.

I wish I could recommend a private study aid to Gujarati as excellent as R.S. McGregor's *Outline of Hindi Grammar*, but as usual with Indian vernacular languages the provisions are lamentable. Bidhu Bhusan Das Gupta's *Gujarati Self-Taught* offers such puzzles as 'See keeping your mouth towards him', 'Do work with your hand' and 'But owing to my bath in the pond two days before, I caught cold'. N.S.R. Ganathe's *Learn Gujarati in 30 Days* displays an equally cavalier approach to vocabulary and correct English: 'Latrine is in outside', 'Don't beat with umbrella', 'Manu is deaf by ear', and 'Come little early'. Like Hindi, Gujarati is written in Devanagari script, with an alphabet of 45 letters, and though it takes considerable effort to learn the Devanagari script, it is quite easy to pick up common spoken words and phrases in Gujarati, some of which are listed below:

What is this?	A shu chhe?
Where is the toilet?	Sundas kyaa chhe?
What is this in Gujarati?	A Gujarati ma shu chhe?
Excuse me!	Maaf karjo
Thank you	Abhar
Yes	Ha
No	Nahin
How are you?	Kem chho?
Fine	Saru
What is your name?	Tamarun nam shu chhe?
My name is Jim	Maro nam Jim chhe
What time is it?	Ketla vagya?
It is eight o'clock	Ath vagya chhe
Where do you come from?	Tame kyanthi aayo chho?
I'm going to Ahmedabad	Hum Ahmedabad jau chhu
I live in Surat	Hum Surat rahu chhu
I have no time	Mari pase samay nathi
I can speak a little Gujarati	Hum thodu Gujarati boli saru chhu
There's no water in the room	Rum ma pani nathi
Give me the bill	Mane bill aapo
Go! Let's go!	Java do!
On the left; on the right	Dabi baju; jamni baju
Straight on	Siddha

In the morning	Savare
Today	Aj
Yesterday, tomorrow	Gai kale, avti kale
Last week	Chellu athvadiyu
Next month	Avta mahine
Next year	Avta varshe
Cheap; expensive	Sastu; monghu
Clean; dirty	Svacch; gandu
Black; white	Kalu; safed
Large; small	Moto; nano
Old; new	Juno; navo
Beautiful, good, bad	Saro; kharab
Very, many; few	Bahu, mani; thodu
Red; blue	Lal; vadal
Green; yellow	Lilo; pilo
Quickly; slowly	Jaldi; dhire dhime
Water; tea	Pani; chha

Numbers and Days of the Week

Many of the numerals can be recognised from Greek, Latin, Italian, French and so on because, like Hindi, Gujarati is derived from Sanskrit and is thus a language of the same Indo-European family to which most other European and Western Asiatic languages (though not Arabic or Basque) belong.

0 shunya 1 ek 2 be 3 tran 4 char 5 panch 6 chha 7 sat 8 ath 9 nav 10 dash 11 agiyar 12 bar 13 ter 14 chaud 15 pandar 16 sol 17 sathar 18 athar 19 ognis 20 bis 21 ekvis 22 bavis 23 trevis 24 chovis 25 pachis 26 chhavis 27 sattavis 28 athavis *but* 29 ogantris 30 tris 31 ektris *but* 39 oganchalis 40 chalis 41 ektalis 48 adtalis *but* 49 oganpachas 50 pachas 51 ekavan 60 sath 70 sitter 80 ensi 90 ekanun 99 navvanun 100 so 1,000 hajar 100,000 lakh 10,000,000 ek karor

Numerals can be written both in Devanagari and also in the form familiar to you. Here are the numbers written in Devanagari script if you want to read signs, price-lists, or timetables:

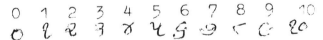

You will find the number 29,148,756 split up in Indian books and newspapers as 2,91,48,756 and written as 2 crores, 91 lakhs, 48 thousand, seven hundred and fifty-six.

Monday	somavar	Friday	shukravar
Tuesday	mangalvar	Saturday	shanivar
Wednesday	budhvar	Sunday	ravivar
Thursday	guruvar	day	var

The Gujarati New Year begins in March, and each of the twelve months over-laps with Western calendar months as follows:

March-April	chaitar
April-May	vaishakh
May-June	jeth
June-July	ashad
July-August	shravan
August-September	bhadarvo
September-October	aso
October-November	kartak
November-December	magshar
December-January	posh
January-February	maha
February-March	phagan

Holidays and Festivals

Gujarat is a dominantly Hindu state and Hindu festivals are fixed in accordance with the Vikramaditya calendar based on lunar months which begin with the full moon and intercalate a thirteenth month of the year every thirty months to ensure that the months stay consonant with the seasons, essential in a largely agricultural country. As years of the Vikramaditya era are often quoted in books and on monuments, remember that these years are 57 or 58 years *ahead* of the Christian calendar. The Indian Government has officially sanctioned a third type of era, Shaka, which is 77 or 78 years *behind* the Christian Era. The Muslim calendar begins with the flight (Hijra) of the Prophet Muhammad on 16 July 622 A.D. and Sura IX, verse 30 of the revealed Qur'an fixed the calendar at twelve lunar months, so that the Muslim calendar does not intercalate an extra month to stay compatible with the seasons, so it falls behind by 12 days every year. This means that A.D. 1994 coincides with part of 1414 and part of 1415 A.H.

You are never far in time or place from an Indian festival: I draw particular attention in the text to those of Daman, which are similar to those of Diu; to the Kite-Flying Festival throughout Gujarat in mid-January; and to the Tarnetar tribal festival not far from Wankaner every September. I just make the best of whatever colourful celebrations block my bus-route, delay my departure, or fill the pavements, and immerse myself in the jubilation.

Republic Day closes many offices and museums on 26 January. In February-March the Hindu spring rites of Holi involve squirting all and sundry with coloured powders and water, so wear disposable clothes at this time (some old India hands never wear anything else!). Parsis celebrate the spring festival as Now Ruz (New Year) in a festival deriving from Iran. This too is the season for the Jain festival of the latest tirthankar, Mahavira, and the Hindu festival cel-ebrating the birth of Lord Rama, as well as the Christian Good Friday and Eas-ter Day. April 13 is an official New Year holiday. August 15 is Indian Independence Day, and so a national holiday. October 2 is Gandhiji's birthday. Dussehra (September-October) and Diwali, three to four weeks later, are Hindu spectacles well worth seeing in any large town, with fairs spread over the next ten days to welcome the new financial year with offerings to Lakshmi, goddess of wealth. December 25 is a holiday for Indian Christians.

Books and Maps

For the topography of Gujarat the basic historic reference tool is the *Gazetteer of the Bombay Residency* in several volumes, and available in only the largest libraries. For the history, M.S. Commissariat's two-volume *History of Gujarat* (1938-57) has been supplemented by his *Studies of the History of Gujarat*, lectures given in 1930-1, and reprinted in Ahmedabad (1987).

The best book on the Islamic monuments of Ahmedabad is K.V. Soundara Rajan's *Ahmadabad* (1980), and two other guides from the Archaeological Survey of India should be acquired: the same author's *Junagadh* (1985), and S.R. Rao's *Lothal* (1985). For Baroda, *Baroda Through the Ages* (M.S.U., Baroda) is regrettably out of print, but at the time of writing it is still possible to obtain from the same publisher V.A. Janaki's *Some Aspects of the Historical Geography of Surat* (1974) and *The Commerce of Cambay from the Earliest Period to the Nineteenth Century* which I am glad to acknowledge here as first-rate sources. The classic work on Jamnagar is Naoroji M. Dumasia's *Jamnagar: a Sketch of its Ruler and its Administration* (Bombay, 1927) and for Kutch there is *The Black Hills: Kutch in History and Legend* (London, 1958) by L.F. Rushbrook Williams, a book reprinted in 1981 and on sale at Aina Mahal, Bhuj.

Your local tourist office will supply you with maps of Ahmedabad and Gujarat. Other maps of smaller towns and archaeological sites are in the indispensable *Penguin Guide to the Monuments of India* (2 vols., Penguin Books, 1989), of which volume I by George Michell covers Buddhist, Jain and Hindu sites, and volume 2 by Philip Davies deals with Islamic, Rajput, and European sites, except for Mehmedabad which is overlooked. A good general map, such as the Nelles *India* or the 1:4,000,000 *Indian Subcontinent*, is of course necessary.

Michell and Davies cannot of course also cover the wealth of vernacular domestic architecture, and for this I recommend V.S. Pramar's excellent *Haveli: Houses and Wooden Mansions of Gujarat* (Mapin, Ahmedabad, 1989).

Chronology

Sultans of Gujarat

Muzaffar I	1396-1411
Ahmed I, founder of Ahmedabad	1411-42
Muhammad Karim	1442-51
Qutb ud-Din Ahmed II	1451-58
Daud	1458
Mahmud I called Beghada	1458-1511
Muzaffar II	1511-26
Sikandar	1526
Mahmud II	1526
Bahadur	1526-37
Miran Muhammad I of Khandesh	1537
Mahmud III	1537-54
Ahmed II	1554-61
Muzaffar III	1561 to the Mughal conquest by Akbar, 1572

Gaekwads of Baroda

Pilaji	1721-32
Damaji II	1732-68
Govind Rao	1768-71
Sayaji Rao I	1771
Fateh Singh	1771-89
Manaji	1789-93
Govind Rao	1793-1800
Anand Rao	1800-18
Sayaji Rao II	1818-47
Ganpat Rao	1847-56
Khande Rao	1856-70
Malhar Rao	1870-5
Sayaji Rao III	1875-1939

Index

calligraphy 213
Cambay viii-ix, 44, 47-56, 77-8, 88,
    140, 193, 234, 238, 286
Cambay, Gulf of 47-8, 211-2, 234, 267
Cambridge University 153, 162, 226
Camões, L. de 112
canals 62
Canevan, A.M. 60
Cantrell, S. *and* W. 90
caracals 226-7
carnelian 54, 232
cars, vintage 152
cartaz 238
caste system 6, 7, 16, 36, 65, 216, 231,
    256
castles. *See* forts
Castro, F. de 244
Castro, J. de 238
cats, jungle 227
caves. *See* names of caves, *e.g.* Khapara Kodia Caves
cemeteries. Ahmedabad 17, 25;
    Broach 60-1; Daman 115; Mandvi
    261; Surat 90-1
Central Salt & Marine Research Institute 225
ceramics 233
chalcedony 232
Chalcolithic Age 231-4
Chalukya Dynasty 107, 137, 168, 206
Champaner viii, 1, 71, 76-82, 242, 275
Chandragiri 217
Chandragupta 216
Changada 232
Changashah 95
Chansad 36
Chaudhuris 16, 105
Chauhan Dynasty 76
Chaul 107
Chavada Dynasty 211
cheetahs 68, 226-7
Chelmsford Market 165
Chhapaya (U.P.) 37, 256
Chhota Udaipur 13, 16, 105
China and the Chinese 47, 92-3, 108

Chintamani 104
Chisholm, R.F. 67, 70
Chishtiyyah 27-30
cholera 281
Chorwad 201-2
Chowdhary, S.N. 208
Christian, V. 60
Christians and Christianity 59-60, 92,
    108-9, 243-6
Christie, E.C. 59
chronology 287
Chudasama Dynasty 181-4, 235
Church of North India. *See* United
    Church of North India
City College, Ahmedabad 18
clothing 282
Coelho *family* 115
Coleridge, S.T. 61
Colimão *family* 115
Commissariat, M.S. 286
Constitution 64
conversion 60
Cooper, R.F. 156
co-operatives 10
copper 36, 233, 238
coral reefs 167
Correa C., 1 7
Costa, C.R. da 110
costume 215
cotton 57, 143, 211
courthouses 184-5
Cousens, H. 22
Couver, J. 175
cranes 140-1, 144, 160, 164, 200, 227
cremation 61
cricket 143, 158, 162, 164, 175, 231-2
crocodiles 164, 188, 197, 199
crows 128, 146, 188
Cunha, N. da 236-7, 242

Dabhoi 71, 85-7
Dabir, *Hajji* ud- 28
Dadhar River 47, 74
Dadra 107, 109
Dakor 40-2

rivers, *e.g.* Sabarmati
roads 4, 61, 87-8
Roda 71, 137
Rodrigues, *P. M.* 109-10
Roe, *Sir* T. 57
Rojdi 159
Rojid 229
Roman Catholics 108-9, 235-9, 243-7
Rosario *family* 115
Roy, N. 114
Rozi 164, 167
Rudra 129
Rudramala Temple 129-31
Rukmini 170
rum 248

Sabarkantha 102, 137, 276
Sabarmati Ashram 1, 7-10, 174
Sabarmati River 47-8, 54, 232, 234
Sagai 252
Sadavrat 61
Sahasralinga Tank 127
Sajan, N. 158
Sakkar Baug Museum 187
salt 139, 142-3
saltpetre 57
Samaldas College 224
sambar 167, 200
Sami 146
Sampayo, R. de M. de 112
sanctuaries, wildlife. Bansda 99-100;
    Dasara 139-43, 150; Hingolgadh
    160, 273; Jamnagar 164, 166-7; Jes-
    sore 269; Sasangir 188, 196-201,
    276-7; Velavadar 227-8; Wankaner
    154
Sander 118
Sanders, M. *and* T. 90
sandstone 37
Sanjan 61, 93-7
Sankheda 13
Sanskar Kendra Municipal Museum
    16
Sapda 249
Saputara viii, 100-5, 276

Sarabhai *family* 10, 14-5, 206
Sarangpur, Ahmedabad 11, 22
Sarangpur, Saurashtra 229-31, 278
Saraspur 5
Saraswati 126
Saraswati River 125, 129, 133, 209
Sardar Sarovar Dam 16, 61-2
Sarkhej 6, 32-5, 49
Sarodar 162
Sarotra 146
Sartanji 153, 176
Sasangir viii, 188, 196-201, 276-7
Sataji 161
Satavahana Dynasty 107, 182
Satchidananda, *Swami* 146
sati 36, 153, 183, 252
Saurashtra 139-234
Savalia, V.D. 196
Sayajirao III 65-74
Sayyid, A.S. 53-4
schools. *See* under the name of the
    school, *e.g.* Rajkumar College
Scindia Dynasty 64
sculpture 71-4, 171
seals 232
seasons 196, 266
Sejakpur 118
Self-Employed Women's Association
    10
Shah, H. 105
Shah, R.D. 214
Shah, S. 249
Shah, U.P. 137
Shah, Y. 249
Shah Alam 21, 25
Shah Jahan 14
Shahi Baug, Ahmedabad 14, 28
Shahinshahis 95, 97
Shahji 212
Shahr-ki Mosque, Champaner 81
Shaikh Farid, Patan 19
Shaivites and Shaivism 75, 138, 168,
    194, 211. *See also* Shiva
shaking minarets 22
Shakir, M. 158

tribes 13-4, 16-7, 71, 73, 100-5, 155
Tripathi, G. 42
Tubraj 105
Tughlaq Dynasty 18, 89, 205-6, 235
Tuna (port) 264-5
Turkey and the Turks 48, 77, 184, 236-8
turtles 164
typhoid 281

Udaimati 125
Udaya Narayan Temple 66
Udvada 95, 97
Ugoji 211
Ujjain (M.P.) 170, 204
Ulugh Khan 57
Union Territory of Daman and Diu vii, 106-17, 235-48. *See also* Daman *and* Diu
United Church of North India 60, 75, 92
United States of Saurashtra 153
Universities. Ahmedabad 16; Baroda 66, 74; Patan 125
untouchability 16, 216
Upanishads 38, 157-8
Uparkot, Junagadh 181-4
Upleta 177
Utelia viii, 228, 234, 274
Utensils Museum 12

V.H.P. 173
vaccination 281-2
Vachanamritam 36, 256
Vadgam 62
Vadnagar 132-4
Vado, S. 15
Vadodara. *See* Baroda
vads 131-2
Vadtal 257
Vagha Talao (Tank) 232
Vaidya, S.B. 68
Vairasimha 32
Vaishnavites and Vaishnavism 36-8, 74-5, 133, 191, 259. *See also* Pushti

Marga Movement; Swaminarayan Movement; Vishnu
Vakatachand, S.H. 218
Vakatachand, U.H. 218
Vakharia *family* 58
Vakil, N. 114
Vala. *See* Valabhi
Valabhi 167, 182
Vallabhacharya 75
Vallabhai 219
Valotri 232
Valsad 95, 102, 198, 267-8, 278
Vamanasthali 182
Vanakbara 240, 242, 247-8
Vansda. *See* Bansda
Vanthali 182
Vapi 97, 242, 266
Varma, R. 73-4
Varthema, L. di 56, 77
Varuna 87
Vasa Haveli 6
Vasai 172
Vasana 32
Vasconcellos *family* 113
Vaso 42-6
Vastupala 118, 190-1
Vatrak River 38-9
Vatva 25
Vavs. See step-wells
Vayudoot 240
Vedas and Vedic ideals 35-8, 61, 129, 257. *See also* the names of individual Vedas, *e.g.* Rigveda
Vegetarianism 36
Velakula 203
Velavadar Blackbuck National Park viii, 227-8
Vendidad 97
Venice and the Venetians 48-9
Veraval 176-7, 198, 202-4, 277-8
Vibhaji 161-2
Vibhuji, K. 156
Victoria, *Queen* 226
Vijay Vilas 261
Vijayarajji 258, 261

RAJASTHAN – AGRA – DELHI

describes the surprises of a great twentieth-century Asian capital and its complex past, the pleasures expected and unexpected of Agra, with its Taj Mahal and I'timad ad-Daula, Red Fort and teeming bazaars. The bulk of Philip Ward's travel guide is devoted to the Country of the Princes: Rajasthan, with its nature reserves of Sariska, Bharatpur and Ranthambore as well as great historic cities such as Amber-Jaipur and Ahar-Udaipur, the frescoed havelis of Shekhavati, the desert cities of Bikaner and Jaisalmer, and the sacred sites of Osiyan, Ranakpur, Nathdwara, Eklingji, Deshnok and Mount Abu. Here are the familiar destinations such as Jodhpur and Pushkar as well as jewels off the beaten track such as Kishangarh, Dig, Kumbhalgarh, Bundi, Kota, and Chittor.

Intended for first-time visitors as well as experienced travellers who want to understand the background to the vision, *Rajasthan, Agra, Delhi* provides a sympathetic and thoughtful companion to India's main attractions.

PHILIP WARD, FRGS, ALA, FRSA, has spent much of his life in Asia and Africa, from Morocco to the Philippines, including eight years in Libya and nearly two in Indonesia. Because of his sympathy with Indian spiritual values, he is an ideal companion to the Mughal and Rajput lands of northern and western India, with their background of Hinduism and Islam. His previous travel books include *Japanese Capitals, Bangkok, Touring Iran, Tripoli, Travels in Oman, Ha'il, Oasis City of Saudi Arabia* and most recently *Finnish Cities* and *Polish Cities*. His meditations on the heart of Rajasthan, beginning in Delhi and continuing to Agra, will enthral and amuse the armchair traveller and become essential reading for any Westerner intending to explore the intricacies of art, architecture and everyday life in modern north-west India.